DATE DUE

D1014639

ALSO BY JOHN POPE-HENNESSY

LEARNING TO LOOK

DISCARD

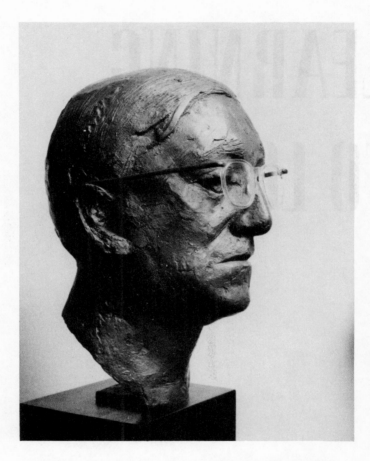

How I should like to look: bronze bust of myself by
Elizabeth Frink (*private collection*)

JOHN
POPE-HENNESSY

LEARNING
TO LOOK

DOUBLEDAY

NEW YORK LONDON
TORONTO SYDNEY
AUCKLAND

709.2
P825L

PUBLISHED BY DOUBLEDAY

a division of Bantam Doubleday Dell Publishing Group, Inc.
666 Fifth Avenue, New York, New York 10103

DOUBLEDAY and the portrayal of an anchor with a dolphin are
trademarks of Doubleday, a division of Bantam Doubleday Dell
Publishing Group, Inc.

Book Design by Barbara M. Bachman

Library of Congress Cataloging-in-Publication Data

Pope-Hennessy, John Wyndham, Sir, 1913–
    Learning to look / by John Pope-Hennessy.
—1st ed.
        p.   cm.
    Includes bibliographical references.
    1. Pope-Hennessy, John Wyndham, Sir, 1913–   2. Art
historians—England—Biography. 3.   Art—Psychology. I.
Title.
N7483.P66A3   1991
709'.2—dc20
[B]   90-3695
                                                        CIP

ISBN 0-385-26141-1

Copyright © 1991 by John Pope-Hennessy
All Rights Reserved
Printed in the United States of America
March 1991
FIRST EDITION

⁰/9/

TO

MICHAEL MALLON,

WITHOUT WHOSE HELP
THIS BOOK COULD
NOT HAVE BEEN PRODUCED.

CONTENTS

LIST OF ILLUSTRATIONS

Frontispiece. How I should like to look: bronze bust of myself by Elizabeth Frink (private collection)

1. My father's father, Sir John Pope Hennessy, as governor of Mauritius (statue by M. Loumeau, 1908, Port Louis, Mauritius)

2. My mother's father, Sir Arthur Birch (painted by Sir William Orpen, private collection)

3. My mother, Una Birch (ca. 1906)

4. Watchtower at Rostellan Castle, County Cork, with Sir John and Lady Pope Hennessy and my uncle, Hugh (ca. 1890)

5. Myself and my brother, James, with our mother in London (1917)

6. Myself and my brother, James, as pages at a wedding (1919)

7. Consigned to school (1923)

8. My father, Major-General L. H. R. Pope-Hennessy (1932)

9. My mother, Dame Una Pope-Hennessy (photograph by Cecil Beaton, 1946)

10. My brother, James, in the gardens at Chiswick House (photograph by Cecil Beaton, 1940)

11. Giotto: *The Presentation in the Temple* (Isabella Stewart Gardner Museum, Boston)

12. Giovanni di Paolo: *The Baptism of Christ* (Ashmolean Museum, Oxford)

13. Giovanni di Paolo: *The Crucifixion* (Christ Church, Oxford)

14. Sassetta: *The Agony in the Garden* (Detroit Institute of Arts, formerly at Ashburnham Place)

15. Domenichino: *Christ Carrying the Cross* (J. Paul Getty Museum, Malibu)

ACKNOWLEDGMENTS

THE AUTHOR AND PUBLISHERS WOULD LIKE TO THANK THE Bertrand Russell Archives Copyright Permissions Committee for granting authorization to quote from the unpublished correspondence of Bertrand Russell in the first chapter of this book.

For permission to reproduce photographs, grateful acknowledgment is made to the following: Massimo Listri: frontispiece, 33; Government Tourist Office, Mauritius: 1; Sotheby's, London: 9, 10, 22; Isabella Stewart Gardner Museum, Boston: 11; Ashmolean Museum, Oxford: 12; The Governing Body of Christ Church, Oxford: 13; Founders Society (Purchase, Ralph Harman Booth Bequest Fund), Detroit Institute of Arts: 14; J. Paul Getty Museum, Malibu: 15; Board of Trustees of the Victoria and Albert Museum, London: 16, 17, 19, 20, 21; Anthony Crickmay: 18; Board of Trustees of the Metropolitan Museum of Art, New York: 23, 24, 25, 26, 27, 28; Archivi Alinari, Florence: 29; Alinari/Art Resource, New York: 30, 31.

PREFACE

THE SEED FROM WHICH THIS BOOK HAS GROWN WAS AN ARTICLE printed four years ago in the columns of *The New York Times*. When it was suggested that the article, "Portrait of an Art Historian as Young Man," should be succeeded by a memoir, I accepted what in modern jargon would be called the challenge, and what I thought of as the task. By nature, I am not introspective—I find it easier to look out than to look in—and the book I had in mind was a curriculum vitae dealing with the positions that I had held, the books that I had written, and the work that I had done. But no sooner did I sit down at my typewriter than the book took charge. One's life is something that one takes for granted, yet when I looked at mine across a span of time, it suddenly seemed very odd. Why did it take this and not some altogether different course? Why had I never entertained some large ambition that was beyond my reach? What were the real factors that contributed to make me what I was? I have never kept a diary, but I have engagement books that stretch back over sixty years. As I opened them, scene succeeded scene and conversation succeeded conversation as though they had occurred only the day before. Amplified by letters, they were the present not the past, and working through them I was reminded how lucky I had been not just in my upbringing and my environment, but in the people—pupils, colleagues, and friends—who so generously offered me ideas and encouragement and support.

JOHN POPE-HENNESSY
FLORENCE
ASCENSION DAY 1990

LEARNING TO LOOK

A FAMILY AND A SON

"IS THAT WHERE YOU WANT TO DIE?" ASKED A FRIEND WHEN I told her I was moving to Florence. "Yes," I said, "but I want to live there a bit first." Florence was not a refuge, it was a goal. I had spent every summer there for forty years, crossing the Ponte Vecchio thronged with sweaty tourists on my way to some gallery or monument. Each summer I thought I learned a little more, but since the relation of art to life, in the period with which I was concerned, was very close, it was frustrating to be a mere observer peering at the city from outside. Today from my terrace I look day in, day out, at the river—sometimes it is silvery and friendly, sometimes brown and hostile—at which Renaissance artists looked, and walk through the same streets. I see, as if within touching distance, the silhouette of Santa Croce and the bell tower of the Badia, the solid mass of the Palazzo Vecchio, the Campanile of the Cathedral, and the marvelous lantern of the Cupola glistening in the sun. They fill me with a sense of reaching port at last.

My life has been devoted to studying works of art and putting them to use. To the material well-being of the world neither activity is of much consequence: it does not make the poor less poor, it does not sustain the hungry, it does not diminish suffering or redress injustice. But works of art have always seemed to me to have a supernatural power, and I believe that visual images constitute a universal language through which the experience of the past is transmitted to the present, and by whose means all lives can be immeasurably enriched.

.   .   .

I have an odd heredity. My grandfather, who had the same name as myself, was born in Cork. His family was poor (I once saw the outside of the small terrace house in which they lived), but he was clever and ambitious, making his way to London and then (in circumstances I have never wholly understood) gaining a seat in Parliament as member for King's County in 1859. A follower, to judge from correspondence an obsequious follower, of Disraeli, he made his mark at Westminster, where Irish Catholic members were something of a rarity. As a Catholic, he became a spokesman for the Polish cause in Parliament. He was evidently charismatic; Trollope's *Phineas Finn* is in part based on him at this stage in his career, and his name is invoked in the brothel scene in *Ulysses*. In 1866, however, he lost his seat, and to fend off his creditors accepted a post in the colonial service, as governor of Labuan, an unhealthy island abutting on Borneo. After some years of incarceration in this miserable colony, he was promoted to be governor-in-chief of the West African Settlements and then successively governor of the Bahamas, Barbados, Hong Kong, and Mauritius. He was a progressive, liberal governor—streets were named after him, and there is a statue of him in Mauritius—and when he saw that things were wrong, he tried to put them right. This is a vice I have inherited.

Like many self-made men he felt an urge to throw down roots, and this he did in County Cork first by buying Sir Walter Raleigh's house at Youghal (where he wrote an elegant, imaginative book, *Sir Walter Raleigh and Ireland*), and then by selling Youghal and buying the former seat of the Earls of Inchiquin, Rostellan Castle, overlooking Queenstown Harbour. As a boy in Cork he had tramped through its demesne and made a vow that he would one day own the house and land. He bought Rostellan in 1888, when he was on leave in London prosecuting a successful libel action against *The Times*. On leaving the colonial service a year later it was to Rostellan that he retired. In his mind, however, retirement from the colonial service did not involve retirement from public life, and in 1890 he again stood for Parliament, successfully, as the anti-Parnellite candidate in the North Kilkenny election. I have the tray from a silver tea service given him by his constituents. But the ill health that was endemic in colonial service cut short his endeavor to return to Westminster, and in 1891, at the age of fifty-one, he died.

In Labuan he married, in 1868, the daughter of Hugh Low, another colonial administrator. Low's background also was unorthodox. His father was the owner of a well-known firm of orchid growers, and as a young man he was sent to Borneo to search for orchids. While there, he was diverted by the Rajah of Sarawak to the colonial service as colonial secretary of Labuan. His name, as Sir Hugh Low, is still revered by lepidopterists, and in Perak, where he was responsible for introducing rubber trees. My grandmother had a strain of Malaccan blood, and when as a child I knew her, she looked like an elderly Malay. Her first son, born in Labuan in 1869, died of dysentery in Freetown in 1872. Her second son, my father, was born in 1875 and was brought up till the age of seven in Government House, Hong Kong. The marriage was unhappy—the range of options in an island like Labuan must have been very limited—and my grandmother grew to detest her husband. After his death she destroyed his papers and dispersed a collection of blue-and-white porcelain to which, rightly or wrongly, he attached importance. A convert to Catholicism, she was superstitious, wasteful, and improvident, mortgaging Rostellan and marrying an Irish neighbor called Thackwell far younger than herself. My father, whose first name was Ladislaus but who was known as Richard, learned of her remarriage from a newspaper. Thereafter her chilly letters to him were always signed "K. Thackwell." My father was commissioned in the 43rd Light Infantry, with which he later served, but was obliged by poverty to volunteer for service in West Africa, while his younger brother, Hugh, was packed off to Canada. Brought up in the expectation of inheriting Rostellan, he never recovered from the heartlessness with which his mother treated him.

My mother's forebears were made of different stuff. Her father, Sir Arthur Birch, was the ninth child of the vicar of Southwold in East Anglia. He was educated at home since money was short and only the three eldest sons could be sent to Eton. One of his brothers became judge of the High Court in Calcutta, and another was tutor to the Prince of Wales, and my grandfather, after a brief period as clerk in the Legacy Duty Office at Somerset House, entered the Colonial Office. After serving as secretary to successive secretaries of state, he was posted to the province of British Columbia and was later lieutenant governor of Ceylon. His wife, Zephine Watts-Russell, was an heiress who, had she lived, would have inherited from her mother a sizable estate, Biggin Hall, near Oundle in Northamptonshire. In Ceylon, however, she contracted a disease known at the time as sprue, and when my grandfather, on leave in London, was on the point of returning to Ceylon he was warned that it would be fatal for her to go back there. Providentially the death of the agent of the Western Branch of the Bank of England was announced, and since one of my grandfather's brothers was a director of the bank he was appointed to the vacancy. The Western Branch was responsible for private accounts, and was established at Uxbridge House in Burlington Gardens, where the Royal Bank of Scotland is today. Business was conducted on the ground floor of the building, and the upper floors, with their fine reception rooms, were the agent's perquisite. The ceiling of the bank has since been raised, to the detriment of the interior, but the eighteenth-century staircase, with its Leoni handrail and its duck's-egg-blue cupola by Joseph Rose, survives. There, for seventeen years after her mother's death, my mother acted as Sir Arthur's hostess.

My mother, named Una after Spenser's *Faerie Queene*, is a prime figure in this story, and I must say something about her here. Born in 1875, she was not subjected to the rigors of colonial life. While her parents were in Ceylon, she had a strict but happy childhood in Northamptonshire under a regime typical of the middle, not the late, nineteenth century. At eight every morning she went to her grandmother's bedroom to read the psalms of the day kneeling by her bed. Her grandmother, who had patches of iodine on her temples to help her eyesight (they were washed off when she dressed), then gave her the previous day's *Times*, with articles ticked off which she would be required to read aloud at two o'clock. This task done, she was encouraged to find her own amusements. "The discoveries of childhood," she wrote many years later in a sanatorium in Switzerland, "remain with us always, the strong lichen-built nests of the tit and the wren, the frail grass structure laid with such apparent carelessness by the lesser white-throat across a bramble joint, the strange home-making habits of the nightingale and nightjar are an abiding memory . . . and then the ways of the fish, the queer friendly tench coming to a withy trap baited with geranium and calceolarias, kept by me in wet moss for a day and then returned to their element none the worse for their outings. Rainy afternoons were spent in the library pulling out book after book. Layard's *Nineveh*, Bewick's *Birds*, White's *Natural History of Selborne*, the *Icon Basilike*, *The Woman in White*, podgy volumes of Tasso, Lowell's *Study Windows*, *The Excursion*, I can see them all and the shelves on which they were ranged under their edging of pinked green leather. In those happy days there was no hurry, day succeeded day in glorious monotony." As a child she had a confession book, in which she wrote her favorite motto, "Be what you seem to be," and she believed until her death that truthfulness of word, deed, and purpose was a human quality of paramount importance. A succession of foreign governesses taught her history, grammar, geography, Latin, French, German, mathematics, and religion. High-spirited and extroverted though she was, she must already, at quite an early age, have been rather an alarming figure. One of the people she intimidated locally was the future Lord Spencer. He was chairman of the Advisory Council of the Victoria and Albert Museum in 1967 when I became director, and I found to my relief that his alarm extended to me too.

At fifteen she was turned over to a curate for more specialized religious instruction, and only at that point did she experience doubt. "An extreme belligerency against the whole ecclesiastical sham seized me. I decided the honest thing to do was to discard everything, and to begin at the bottom of the pole. Every other day I read philosophy with a tutor. I began my course of reading with Descartes and his proofs of one's own existence. I read on and on, Leibniz, Spinoza, Fichte, Kant, Hegel and finally Nietzsche, and in Nietzsche, for a time, I found a new gospel." At Biggin, she stenciled phrases from Nietzsche onto her bedroom walls. But her interests were not purely intellectual, and after she came out, in 1893, she led a conventional social life. Society then must have been more amusing than it is today. It had a pronounced feminist slant. I have an enchanting account of a dinner given by Millicent, Duchess of Sutherland, based on the premise that the surnames of all the distinguished women in London began with the letter *B*.

It is hard to establish what the character and the convictions of someone one knew well were in the days before one knew her. Not long ago, however, I came upon a book entitled *Golden String: A Day Book for Busy Men and Women*. It is an anthology published in 1902 by Susan, Lady Malmesbury, and Violet Brooke-Hunt to which my mother contributed. The passages she chose are asterisked. They come from a great variety of sources, but most of them deal in one way or another with the need for action. There are quotations from Carlyle ("Our grand business undoubtedly is, not to *see* what lies dimly at a distance, but to *do* what lies clearly at hand"), and Lavater ("Act well

at the moment, and you have performed a good action to all eternity"),
and Landor ("Those who are quite satisfied sit still and do nothing;
those who are not quite satisfied are the sole benefactors of the earth"),
and Amiel ("The man who insists on seeing with perfect clearness
before he decides, never decides"), and Novalis ("Character is perfectly
educated will"), and Goethe ("To be active is the primary vocation
of man"). I suspect that these are the convictions my mother entertained in the first decade of this century. Certainly they were the
principles on which I was brought up.

For my mother two influences were of special consequence. The
first was that of William Hale White, whose *Autobiography of Mark
Rutherford* describes the spiritual development of a young dissenter,
and one of whose later books, published under the pseudonym Mark
Rutherford, *The Revolution in Tanner's Lane*, overwhelmed her. She
wrote to him and a correspondence ensued. "Undoubtedly," he writes
in one of his letters, "we must have a religion if we are to live. We
must build for ourselves some kind of a shelter, and it will, in the
true sense of the word, be metaphysical. It has to be the work of our
own solitary labour." They met in the London Library. He was, she
wrote years afterwards, "a small man with close cropped grey beard
and hazel eyes. Deprecating the idea of being taken for a prophet or
teacher, he told me that his life had been quite unsuccessful. I explained how much his books had meant to me, and in a quiet sort of
way he seemed pleased. His limpid English still gives me great peace,
but the problems discussed in his books are no longer to me of the
compelling interest they once were. Books which become integrated
in one's personal life are in a different category from those which have
merely interested or amused us, and when we have lived them into
our lives they lose their savour."

The second influence was that of Coole, the home of Lady Gregory
in County Galway, where my mother and her two brothers often
spent holidays. Their connection with Lady Gregory was through
Ceylon, where Sir William Gregory had been governor and Sir Arthur
Birch had also served. Years later, at Lady Gregory's request, my
mother wrote down her memories of Coole, "one of the most comfortable and most beautifully arranged houses I have ever stayed in.
There was an enchantment about the approach, first the arrival at
Gort, then the swift swinging drive through the bracken and grassland
of the park and then the plunge under an avenue of dark ilexes and

a sweep round a nubby patch of grass that used to serve us as a cricket field. One of the strange things about the place was that one never saw a map of it or got a clear idea of it in one's mind as one does with most estates. It always remained mysterious, was always the sort of place in which anything might happen. The seven woods, of which Yeats wrote, wound about the lake and by a river, and in them we used to canter on ponies." On one occasion Yeats and George Moore were fellow guests. "One morning Lady Gregory said to me: 'We want some rabbits for the house. You know Yeats can't shoot. George Moore was brought up on an estate and knows how to handle a gun. Will you take him out and show him where the rabbits are and beat the bracken.' George Moore was not an attractive man to look at, and probably looked as unattractive as he ever did in his life when he appeared ready for our expedition. He wore a bowler hat, and somebody had lent him some knickerbockers. With them he wore thread stockings and black laced boots. He was given one of Robert Gregory's guns to carry, and we wandered down the avenue to the warren. A rabbit belted from the bracken. I said 'Rabbit!' He lifted the gun to his shoulder and there was a click. Another rabbit belted out and I shouted 'Fire!' The same thing happened again. So I walked up to him and said, 'That gun must be at half cock.' 'Oh yes, it is,' said he, and immediately released the trigger. We then walked on a little farther when another rabbit appeared, at which he really did fire, but of course missed. Then throwing the gun petulantly on to the ground he said to me: 'I won't have anything to do with the nasty thing.' I returned home to tell Lady Gregory what a failure our walk had been. I don't know the date of this, but it could not have been very long after *Esther Waters* was out." Moore's *Esther Waters* was published in 1894.

At first my mother found Yeats a mysterious and rather alarming figure. "His enormous shock of black hair, his large black tie, his black trousers and black coat, large black wideawake and in cool weather his long black cloak made him appear to me very strange, stalking slowly along the rides in the woods. At meals we used to sit entranced while he talked to Lady Gregory of leprechauns and fairies and what some old man or woman had told him. He disappeared after breakfast, and used to come down to luncheon often looking dishevelled and worn out. One day I had the temerity to say to him: 'You look as though you have had a very hard morning's work,' and he said to me:

'I have. I have written four lines.' " In London my mother used to visit him "in a little alley behind St. Pancras over a lapidary. The entrance to his rooms was very small and the staircase steep and narrow, and when one got to Yeats's sitting room one found the walls hung with black velvet. In the middle of the room stood the Kelmscott Chaucer on a high reading desk, which I, together with many others of his admirers, had subscribed to buy for him. There I sat listening to him reading his own poems." In 1932 Yeats sent my mother an emotional letter describing Lady Gregory's death (I gave it to the Berg Collection at the New York Public Library), but she could never forgive him for the complacency with which he allowed Coole to be destroyed. One of her last pieces of writing was a review in 1949 in the *Spectator* of the autobiography of Sean O'Casey in which she described how Yeats "after he had become a Senator and one of the leading men in Ireland, made no effort to save Coole as a shrine of culture, but permitted it to be razed to the ground and degraded to a nettlebed."

Inevitably my mother became involved with the Abbey Theatre, not in its initial phase but in 1910 when the withdrawal of a subsidy threatened its continuance. A meeting was arranged by her at her father's house in Old Burlington Street, at which Lady Gregory, Yeats and George Bernard Shaw spoke on the need for an Irish theater. The appeal was successful, and one of the guests, a naturalized Dutchman, at once put up a quarter of the sum required.

My mother's purpose, from which she never deviated, was to write. One of her first books was a translation of Novalis's *Disciples at Saïs*, and another was the life of a woman modern feminists have overlooked, the Dutch mystic Anna van Schurman. Two engravings of Anna van Schurman still look down at me with quiet confidence in my study in Florence. To me the most compelling of her early books was a little volume called *Maxims of a Queen*. It lived in a lavatory at the turn of the staircase, and as a child I read it till I knew it almost by heart. The Queen was Christina of Sweden, and the maxims were apothegms written by her in 1680 in the Palazzo Riario in Rome. She warned one against marriage. "It requires more courage," she declared, "to marry than to go to war." She inculcated skepticism: "We should never believe anything we have not dared to doubt." She disapproved of patience. "Patience," she insisted, "is the virtue of those who lack either courage or force." And she believed that "we should be more miserly with our time than with our money." Looking back, I think that the influence of the *Maxims* must have been very strong, and it was reinforced in the 1960s when I reread them before lecturing at the Council of Europe exhibition on Queen Christina of Sweden organized by my friend Carl Nordenfalk in Stockholm.

A decisive point in my mother's development as a writer was an invitation from Arthur Elliot to contribute articles and book reviews to the *Edinburgh Review*. The *Edinburgh Review* around 1900 was no longer the "kind of Delphic Oracle" described by Carlyle, but it was a paper of great consequence, and through her work for it my mother formed a friendship with the editor which lasted till his death. The manuscript of *Anna van Schurman*, like that of its successor, *Secret Societies and the French Revolution*, was submitted for criticism to Bertrand Russell. "Your style," he wrote of *Anna van Schurman*, "is not as good as it ought to be, partly from trivial faults, partly from an anxiety to give authority to your opinions. Facts need the backing of authority, but opinions do not." *Secret Societies*, which consisted of articles reprinted from the *Edinburgh Review* and the *Nineteenth Century*, he approved but for "the absence of proper movement and development in the treatment of your theme. . . . It seems to me that anything that ends with the Revolution should give the feeling of shooting Niagara; faster, faster and more delirious and wildly intoxicating, and then the sudden crash." The relationship on both sides was one of confidence. "I hope you won't mind my mentioning these things," says Russell in one letter. "I should not think it worth while if I did not have a great belief in your powers." "Please remember," my mother replies, "how grateful I always am to be told the truth."

My mother's interests before the First World War lay in the French Revolution and in the lives of women who left their mark upon events. Her heroine was Madame de Staël, and a view of the Lake of Geneva, the waters of freedom, always hung above her desk. Before the war she began work on a biography of Madame Roland, and this appeared in 1917. "Individual life," she wrote in the preface, "at its best is a profound and passionate business, and the work of the biographer should also be a profound and passionate business, but for the most part it is nothing of the kind, and is a mere refuge for the manufacturer of books." She wrote well but was not a natural writer; the interest of her work, till middle life, rested in what she wished to say, not in the way in which she said it. But what she said was shrewd, penetrating, and frequently original. Her work culminated in old age in two highly regarded and extremely able biographies, of Dickens and Charles Kingsley. She instilled in me and in my brother the conviction that we were meant to write. Her greatest sadness was that she produced, in my brother James, a writer of extraordinary natural talent but with a character so flawed as to prevent his fully realizing his gifts. "If he had had a different character," she used to say, "what a great writer he would have been."

My parents married when they were both thirty-four. They had met some years earlier when my father was on leave from service in Somaliland, but their marriage was delayed by Sir Arthur Birch's unwillingness to accept him as his son-in-law. He objected especially to his daughter marrying the son of a former colonial governor of whose personality and politics he disapproved. To regular members of the colonial service my father's father was anathema. He was looked on as a politician turned administrator (which indeed he was). A ready sympathy with the underdog that was second nature to someone born on the wrong side of the tracks in Cork was blamed for raising trouble even in peaceful colonies like Mauritius and Hong Kong. Sir John Chancellor, one of his successors in Mauritius, told me one night at dinner that he was a disloyal governor. The opposite case was presented in a profile in the *Whirlwind* in 1890 that accompanied a poor drawing of him by Walter Sickert: "In 1865 he left Parliament and entered upon a long series of Colonial Governorships, which enabled him to give very practical expression to his nationalist views. He at once set pluckily to work to reform the whole system of corrupt patronage, conferring posts upon competent natives in preference to the *mauvais sujets* who are foisted on new countries after failing in the old. Sir John has also accomplished wonders for the cause of Home Rule in the Colonies." Sir Arthur also objected to the marriage on religious grounds. From my mother's standpoint the decision was a grave one. She asked the advice of Bertrand Russell, who replied: "It is not right to sacrifice marriage on account of parents. And generally, in important matters, the young have the greater right, because the future depends upon them. When the young sacrifice themselves to the old, the latter half of their lives is rendered useless. Generally it is worse than useless, because when they become old they exact a similar sacrifice from whatever young person can be induced to make it. You say you wonder whether you have a right to be selfish. But much more than your own happiness is involved, and it does not do to be afraid of happiness when it comes. Yes, you may rely on my keeping silence absolutely; also upon my being very much your friend."

With Sir Arthur's concurrence but not with his approval, the marriage took place in June 1910. My father at the time was at the Staff College, so married life began at Camberley and continued in York, after my father's appointment to a post at Northern Command. "Our happiness made my life seem complete," wrote my mother later. "We hardly wanted to go outside our own garden, and had no need of anything more than we had in each other." At twenty minutes to midnight on December 13, 1913, at a house in Grosvenor Place overlooking the garden of Buckingham Palace, I was born. One of my godfathers was a general, Sir John Gough, who won a VC in the First World War, and the other was an air marshal, Sir Robert Brooke-Popham, who lost the whole of Southeast Asia in the Second.

I was fond of my father though I never knew him well. At the time of my parents' marriage he must have seemed a romantic figure, but I could never see him in that light. His favorite poet was Swinburne, his favorite novel Meredith's *Ordeal of Richard Feverel*, and his favorite painter Renoir, whose *Parapluies* we used sometimes to visit at the Tate Gallery. He was a keen but clumsy watercolor painter. Not long ago I was shown his elaborate paint box and palette, which are now used by an Australian painter in the Val d'Arno. Kind and sensitive though he was, he was difficult to talk to, and only once or twice at the end of his life did we skirt the edge of intimacy. He idolized his father's memory, and was, along with my mother, an enthusiastic supporter of the Irish Dominion League, for which he produced in 1920 a well-argued booklet, *The Irish Dominion: A Method of Approach to a Settlement*. His aspirations were political, but there was no way in which they could be realized. He was in the Army when he married, and there, till his retirement as a major general, he remained. His outward appearance was distinguished, but he was haunted by a sense of failure to become whatever he had hoped to be. A passionate Liberal, he wrote competently and spoke well, but his judgment on people and events was emotional and often wrong. For my mother he became something of a liability. He was wasteful and unpractical, and was not allowed to handle money or to carve. My brother (whom he detested and who detested him) inherited many of his weaknesses.

My mother, from the time that I first knew her, was a dynamic and formidably able woman. "Mummy tiger" I called her when she irrupted into the day nursery. After the Great War broke out, she became a member of the Central Prisoners of War Committee, and was responsible, under the British Red Cross Society, for organizing aid to British civilian prisoners of war in Germany. The only surviving evidence of this activity is a paper she edited, *The British Prisoner of War*, which was designed "to give a more useful and accurate survey of the needs, circumstances and experiences of British prisoners than would be possible in any other way." For her war work she became a Lady of Grace of the Order of St. John of Jerusalem—I remember a mysterious ceremony when the Duke of Connaught, wearing a long black cloak, bestowed the decoration on her—and was invested with the new honor of Dame of the British Empire (DBE). Thereafter she was known as Dame Una.

These are the genes that I inherited.

2

A VOCATION

I AND MY BROTHER JAMES (WHO WAS THREE YEARS YOUNGER; HE was born in November 1916) were brought up in that blessed period when children led private, secluded lives. James was more temperamental than I was. Like me, he had been born at home, as most children were then, and the first thing that I remember vividly is looking down into his cradle in my mother's bedroom. This was the start of a protective relationship, but from the first he demanded attention in a way that I did not and threw his shoes at me across the nursery if he did not receive it. We saw our mother after breakfast and at tea time, and life was controlled by a nanny, Agnes Treloar, who later became my mother's maid and remained with her till her death. She was an excellent letter writer, and she believed in knowledge. From her penurious wages she subscribed to *Harmsworth's Universal Encyclopaedia*, which came out in monthly parts, giving us nine bound volumes on the day she had been with us for eight years. She outlived my mother, and when she died I wrote to James: "She believed in us in a simple, direct, unquestioning way, and we both owe her an awful lot for those long lessons in industry and determination, and for the sense that the completion of a task is its own reward." Though I was not conscious of it at the time, mine was a planned childhood. My mother taught me the value of time. She had a gold watch with the same Greek inscription that Dr. Johnson had on his: For the night cometh. It was inherited and lost by James, who did not believe the night would ever come.

I was excited by railway engines, and staying in Devonshire with my grandmother, who lived at Teignmouth, I used to watch them

from the seawall and take down their names. Few people nowadays
will remember what instruments of education Great Western railway
engines were; for me *Rob Roy* and *Quentin Durward* were engines long
before they became books. In the day nursery, the main sources of
pleasure were large, elaborate jigsaw puzzles (how important they
must have been for the training of visual memory); a model theater,
produced by a firm called Pollock in Hoxton, which left me with an
abiding interest in nineteenth-century stage design; a typewriter (a
very small one with a mauve ribbon); and a scratchy gramophone.
On the typewriter I typed plays, which I sent to my mother's friend
Lady Gregory, who sent me her own plays back (a photocopy of a
letter to Lady Gregory written when I was six reached me not long
ago as a Christmas greeting from the New York Public Library). On
the gramophone I played the few records I was allowed; a little Mozart,
the *Freischütz* overture, and some Rossini, Verdi, and Bellini, but no
Puccini and no Wagner. The HMV yellow-label records had a thin
sound, but in their own way they were standard-forming, and when
nowadays I hear singers plowing their coarse way through "Parigi, o
cara" and "Batti, batti, o bel Masetto," I still have a faint auditory
memory of how they were once sung. In childhood music for me
meant opera. I was not taken to the opera in the way children are
now, but my interest was fanned by visits to a shop window in Oxford
Street, where, when the *Ring* was on at Covent Garden, there was a
tableau of Brünnhilde on her rock, and by grotesque but fascinating
photographs in a book called *Opera at Home* of Tetrazzini as Lakmé
and Titta Ruffo as Rigoletto. The first film I saw was of myself posting
a letter to my father in Mesopotamia, and the first time I went to the
theater was to see a play called *Where the Rainbow Ends*, about some
orphan children who were reunited with their parents as the curtain
fell. I sobbed through the last act, and only when I saw the play again
two years later did I realize how false and vulgar its symbolism was.
This was the first occasion on which I was conscious of seeing through
a fake. I was sent prematurely to a music school, which I disliked
since I knew nothing about keys or harmony, and it was decided that
I was unmusical; never thereafter was I allowed a music lesson. When
I learned to play the piano, it was through a form of self-tuition called
Naunton's National Music System. I was also taken to an art school
in Jermyn Street, where one drew live guinea pigs and rabbits in
crayon on brown paper. I disliked this too, and to this day I cannot
draw.

More important were books. First they were read to one, and then one read them for oneself. The diet was the conventional one of the time. There were heartrending stories about animals, like *Black Beauty* and *The Story of a Red Deer*, and Charles Kingsley's *Water Babies*, which in pre-Freudian days was regarded as a healthy book, and Captain Marryat's *Children of the New Forest*. In the nursery I read *The Children of the New Forest* again and again. When, not long ago, I bought it in paperback at a bookshop in Pisa, I realized that it was only the ability in children to empathize with other children that lent suspense to its slow-moving narrative. In *Swiss Family Robinson* I remember with fraught pleasure a description of an anaconda moving like a sail along the beach and swallowing a donkey; the incident is omitted from modern bowdlerized versions of the book. I was enthralled by historical novels, especially Henty's, where the same lay figures were moved at will from one century to the next, and Harrison Ainsworth. How, I wondered, as I looked again the other day at Ainsworth's *Windsor Castle*, could this ungainly, leaden story have stimulated anyone's historical imagination? I liked listening to early Dickens novels but not reading them, because the edition in the nursery had the deterrent of Phiz's illustrations. Conversely I enjoyed reading Ruskin's *King of the Golden River* because its illustrations buoyed up the text. If somebody sent me a lavish book for Christmas whose illustrations might cause bad dreams, it was confiscated and replaced by some less harmful book. Edmund Dulac and Arthur Rackham were victims of this policy. I admire them today, but in my childhood they were forbidden fruit. One intruder found its way into the nursery bookcase, Pope's *Rape of the Lock* with Beardsley's illustrations. It generated a dislike for Beardsley I have never wholly overcome.

In the night nursery there was a Medici print of Velázquez's *Don Baltasar Carlos*—as I undressed I watched him cantering with his deadpan face through the lowering countryside—but in the day nursery there were no works of art. The things I was encouraged to collect were natural objects, shells and birds' eggs and butterflies. Some of the seashells were collected during summers at St. Briac, and some, the prettiest, were bought from a shop near the Hammersmith Broadway. I was also given a collection of Southeast Asian land snails assembled by one of my father's forebears. Among the moss-green and rust-brown shells was a sapphire-blue snail shell from Sumatra. When I took it to the Natural History Museum I found that the examples there were all but colorless, but mine had never been exposed to light, and when I look at it, it still gives me the shock of pleasure it gave me when I first handled it seventy years ago.

Gradually, however, nature gave way to art, in the form not of the Italian paintings which hung on the drawing-room walls, but of Chinese ceramics and archaic Chinese jades. My parents' collection was a very modest one compared with the great collections of Eumorfopoulos and Oscar Raphael that existed in London at the time, and the Korean ceramics which were its centerpiece were sold in 1926. But it was formed with great enthusiasm, especially on my father's side, and photographs of piece after piece were submitted for professional judgment to Salmann in Cologne or Laufer in Chicago. As a child I simulated interest in each acquisition as it was made, and then became genuinely interested. My favorite object was an early Ming cloisonné begging bowl, with purple and white horses galloping round it, which still stands on my mantelpiece. In 1920 my mother was commissioned to write an illustrated book, *Early Chinese Jades*. It is now long out of date, but was in its time a serious piece of work, and in a rudimentary fashion it introduced me to the problems of connoisseurship.

The families of soldiers were condemned to a process called "following the drum." This meant that I was brought up in a succession of rented houses, not in a house my parents owned. Home, therefore, did not signify a house; it signified the objects with which the house was filled. My father, after the Great War, served a term in the War Office in London, where we lived on Primrose Hill near the north entrance to the Zoo. The Zoo was less up-to-date than it is now, but the proximity of animals and the sounds they made at night brought the jungle very close. Visitors were allowed to feed the animals more freely than they are today, and I especially remember the dirty yellow teeth of the rustling porcupines and the serrated violet surface of the giraffes' tongues. I have retained a spasmodic interest in zoos, which led me years later to the reptile house at San Diego (where the snakes with their fresh skins look as though they have been scrubbed by some overzealous painting restorer), to the romantic wildlife park, and to the monkey cages at Seattle.

London was succeeded by a period in Berlin on the Commission of Control, where we lived in a dark apartment in the Pariserstrasse. It belonged to a lesbian, Baroness Wollwart-Wesendenck, with whom my father had rather unsuitably made friends, and on the far side of

the engraved glass doors separating the drawing room from the dining
room was one of the pianos on which Wagner is said to have composed.
On the journey to Berlin my nurse was taken off the train at Bentheim
for lack of some essential visa, and James and I were delivered to my
parents on the platform at the Zoologischer Garten station by a heavily
powdered old lady called Princess Helena Victoria. I played whist
with a German governess and read Schiller, earlier than I should have
done, since I was surprised that in the first scene of *Maria Stuart*
Paulet, whom I supposed to be a woman, seemed grammatically to
be a man. A stolid butler called Max took us to Sans Souci and the
Neues Palais (I never went back to either till after the Second World
War), and I slid with my mother in felt overshoes round the palace
at Charlottenburg.

In Berlin I became passionately interested in butterflies. The surrounding woods harbored butterflies which were almost extinct in
England. "I am dreadfully excited," I wrote to my mother, who was
at St. Moritz. "Yesterday we went to Seegefeld, Finkenkrug and
Finsterberg, and at Seegefeld I caught a Camberwell Beauty. It is a
perfect specimen with a brilliant yellow edge. We saw several others,
but they were in the top of the willows." At Kufstein in the Tyrol I
chased transparent, fast-flying Parnassus Apollos, with a pedantic
entomologist who pinched the heads of butterflies instead of putting
them in a killing bottle and insisted that they should be set on boards
lined with *Torf*. I pursued them because of the aesthetic satisfaction
they gave me, not, like Nabokov, from genetic interest. Looking at
the green-and-brown pictures painted by Braque in the 1930s, I am
reminded of the markings of an oleander hawk moth that I hatched
out in a clothes cupboard in Berlin. When I took one of my Camberwell Beauties from Berlin to be set professionally in London, I was
asked excitedly if it had been caught in England. "Yes," I replied.
This was the first lie that left me with a long-term sense of guilt.

There followed another period in London when my father was once
more at the War Office, and then the prospect of an appointment as
military attaché. Initially this was to have been in Peking, and I spent
my holidays copying Chinese characters in black ink on small white
cards. In 1926, however, the appointment was switched to Washington.

In 1923 my mother became a Catholic. Her conversion was directed
by a devout Dominican, Father Bede Jarrett, who became first a friend

of my mother's and then, when I was at Oxford and he was at Black-friars, a close friend of my own. The conversion was laborious, not for any lack of sympathy with Catholicism—in the middle of the nineteenth century a Watts-Russell in the local living of Benefield had become a Catholic in the wake of Newman, and one of his sons, Julian Watts-Russell, died as a Papal Zouave at Mentana—but because of the restrictions it imposed upon free thought. Before and during the Great War she enjoyed perfect health, but in Berlin she developed the first symptoms of an illness, involving bronchial hemorrhages followed by high temperatures, from which she suffered for the remainder of her life. In Germany it was explained as tuberculosis, in England it resulted in an empyema, and in Switzerland it was treated by flooding the lungs with iodine. It was correctly diagnosed only in 1933 by Sir Aldo Castellani, who on my mother's first visit to him produced a pamphlet in which every symptom was described. It was called bronchomycosis, and in those days could be treated but not cured. From then on my mother's life was a courageous struggle against ill health.

At the age of nine, I was, in the usual fashion, sent away to school. My father had been unhappy at a Jesuit school, Beaumont, and was determined that I should not suffer Jesuit discipline. The alternative was to be educated by Benedictines at Ampleforth or Downside. The choice fell on Downside, where the ratio of boys who became priests was said to be lower than at Ampleforth. At that time the Junior School was on the same site as the Upper School, so I was consigned to Somerset for nine interminable years. By temperament I am not gregarious, and I have always disliked group activities. I hated rugger and was extremely bad at it, and since the summers were a torment from hay fever I hated cricket too. My letters from school are uninformative. If I gave my mother any information, she was prone to act on it and protest to the headmaster, so I told her as little as was possible. The letters record deep unhappiness, but though I was not positively happy till the last two years that I was there, I do not recall being nearly so unhappy as I claimed. There was a passable library, and the corridors on the ground floor were punctuated with Medici prints. I recall them every time I see the Albertinelli *Visitation* in the Uffizi. I enjoyed reading Tacitus and Ovid and Juvenal, and I learned the whole of *Macbeth* by heart. There was a weekly film (a silent film, generally with Harold Lloyd) and there were occasional concerts by the Abbot, who was an ambitious, slapdash pianist, and by John McCormack, whose son was at the school. A portly figure, he sang the sort of music that was thought suitable for schoolboys, a little Handel and some Irish songs. Not till years later did I hear, in the Albert Hall, his incomparable singing of *Lieder* by Hugo Wolf. One could bicycle to Wells Cathedral—it took the best part of a day there and back—and once a year there were collective visits by charabanc to Stourhead and Longleat. I was rebellious, but I got a large number of prizes. To this day I do not understand the self-assurance with which I set out to secure, one after another, all six volumes of Crowe and Cavalcaselle's *History of Painting in Italy* and the three volumes of Berenson's *Study and Criticism of Italian Art*.

As one grew up the presence of a monastery conferred two inestimable benefits. The first was liturgical. The choral singing of Palestrina at Mass and of Vittoria at Tenebrae in Holy Week was of superlative quality (it was spoiled only when the Junior School, and with it the trebles, moved elsewhere). Years later, scrambling through the pine forest at Vallombrosa, Berenson asked me what I believed. I said I believed tenaciously in a number of things that were inherently improbable, and that the fixative by which I was attached to them was ritual.

To sit on a firm cushion of orthodox belief had, I thought, many advantages. It meant that you need not waste your time speculating about fundamentals, but could concentrate your skepticism on the subject with which you were concerned. It meant also that one's standpoint was closer than it would otherwise have been to that of the artists with whom one dealt. They believed in the immanence of the supernatural and so did I. Like them, I would not be surprised if a saint suddenly plunged through the ceiling of my room. It meant that you believed in the access of what creative artists would call inspiration and what noncreative people like myself would consider grace. To pray as you pray in the Palm Sunday liturgy that your humility may be protected from the horns of unicorns (unicorns in that context meaning, I presume, rhinoceroses) adds a poetic dimension to ordinary life.

The second benefit was the presence in the monastery of monks who did not teach. In my last years at Downside when I was being groomed for an Oxford scholarship, I built up an enduring debt to three of them. One was Dom David Knowles, the historian of monasticism and later Regius Professor of History at Cambridge, whose mastery of historical method sets a standard to which I still aspire. Another was a former clergyman, Brother Christopher Butler, later abbot of Downside, whose first Mass I served when he was ordained. The third was the music master, Dom Thomas Symons. A nephew of Arthur Symons, he took me analytically through the Mozart piano concertos, and I listened on his wireless when Toscanini gave his first London concerts with the New York Philharmonic Orchestra and when Ponselle's Norma and Stabile's Falstaff were broadcast from Covent Garden. Whenever I hear the magical opening of the last scene of *Falstaff*, I recall the smoke-filled study in which I heard it first. I wrote to Dom Thomas many years later to say how greatly he had enriched my life.

In the 1920s America seemed a long way away, and would have seemed still farther had two of the sons of the ambassador, Sir Esme Howard, not been my contemporaries at Downside. Before the days of air conditioning the British Embassy in Washington was accustomed to move for the summer to the north shore of Massachusetts, so in June 1927 our whole household (quite a modest household—my mother, my brother and myself, my mother's maid, a cook, housemaid and parlor maid) sailed for Boston. I should like to say that this was the beginning of my love affair with the United States, but it was nothing of the kind. The United States of 1927 was very different from the United States of today. It was a chauvinist, illiberal country—it was there that I first heard of anti-Semitism—and since national characteristics are generally more pronounced in the young than in adults, the transition was a far from easy one. One's contemporaries were more efficient; they seemed to have a higher level of physical vitality—playing better tennis and swimming more strongly—and they made me feel for the first time in my life that I was provincial. Tennis nonetheless became the only game in which I have ever felt real interest. In the annual tennis tournament at Marblehead I sat enthralled as Helen Wills won match after match, and in Washington on an indoor court I once saw Bill Tilden play. Before the advent of television I used to go from time to time to Wimbledon, and at the Victoria and Albert, having no television of my own, I imported a television set for the duration of the tournament. Now in Florence I still look forward avidly to the telecasts from the Stade Roland-Garros and Wimbledon and Flushing Meadow.

In two summers at Manchester-by-the-Sea I learned something about New England—my parents were inveterate sightseers—but only during Christmas holidays in Washington did there spring up the overpowering liking for America I have felt ever since. The residential parts of Washington have changed very little and I feel nostalgia whenever I go back there. At Manchester we lived for one summer in a rather unattractive roadside house, which I remember only because the next house was owned by a Mrs. Anthony, whose son Edgar was a graduate of the Fogg and wrote good books on the Florentine Baptistry and on early Florentine architecture and decoration. The Anthonys were cared for by a young Italian manservant. This seemed to me an ideal form of life, and when years later I set up in London on my own, I made an ill-fated experiment on the same lines. The following summer we moved to a secluded house behind the Singing Beach called Thunderbolt Hill, which had been built for a Boston publisher. Dickens had stayed in it, and in a drawer there was what purported to be a piece of Cortez's shroud and a small Shakespeare that had belonged to Leigh Hunt and had markings by Shelley. My brother went to school in Washington, but I remained at Downside, traveling to America in the summer and at Christmas only. In the short vacation after Easter I stayed in Essex with my uncle, Wyndham Birch, at whose marriage I had been a page in 1923. My aunt, Lady Susan Birch, was a close friend of Melba, and at the wedding service I heard Melba sing. Born a Yorke, my aunt seemed, like all the members of her family, to have been transposed in some mysterious fashion from the Regency. She was short and warm and funny, and through her I had a foot in a world I would not otherwise have known.

Brief as they were, my months in America were decisive, in that they provided me with a vocation. From then on I knew I would devote myself to studying works of art. It is difficult to define how this occurred. If you saw works of art in English houses, it was bad manners to admit that you had noticed them. In America, on the other hand, you were shown every Hoppner over every mantelpiece. I listened to discussions about the Isabella Stewart Gardner Museum in Boston, which was opened to the public in 1926, and the new Fogg Art Museum, which opened its doors in 1927, and whenever I was taken into Boston to have my hair cut, I went to a museum. Revisiting Fenway Court the other day, and sitting in a wooden chair in front of Giotto's *Presentation in the Temple*, I recalled the sensation of sitting in the same chair at the same desk sixty years before. I was not interested then in the attribution of the picture or in its structure; I was fascinated by its content. It was an illustration but it differed from other illustrations in the gravity of the emotions by which the figures were inspired. In the same way the tremulous *Crucifixion* of Simone Martini in the Fogg Art Museum became part of the visual baggage one would carry throughout life. It was many years before I regarded the language used by painters as an entity called style, or looked at pictures as works of art. To me, at that time, painting was visual literature and its interest derived from the authority or the imagination with which each subject was described. In Boston there was a firm known as Perry Pictures, which sold inexpensive, wrinkly sepia reproductions of a great range of paintings. Illustrated art books were less common then than they are now, and it was through Perry Pictures that I first became acquainted with the Rubenses and Rembrandts at Munich and the Titians in Dresden and Vienna.

One day in the summer of 1928 I was taken by my mother to tea with Miss Helen Clay Frick and her mother at Pride's Crossing. She lived in an enormous red brick house with a phalanx of white gardeners pulling up plaintains from the lawn. I remember the visit for three reasons. The first is that on the wall there hung two pictures she had bought for the Frick Collection that spring, the Duccio *Temptation of Christ* (the first Duccio I had ever looked at seriously) and the *Christ Carrying the Cross* attributed to Barna da Siena. The graphic dialogue between Christ and Satan in the Duccio and the patient, submissive figure of Christ in the Barna stamped themselves upon my mind. The second reason is that my mother mentioned the name of Berenson. "Berenson," said Miss Frick stiffly, "never let me hear the man's name again." As I had not heard it before, this also made an indelible impression. When I told the story years later to B.B., he was not amused. The third is that I learned for the first time about Siena, for which Miss Frick and her mother were leaving on the following day. It was a place, I was told, where there was nothing to eat and to which one was compelled to take tinned hams and other food sufficient to support a garrison in a state of siege. On the tea table there was a splendid silver service. Miss Frick poured from the kettle into the teapot, but nothing happened. She poured again, with the same result, and then opening the kettle lid, she pulled out a dishcloth.

In Washington there were fewer pictures to look at—the only Old Masters were in the Corcoran Gallery of Art—but I was taken to see Duncan Phillips and his collection, and I still remember the impression made by the Delacroix of Paganini and by one of the Courbet winter scenes. I thought Arthur B. Davies, to whom an entire room was at the time dedicated, a remarkable painter, and I think this still. On one memorable occasion I saw the magnificent paintings that are now in the National Gallery of Art hanging frame to frame in Andrew Mellon's apartment. At the Grenville Bookshop on Connecticut Avenue my father bought me Berenson's *Sienese Painter of the Franciscan Legend* and I bought for myself the three volumes of Crowe and Cavalcaselle's *History of Painting in North Italy*, which I read with obsessive attention during a rough crossing to Southampton on the *Mauretania*. Back at school I formed the habit of retreating to a classroom in the evenings to annotate the book. "The attribution of this picture to Catena," I wrote in what was then prim handwriting, "is most unlikely. Possibly by Basaiti?" The only person there who encouraged this development was the abbot of Downside, Dom John Chapman, who had a photographic memory of the contents of museums in northern Italy. He gave me early catalogues of the galleries at Bergamo and Verona and Vicenza which I still own. They were useful in a practical sense since they were illustrated, but they were useful morally as well; he was the first respect-worthy person who realized that my field of interest was not an eccentricity.

In the summer of 1929, when my father came back to Europe on leave, we lived for a time in a bat-ridden Saracen tower called the Maison du Diable on Lac du Bourget (where I was steeped in Lamartine and read Virgil with the local priest, who pronounced Latin as though it were French), and then at Chexbres on the Lake of Geneva, where Hodler painted some of his greatest landscapes. A specialist in Lausanne reported that I had a double spinal curvature ("*Ne bougez pas,*" he said as my spine was photographed, but time after time I budged). My parents forbade him to operate, but thanks to his diagnosis I was removed from school for two terms, and when I eventually returned there was exempted from everything I did not wish to do.

In the months spent with my mother on the Lake of Geneva my true education began. I read voraciously, and typed my mother's books. I was paid for typing them, and fined when I made mistakes.

I was pleased at the time to have the money—I spent it on Old Master drawings, which could then be bought inexpensively by post from a London firm called Parsons in the Brompton Road—but in retrospect I am still more grateful for the discipline the work imposed and for the range of interests that it opened up. It has been second nature for me ever since to sit for hours on end at a typewriter. One of the books I typed, *Three Englishwomen in America*, about Fanny Kemble and Fanny Trollope and Harriet Martineau in the United States, was reissued not long ago. The most exacting job was that of transcribing, from a faded manuscript, the American journal of Mrs. Basil Hall, later published as *The Aristocratic Journey*. When I myself started lecturing in America, I found that many of the places I visited were vested with a historic dimension through my memories of this work. Mrs. Hall's husband, a naval captain, made drawings with the camera lucida; I bought one, but found it was intended for people less impatient than myself. In the Hotel Victoria at Glion, where we lived— my mother was under treatment at Valmont nearby—I learned about Rilke, who had been treated by her doctor, and read *The Notebooks of Malte Laurids Brigge*. A regular visitor to the hotel was Santayana, who when we arrived had just returned to Rome, leaving behind his secretary (who later wrote his life) and some annotated copies of Desmond MacCarthy's paper *Life and Letters*. A Frenchwoman, Madame Gouin, had tried to scrape acquaintance with him in the elevator, without result, since he had always pressed the button for his own floor and never asked her which was hers. "*C'est un homme extraordinaire*," she said, "*il déteste les femmes*." A Dutch friend of my mother's was in the habit of spending part of the winter at the Palace Hotel in Montreux. He was named Drucker, and was responsible for forming the great collection of Hague School pictures in the Rijksmuseum and for building the annex in which they are housed. Nowadays visitors go to the Drucker-Fraser galleries mainly to see Prud'hon's *Schimmelpenninck Family*, but to me the Marises and Bosbooms, which I knew first from postcards given me by Drucker, are old friends. I used to own a pastel by Isaäc Israëls which Jozef Israëls had given to my mother, when she was staying with the Druckers. I passed it on to a friend, and I am sorry that I did so; it was as good as a second-class Manet. From my months in Switzerland I cherish the memory of a day at St. Maurice d'Agaune, with its incomparable treasury and its Byzantine textiles; a visit to the Reber collection outside Lausanne, with its great Picassos and Juan Gris, where I first yielded to the seduction of Cubist paintings; and of a concert in Lausanne Cathedral, where Kreisler played the Brahms and Beethoven violin concertos in one program with Weingartner conducting. I had never heard either concerto live before, and to listen to ideal performances of both on one occasion was a never to be forgotten experience.

At Downside my education had been strictly classical, but in 1931 it was decided that my Greek was not strong enough to enable me to get a scholarship, and I was summarily switched to eighteenth- and nineteenth-century history. Was I to go to Oxford or Cambridge? My father favored Cambridge, so I was sent to see Sir Sidney Cockerell at the Fitzwilliam Museum. A disciple of Ruskin and a creative museum director, he was also a snob of a rather unusual kind; he used to give away not letters written to him by the great but the envelopes in which they had arrived. To my embarrassment he gave me, as a special treasure, an envelope addressed to him by Charles Doughty, and I accepted it not having heard of *Travels in Arabia Deserta* and ignorant of who Doughty was. My own preference was for Oxford, not Cambridge, and in 1932 I was awarded a Williams Exhibition at Balliol College.

In 1931, while I was still at school, a friend of my mother's, Logan Pearsall Smith, sent me down to the London suburb of Richmond to visit a new meteor in the artistic sky named Kenneth Clark. His reputation stood very high; he had worked with Berenson on revising *The Drawings of the Florentine Painters*, he was cataloguing the drawings of Leonardo da Vinci at Windsor, and he was working on the Commemorative Catalogue of the Italian exhibition at Burlington House. When I rang the bell at the Old Palace, the door was opened by a young man of extraordinary charm, confidence, and suavity. He proved helpful—he gave me proofs of the plates from the Commemorative Catalogue, some of which I framed for my study at school—and he showed me his drawings. Would I like him to tell me who did them, he asked, or would I prefer to form my own impressions? I said I had rather be told. At the end we came to a dim French drawing in red chalk. "I call this my *faux Vatteau*," he said, and I felt then (and for some years afterwards) that he was everything that I aspired to be. This was the opening of a long relationship, which ended only in 1983 when I came over from New York to speak in St. James's, Piccadilly, at his memorial service. At the time I went up to Oxford,

Kenneth Clark was the keeper of Western art in the Ashmolean Museum.

My father's last post after leaving Washington was as commander of the 50th (Northumbrian) Division. Its headquarters were in Darlington, and through my last years at school and the whole of my period at Oxford we lived in an ugly house with a rose garden looking over the river at Hurworth-on-Tees. It is always said that you cannot know England if you have lived only in the South. But around 1930 living in the North of England was a dispiriting experience. The Depression was at its worst. Colliery towns through which one drove were filled with unemployed sitting idly outside their houses, and the territorials who came annually to camp were emaciated and underfed. By temperament I am nonpolitical, but I would have been insensitive indeed if this had not affected my attitude toward politics and toward society. Years later, as a museum director, I felt greater sympathy with Socialist than with Tory governments.

The cultural resources of northeastern England were then very thin. The York City Art Gallery, which is now an excellent museum with a strong collection of paintings, was a mausoleum filled with pictures by Etty; and the Laing Art Gallery at Newcastle upon Tyne was also of little interest. The only significant public collection was the Bowes Museum at Barnard Castle, an elephantine copy of the Tuileries built by John Bowes and his wife, the Comtesse de Montalbo, an amateur painter, to house their collection of ceramics, their sometimes excellent French furniture and tapestries, and almost a thousand paintings, ranging from an important Dutch triptych by the Master of the Virgo inter Virgines to an early Fantin-Latour. The strength of the collection lay in its Spanish paintings—they included a magnificent El Greco and a Goya prison scene—but among them was a Sienese panel from the predella of Sassetta's Arte della Lana altarpiece. The museum was neglected and ill run, and most of its few visitors were people who had come to Barnard Castle to see the site of the school described in the early chapters of Dickens's *Nicholas Nickleby*, Dotheboys Hall. But when I returned there in 1967, to open an exhibition of Spanish paintings, I found that, thanks to an energetic local committee and an efficient director, the museum had been reanimated.

The pictures in the Bowes Museum were not the only Spanish paintings in the neighborhood. At Auckland Castle, the seat of the Bishop of Durham, the dining room was filled with twelve life-size paintings by Zurbarán of Jacob and his sons. They were very dirty, and were said in books on Spanish painting to have been painted for export to the Spanish colonies. When Kenneth Clark came up to stay, I drove him over to see them. A tea party was in progress, and we sneaked away to look at other rooms. One of them was decorated with excised illuminations attached with drawing pins to velvet mounts. I asked the bishop's wife, Mrs. Hensley-Henson, about them through her ear trumpet. "We call them Uncle Denny's scraps," she said, and they proved indeed to have been collected by James Dennistoun, the author of that fascinating book *The Memoirs of the Dukes of Urbino*. Negotiating for them afterwards, Kenneth Clark landed the whole collection (and very splendid it was; it included a quantity of illuminations by Niccolò da Bologna and many other miniatures of first-rate quality) at cut price.

Not far away was the Morritt house of Rokeby. It is now remembered as the home in the nineteenth century of one famous painting, Velázquez's *Rokeby Venus*, but when I went there in the early 1930s, the grounds, with their ancient yews and fir trees flanking the fast-flowing river Greta, were the quintessence of romanticism. I had an old-fashioned liking for narrative poetry, and my response to the North of England, especially to Durham and Rokeby and Barnard Castle, sprang from the poems of Sir Walter Scott. In 1930, in anticipation of the centenary of Scott's death in 1832, my mother was commissioned to write a life of Sir Walter; it appeared in 1932 in the same year as Buchan's more orthodox biography. At Hurworth, therefore, I read all the Scott novels (even *Count Robert of Paris*) and started work on a catalogue of his portraits. In number the portraits of Scott are second only to those of the Duke of Wellington, and they cover a fascinating transitional period between the elitist portraits of Reynolds and Romney and the bourgeois portraits of the nineteenth century. Portraits are the outcome of a bilateral relationship, of whose nature there is commonly no record. But there is abundant evidence, from Scott's letters and diaries and Lockhart's life, of exactly why each of the Scott portraits took the form it did and of what the sitter thought of it. Had the catalogue been printed it would have been my first work on art history. As it was, I returned to it from time to time over the years, and then gave the manuscript to Francis Russell, who in 1987 published an excellent catalogue of his own.

The most interesting aspect of my mother's work on Scott was an attempt to apply the concepts of style criticism to the Scott novels. Scott published no novels till the sale of his narrative poems declined, and then, after 1814, novel after novel poured from the press. My mother's case was that Scott's superhuman productivity could be explained only if he had been writing prose romances at a far earlier time, and that certain novels, *Redgauntlet*, *Rob Roy*, and *St. Ronan's Well* among them, were composites of earlier and later work. This theory (which was also taken up by another student of Scott, Donald Carswell) still seems to me plausible, but to the best of my belief it has never been further investigated.

Not far from Hurworth, on the far side of the Tees, lay Halnaby Hall, the scene of Byron's disastrous honeymoon. A charming middle-sized William and Mary house, it was demolished after the last war. The bedroom and bed in which Byron and his wife had slept were preserved, but the crimson bed curtains, through which he saw the firelight and thought he was in hell, had been cut down for chair seats. James and I were given some surplus pieces of the fabric by the owner, Lady Wilson-Todd. Years later, he gave his to Harold Nicolson and I passed mine on to Elizabeth Longford. With my mother I went to Seaham, an elegant house looking over the North Sea which by then had become a tubercular hospital, to see the room in which the marriage took place, and to Elemore, where Lady Byron was brought up. I recall only that the owners of Elemore, who were called Baker-Baker, had a Cranach and that there was a coal pit at the bottom of the garden. The memory of these visits persisted, and the other day (I am speaking of the year 1988) I went round a Byron centenary exhibition in the Biblioteca Classense at Ravenna, looking at the relics from Newstead that Byron gave to Teresa Guiccioli.

From Newcastle small boats plied along the Tyne past Jarrow and Tynemouth and over the North Sea to Rotterdam, and in one of these, with my father, I paid my first visit to Holland. The forged Vermeer *Supper at Emmaus* was in the news (the only person to my knowledge to question it at that time was the dealer Alfred Scharf), and I looked at it from a respectful distance over a rope in the Boymans Museum. My father was highly responsive to painting, and it was a great pleasure looking with him at pictures in the Rijksmuseum and the Mauritshuis. What impressed me most on this exploratory visit was Haarlem, partly for the two late portrait groups by Hals (when I go back to see them now I still wonder at their explosive force) and partly for the drawings in the Teyler Museum. The photographs that I took back were of the Teyler drawings by Claude.

At Oxford the 1930s were a halcyon time. School relationships were ruptured and one made friends in the world in which one would in future live. Looking through old engagement books, I see repeatedly the names of Jo Grimond, who got the Williams scholarship when I got my exhibition, and Lionel Brett, who became rector of the Royal College of Art and a member of my Advisory Council at the Victoria and Albert, and Charles Mitchell, later at the Warburg Institute and Bryn Mawr, and Stuart Hampshire, the philosopher, and Jeremy Hutchinson, a future chairman of the Tate Gallery, and Giles Robertson, the biographer of Giovanni Bellini, and Duncan Wilson, who became ambassador in Moscow and wrote a first-rate life of Gilbert Murray, and Con O'Neill, who negotiated the British entry to the Common Market. At one college dinner, Ronald Knox, the Catholic chaplain, opened his speech with the words: "I belong to a generation of which only the unfit have survived." Of the Second World War this could not have been said, but the names of the survivors among my contemporaries are mingled in my mind with the names of those who died, like Jasper Ridley, who had some of the highest standards of conduct and judgment I have ever known, and Richard Kay-Shuttleworth, and David Wallace, and Guy Branch, whose Lysander in Max Reinhardt's production of *A Midsummer Night's Dream* I still recall each time I see the play. Fortunately, I am not the only person to do this; Isaiah Berlin tells me that he does so too. Each Oxford college in those days left a mark upon its undergraduates, and Balliol left its mark on me, in the form of a self-confidence that sometimes verged on arrogance and a clear understanding of the difference between success and a *succès d'estime*. One was proud to be the heir to an intellectual tradition of such distinction and austerity, and though I did not afterwards maintain close contacts with the college, one of the honors I most prized in later life was to have been elected to an Honorary Fellowship.

Areas of pleasure were broadened or opened up for the first time. The most significant was music. I could sight-read, incompetently, on the piano and had long collected gramophone records, which I played on a then fashionable gramophone with triangular needles and a large mottled horn. But in those days the gap between real and recorded performances was much greater than it is today. From

Downside I had occasionally gone to concerts at the Colston Hall in Bristol, to hear Mengelberg conducting the Brahms Third Symphony and Rachmaninoff playing the Beethoven Tempest Sonata, but otherwise I was starved of live performances. At Oxford the sky opened. The world was filled with people with whom music could be seriously discussed. There were local operatic productions, of Dvořák's *Kate and the Devil* and Gluck's *Iphigenia in Aulis* (and very bad the *Iphigenia* was; as I came out I ran into Kenneth Clark, who said: "It only shows that one can't kill a work of art"). In the Holywell Music Room there were recitals, by Friedrich Wührer, then a promising romantic pianist, and Harriet Cohen and the Mangeot Quartet. In the hall at Balliol the young Rubinstein played Brahms intermezzi and Chopin mazurkas miraculously well, and the Oxford Town Hall offered recitals by Edwin Fischer (one of the most private of all pianists) and by a stupendously gifted young man who commonly played with the Busch Quartet, Rudolf Serkin. The memory of some performances is ineffaceably implanted on one's mind, and when I hear the Beethoven Opus 22 sonata I still recall it as Serkin played it then. In the chapel at New College the Busch Quartet played the Haydn *Seven Last Words* and in the Town Hall they played the great Schubert G major quartet. London was within easy reach, and at weekends or in the vacation one could hear Rachmaninoff, in a concert I remember not for the work that took me there, the first performance of his *Variations on a Theme by Corelli*, but for the *Nachtstücke* of Schumann, the most eloquent piano playing I have ever listened to. At the Wigmore Hall, Lhévinne rattled through the Waldstein Sonata and Balakirev's *Islamey*, and at Queen's Hall Josef Hofmann played the Chopin E minor concerto. There was a covey of great string players, Piatigorsky in the Schumann cello concerto, and Huberman playing Tchaikovsky, and Flesch and Milstein, by whom I heard not long ago a superlative unaccompanied Bach recital in New York. Horowitz played Liszt and Gieseking played Debussy, and you could encounter Busoni in recitals by Petri and in Szigeti's playing of the violin concerto. There were vivid concerts by Beecham and dull concerts by Boult, and there were visiting orchestras like the Berlin Philharmonic with Furtwängler and visiting conductors of whom the most underrated was Klemperer and the most acclaimed was Toscanini. In the years that led up to the war the subconscious prejudice against German music-making was very strong, and each Furtwängler concert was trounced in the *Sunday Times* by Ernest Newman, the leading critic of the day. How injudiciously one can now hear for oneself on compact disc. Every generation requires a pianist who will reinterpret the Beethoven piano sonatas. Today the mission has fallen to Alfred Brendel, but before the war it was the prerogative of Schnabel, and I am deeply grateful that it was through Schnabel's mind, in performances more thoughtful and less clear-cut than those of Backhaus, that I first got on close terms with them. Mahler and Bruckner were private cults. Mahler's idiom seemed elusive—I remember sitting through a deplorable rehearsal by Sir Hamilton Harty of the *Lied von der Erde*—and to hear his symphonies you had to subscribe to the Courtauld-Sargent concerts. When I listen to Bruckner's Seventh Symphony today, I still recall it as I heard it first on Polydor records in Berthold von Bohlen's rooms at Balliol. Opera played a smaller part in my life than it did later. At Covent Garden, where a white tie was de rigueur, it was sometimes possible to get tickets for the individual operas of the *Ring* (I did not hear *Götterdämmerung* till after the war), or for *Tristan*, which I heard for the first time soon after I left Oxford, with a new soprano called Kirsten Flagstad and Melchior and Janssen conducted by Fritz Reiner, or for *Elektra* with Kerstin Thorborg as an incomparable Clytemnestra, or for *Parsifal* with Torsten Ralf and one of the best of all Wagner sopranos, Germaine Lubin, or for an *Aida* with Martinelli singing Radames, or for a *Rigoletto* in which "Bella figlia dell'amore" was phrased by Lauri-Volpi with a seductive elegance I have never heard surpassed.

Another source of intense pleasure was contemporary art. In the mid-1930s this meant *Minotaure* and Picasso and Matisse, and Cocteau films, and Gertrude Stein in a dress made of sackcloth taking curtain calls after *The Wedding Bouquet*. The avant-garde today is stale and dull—I hold no stock in Carl Andre or pieces of felt suspended from the wall—but in the 1930s it was vital and positive, and it produced now forgotten masterpieces like Miró's decor for *Jeux d'Enfants*, where the curtain rose on a huge snowball with a scarlet arm protruding like the hand of a clock. The prices of works of art were still low, and it was no surprise to find small Picassos on one's friends' parents' walls.

Standing in Oxford was gauged by the number of invitations you received to raucous meals with Maurice Bowra, but I learned much from my friendship with Tom Boase, who exercised a civilizing influence from his rooms at Hertford, from Sligger Urquhart, with whom, like other undergraduates, I sometimes breakfasted at Balliol, and from Roy Harrod, with whom I dined at Christ Church. The master of Campion Hall was Father D'Arcy, the Catholic chaplain was Ronald Knox, and Blackfriars boasted a Byzantine scholar who became a close friend, Father Gervase Mathew. But the reason for going to a university is to learn and not to talk, and the historical teaching at Balliol was at the time incomparably good. Initially my tutor was Vivian Galbraith, from whom I learned almost all I know about documents and their interpretation. Since my special period was a rare one which could not be taught domestically—it ran from A.D. 476 up to the death of Charles the Bald—I was farmed out to Nowell Myres, later Bodley's librarian, at Christ Church. I was enthralled by Carolingian and Byzantine history, and when I first went to Italy, for three weeks in the summer of 1934, my prime interests lay in Monza and Ravenna, not in the Renaissance. Most people have the illusion that at their university they did very little work. I believed that too until I turned up an old volume of notes which seemed to show that I worked methodically and very hard. The number of Jews in the Byzantine Empire, the reliability of Ermoldus Nigellus, late Roman and early medieval commerce, rural economy in Merovingian France—I remember nothing of them now, but then they were grist to my mill. The seminar from which I learned most was given on hot summer afternoons in the Schools by that great paleographer E. A. Lowe. It embodied lessons in visual analysis that were applicable far outside the reading of Carolingian minuscule, its ostensible field, and it convinced me that every art-historical curriculum ought to include a compulsory course in paleography.

Much of my life at Oxford centered on the Ashmolean Museum. While Kenneth Clark was there—he became director of the National Gallery at the beginning of 1934—one could spend afternoons with a stack of Raphael drawings or with some painting taken off the wall. Under his successor, K. T. Parker, a great connoisseur of drawings, the museum suddenly shrank into a beautifully regulated print room. This was my first experience of the sterilizing influence of a training in the British Museum. Much of my time in the Ashmolean was spent searching for the subject of a monograph. The political background was menacing, and certain topics, on grounds either of size or of complexity or of my own immaturity, were ruled out. But there was one picture in the Ashmolean for which I felt special affinity; it was a *Baptism of Christ* by the Sienese fifteenth-century painter Giovanni di Paolo. It was direct and highly personal—the story seemed to be told by an eyewitness—and celestial light from a small God the Father at the top irradiated the whole scene. There was also a second panel by Giovanni di Paolo at Oxford, a small *Crucifixion* at Christ Church with a background of patterned fields and traces of fantastic silvering. This was the artist on whom I decided to work, since his paintings seemed to me as decoration to be of the first quality, and to present critical or aesthetic problems of real interest. Above all, his personality was compatible. In any monograph (or any dissertation, for the matter of that) the factor of compatibility is of paramount significance.

The history of art was not part of the Oxford curriculum, and the Slade Professorship throughout the period I was there was held by a nonentity. From time to time outside lecturers spoke in the Ashmolean. One of them was the Raphael specialist Oskar Fischel. His lecture was tired and sentimental, and for all his considerable merits he was a type of art historian I did not wish to be. The most compelling art lectures that I heard at Oxford were by Kenneth Clark; they were a preview of the brilliant book on Leonardo he published in 1937. The lecture room in the Ashmolean in those days was very small, and before each lecture began it was charged with magnetic excitement.

The Clarks lived at Headington, in a house filled with Cézanne watercolors and Vanessa Bells and Duncan Grants, and there one evening at dinner I had my only meeting with one of the tutelary deities of the art pantheon, Roger Fry. His appearance was unattractive—he had coarse, roughly parted hair and dirty fingernails—but his speaking voice was of extraordinary resonance and charm. We discussed Giovanni Bellini, on whose chronology he was by then a little shaky but on whom he had written an excellent early book.

One day in 1933 Kenneth Clark passed on to me for review in the *New Statesman* a book by Sir Charles Holmes on Raphael. It was a poor book, as I said in my review, but what I wrote elicited an enthusiastic letter from a scholar I had not previously met, Tancred Borenius. I had no idea whether his letter was prompted by the quality of the review or by dislike of Holmes. A Finn by birth, Borenius was something of a polymath. He had written well on Montagna and Vicentine painting, he had edited Crowe and Cavalcaselle, he had formed part of the Harewood collection and made countless catalogues, and he had directed the excavation of Clarendon Palace. Had he been English by birth all posts would have been open to him.

As he was not, all posts were barred. He had two bêtes noires at the time; one was Lord Lee, the chairman of the National Gallery Trustees, and the other was the founder of the Witt Art Reference Library, an old lecher called Sir Robert Witt. To them was added the new Surveyor of the King's Pictures, Kenneth Clark. When Clark, in 1937, bought for the National Gallery four little Giorgionesque pictures by Previtali that would have been good purchases for the Ashmolean but had no place in Trafalgar Square, Borenius orchestrated a press attack on him which all but evicted him from his post. Visiting Borenius's gloomy house near Kensington Gardens, I found him genial and encouraging, and he gave me much practical help, providing introductions when I went abroad and reading the proofs of both my early books. When I think of him today, I see him in 1937, at the opening of the opera season in the royal box at Covent Garden, blazing with foreign decorations, at Queen Mary's side.

At Oxford I reviewed other books for the *New Statesman*. I had, or seemed to have, no natural gift for writing, and they were couched in long, laborious sentences. The literary editor, Raymond Mortimer, helpfully split them up, putting the word "moreover" in the joins, but I was still dissatisfied with the result. I learned more from Joe Ackerley at the *Listener*, and still more from Logan Pearsall Smith, who was responsible for teaching Kenneth Clark to write (his influence is apparent halfway through *The Gothic Revival*) and for honing the fluent styles of Hugh Trevor-Roper and Cyril Connolly.

The dean of studies in Italian painting was Bernard Berenson, and it was essential for my work to secure admission to I Tatti, his villa in Florence. So it was arranged, once more by Logan Pearsall Smith, that I should be screened by his sister, Mrs. Berenson. It was an intimidating experience. A monolith in gray satin, she sat under the painting by Duncan Grant that hung between the windows in Logan's drawing room, and to the end of a stilted conversation I had no idea whether I had made good. But on my way downstairs I heard her say, with the solemnity of a sibyl, "Follow your star." "That was meant for you," said Logan, and I called back, "I shall."

In the summer of 1934 I went to Italy for the first time. It was a brief exploratory visit. On my way to Arezzo I got out of the train in Florence to draw money at a bank near Santa Maria Maggiore on one of the letters of credit with which one traveled in those days. It was raining, and my first sight of the city which would eventually become my home was strikingly unmagical. From Arezzo I went on to Perugia and Assisi and thence to Siena. Filed in my mind among the faded snapshots of this journey are the Iron Crown and the ivory *Poet and His Muse* at Monza (the ivory seemed to me then, as it does still, one of the most beautiful of all carvings in relief); the white oxen which used then to plow the fields round Classe; the pellucid Raphael fresco at Perugia and the glass vase in the Signorelli altarpiece in the Cathedral; the green and gold polyptych of Pietro Lorenzetti in Santa Maria della Pieve at Arezzo; and the Pinacoteca at Siena newly and brilliantly installed by Cesare Brandi. From Siena I returned for a fortnight to Florence, where I stayed with a family in Borgo San Jacopo. Mrs. Berenson, who had a talent for helping people at other people's expense, described their flat as modest, and so it was. But this was balanced by a piece of sage advice, that I must, if I wished to understand Trecento painting, take lessons from Evelyn Sandberg Vavalà. Her lessons were expensive (they used up all of my spare cash) but were memorably good. In the evenings we went through photographs, and the following day, in the Accademia or in some church, we looked at the subject of the photograph in the original, and I learned to distinguish the chubby children of one painter from the chubby children of another. Evelyn Vavalà became a mentor and a valued friend, and remained so till she died. She was, in an unostentatious fashion, one of the most disciplined scholars I have ever known—her books on the painted Cross and on Veronese Trecento painting have never been surpassed—and the debt I owe her is immeasurable. On my last day in Florence I was asked to stay by the Berensons, who were at Consuma, but I thought that this encounter might well be postponed. At Seeber's bookshop in Via Tornabuoni I bought a copy of Roberto Longhi's newly published book about Ferrarese painting, *Officina Ferrarese*, and read it, with mounting excitement, through the night in the train to Paris.

After this short journey I had another year at Oxford, in which I worked intensively on my projected monograph and less consistently on academic subjects, and my degree in 1935 was a second, not a first. But I had a little capital—my father's brother, Hugh, in a will made in France in 1916, had left me some coconut islands off Borneo called Karaman, and the capital resulted from their sale—so I decided to use the money as income and to devote two years to traveling and to the preparation of a book. When I came down from Oxford, therefore, I had a life plan in my mind.

3

AN ABBREVIATED PILGRIMAGE

MY *WANDERJAHR*—IT WAS REALLY ONLY HALF A YEAR—BEGAN IN 1935 and was geared first to museums and the works of art that they contained and then to the book I proposed working on. The Abyssinian War had already begun, and relations with Italy were at an all-time low, so it seemed prudent to begin the journey in Northern Europe before heading south. There was also a practical reason for doing so, since in the middle of July there opened in Amsterdam the finest of all Rembrandt exhibitions. Well selected and beautifully arranged, it was organized by Schmidt-Degener, who reframed a number of the foreign loans. The effect that it made was overwhelming, and when in 1969 I returned to Amsterdam for the opening of the tercentenary Rembrandt exhibition, I thought it less effective than the earlier exhibition. Its range was greater—it included some of the large machines like the Dresden *Wedding Feast of Samson* and the *Claudius Civilis* from Stockholm—but never did one get the sense, which the earlier exhibition gave, of penetrating the recesses of Rembrandt's mind. One of my illusions as a boy was that I was intended to devote my life to studying Rembrandt and his school, and I sometimes wish I had done this. Nowadays a Dutch committee is at work sifting and rejecting a great part of what was once regarded as Rembrandt's work. Diligent weeding of the garden has deprived it of a great deal of its allure, and when I am assured today that the huge and moving *Sacrifice of Manoah* at Dresden is by a pupil and not by Rembrandt, I fall back on the conviction that Dutch painting is too good to be studied only by the Dutch. Schmidt-Degener put me in touch with two young members of his staff who remained lifelong friends, Bob de Vries, a future director of the Mauritshuis who wrote admirably on Vermeer, and Artur van Schendel, a future director of the Rijksmuseum. With them I made an expedition to the Kröller-Müller Museum, where a small and rather indifferent panel by Giovanni di Paolo lay afloat in a turbulent sea of van Goghs. I have always been skeptical of artists who wear their hearts on their sleeves, and from quite an early time, when I knew most of van Gogh's paintings only through color reproductions, I resented their intemperate appeals for sympathy. He was a great painter indeed, but never in the 1930s would one have suspected that half a century later he would become the most expensive artist in the world.

At that time Amsterdam could boast two excellent private collections of Italian paintings and works of art. The first was that of Otto Lanz, who had died not long before. It was possible to handle the paintings—they included three beautiful panels by Lorenzo Monaco —and some very fine Paduan bronzes and plaquettes. The owner of the second, vom Rath, was a courtly old man with a frescoed house on the Herengracht who owned a Botticelli, an Ercole de' Roberti, and a small Signorelli *St. George and the Dragon*, which are now in the Rijksmuseum. I knew most of the main Dutch picture galleries from earlier visits, but not Utrecht, where the Central Museum then incorporated the Archiepiscopal Museum. The medieval objects were very fine, and included a small group of Sienese paintings, now consigned to limbo since the reconstructed Archiepiscopal Museum deals only with religious art north of the Alps.

Utrecht led on to Münster and Cologne. Nobody visiting West Germany today can have the least idea of the excitement of encountering German art when the cities in which it was produced were still intact. In the war Hanover and Bremen as urban entities were all but effaced, and Cologne too would have lost almost all its character but for the Cathedral, which seems today, as it did then, the most inspiring of all Gothic churches. Its contents, from the shrine of the Three Kings to the great triptych of Stephan Lochner, represent a continuous devotional tradition stronger than that of any other cathedral in the north. But its context has been lost, and nowadays, in the bustling pedestrian street that runs through the middle of the city and the ring roads that surround it, it is hard to envisage the medieval town. The urban plan has been preserved, but little more. In 1936 the Wallraf-Richartz Museum (which derives its name from a forebear of my friend

Paul Wallraf) was an old-fashioned institution, quite unlike the bold, clinical museum of today, and the paintings were shown in a natural, unpretentious way. To anyone interested in Northern Gothic paintings the prime areas are the Rhineland and Bohemia. I did not visit Prague until the 1950s, but at Cologne I found myself wondering, heretically, if the Lochner of the *Last Judgment* were not, in some respects, a greater painter than Fra Angelico. The same suspicion crossed my mind on my last visit to Cologne, when I left its congested streets to look once more at the backs of the heads of Lochner's Blessed queueing up at the heavenly door.

Frankfurt too was an altogether different city when the historical sections of the town were still preserved. Its associations with Goethe were very real, and even at the time that I was there a number of Jewish private collections still survived, though the most important of them, the von Hirsch collection, had been moved to Switzerland. There was a prevailing sense of secretiveness, and I failed to secure access to the only collection I required to see in which there were two predella panels by Giovanni di Paolo. Then, as now, the focus of interest was the Städel Institute, and the area round it and the lime walk along the Main looked then much as it does today. Walking through it recently, I was reminded of how much I had learned from my early visit there, first about Jan van Eyck and Rogier van der Weyden, and then from the miniature-like early Fra Angelico (I have since paid day visits to Frankfurt from London to look at it) and from the beautiful Barnaba da Modena and the Lorenzettis. The appeal of the museum was not just that it was discriminating but that it was so small as to be assimilable. In the print room it was possible to go through the Italian drawings without formality. In those days it was the practice for specialists on drawing to write their opinions in pencil on the mounts. As I held the Pesellino drawing for the altarpiece in London up to the light, I wondered when I should be in a position to do this too. Most of the Italian paintings in the Städel Institute I knew in reproduction, but the adjacent Liebighaus was a surprise. It was filled, thanks to the genius of Georg Swarzenski, with sculptural masterpieces of every kind, marble caryatids by Tino di Camaino, a superb Carolingian ivory from the Cathedral, and an enchanting series of baroque and rococo pigmented wooden sculptures. Swarzenski's sense of quality was impeccable, and the eighteenth-century sculptures he bought, highly regarded as they are today, ran counter to contemporary taste. When he left Germany he moved to the Boston Museum of Fine Arts, where he was again responsible for many remarkable purchases. I am sorry that I never met him, though I became a friend of his son Hanns, who had a captivating character and an erratic eye.

My goal, however, was Altenburg, which lies south of Leipzig and north of Chemnitz, and its little visited Lindenau Museum. Bequeathed to the city in 1854 by Bernhard von Lindenau, it contained two collections of great importance, of Greek vases and Italian primitives. The pictures posed a vast variety of problems, since they had not been adequately studied, and many of them were overpainted. They have since been restored and admirably catalogued, but in 1936 one was dependent on a green paper-covered reprint of a catalogue of 1898 and on the Berenson lists. Lindenau was a collector of exceptional discernment, with a preference for small-scale paintings and especially for predella panels. He owned two great Lorenzo Monacos, a romantic picture of St. Jerome by Fra Filippo Lippi (an early work I thought it then, and I still do today though that view is not shared by Lippi specialists), a strange panel of the Agony in the Garden and St. Jerome in prayer, which I rejected as a Masaccio when I first saw it but which I now regard as autograph, and a large number of Sienese paintings, including works by Barna and Lippo Vanni and Lippo Memmi and Pietro Lorenzetti and four panels by Giovanni di Paolo. I stayed for a week in Altenburg till I knew each stroke on them by heart. Two of the Giovanni di Paolo *Crucifixions* proved to come from known predellas, and this and other discoveries there convinced me that, given time, I could forge a personal style-analytical technique. The only problem was that the pictures were sealed in glass boxes. It was supposed that the *Kammerherr*, who had died not long before, had arranged this, and his successor, a young specialist in Greek vases, did not know how to open them. Altenburg was a dull place, as it still is today, and when the gallery was shut I sat in my bedroom in a once grand hotel reading *Ulysses* and picking my way through reports in the *Völkischer Beobachter* of speeches made at Geneva by those disaster figures Pierre Laval and Sir Samuel Hoare.

Today, seen from a hotel window across the Elbe, Dresden, with its ruined and decaying buildings, looks like a ghost city, but in the 1930s it was a delight, both for its architecture, which then played a smaller part in my responses than it would do now, and for its paintings. The collection in the Gemäldegalerie is still, in sheer paint quality, the most sensuous in the world, for its Titians (knowing it only in color reproductions, I was quite unprepared for the weight and scale of the *Tribute Money* or for the voluptuous surface texture of the *Woman in White*, which seemed to me then, as it still does today, one of the half dozen greatest portraits in the world), for its Giorgione (which ceases, when one stands in front of it, to be a problem of attribution and becomes what it was in the beginning, a supremely satisfying work of art), for its Palma Vecchios (above all the lyrical *Jacob and Rachel*, a parable of affection set in a Bergamasque landscape of incomparable warmth and naturalness), and for its Correggios. With the sublime exception of the *Notte*, I found Correggio a difficult artist. I was not fully attuned to Mannerism—before the war very few students of my generation were—but by applying the criteria of Wölfflin's *Classic Art*, I could establish contact with the early *Virgin and Child with St. Francis*, though not for many years, not indeed till I had worked on Annibale Carracci and Domenichino and until Correggio's two great cupolas in Parma could be studied under restoration from the scaffolding, did I experience the sauna-bath pleasure that Correggio's *St. Sebastian* altarpiece and his *Virgin and Child with St. George* at Dresden give me now. The case of Raphael's *Sistine Madonna* was different. Whatever impediments could be put in the way of its appreciation were present in the Dresden Gallery; it was shown in nineteenth-century fashion, in a tabernacle with a red plush seat in front of it as an icon to respect, not as a masterpiece to cherish or to love. Even so, as I sat before it reading the great description by Wölfflin, I felt the first stirring of the enthusiasm that was to lead me later to devote a book to Raphael.

Another source of pleasure in Dresden was music. The standards at the opera were exceptionally high, and I was fortunate enough to hear my first *Fidelio* in the Semper Opera House conducted by the young Karl Böhm. Not only was it well directed and well sung, but the context of the time gave it a tension that it lacks today. The production was faithful to the human scale of the libretto and did not degenerate into the symbolism now common in large opera houses. The standard of staging at Dresden was distinguished, and nowhere more so than in Strauss's *Ariadne auf Naxos* and Weber's *Oberon*. I recall the setting in which Marguerite Teschemacher sang "Ozean, du Ungeheuer" as one of the most accomplished pieces of stagecraft I have ever seen. Nowadays *Oberon* is thought of as an intractable opera—I repeatedly pressed it without result on the board of Covent Garden—but in the 1930s, when romanticism was less distant than it is today and the nature of pantomime, with its combination of the serious and the absurd, was better understood, it seemed an entrancing work. The beautiful *Ariadne* was taken by the Dresden Staatsoper later in the year to London, with simplified staging under the limp direction of Richard Strauss.

In Berlin I found, to my surprise, that after a ten-year absence I still knew the way about. I do so in West Berlin today, as a matter of fact, since the streets have the same names, though they look quite different from the streets I originally knew. Nowadays one's goal there is the Staatliche Museum at Dahlem, but in the 1930s it was the Kaiser Friedrich Museum. When its collection was intact, it was, for someone like myself who was concerned mainly with Italian art, the most invigorating collection in the world. Revisiting the derelict museum since the war, I have found it hard to recapture the pleasure of my early visits there, but on the last occasion I saw to my delight that a belated but successful effort had been made to reconstruct some of the galleries on the principles that obtained before the war. Though the Sassetta altarpiece of the *Assumption of the Virgin* and Signorelli's sublime *Triumph of Pan* were both destroyed, the spaces that they and the paintings now at Dahlem occupied could once more be identified. I looked, as I have always done, at everything, but my concern lay with the Italian paintings and centered (to judge from a catalogue I annotated) on problems of authorship. Each evening when I returned after the museum shut to my squalid hotel in the Mittelstrasse, I noted the attributions of earlier scholars in pencil in the catalogue. But in Berlin I also learned a great deal of which I was unconscious at the time. In the Italian Renaissance galleries, painting and sculpture and the decorative arts were shown side by side, producing a historically valid synthesis that was impressive in its range and opulence. When, at the Victoria and Albert Museum fifteen years later, I was faced by the task of reinstalling the Gothic and Renaissance galleries, memories of the Kaiser Friedrich were in the forefront of my mind, but I rapidly discovered how difficult a seemingly effortless display was to achieve. Only later when I had a second shot at it did I produce passable results. Wilhelm von Bode, the presiding deity of the collection, had died over ten years before, but his controlling mind and his almost unfailing sense for quality could still be felt. Young as I was, I was treated with the utmost kindness by members of the museum staff, especially by Dr. Irene Kühnel-Kunze, who wore a white coat like a dentist and had written about Previtali. Everything that could be done to help she did. Pictures were taken off the wall so one could see the backs, and when the museum was closed on Mondays one was made free of the stored paintings. Later, when I was myself responsible for public collections, I tried always to ensure that the facilities offered to students were commensurate with those I had myself enjoyed in the 1930s in the otherwise hostile climate of Berlin.

I knew very few people in Berlin, and evening after evening was spent in the Staatsoper, where the inexpensive seats in the top gallery were so steeply raked that one had the sense of sliding down into the stalls. The principal conductors were Clemens Krauss, who had moved to Berlin from Vienna, and Robert Heger, and among the singers were Anna and Hilde Konetzni, and Margarete Klose, and Frida Leider, that great artist Tiana Lemnitz, and Franz Völker and Helge Roswaenge. A great deal of Verdi, sung in translation, was included in the repertory, and it was in Berlin that I first heard the *Macht des Schicksals* and the *Maskenball*, Völker in a splendid *Otello*, and Tiana Lemnitz in a sublime *Lohengrin*. A slow, majestic *Zauberflöte* was conducted by Sir Thomas Beecham, in adaptions of the sets by Schinkel, through which the pantomime Mozart conceived became the grave neoclassical allegory we know now.

Since the Italian situation was still unresolved (as indeed it remained until the war), I decided to go on from Berlin to Basel and thence to Munich, Vienna, and Budapest. In Basel there were three objectives, the Holbeins in the Öffentliche Kunstsammlung, the Holbein scholar Paul Ganz, to whom I had an introduction, and the collection of Robert von Hirsch, which included the central panel from an early Giovanni di Paolo altarpiece. I had always had a deep interest in Holbein, less on historical grounds, important as those are, than as a painter of genius whose true stature was not properly described in any published book. Only in an essay by Fritz Saxl on the illustrations to Erasmus's *Praise of Folly* does one get some impression of the intellectual level on which he worked. But at Basel this was, and still is, spelled out unambiguously on the gallery walls. Beside his *Dead Christ*, Mantegna's *Dead Christ* in the Brera looks tentative and insecure; beside his *Lais Corinthiaca*, the comparable paintings by Luini look flaccid and dull; and beside his early portraits, like the *Bonifacius Amer-bach*, Florentine portraits look generic and rhetorical. These were my impressions in 1935, and I would stand by them today. Paul Ganz's reputation at the time was tarnished by his publication of a weak panel of King Henry VIII known as the Castle Howard Holbein and of a number of other questionable paintings. He was, however, a man of extraordinary warmth with a wife who looked like Holbein's in his painting *The Artist's Wife and Family*. When I lunched with him, I found that he knew very little about English history or literature in the first half of the sixteenth century; this is indeed apparent from his books. But he had a passion for that then underrated figure Fuseli. Going round his Fuseli paintings (there were forty of them, as I recall) and over his excellent Fuseli drawings, I was magnetized by their imaginative quality, and when, almost half a century later, I found myself buying one of Fuseli's Milton scenes for the Metropolitan Museum, the criteria I applied to it derived from my memories of Ganz's Fuseli collection.

For tea I was passed on to von Hirsch, newly established in the Engelgasse, with the whole of his extraordinary collection less some paintings he had been compelled to leave behind in Frankfurt in order to obtain permission to export the rest. I went to see him many times after the war. On this first visit the tea consisted of caviar and wild strawberries. If ever there were a collection designed to give sophis-ticated pleasure on many different levels, it would be his. His Giovanni di Paolo was extremely fine but had been heavily repainted; it is now, in much improved condition, in the Norton Simon collection. The only other guest was a coarse-looking man with pyorrhea, the collector Königs, whose magnificent Old Master drawings are now at Rotter-dam. I watched von Hirsch and Königs handling drawing after draw-ing and bronze after bronze, and realized that I had been admitted to the hypercritical, hothouse atmosphere in which the great continental collections of artifacts and works of art, like those of Spiridon and Figdor, had been formed.

Another interest generated by this visit was in the work of Böcklin. From photographs I had never guessed that Böcklin was an artist of exceptional quality. Thirty-five years later I found myself, at the Arts Council, collaborating with Michael Stettler on a Böcklin/Hodler ex-hibition for the Hayward Gallery. At Berne I was shown, in storage, the Duccio and the fascinating group of Italian primitives that are now publicly exhibited (they were then so private that I was forbidden to reproduce or to discuss them.) Letters record that the Swiss National Museum at Zurich seemed to me a vivid and progressive place. Revisiting it now, I cannot conceive why I thought this.

The riches of Munich were immense, and though I visited the Glyptothek (much less well installed then than it is today) and the Bayerisches Nationalmuseum, most of my efforts went into memorizing the paintings in the Alte Pinakothek. The only catalogue available was a summary volume issued in 1922. The Pinakothek is now one of the best catalogued of all galleries, and I often envy the students of today to whom a modern catalogue offers a head start that I did not enjoy. There was much to memorize, from the Taddeo Gaddi scenes from the life of St. Francis to the four great panels from the predella of Fra Angelico's San Marco altarpiece. I did not then know how closely my own work would be bound up with Fra Angelico. Within a fortnight I became familiar with a great many paintings that would be part and parcel of my future life, some of them, like the Leonardo da Vinci *Madonna and Child*, resistant to analysis, others, like the Perugino *Vision of St. Bernard* from Santo Spirito, that I accepted as the masterpieces they still seem to be. The three great Raphaels, the then much overpainted *Canigiani Holy Family*, the *Tempi Madonna* and the *Madonna della Tenda*, were in less brilliant condition than they are now. Though they are some of Raphael's most cogitated panel paintings, they then gave me less pleasure than the two great Tintorettos, the *Christ in the House of Martha and Mary* and the *Vulcan, Venus, and Mars*, and much less pleasure than the explosive paint surface of Titian's late *Christ Crowned with Thorns*. But in a collection that contains Dürer's *Apostles* and *Self-Portrait*, and Altdorfer's *Birth of the Virgin*, and the *Pearl of Brabant* and the Massys *Danaë*, Italian pictures were only part of the story and my attention inevitably spread from south to north. The only artist with whom I found it hard to get on easy terms was Rubens. When we addressed each other, we used the second person plural, not the second person singular.

I used to stay in the Pinakothek all day, with an hour off for lunch, and my only relaxation once more was opera. Performances were then given in the Prinz-Regenten-Theater, and were distinguished musically but were visually unmemorable. I saw *Der Freischütz* and *Macbeth*, in both of which the stage and auditorium were filled with smoke. One of the few smoke-free operas was *Der Rosenkavalier* in a superb performance with Felice Hüni-Mihacsek. *Macbeth*, though it was conducted by Hans Knappertsbusch and sung by Heinrich Rehkemper, seemed a crude, uneven work, and only when it was put on a few years later at Glyndebourne by Fritz Busch did I realize it is a masterpiece.

At this point, the threat arose that I might have to break off my journey. My father had long had political ambitions, and in the general election of 1935 he was adopted as the anti-appeasement, Liberal candidate for Tonbridge, a strongly Conservative constituency where no Liberal had the chance of so much as saving his deposit. He asked me to come back to canvass for him, but I refused to do so. "I know," I wrote in a needlessly blunt letter, "precisely what I want and ought to do, and short of war I shall do it. I have a very short period of completely free time, and it is vital that I do not waste it by coming back to London prematurely." So from Munich I went on to Vienna. Before going there I had written to Ernst Buschbeck, the assistant director of the Kunsthistorisches Museum, with whom at least one of my contemporaries at Oxford had, while learning German, stayed as a paying guest. He was a charming, principled, voluble man, and I learned a great deal from staying with him. Not only about art, for he had a son called Herwarth, a pimply boy of sixteen, who was a member of the Nazi Party. In the clash between Buschbeck's liberalism and the callow convictions of his son one saw played out a drama which must have been repeated in countless other Austrian households at the time.

Before the Anschluss, Vienna was the mecca of art history, and the Kunsthistorisches Museum was the leading art museum in the world. It was a center of research, the results of which were transmitted through the Vienna *Jahrbuch* and in countless catalogues that are still standard works of reference today. Leo Planiscig on bronze statuettes, Ernst Kris on hard stone carvings, Julius von Schlosser on the literature of art history were names to conjure with, while Johannes Wilde (whom I did not meet till later) had broken new ground with the application of X rays to the study of Giorgione and Titian. As a result, one looked at the magnificent collections critically, and the lessons that one learned from them were manifold. Returning there today, I still recall the long mornings (the museum then closed, as it does now, at three o'clock, and lunch at Buschbeck's flat was at three-fifteen) spent looking at Giorgione's *Three Philosophers* and the resonant purple-and-green *Lucretia* of Veronese and the ingratiating *Jacopo Strada* of Titian. It was in Vienna, not in London or Venice, that my lifelong fascination with Titian's human personality began. But the riches of Vienna were not confined to the Kunsthistorisches Museum. There were the Albertina (where more drawings were displayed in the original than are today) and the Kunstakademie (which happens to own a key work by Giovanni di Paolo, a scene from the life of St. Nicholas of Tolentino, which I was allowed to handle) and the Czernin collection (with its magical Vermeer) and the Galerie Harrach. The Liechtenstein collection, then exposed in its entirety, still included Leonardo's *Ginevra de' Benci* (which is now in Washington) and the jewel-like portrait diptych by Jacometto (which is now in New York). All these were open to the public, but the Lanckoronski collection was not. I was introduced to its owner by Buschbeck, and when I went there I saw works by two artists with whom I was later to be involved, Uccello's *St. George and the Dragon* (later bought by the National Gallery in London) and the mythological frescoes by Domenichino from the Villa Aldobrandini at Frascati. No collectors were more welcoming than the Lederers, who had a number of Sienese paintings, including a great Simone Martini (now at Malibu), and a group of bronzes formed under the eye of Planiscig. The Lederers were patrons of Schiele and Klimt, and I remember looking at their Klimts in consternation that people who collected pictures in good taste could collect Klimt too. This seems an archaic misjudgment today. Forty years later I found myself buying for the Metropolitan Museum a fine early Klimt of Frau Serena Lederer which I had first seen in Vienna in 1935. My visit led to a friendship with Erich Lederer which was resumed after the war in London and Florence and Geneva, when I bought a Paduan bronze from him for the Victoria and Albert and published a bronze model in his collection by Benvenuto Cellini. The Cellini had been found by his mother one wet morning at Böhler's in Munich, in use as a doorstop, and is now in the J. Paul Getty Museum.

Buschbeck was endlessly informative. I learned from him how the Kunsthistorisches Museum was administered, and what were the Achilles' heels of art historians like Wilhelm Suida and Hermann Voss and Leo Planiscig. But staying with him had one handicap: excellent linguist that he was, he had an endless fund of not very amusing stories in German and Austrian and English dialects. So I generally dined out and more often than not went to the opera, which at that time was directed by Weingartner. I remember especially a *Don Giovanni* (which at Vienna was performed without its final scene) with Alfred Jerger as the Don, Maria Nemeth as Donna Anna, Luise Helletsgrüber as Donna Elvira, and Elisabeth Schumann as an entrancing Zerlina. This was the only time I saw Elisabeth Schumann on the stage, and I recall her beguiling phrasing of "Vedrai, carino" each time I hear the opera now. Weingartner was a great Wagner conductor. In London I heard his *Parsifal* and in Vienna a near-perfect *Meistersinger*. I also remember with special emotion a Liszt memorial concert, at which Weingartner, a Liszt pupil, conducted the Dante Symphony and Emil von Sauer, also a Liszt pupil, played the A major piano concerto. In those days Sauer, with his unruly white hair, looked like a reincarnation of Liszt, but when, not long ago, I visited the Liszt house at Weimar, I saw a photograph of him as the trim, sharp-featured boy Liszt trained. In Vienna one was free of the menacing presence of Nazi police and troops, and I left for Hungary with reluctance and regret.

The principal Sienese paintings in Hungary were, with one exception, not in Budapest but in the collection of the Prince Primate at Esztergom. The Prince Primate, Cardinal Seredi, was a Benedictine, and I secured a letter to him from the abbot of Downside which elicited an invitation to spend a night at Esztergom. Esztergom is easily accessible now from Budapest, but it was not so then. The journey from Vienna involved changes at Komárom and Almásfüzitö, and at Esztergom, which lies on a bend in the Danube, I was met by the cardinal's administrator, Nicolao Este, a middle-aged man who spoke a little, but only a little, English and Italian and French. We drove together in a coach with two horses and a coachman in a bright blue uniform through muddy streets to the Archiepiscopal Palace. The picture gallery, containing Italian primitives and Hungarian panel paintings rescued by an earlier Prince Primate from local churches, proved of great interest. At six I was taken to tea with His Eminence, a big-built man with fingers covered with rings and a monumental, rugged brown face. He wished, he said, to practice his English, which proved exiguous, and tea did not go easily. Conversation was in the third person singular and one could apparently talk of nothing in his presence but the cardinal. ("His Eminence is the last great canonist," said one of his staff helpfully. "He has just finished editing the seventieth volume of the canon law. I expect you used his edition in your studies at Downside.") The cardinal spoke in the first person plural. I was bidden to dinner at half past eight, and before I was shown in, the monsignor deputed to look after me said, "His Eminence will talk Latin." But try as I might, I could not describe my railway journey (or anything else, as a matter of fact) in Latin, and the conversation, such as it was, lapsed into pidgin German almost at once. But the dinner taught me what life in the sixteenth century must have been like. The cardinal and his staff ate very fast, using their fingers as well as their knives and forks, and there were two napkins, one with an embroidered monogram for one's knees and the other to wipe one's fingers on when they went in the sauce. There was no hot water in the palace, and the sanitation was disgusting. I have been back to Esztergom since—it is now a Museum of Christian Art—and as one looks at what was the formal garden, with its white peacocks and its willows reflected in the river, the Esztergom of the 1930s seems a mirage. But my visit had a later by-product in the form of an exhibition at the Victoria and Albert Museum of Hungarian Renaissance art which included excellent metalwork from the treasury of the Cathedral and a fine group of Danubian primitives from the gallery at Esztergom.

Budapest was something of a disappointment. There was no guide-book that explained, as Lukasz has since done, why almost all of its grotesquely ugly public buildings date from the last decade of the nineteenth century. It was cold, and the Szépmüvészeti Múzeum and the print room were unheated. Shivering in an overcoat, I spent three or four days looking at the paintings, warming my hands at the pallid flame of Raphael's *Esterházy Madonna*. The collection of Italian sculpture (which had been bought in a hurry before the opening of the museum) seemed to me uniformly poor. But Budapest also possessed two luxurious private collections. One belonged to Baron Hatvanyi, whose house was jammed with nineteenth-century French paintings. The other, that of Baron Herzog, had as its nucleus a group of seven El Grecos and five substantial Goyas. Impressive as they were, both collections were too dealer-like to be congenial. When I returned to Budapest officially nearly thirty years later, to open relations between the British Academy in London and the Magyar Tudomanyos Akademie, only one private collection remained. It was of baroque bozzetti which the impoverished owner was progressively handing over to the state. "We say he is eating his collection," joked a hard-hearted member of the museum staff.

Cracow, which I longed to visit, seemed very far away (I got there under the auspices of the British Council only in 1975), and since it was now autumn I decided to take the train from Budapest to Venice. I arrived there in the middle of an *acqua alta* to find the Piazza San Marco flooded and the walls covered with anti-British, anti-Eden slogans. Much of the agitation was artificial, but to anyone who believed in the ethical issue involved it was unpleasant to be surrounded by vociferous hostility. The days were bright and cold, and I seemed to be the only tourist. I was very conscious of how easy it would be for any fascist zealot to edge one off the wooden walkways into the knee-deep water covering the Piazzetta. The tempo of sightseeing in Venice is different from that of other places, and I realized that the Accademia and the Frari and Santi Giovanni e Paolo could not be taken by storm. At Padua I got myself locked into the Arena Chapel and the Ovetari Chapel in the Eremitani, unaware that Giotto's frescoes would survive to form part of the architecture of my own and other people's lives, whereas Mantegna's within a few years would be all but obliterated.

Siena, however, was the goal, as it had been from the start, and I went there direct from Padua. Money was short, and I put up in a hotel in the Via del Re in a frigid room on the fifth floor with a view over the Mangia and the Palazzo Piccolomini. It cost only thirty lire a day, and served its purpose well enough. There I embarked on a routine, in which the morning was spent in the Pinacoteca, while in the afternoons I laid the foundations of what later became a very thorough knowledge of the churches of Siena. The days were closing in, but it was still possible to see a limited number of places outside the city, San Gimignano (which is at its nicest in early winter) and Buonconvento and Asciano. Bus journeys were slow, but never since has the barren countryside beyond Asciano looked as it did in the setting sun from a bus window then. There was no option but to stay the night in each small town. Some of the hotels were viable, and are still so today—the Marzocco at Montepulciano was one of them, and another was at Montalcino, where I was kept awake by the noise of a boisterous fascist meeting downstairs; others were barely tolerable. A practical consequence of this form of transport was that you were forced by the bus schedule to stay in each town a little longer than you wanted to, and since there was nothing to do but look at works of art, I got to know them more thoroughly than students who visit them by car today. Everywhere there were slogans on the walls, "*Duce, siamo pronti,*" "*A noi il Duce,*" "*Noi tireremo dritto,*" and stencils of the

Duce's head, which could be transferred to any space available, were on general sale. The only introduction I employed was to the super-intendent, the archivist Peleo Bacci, a big, nervous, voluble man with a large black felt hat, who gave me a rhetorical talk on the study of art having no national boundaries and expressed his pleasure at being able to give practical proof of the esteem in which he held his British colleagues. The outcome was a permit to go through the choir books in the Piccolomini Library, and invaluable joint expeditions to the Duomo and San Domenico, where Bacci knew the pre-Tridentine layout of the altars like the palm of his hand. At the annual inspection of the Pinacoteca by the minister, Bottai, which took place a few days later, I saw Bacci again, in riding breeches and a black shirt with medals, marshaling the gallery guards, who likewise wore black shirts and ties, as the minister, who was also in uniform, paraded slowly through the gallery.

The virus that I caught at Oxford was emotional, and I have never recovered from it. Sienese pictures spoke to me (as they must have done to many other people) in accents so seductive and so intimate that to look at them was like a conversation on a scrambler telephone. One had the illusion of responding to a message no one else could hear. For many years a little band of Americans and Englishmen had felt, as I did, that they had a hot line to Siena. Their leader was F. Mason Perkins, whose views on the attribution of Sienese paintings were, in terms of the knowledge then available, all but infallible. Another was a London dealer, Robert Langton Douglas, who had published at the beginning of the century a good book on Fra Angelico and a valuable history of Siena. A third was Edward Hutton, who wrote admirable books on Tuscany and Umbria. A dealer, but a man of transparent honest-mindedness, he was an enchanting conversa-tionalist, from whom I heard long stories of life in Siena before the First World War. From Hutton I had a note of introduction to Perkins at Assisi.

Arriving at Assisi, I found he had no telephone, so I sent a note round to his house, and early the following morning I received a message to say that he was waiting for me in the piazza outside San Francesco. His Bostonian appearance—he was a small white-haired man with a trim, clipped mustache—was one of absolute normality. But once inside the upper church (and we stayed in it for an hour and a half) he was transformed, talking of the frescoes with a wealth of feeling that was inspirational. I had other long and helpful talks with him. Though he was quite well off, his life was governed by a neurosis over money. He could not afford electricity or fires, the reception rooms on the ground floor of his house in the Piazza del Vescovado were uninhabited, and his work was done in a kind of cupboard upstairs. His articles were laboriously composed in sprawly handwriting because he had no typewriter. Though a pupil of Leschetizky, he had left his grand piano in an abandoned villa at Lastra a Signa, which was infested by ants (when he mentioned it, it was with the relish with which John Donne wrote of human decay), and his collection of paintings was stacked in Florence to avoid paying something called the paterfamilias tax, which had been levied in 1917. He spoke with envy of the "princely income" paid to Berenson by Duveen. Mrs. Berenson, he said, was a cruel, hard woman who was responsible for most of her husband's quarrels. Left to himself, Berenson was kind and tolerant. In London he recommended me to visit Langton Douglas (who, when I did so, proved extremely helpful). Perkins's welcome gave me the sense of becoming a member of a very select club, and the Siena I first knew was Siena seen largely through his and Douglas's and Hutton's eyes. "Club" is a rather inappropriate word. A better term would be "sodality," for what they reverenced was the content and not just the style of Sienese paintings. Hutton was a Catholic—when I knew him in London he helped to subsidize the choir at Westminster Cathedral—and Perkins also was a Catholic. At Assisi he went to Mass each morning in the lower church, and on a later visit I remember refusing, on the feast of the Perdono, to tramp four miles with him to Santa Maria degli Angeli to secure access to the Porziuncula and then to climb four miles back uphill. Douglas also became a Catholic. I last visited him, at the request of Father D'Arcy, at San Girolamo at Fiesole, where one of the Irish nuns told me in a shocked voice that he did not believe in Adam and Eve. Neither, I said, did I.

Perkins enthusiastically endorsed my proposal for a book on Giovanni di Paolo, and when I got to Perugia, Raimond van Marle, whose *Development of the Italian Schools of Painting* was in those unregenerate days a standard work of reference, endorsed it too, on different grounds. For some time his archenemy Cesare Brandi had been preparing a monograph on the artist, and he was determined to do Brandi down. When I dined with him outside Perugia, I found him warm and amiable. A self-indulgent *bon viveur*, he had on paper a talent for using language to say nothing at all. Only one early book, *Simone Martini et les Peintres de Son Ecole*, is still of use. From Perugia I returned to Florence, staying for prudence sake at a Swiss- not an Italian-owned hotel, and from Florence I went back to London.

When I was still an undergraduate, it was proposed by Kenneth Clark that instead of taking my degree I should move with him to the National Gallery, of which he was then director designate. My father, very sensibly, refused to allow this. In 1935, however, when I was still abroad, I made arrangements to serve as an Honorary Attaché at the Gallery for three months in the spring of the following year. This was not a fruitful period. I sat at a desk in one corner of the library, occupied partly with my own research and partly with sorting photographs of drawings by Cuyp, while in another corner, at the opposite end of the room, sat a second Honorary Attaché, Denis Mahon, already immersed in the study of Bolognese painting. As we were both nominees of the director, we were viewed with suspicion by the staff. A good deal has been written on the uneasy staff relations at the Gallery under Kenneth Clark's directorship. The academic staff was small, inward-looking, and, with one exception, untalented. The exception, Philip Pouncey, was destined to become the most distinguished connoisseur of drawings of his day, but in 1935 even he gave no indication of the stature he would eventually assume. The keeper was a nonentity named Isherwood Kay, who had once written on the watercolor painter Cotman, and the deputy keeper a prissy, thin-faced figure called Martin Davies, with whom I found it difficult at that time to keep my temper. Later, when he became a poor director of the Gallery and I was director of the Victoria and Albert, a working accommodation was reached. The interests of the staff centered not on their public duties but on the preparation of new catalogues, and their attitude to the director (whom they neither liked nor understood) recalled that of Puccini's Bohemians to their landlord Alcindoro. Responsibility for the trouble rested firmly on the shoulders of the staff, but it was compounded, on Clark's side, by a lack of ruthlessness which continued throughout his life to impair his value as an administrator.

Work on Giovanni di Paolo continued in London till the summer, and at the end of June I left again for Italy, first for Pisa, where I had never previously spent any time, and then Florence. I had an introduction from a friend of my mother's to Olga Loeser, the widow of Charles Loeser the collector, best known as a pianist who performed with the Lener Quartet. On her terrace at Torre Gattaia, amid yapping Pekinese dogs, I made two friends who were, in different ways, to affect my life. The first was a girl who seemed to have written a successful book. What distinguished authoress, I wondered, could this be? The book was about Parnell and her name was Joan Haslip. I saw more of her in Florence—her enchanting Austrian mother lived in a villa off the road to Settignano just above I Tatti—and we met frequently during the war in London. She has continued to write biographies, and very good biographies they are, and half a century later she paved the way for my own move to Florence. The second friendship, with Richard Offner, was professional. I knew Offner through his books and articles, and from the time I first read it at Oxford I looked on his *Italian Primitives at Yale University* as one of the most brilliant and suggestive books published on Tuscan painting. Sleek, sallow and personally rather vain, he spoke with great deliberation, and had he been less malicious it would not always have been easy to concentrate on what he said. He asked me to his flat in Borgo degli Albizzi to look through photographs. This was the beginning of a long and for me a highly fruitful relationship.

Relations with Berenson began less easily. I went up to tea at I Tatti, but I recoiled, as I recorded in a letter at the time, at the stream of vituperation directed by Berenson against Richard Offner and Erwin Panofsky. When I lunched at I Tatti later that week, things went rather better, owing to the presence of John Walker (who in the course of time became a close and esteemed friend) and his fiancée, Margaret Drummond. B.B. explained in front of his Domenico Veneziano and Neroccio Madonnas the difference between contour and outline (it was an explanation he must have given to countless visitors) and spoke for five inspired minutes about Ingres. This was the seed from which our later friendship sprang. "If he were not going off to Ragusa tomorrow," I wrote, "I believe that I should genuinely like him." Anyway, I was given free use of the library at I Tatti, where the Shapleys were working on the revised Chicago edition of Berenson's *Drawings of the Florentine Painters*.

I did not then realize that I Tatti, as structure and idea, was a theme that would recur through my whole life. When I first went there I knew the outside of the villa from photographs of the two great *Olea fragrans* flanking the path down to the *limonaia* and the terraced garden sloping down the hill. But I found the inside, despite the presence of great works of art, a little daunting. There, in the downstairs room in which I first met Berenson, was the great *St. Francis in Ecstasy* of Sassetta with its two accompanying saints and a miraculous *Madonna* of Bernardo Daddi. It was midsummer, so daylight was excluded, and by dim electric light they looked like visions of works of art rather than originals. The upstairs corridor was lined with pictures, the Giotto *Entombment* and the Signorelli portraits of the Vitelli and small panels, some of which, to my embarrassment, I could not identify. In the library, round which I was taken by the librarian, Alda Anrep, I looked with alarm at the long wooden table at which I should eventually find myself studying photographs and the deep leather armchairs in which Cyril Connolly had sat reading *Ulysses*. The most unnerving feature of the house in those days was its quietness. It was a temple where the prevailing silence was never, save at mealtimes, broken by a human voice.

From Florence I went on to Siena, where I stayed in the Pensione Santa Caterina, in a room that looked across the tanneries in Fontebranda to the Cathedral. My first objective was a *Madonna* by Giovanni di Paolo at Castelnuovo Berardenga. People stared at me as I got off the train, and I realized why only when I discovered that the village was eight kilometers from the railway station. I have found since that one's impressions of works of art become more vivid in the ratio of the trouble that one takes to see them, and though the panel has since been cleaned my dominant image is of how it looked on that first day. Gradually my picture of the Sienese *contado* built up, with visits by bus to Colle di Val d'Elsa and Casole d'Elsa and Grosseto and Pienza and Montalcino and Massa Marittima, though it was still far short of what it would eventually become. From Siena I went on to Orvieto and from Orvieto to Rome, of which my knowledge (outside the Pinacoteca Vaticana and the Borghese Gallery) was still woefully inadequate.

My timetable was determined by one external fact, that I had been invited to the Salzburg Festival, which in those days was of a quality that would have made refusal unthinkable. So from Rome I went by train to Spoleto, to see the Lippi frescoes, and Pesaro, to see the *Coronation of the Virgin* of Giovanni Bellini. The Albergo Zongo at Pesaro had no mosquito nets, and my only reading matter was a yellow-bound copy of *Salammbô*. By the morning its cover was red with blood. Pesaro was then, as it still is, the taking-off point for Urbino, where the Ducal Palace was more evocative than it is in its repristinated state today; it was then a credible setting for the conversations in the *Cortegiano*. From there I went on to Bologna and Verona en route for Salzburg.

Salzburg in 1936, with Toscanini and Bruno Walter, was Elysium, and Toscanini's *Falstaff* with Stabile, his *Meistersinger* with Lotte Lehmann, and Walter's *Orfeo* with Kerstin Thorborg were of a quality one will never hear again. One of life's exasperations is that one sometimes hears the best performances of great works before one knows them properly. Toscanini's *Falstaff* was my first *Falstaff*. The score of *Fidelio*, on the other hand, I had worked through carefully in London. "I could never have imagined a performance as fine," I wrote at the time. "One realised exactly what emotional state every bar of the music is intended to convey and exactly what the whole story signifies. I have never heard anything to compare with the strength and poignancy of Toscanini's playing or Lotte Lehmann's singing. It was an extraordinary experience hearing that very sophisticated audience shouting and shouting after Toscanini finished the Leonore III overture. I have never felt anything so intensely." At Salzburg I once more encountered Berenson. He was sitting in the stalls during the interval as one smart lady after another brought him sandwiches. I said that the *Fidelio* was so fine I doubted if, on the following morning, I should go to Walter's performance of Mahler's Third Symphony. "My dear, you would be making a great mistake," he said. "Mahler is a very considerable phenomenon." The following evening he was there again, and I told him how grateful I was that he had advised me to attend the Mahler concert. "How can you be taken in by stuff like that?" he replied. I found this disconcerting.

I stayed at Schloss Auersperg, where the guests included the U.S. Secretary of Labor, Frances Perkins, and her daughter. Madam Secretary was dynamic and immensely likable. She and I went together to *Jedermann* (she thought, by some confusion, it was called *Fledermann*, but after it was over she gave some alms to a beggar across the street) and to Liszt's *Psalm XIII* in the Cathedral. I dined with her years later in Washington, where she lived in Leroy Place in the house my parents had leased forty years before. After Salzburg we went on to a pension—too much like a chalet for my taste—at Garmisch, Haus Hirth, where Olga Stokowski was staying with a talented boy who became the pianist Eugene List. Escaping as early as was feasible, I headed north to Aachen and Münster and thence to Brussels, where I had arranged to see the legendary Stoclet collection. You sat at a table and were shown the paintings one by one; this was a good way of looking at them, but unfortunately there was another guest, from the British Museum, who was concerned solely with the Japanese part of the collection, so we sat facing each other at a table while artifacts from the two cultures alternated. The Stoclet Giovanni di Paolos, the celebrated scenes from the life of St. Catherine of Siena, were the only recorded works by him in Europe I had not seen in the original, and once I had been over them it was possible, when back in London, to complete my book. It appeared in 1937 from Chatto & Windus and received a surprisingly favorable press. I had the sense of emerging from the chrysalis.

My instinct at this point was to sell my stock in Siena and begin work on Florence in the person of a then unfashionable painter, Domenico Ghirlandaio. I went to the National Gallery to seek Kenneth Clark's advice, and found him lying on a sofa in his office without shoes. I put my proposition to him, and he dismissed it instantly. My approach was theoretical, he said, and I must instead stick to Siena and begin work on Sassetta. This I obediently did. There were a number of difficulties, however. The first was the time factor; it was clear in the first half of 1937 that war with Germany was imminent. Whatever was done had therefore to be done rapidly. The second was that Sassetta was in a rather special sense the property of Berenson; his *Sienese Painter of the Franciscan Legend* was among his most attractive and accomplished books. The third was that whereas Giovanni di Paolo could be studied in the local context of Siena, Sassetta was more broadly based; his style abutted at one point on Masaccio and at another on Piero della Francesca. As so often, the deciding factor was chance. I was asked to lunch by Lady Catherine Ashburnham, and driving down there with a friend, I predicted that we should see a Sassetta. Most of the park gates were shut and we were late for lunch, but when I sat down in my place with my back to the windows and my face toward the wall, I saw hanging on it the *Agony in the Garden* by Sassetta that is now at Detroit. Martin Davies, who had been to Ashburnham not long before, and who for three years had lived with seven Sassettas in the National Gallery, had failed to recognize it, but there, unmistakably, it was. I took this as an omen, and started working on the book.

Sassetta involved more visits to Italy. By way of Milan (to see the frescoes by Masolino at Castiglione d'Olona) and Venice (where Barbantini's great Tintoretto exhibition was crowded with visitors), I went on to Florence, where the main focus of interest was the Mostra Giottesca. For the historiography of Trecento painting this was a landmark event. If one looks at the retrospective catalogue today, most of its conclusions seem self-evident, but they were not self-evident at the time, since it was the first occasion on which many of the paintings could be properly seen. The *Rucellai Madonna* was moved for the first time from Santa Maria Novella, and the doubts about its authorship which were entertained by Berenson and many other scholars were suddenly resolved. There could be no question but that it was a work of Duccio. The great painted crosses from Santa Maria Novella and San Felice and the Ognissanti and Padua were shown together, and so were the Giotto *Dormition of the Virgin* from Berlin and the *Coronation of the Virgin* from Santa Croce and the *Scenes from the Life of Christ* from Munich and Settignano and New York. There was a wide spread of Dugento paintings, and the secondary Trecento artists, whose reintegration was due in the main to Offner (the Master of the Fogg *Pietà*, the Master of the Dominican Effigies, Pacino di Bonaguida, and Jacopo del Casentino), for the first time assumed an intelligible form.

The atmosphere was overtly competitive. At tea in the garden at I Tatti, Mrs. Berenson warned me against Offner. She would continue to ask me to meals, she said, but unless I promised not to see Offner she could not ask me when B.B. was there. But B.B., when a few days later he returned from Crete, was very cordial. At Siena, I saw the Palio from the balcony of the Palazzo Chigi-Zondadari (this was an occasion I later came to hate; nothing makes one feel so unclean as simulating enthusiasm). At Assisi, Mrs. Perkins warned me that in the hill towns and especially at Cortona witches blew herbs into one's pillow that caused a wasting disease no doctor could cure.

Sassetta also required a further visit to Berlin. I went there in the spring of 1938, just before the Czech crisis, to stay with Con O'Neill in the only street I have ever lived in whose name I could not pronounce, the Woyrschstrasse. I heard some good opera—*Der Rosenkavalier* with Frida Leider as a rather coarse Marschallin, *Tiefland*, and *The Bartered Bride*—but what I especially remember is the warmth of the professional relationships. Pictures were taken down in the gallery so that I could examine them with the gallery restorer, von Danzas. In the depot of the Schlossmuseum, to which I was taken by a descendant of the Dresden painter Schnorr von Carolsfeld, I found under a filthy glass shade a supposedly lost Sienese secular object of great importance, a gilt and silvered box painted by Domenico di Bartolo which had been in the Figdor collection. It disappeared when the palace was bombed during the war, and I regret that I did not make a detailed description of its paint surface.

In the spring of 1939, there opened in Italy two of the finest exhibitions I have ever visited. One was a Veronese exhibition in Venice, organized by Rodolfo Pallucchini and hung with impeccable skill. That I have so often since then left the train at Verona when I did not plan to, to see the Veronese altarpiece in San Giorgio in Braida, or at Vicenza to see the Veronese *Adoration of the Magi* in Santa Corona, is due solely to this exhibition. The second exhibition was of Brescian painting. Though there have since been individual exhibitions at Brescia of Romanino and Moretto, the exhibition of 1939, which included a roomful of Savoldos, still seems to me unsurpassed. At Brescia, I caught a train to Lugano, where I had been invited by Rudolf Heinemann to lunch with the old Baron Thyssen-Bornemisza and went round his spectacular collection.

Late in 1938 my book on Sassetta was delivered to the publishers—rereading it, it seems to me it could have done with another twelve months' work—and it was already in the bookshops when war was declared.

FROM PEACE
TO WAR

4

MY VISITS TO ITALY AND GERMANY IN 1938 AND 1939 WERE shorter than they had been before, since in the spring of 1938 I joined the staff of the Victoria and Albert Museum. The vacancy to which I was appointed was caused by the death of Basil Long, whose book on English portrait miniatures is still a standard work of reference, and was in the Department of Paintings. In those days there were two categories of national museums, those that were integrated in the Ministry of Education and those that were trustee-controlled. The staffs of the second group (which included the British Museum, the National Gallery, the Tate Gallery, and the Wallace Collection) were employed by trustees on the same terms as civil servants, while the staffs of the first group (the Victoria and Albert Museum and the Science Museum) were civil servants in the full sense. The difference lay not in status but in procedure. In the Victoria and Albert, civil service procedures were strictly observed; you wrote reasoned minutes that were kept in files held in a central registry. This may sound time-wasting, but in practice the system was a good one, and I am very happy to have been trained in it. Whereas in the British Museum handwritten letters were sent out of which no copies were made, at the Victoria and Albert there was a complete record of each transaction.

The director, Sir Eric Maclagan, was an old friend of my parents. He was a wide-ranging and highly respected scholar and an excellent linguist, and had a well-developed directorial technique. On the first morning he explained that he would no longer call me John as he had always done; he had, he said, a cousin on the museum staff whom he also addressed only by his surname. The Department of Paintings was a subdepartment of the Department of Engraving, Illustration, and Design, of which the keeper was James Laver. "You will find him a delightful colleague," Maclagan said. Laver, of whom I saw relatively little but came to like, was the author of a best-selling book, *Nymph Errant*, which in turn became a successful play. Ebullient and lightweight, he continued during my time in the museum to publish fluent books, on fashion, Nostradamus, Whistler and Tissot and Huysmans, but never again did he strike gold. With the head of the Department of Paintings, an Australian, Carl Winter, who was later a highly effective director of the Fitzwilliam Museum, I formed an immediate friendship; he was funny and outspoken and anarchical, and had an excellent, unprejudiced eye. His greatest asset was contagious honest-mindedness. We worked closely together for only a short time—till the outbreak of war indeed—but in a period of eighteen months I learned more from him than I can acknowledge here. The responsibilities of the department were strictly circumscribed. It maintained a collection of oil paintings, some of them of great distinction. It included the Constable collection (with its full-scale studies for the *Hay Wain* and the *Leaping Horse*), a big collection of Victorian paintings assembled by John Sheepshanks, and the Ionides collection, with a splendid Nardo di Cione and a great Degas. To obviate competition with other museums, oil paintings were a closed collection; they could be bought only if they were of value as illustrations of costume. The department also housed a significant collection of English watercolors and the national collection of portrait miniatures. When I joined the staff, I already had a deep interest in Holbein and in the Elizabethan portrait miniature, and as I worked there I developed an interest in eighteenth-century portrait miniatures as well. The best of them still seem to me outright masterpieces, and they have risen in value hardly at all; I am surprised that no one collects them today. Members of the public brought in miniatures and watercolors for inspection, and one Saturday not long after I took up my post I found myself confronted by Sir Alfred Munnings, the racing painter, with a spurious Constable sketchbook. I explained to the peppery little man the reasons why it could not be by Constable. "You're too young to know," he shouted as he left the room. Watercolors are a difficult study, not on the top level but on a level beneath, since most of the great watercolor painters, de Wint and Cotman among them, taught, and it is very difficult to establish criteria by which dull autograph works can be distinguished from touched-up copies.

One of the things for which I am most indebted to Carl Winter is that he encouraged me from the first to buy for the collection. I found at a dealer's a beautiful drawing of Lord Rivers in soft chalk by Gainsborough, and it was bought. The same thing happened with a more spectacular purchase. In Italy I had made friends with a dealer of exceptional talent, a friend of Roberto Longhi's named Vitale Bloch. One morning he came to see me bearing a parcel. It contained an album with fifty-three oil sketches by Canaletto's contemporary Luca Carlevaris. The book had been offered to the Museo Correr in Venice, which was unable to buy it, and the asking price was a mere two hundred and fifty pounds. It was eligible for purchase since it contained sketches of figures in Venetian dress, and it was bought. After the purchase it transpired that the sketches were used by Carlevaris in painting after painting, and were indeed the unique surviving examples of a form of life sketch which must also have been made by Canaletto. I published them, and only the other day, when I was writing the catalogue of the Robert Lehman collection, did I find that three of the four Lehman Carlevarises contained figures depending from them.

At this point a curious thing occurred. The Department of Engraving, Illustration, and Design owned a large number of sketchbooks, and one day I was looking casually at the shelves where they were stored. I took down one inscribed "Luke Callevaris," who was catalogued as an otherwise unknown English painter. It was in fact an unrecorded volume of bistre drawings by Carlevaris, and I published that as well.

The world of English watercolors was an exclusive, rather parochial one, but I went through most of the significant collections. One of my guides was Charles Bell, a former keeper of Western art in the Ashmolean Museum, who had earlier been the mentor of Kenneth Clark. A small man with a waxen face and a venomous tongue, his relations with K. had gone from bad to worse. "I stood behind Kenneth Clark on the platform of a bus this morning," he once said to me. "I could have pushed him off." From his tone it was clear that he had indeed been tempted to do exactly that. Bell was a xenophobe—access to the Ashmolean drawings when he was in charge was often denied to students with German-sounding names—but he had a very real sympathy for eighteenth-century Italy and was responsible for the first serious articles on John Robert Cozens, who traveled in Italy with William Beckford. They are academic in that they are concerned with the pattern of Cozens's movements in Italy, not with his style or with the qualities that made him a great landscape painter. I believed even then that Cozens was one of the finest English interpreters of the Italian scene, and when, years later, as director of the Victoria and Albert I opened the great Cozens exhibition organized at the Whitworth Art Gallery in Manchester I had an opportunity of saying this.

In the late 1930s watercolors could still be bought for the collection, and a good many were secured. The only cases in which I was personally concerned were gifts. The first, from the estate of S. D. Kitson, the biographer of Cotman, consisted of a large number of Cotman watercolors which complemented in a very satisfactory fashion the Greta watercolors by Cotman that were already in the collection. The other was of some albums containing drawings by members of the Sketching Club. At each meeting the members of the club were given a literary quotation to illustrate. The works that resulted are not, or are very seldom, serious works of art, but they provide firsthand evidence of how the romantic imagination worked. The only exhibition Winter and I organized in the short period before the war dealt with English watercolor painters in Italy. Walking across the Ponte Santa Trinità in Florence today, or crossing Lago Maggiore to the Borromeo Palace at Isola Bella, I often recall the drawings in this exhibition. A larger version of it was organized after the war to celebrate the state visit of the Italian President, Giuseppe Saragat.

More valuable than any of the other interests Winter stimulated was a devotion to the miniaturist Nicholas Hilliard. I believed (and the belief was not fashionable at the time) that Hilliard was a less insular artist than was generally supposed, that he was influenced by French court portraiture, and that his book on the portrait miniature, *The Art of Limning*, could be understood only in the light of Italian High Renaissance texts on the theory of painting. Recovering from pneumonia in the middle of the war, I returned to the third of these theses in an article in the JOURNAL OF THE WARBURG INSTITUTE entitled "Nicholas Hilliard and Mannerist Art Theory," and when the war was over I lectured at Rotterdam, Utrecht, and Amsterdam on the Elizabethan miniature; this lecture was later published in book form as *A Lecture on Nicholas Hilliard*. After it appeared, evidence turned up proving that Hilliard had indeed worked in France.

In 1939 the International Congress of Art History held its biennial meeting in London. The president was Eric Maclagan, and its sessions reached a climax in an evening party at the Victoria and Albert Museum attended by Queen Mary and Prince Paul of Yugoslavia, a svelte, beautifully groomed figure who looked as though he had been poured into his exquisitely cut tail coat. The interest of the occasion, however, was not the party but the simultaneous presence in London of most of the major living art historians. There I met Antonio Morassi (who presented a lecture, later reprinted in *Le Arti*, on the figures revealed by radiography in the Giorgione *Tempest*), Carlo Lodovico Ragghianti, a future hero of the Italian resistance, Ruth Wedgewood Kennedy (whose book on Baldovinetti had recently been published), Giuseppe Delogu, the historian of Venetian painting, Ranuccio Bianchi Bandinelli, the author of *Classicità dell'Arte Classica*, and many more. For someone interested as I was in art historians as well as in art history this was a Lucullan feast. The cynosure of interest was the leader of the Italian delegation, Roberto Longhi, the most brilliant art historian of his day. To the horror of the organizers, when he arrived in London he retired to the Strand Palace Hotel, canceling his lecture. I had great admiration for Longhi's work; his *Piero della Francesca* and his *Officina Ferrarese* seemed to open the door to a new kind of appreciative, nonacademic, literary art history. With Maclagan's approval I asked Bianchi Bandinelli, the only member of the Italian delegation whom I knew, to visit Longhi at his hotel and find out what was wrong. The trouble was that he had been put on to lecture on the same morning as Delogu, and arrangements were therefore made to extend the conference by half a day so that he had a whole morning for his lecture.

It dealt, in a highly original fashion, with the followers of Caravaggio and was later printed in an expanded form in *Proporzioni*. I asked Longhi and his wife, the novelist Anna Banti, to dinner with my parents. The meal went better than I expected; Anna Banti was civil and easy, and Longhi was witty and extremely likable. I did not see him and his wife again until, after the war, I went to their house in Via Benedetto Fortini in Florence.

Longhi, as was well known at the time, had been for many years bound up with the dealer Contini-Bonacossi. I first encountered

Contini-Bonacossi when I was taken by the collector Peter Lycett-Green to visit him at the Savoy Hotel in London, where he was staying before embarking for the United States. A huge, rather menacing man with a thin veneer of geniality, he was surrounded by the pictures he then sold to Samuel B. Kress—the Piero di Cosimo *Propagation of Coral* in the National Gallery in Washington was one of them. I visited him again in Florence to see the Sassetta altarpiece of the *Madonna of the Snow*, which had till then been in a small church at Chiusdino. Contact was resumed after the war, and continued till I omitted one of his paintings from my book about Uccello. I did not see his collection again until it was installed in the Meridiana of the Palazzo Pitti.

The meeting place of the art establishment in London was the Burlington Fine Arts Club. It had a long and creditable history and an excellent library, and a number of extremely important exhibitions had been organized in its gallery. The catalogues of them form important works of reference. I was elected a member not long before the war and charged with the preparation of an exhibition, but the war put paid to that as well as to the club, which was dissolved. The works exhibited were commonly drawn from private collections, and in the 1930s these were still very rich indeed. Some were easy of access, like the Cook collection at Richmond, where an incredible array of masterpieces was shown by appointment to visitors. Another was Bridgewater House, which could be visited by arrangement with the curator; it included the Titians and Raphaels and Poussins which are now on loan to the National Gallery of Scotland and magnificent seventeenth-century Bolognese paintings. There one day I met Wilhelm Suida, a gentle, bland old man, who explained to me, quite correctly, that a painting labeled as Palma Vecchio was really by Titian. For other collections it was necessary to obtain some personal introduction. When I first saw the Crawford pictures in Audley Square, I was taken round by the old Lord Crawford, who kept up a monologue about the threat offered by the Russians on the Indian frontier. I was first shown the Gambier-Parry pictures at Highnam, which are now in the Courtauld Institute Gallery, by a charming old bearded Major Gambier-Parry, who said to my mother, "Do not let him burn himself out too fast." From Oxford I went for the first time to George Spencer-Churchill's at Northwick, where the park ran right up to the house, as it does in eighteenth-century topographical paintings. He was a retiring man, who had suffered since the war from noises in his head and had a wireless tuned to a single program in the living room and dining room, and he knew Shakespeare's plays by heart; give him half a line from *The Winter's Tale* or *Coriolanus*, and he could continue it. His prime interest was an enthralling collection of antiquities and built onto the house was a large gallery of paintings. Later I stayed at Northwick on a number of occasions. There were many deterrents to doing so—the bedrooms were damp, there was nothing to drink but one glass of sherry before lunch and dinner, and almost always the party included an unknown colonial guest from the Victoria League—but weekends there were enjoyable.

In some houses time seemed to have stood still. One of them was Holkham, where I was taken to stay by my aunt, Susan Birch, with the old Lord Leicester. Going round the pictures, we reached the great Batoni of Coke of Norfolk of 1776. "This is my grandfather," said Lord Leicester, pointing at the elegant figure in fashionable eighteenth-century dress, and indeed it was. After dinner Lord Leicester was persuaded to part with the key to the library safe, and from it there emerged a celebrated codex by Leonardo da Vinci (now in the United States) and marvelous illuminated manuscripts. More taxing were visits to Lord Lee of Fareham. The last time I went to see him, after the outbreak of war, in Gloucestershire, he had, in addition to his own pictures, secured some pictures for temporary safekeeping from the National Gallery. One of them was the Mantegna *Agony in the Garden*. "I don't like this picture," he said. "The angels have only one wing. what do you call chaps in the Air Force with one wing? Observers, that's it, observers."

Sometime before the war I met for the first time a distant cousin, Norah Methuen. I never understood our exact relationship, but her maiden name was Hennessy and photographs of her father looked just like photographs of mine. Paul Methuen, in reaction against his father, the field marshal, had become a painter. A pupil of Sickert, he was a talented but not a very talented artist. Watching him painting branches of magnolia, I used to wonder that live flowers could become so muddy and dull, but his small sketches of buildings in Bath or Bristol in mixed media were more vivid and more personal. At Corsham, where I stayed with the Methuens repeatedly, the gallery of paintings with its Gainsboroughs and its great Van Dyck *Arrest of Christ* has to this day been preserved. After the war I became closely involved with the Methuens' affairs as a member of the board of the Corsham Estate Company, from which I learned something of the responsibilities involved in estate management. This was of use later when, as director of the Victoria and Albert Museum, I became an ex officio trustee of the house bequeathed to the state by Lord Stanhope at Chevening. Life at Corsham was enchantingly informal—unless guests were expected Paul Methuen wore no tie, and Norah spent her time repairing the purple velvet curtains in the library. Part of the house was on long lease to the Bath School of Art, but Paul Methuen's view of art as an interpretation of life was very different from that of the would-be avant-garde students who painted there. My last visit to Corsham was to Paul's funeral. Traveling back to London by train from Chippenham with John Betjeman, I found we shared a sense of gratitude at having been admitted for so long to the intimate, highly principled private life that Paul and Norah had imposed upon the rather forbidding house.

One day from the window of my office in the Victoria and Albert I was watching a window cleaner on a high ladder on the far side of the yard outside. He missed his footing, fell, and was killed instantly. This seemed to me a sign that my peaceful existence at the museum was near its end. There followed the Munich crisis, when days were spent packing up the major works in the collection, some weeks in which they were once more unpacked, and finally, after the German-Soviet pact, a period of definitive dismantling in preparation for their dispatch to disused tube stations and to Montacute. The onset of war was like a thunder cloud. It moved ineluctably forward, and when it broke there was no escaping it. I had known enough Jewish colleagues in Berlin and Munich who had vanished without trace to be convinced of the moral issues involved. People nowadays deride Chamberlain's policy at Munich, but the fact that some effort to reach an accommodation was made and was seen to have failed was a sine qua non for the resigned unanimity of public opinion when war was declared. Since the personnel of the Victoria and Albert were civil servants, they were, save for a small skeleton curatorial staff, redirected to other essential work. I was sent out on offer to the Lord Privy Seal, Sir Samuel Hoare, but Hoare could not make up his mind whether he wanted an Assistant Private Secretary or an auxiliary Principal Private Secretary, so the proposal, luckily, was allowed to lapse. Instead I found myself in the Intelligence Department of the Air Ministry, and there I spent five frantically busy and far from sterile years. Initially I went there as a civilian, but later I was commissioned in the RAFO. My military duties were minimal, save for a brief period when I found myself doing night duty at the main Air Ministry building and inspecting sentries posted among the barbed wire in St. James's Park. I had never met ordinary people before (people whose interests did not in some way conform to my own, I mean), and to my surprise I found them congenial and interesting.

The first impression, however, was one of eccentricity. My section was concerned with intelligence about the French, Belgian, and Dutch air forces, and the head of it, a retired major, believed that colds could be cured by having one's hair cut. A great deal of our intelligence was imaginary; the lists of Belgian aerodromes represented little more than fields in which, in emergency, runways might be laid down. But gradually knowledge became more systematic, and it was just as well it did. On the day of the German attack on Belgium and Holland I was taken by the Director of Air Intelligence to a meeting of the Joint Intelligence Committee in Richmond Terrace, presided over by Bill Cavendish-Bentinck, where the scale of the German advance in France was revealed. I had been at my desk all night, and in the hour that I had off for lunch I retreated to the reading room of the London Library and read Croce's essay on Góngora. Soon afterwards, the intelligence directorate moved to subterranean offices in Monck Street. The staff contained a number of extremely intelligent people, a future Speaker of the House of Commons, and Reggie Maudling, a mainstay of post-war Tory governments, and a delightful elderly liberal-minded Socialist, Wedgwood Benn. John Strachey sometimes strayed into one's office with a volume of Proust under his arm. "I find it a great nature poem," he explained. For a short time Harold Acton, in transit to India, was attached to my section. I often recall this first meeting when I go to his house, La Pietra, today. After the French collapse and the German occupation of France and Belgium, there was no need for an independent section dealing with any of these countries, and I was put in charge of general political intelligence and of the Air Ministry Weekly Intelligence Summary, which went out to Air Force units throughout the world. I have no file copies of it, but the work was taxing and I suppose it was useful, as in 1944 I was awarded a military MBE on its account.

After Pearl Harbor an American component was added to the staff.

This was agreeable and invigorating, but I was often surprised at the freedom with which American intelligence officers, operating on the same data as our own, slanted their interpretations toward the policies they espoused. At the time this lack of objectivity did not greatly matter, but some of the officers who were in London then occupied positions of influence in Washington during the wars in Korea and Vietnam, where many political decisions were taken on the basis of wrongly interpreted intelligence.

The problem of the war was one of intellectual not physical endurance. Like other people, I took my chance in air raids with an irrational belief that I was likely to survive. When, one evening during a raid, as I was working in my study in my parents' house in Avenue Road, my typewriter jumped up and hit me on the head, I was not much surprised. Nothing indeed was surprising, not even a night when Field Marshal Sir Philip Chetwode and his family slept in our drawing room because they thought, mistakenly, that an unexploded bomb had fallen in their garden at the bottom of the road. After the bombing our house was drafty and the front door was insecure. My father was the district air raid warden, a post that, in the period of heavy air attacks, was more onerous than it sounds. To me and to my mother it seemed that his peace of mind was seriously disturbed by night duty and by long periods in which he was on call. He became nervous and irritable (as many other people in similar positions must have done) and this was exacerbated by periodical articles on strategy written by him for the *Evening News*. They were collected in a little book under the title *Can Britain Attack?*, which recorded defeat after defeat. He was disturbed that my brother, whom he thought irresponsible and indiscreet, had been appointed to the intelligence directorate at the War Office. This was, indeed, the subject of the last serious conversation I had with him. One evening in 1942 I returned at seven from the Air Ministry to find he was in pain, and hardly had the doctor come than he collapsed and died. My brother, who had had a stand-up row with him that morning at breakfast, came home to find him dead. In wartime even funeral arrangements are difficult, but I arranged for a Requiem Mass to be said by Archbishop David Mathew and for his burial at the Franciscan Friary at Crawley. His tombstone, designed by my mother and carved by a pupil of Eric Gill, is inscribed with the words "*Ubi thesaurus ibi cor.*"

After my father's death my mother and I moved to a borrowed

house in Ladbroke Grove, where we lived for the remainder of the war. It was a trying, anxious time, which is still associated for me with the fetid smell of the tube at the Holland Park Station, when one reached it in the morning after it had been slept in by crowds overnight, or in the evening after dinner, when one picked one's way over recumbent figures to the lift. The reality was totally unlike the hygenic drawings of Henry Moore. Air raids are not conducive to prayer; they are too noisy and exciting. But flying bombs were very different, and each time a flying bomb was overhead one prayed. It was no use praying to major saints, whose switchboards would almost certainly be busy, so I prayed to St. Rose of Viterbo, whose line seemed always to be disengaged.

The key to intellectual survival was scholarly contacts, and here the conduit was Fritz Saxl, with whom I lunched almost every week on Wednesdays at a small Italian restaurant in Frith Street in Soho. The arrival in London of the Warburg Institute in the 1930s had been a turning point in the development of art history in England. That this was so was due not so much to the Warburg library, fine as that was, as to the personality of its director, Saxl. He was an *imaginative* scholar of extraordinary range. He believed, in Ernst Gombrich's formulation in the preface to *A Heritage of Images*, "that visual images should and could be used as historical documents and that the insights they may give us are in no way inferior to those derived from the study of written sources." But he had at the same time an intuitive, almost uncanny sense of the potential of whatever younger scholar he was dealing with. He transformed Anthony Blunt from a jejune Marxist journalist into one of the most accomplished art historians of his day, and my own debt to him was boundless. People nowadays talk about interdisciplinary or contextual studies, but Saxl's objective was more precise, to invest two-dimensional art history with a third dimension. As each week began, I looked forward eagerly to our meetings, and it was through them that I was introduced to Riccio's Paschal Candlestick in the Santo at Padua and its implications for Paduan humanism (Saxl was working at the time on an article published as "Pagan Sacrifice in the Italian Renaissance"), to the Reformation in Basel, and to the Neapolitan battle pieces of Aniello Falcone.

When one is overworking, the best form of relaxation is other work. Initially this involved the study of a codex of the *Divine Comedy* in the British Museum, illuminated for Alfonso V of Aragon by Giovanni

di Paolo and an unknown miniaturist whom I believed (wrongly) to
be Vecchietta. It compelled me to read not only Dante but the whole
range of Dante commentaries. My interest in it was not, or was not
primarily, attributional; it was rather, through analysis of iconography
and textual sources, to establish the visual images which rose to the
surface of the minds of readers of Dante in a not very progressive
cultural center in the second quarter of the fifteenth century. The
codex had been sent for safekeeping to the National Library of Wales,
and I spent two periods of leave in a horrible seaside hotel at Aberystwyth. The British Museum drawings that had also been evacuated
there were in the charge of A. E. Popham, and in the hotel I found
a scholar whom at that time I knew only slightly but whom I much
admired, Johannes Wilde. Wilde's tiresome wife, herself a scholar,
was there too. "Every day you look more tired," she said when I came
down to breakfast. She had a torch, which she brandished indiscrim-
inately in the blackout, and an insatiable curiosity as to the contents
of any parcel a soldier might be carrying. As a result, after my second
visit, Wilde, the most innocent and peace-loving of men, was arrested
as a spy and deported with a group of dangerous Nazis to Canada.
The task of retrieving him fell on Anthony Blunt.

The early drawings from the Royal Collection at Windsor had also
been moved down to Aberystwyth, but the very large and very important collection of seventeenth-century drawings remained in the
Royal Library. Cataloguing the collection had been begun before the
war under the direction of the Royal Librarian, Owen Morshead. Its
beginning was inauspicious, a slovenly catalogue of the Flemish drawings by a Belgian scholar, Leo van Puyvelde. Puyvelde, when I later
met him at Windsor, proved a bogus figure, dressed in a Belgian
uniform covered with decorations commemorating various exhibitions. When the management of the catalogue passed to Blunt, it at
once assumed an entirely different character. A volume on the drawings of Guercino was commissioned from Denis Mahon, and Anthony,
to my surprise since I was not a Seicento specialist, offered me the
choice of cataloguing any one of the other major blocks of drawings.
The options at first seemed very wide, but they worked down in
practice to two areas in which the collection was especially rich. These
were the drawings of the Carracci and the drawings of Domenichino.
After going carefully through the sheets, I opted for Domenichino;
and the Carracci catalogue was then commissioned from Rudolf Witt-

kower. The reason for my choice was first that the Domenichino drawings represented most of the whole contents of the artist's studio at his death, and five-sixths of his surviving graphic work; in number and importance they were comparable to the Ingres drawings at Montauban. The second and decisive reason was that Domenichino represented a critical problem of a very special kind. Until the late nineteenth century he had been thought, after Raphael, to be the greatest painter in the world; thereafter his stock had slumped. His paintings moved Taine to admiration, Goethe to rapture, and Stendhal to tears, but his work was then demolished by Ruskin, who with "safe universality of reprobation" drove his bulldozer through the painter's reputation. The problem therefore was critical as well as art-historical in a narrow sense. I found it difficult to believe that idealist critics in an earlier period had been wholly wrong, and it seemed that the preparation of the catalogue could not but result in a re-estimate of Domenichino's value and personality. The catalogue proved an immensely laborious task. Whenever I was free I went to Windsor, and stared at sheets of putto heads smiling up from gray-blue paper, as though challenging one to discover for which work they were made. Fortunately a very large number of drawings could be satisfactorily identified, and when today I look at the *Last Communion of St. Jerome* in the Vatican, with the studies for the individual heads and figures in my mind, I find it as moving as did spectators in the early nineteenth century. Blunt's name is now vilified, but throughout my work on the Windsor catalogue and in many other contexts I found him generous, supportive, and disinterested.

Paradoxically my most vivid memories are of three days in October 1944, when I was sent over to Paris to see Air Marshal Tedder, whose headquarters were at Versailles. It was the first time I had left England for five years, and I shall never forget the sense of liberation as I walked through the misty, derelict park with chestnuts crackling underfoot while I waited for my appointment. It so happened that the Salon d'Automne in Paris opened at the time, with a buoyant exhibition of new paintings by Picasso and Matisse. It imparted, as did nothing in London, an enheartening sense of continued creativity. I wrote about it for the *Listener*, and I recall it whenever I see one of the Picassos that were shown there on the wall of Louise Smith's apartment in New York.

In the middle of the war, my brother, then in the intelligence directorate at the War Office, was transferred to Washington. He lived there in the house of an astrologer, Miss Bartleman, whose horoscopes were in great demand. She cast his horoscope, and in March 1945 I had a letter from him saying that she had also cast mine. The letter read:

It is such a hot spring night, about ten o'clock, and I have been buying flowers (from a barrow by lamplight) for my room. I took some down to Miss Bartleman for her "German bunny" of white china, which is a vase on the mantelpiece of a rabbit with a lop ear, and we then settled down to business over your horoscope. Here it is. Don't blame me if you are frightened by its uncanny accuracy. All I can faithfully say is that I have added *nothing*, simply assembled my scribbled notes (she reads very fast) and used her wording whenever possible. I am as usual rather stunned by it. It cannot be thought-reading, for it is all mathematical and one can see her working it out section by section. I had told her nothing but, once long ago, that you were a scholar and a student of Italian primitives. She was standing in the kitchen when I came in with the flowers, peeling a lettuce, and asked your time and date of birth. I gave them to her and she said, "What does he do now?" I said Air Force, and she said, "But don't say that. He couldn't possibly fly with his moon and sun in that position, at least I hope for his own sake he has never tried; he couldn't do it."

A summary of the chart was enclosed in the letter. It read:

This person is born for fame and will have a very long life. He is "a lovely gentle soul" and has a phenomenal brain, is "seething with emotion" but never towards human beings, and is so sensitive that "he cannot stand the shriek of a train whistle or any sudden noise." He is at the moment working much too hard, "definitely over-working" at some kind of work he does not like. He has, however, a lot of plans (since he always plans ahead) for literary work during the coming eighteen months, and these will all succeed. He will achieve great fame and money by his work, which will become more strictly creative than anything he has done hitherto. He will produce some great work of a visionary or occult nature, which could have to do with the Italian Renaissance. Astrologically he can

never wish to live in England, but must and should live in Italy;
he cannot go there, however, before next year. His planets absolutely prevent his having emotions about people or even liking them.
He will never really enjoy social life, and must at all costs be left
alone since he is entirely happy in himself at his own ploys. It
cannot be too much emphasized that he *must* be left alone. Hardly
anyone can understand him, and neither his mother nor his brother
will ever be able to do so fully, although there is the greatest harmony of affection between all three. He can become very irritable,
even very disagreeable when crossed or if anyone tries to force him
to do what he doesn't like. People, including his own family, sometimes irritate him to excess. He is not of a spending disposition,
indeed in preference saves, but will readily spend money "on some
valuable book or, it seems to me, a picture."

In a gloss on the chart James added:

You chose a life in which all outside interference would be impossible and you would be automatically immune to people. What
surprises Miss Bartleman most is how happy you are in yourself
and will always remain; it is most unexpected, as you could easily
have been melancholy and unhappy by a few hours difference.

Ten years later I myself visited Miss Bartleman. I did so only once,
as I have a cat allergy and her house was filled with cats. She added
one rider to the chart, that I should never marry.

I would have expected before the war to have felt strong emotional
recoil at the destruction by bombing of so many monuments in Germany. Today I ask myself, when I return to some almost effaced city,
how necessary it was. But at the time, partly because one knew so
many people who were the courageous agents of destruction, there
was no room for thinking of this kind. The case of Italy was different.
The potential for destruction was immense, but major monuments
were listed and were treated with real, not simulated, circumspection;
in relation to the tonnage of bombs dropped the level of cultural
destruction was very low. There were miscalculations or plain acci-
dents—two of the most serious were at Treviso and Padua—but by
and large the record was creditable. There was, indeed, only one
notable exception. It occurred in 1944 after the fall of Mussolini, when

the Badoglio government was in charge. I did not normally see Cabinet minutes, but on this occasion an extract reached my desk, reporting that Eden, the Foreign Secretary, concerned at the delay of the Badoglio government in opening up negotiations, had urged that an attack be launched on Milan. The air attack was mounted—one could hear the menacing hum of the bombers crossing London—and grave damage was done to the Ambrosiana, La Scala, Sant'Ambrogio, and countless other monumental buildings. A vigorous protest at this barbaric occurrence came from the Minister to the Vatican, Sir D'Arcy Osborne.

In 1945, when the war in Europe was barely ended, I was one of a small group of officials invited by the Italian government to study the reconstruction of local monuments. The party consisted of James Mann, the director of the Wallace Collection, William Gibson, the keeper of the National Gallery, Benedict Nicolson, and myself. We were received by the Director General of Fine Arts, my friend the archaeologist Ranuccio Bianchi Bandinelli. In Naples, Bruno Molajuoli outlined what seemed an impracticable scheme for transferring the picture gallery from the Museo Nazionale to the palace at Capodimonte (it was in fact realized successfully a few years later) and took us through a number of devastated churches, in some of which the baroque marble casing of the chapels had been stripped off, leaving Gothic architecture exposed beneath. In Rome we visited the Istituto Centrale di Restauro, where Cesare Brandi was patiently reintegrating patches of Mantegna's Eremitani frescoes from such fragments as survived. In Florence the Ponte Santa Trinità had been destroyed and the bomb-damaged west end of Via de' Bardi was a horrifying spectacle. From Florence by way of Perugia I traveled back to Rome in a lorry in the sympathetic company of Stanislao Lepri, who was already an aspirant surrealist painter though still on the staff of the Italian Foreign Ministry. The sides of the roads were littered with wrecked armored cars and tanks. How long would it be, I wondered, before nature could reassert itself? If I had been told then: "A couple of years," I would not have believed it. In Siena for the first time I met Enzo Carli, who became an intimate friend, and in Florence, Ugo Procacci, of whom the same is true. It was a confidence-inspiring experience, and laid the foundation of years of collaboration which have continued to this day.

5

FROM WAR TO PEACE

IN 1945 LIFE BEGAN AGAIN. THE FUTURE COULD BE MEASURED IN decades not days. To what use should it be put? There seemed to me to be three alternatives. The first (toward which I was led by my experience in the war) was to indulge the talent for administration that I seemed to have and enter some different profession. I dismissed this possibility. The second was to continue the work which had been interrupted by the war and resume the study of painting and sculpture in Siena. I questioned the advisability of this in the long, not the short, term; old mistakes (and there were quite a number of them) could be rectified and new discoveries might indeed be made, but the subject was a narrow one and its possibilities were circumscribed. The third was to embark on a new field of research that might, if it were studied resolutely and methodically, exert some wider influence on the history of art. I opted for this third course, and as soon as the war ended I agreed to return to the Victoria and Albert on condition that I be appointed to the Department of Sculpture.

I had looked at sculpture before the war in Italy and Vienna and Berlin, but less seriously than I had looked at paintings, and I was sadly ignorant of the whole field. The little I had read about it was sufficient only to establish how understudied the subject was. At Oxford I had bought a copy of the English translation of Bode's *Florentine Sculptors of the Renaissance*, but had found nothing in it to kindle my interest. "Florence," one read on the first page, "is the home of modern art; here in the soil of Arno city the tender plant first took root. . . . What may be said of Italian sculpture of the Renaissance in general is true in particular of that of Florence. All the peculiar qualities of that art are here developed in their purest and most characteristic form, for they were the product of the soil, springing from the very soul and life of the people, unalloyed by alien admixture or influence." The first break in the ice was due to a book called *Stones of Rimini*, in which Adrian Stokes described what was essentially a sensory response to the marble sculptures of Agostino di Duccio in the Tempio Malatestiano; it succeeded in communicating through the printed page in a perverse, ill-reasoned form the experience of physical tactility that is central to an understanding of sculpture.

The decisive stimulus came, however, as it so often does, from an individual, not a book. He was a young Hungarian named Jenö Lányi, who had a fine-tuned, skeptical mind that was intolerant of received opinion. The prime difficulty in studying Italian sculpture, Lányi recognized, was the absence of an independent methodology. The means by which sculpture was studied were means derived from the study of painting. Sculptures were in three dimensions, but they were analyzed as though they were in two, and the criterion of resemblance was based on the external appearance of the sculpture not on the thought processes or the technique by which its appearance was achieved. Lányi was looked on with some suspicion in London ("Nothing new in this," said Eric Maclagan, the director of the Victoria and Albert, and Margaret Longhurst, the head of its sculpture department, coming away from a revolutionary lecture given by Lányi at the Warburg Institute), but the handful of articles he produced are still required reading for students of sculpture. His aim was to produce a monograph on Donatello, in which every work would be truthfully rephotographed and freshly analyzed. He and his wife, a daughter of Thomas Mann, lived near Swiss Cottage, and there in the evenings the Donatello project was a constant subject of conversation. But it was not, alas, to be, for in 1940 the boat in which Lányi embarked for New York was torpedoed and he was drowned. After the war the problem of his scholarly legacy was discussed, and his notes and photographs were handed over to what was seemingly the only eligible candidate, a young German-American student called H. W. Janson, who had written a dissertation on the sculptures of Michelozzo. Janson was the antithesis of Lányi—he believed in reasoning, not in sight— and the outcome was the antithesis of the book Lányi conceived, a blind, heavyweight, argumentative catalogue that is still the standard book on Donatello.

It was due in great part to the posthumous influence of Lányi that I decided to join the Department of Architecture and Sculpture at the Victoria and Albert. The decision proved to be a wise one, and I stayed there for twenty-two contented and constructive years, first as an assistant keeper and then as keeper of the department. That they were contented and constructive years was due to a variety of factors. The policy of the museum was to encourage and not just tolerate research. The keeper of the department, Delves Molesworth, was not himself a scholar, but he was liberal and funny and farsighted and had an excellent sense of quality. I learned a great deal from him, and without his support much of the work I did there would have been impossible. In later years when I was myself in charge of staff, my endeavor was always to give them the same opportunities and the same encouragement that he gave me. Sculpture cannot be studied from books. It must be touched and handled and moved about if it is to be properly understood. It can be dealt with effectively, that is to say, only in the conditions obtaining in museums. The sculpture collection at South Kensington is preeminent both for its richness and for its range. One was dealing not only with the Italian sculpture in which one specialized but with a superlative collection of Early Christian and Byzantine and medieval ivories, with English alabasters, with German limewood sculptures, with French terracottas and portrait busts, with English eighteenth-century sketch models and portraits, and with a great collection of Rodin. They were not plates in a book, they were works made by human hands, and one came slowly to accept that sculpture, unlike painting, was a single field, that through the centuries its creative processes had been subject to little significant change, and that only in the light of firm qualitative judgments based on a broad range of experience could the psychology of individual sculptors be understood. There was, moreover, at South Kensington an inestimable boon in the presence of a systematic cast collection. It was formed for the benefit of artists at a time when painters still copied casts, but its current beneficiaries were art historians. One could look at photographs of Bamberg or Compostela, of a Pisan pulpit or some Flemish chimneypiece, and then, turning to the cast, test for oneself how deeply it was carved and just how it was made. Cast collections, generally of a less comprehensive kind, used to exist in American museums, but they have one and all been broken up by directors who coveted their space for showing works of art.

The switch from painting to sculpture, however, was less clean than this account suggests. Studying works in three dimensions is very different from studying works in two, and not till 1949 did I publish two essays on Italian sculpture which seem to have stood the test of time. While I was gaining my sea legs, my private time was taken up with books and articles on painting, the Domenichino catalogue and the *Sienese Codex of the Divine Comedy*, which I had worked on through part of the war, a popular book on fifteenth-century Sienese painting, and monographs on Uccello and Fra Angelico. Before the war, moreover, I had begun a book on the Sienese fifteenth-century painter Matteo di Giovanni, and I continued working on it in Siena when the war was at an end. I have never been much good at original documentary research, and I once transcribed a whole series of documents about another Matteo di Giovanni, only to find that he was blind. But that was not the reason why I gave up the book. Sometimes one gets exasperated with the limitations of one's friends and expels them from one's life, and I did exactly that with Matteo di Giovanni.

When the war ended I continued to live with my mother. Her biography of Dickens, which appeared at the end of 1945, had a substantial and well-deserved success. The first to be written after the Nonesuch publication of his correspondence, it shocked hidebound Dickensians, but it still seems to me, biographically not critically, an excellent book. The new focus of her interest was Charles Kingsley, and when *Canon Charles Kingsley* appeared in 1948, she moved on to a connection by marriage, Alphonse de Lamartine, whose wife was Marianne Birch. Given her physical condition it was impossible she should live without companionship, and since James, when he returned reluctantly from Washington, had his own establishment, I continued to look after her. Her character was, if anything, stronger and more exigent than it had ever been, but since she was physically less active she tended to live vicariously. Hers was a far from empty life. There were countless guests, Rose Macaulay foremost among them, and friends of my brother's, headed by the cellist Maurice Gendron, were one by one absorbed in a kind of family relationship. My mother was astringent and extremely funny—Jim Lees-Milne complains in one of his published diaries that she had no small talk, and this providentially was true—and though I sometimes longed for freedom I did not resist captivity. James generally remained

1. My father's father, Sir John Pope Hennessy, as governor of Mauritius (*statue by M. Loumeau, 1908, Port Louis, Mauritius*)

2. My mother's father, Sir Arthur Birch (*painted by Sir William Orpen, private collection*)

3. My mother, Una Birch (*ca. 1906*)

4. Watchtower at Rostellan Castle, County Cork, with Sir John and Lady Pope Hennessy and my uncle, Hugh (*ca. 1890*)

5. Myself and my brother, James, with our mother in London (*1917*)

6. Myself and my brother, James, as pages at a wedding (*1919*)

7. Consigned to school (*1923*)

8. My father, Major-General L. H. R. Pope-Hennessy (*1932*)

9. My mother, Dame
Una Pope-Hennessy
(*photograph by Cecil
Beaton, 1946*)

10. My brother, James, in
the gardens at Chiswick
House (*photograph by
Cecil Beaton, 1940*)

11. Giotto: *The Presentation in the Temple (Isabella Stewart Gardner Museum, Boston)*

12. Giovanni di Paolo: *The Baptism of Christ (Ashmolean Museum, Oxford)*

13. Giovanni di Paolo: *The Crucifixion (Christ Church, Oxford)*

14. Sassetta: *The Agony in the Garden (Detroit Institute of Arts, formerly at Ashburnham Place)*

in London when I went to Italy. In 1949 my mother developed cancer and was operated on in London. I remember returning home after the operation to find Rose Macaulay sitting in the drawing room to find out what she could do to help. Most people after an operation recover their strength with deceptive speed, and initially my mother did so too, but the first operation was followed by a second, and I left in the summer with much misgiving for Italy. In Siena I received a letter in which my mother's handwriting had changed: it was malformed and loose, not the neat, disciplined writing one had always known. James, on the telephone, begged me to stay away, but I took the first train to Paris, and there, buying a copy of *The Times* at the bookstall in the Gare de Lyon, I read of my mother's death. James's character was tempestuously emotional. Earlier in the year, when I thought he should be back in London, he had stayed obstinately in the South of France, accusing me of using my mother's illness to force him to return, and his behavior later, however ill conceived, was an act of expiation to prevent my witnessing my mother's death.

A fortnight after my mother died James received a letter from his landlord in Ladbroke Grove saying that the flat above his own had become free and was at his disposal if he wished to lease it. My mother's apartment in Lansdowne Road was much too large for me alone, so for three years I lived in cramped conditions on top of James. A second thing occurred at the same time. Among James's friends was a hockey player from Amiens who had met him in a doctor's waiting room in Nice and thought him so ill that he should be brought back to London. My gratitude to him for doing this was redoubled in 1949 when, after my mother's death, he put me in touch with a talented South African undergraduate at Oxford named Andrew Porter who wished to write on music. The most distinguished Anglo-Saxon music critic of his generation, he has been a pillar of my life for forty years.

Up to this point I had never known James really well. I had boundless admiration for his talent, but his life seemed secretive (more so to me than to other people, I suspect), and I looked upon his forays into low life and smart society with some reserve. Years later, a close friend, Maud Russell, described him to me as "two characters lodged in one shell. The serious, hardworking, self-critical (so far as his writing was concerned) workmanlike being, and that other self, wild, careless, unheeding. A person might easily have known only one half of him and not had a clue to the other half." With concessions on both sides, however, we contrived a compromise existence, I in my study writing on Fra Angelico and he entertaining Guy Burgess and Derek Patmore downstairs. In August 1950, on the anniversary of my mother's death, I wrote to him from Vallombrosa: "In a sense, as you say, this has been a horrid year, but in another it has been so much happier than I could ever have expected, and this is due almost entirely to you, and to your constant affection and helpfulness. There is a passage in Sophocles where Antigone says that the bond between siblings is the most irreplaceable of all relationships, and I begin to think that this is true." James had a gift for friendship and a vast circle of friends, some of whom, like Maud Russell and Ann Fleming and Riette Lamington, became firm friends of my own. I remember watching Greta Garbo leaving her taxi, with her head swathed in a mackintosh, when Cecil Beaton brought her to lunch. I have never been able to recognize people, and when I met her again five or six years later at a party in New York I had no notion who she was.

James was already a successful writer. His first book, *London Fabric*, won the Hawthornden Prize in 1939, and still reads as freshly now as it did then. But from the time he left school, he had been looked on as a problem. He followed me to Balliol, but was unhappy following in my footsteps and went down after a year. For a few months he was employed by a Catholic publishing firm, Sheed & Ward, and then, in 1938, was packed off to the West Indies as secretary to the governor of Trinidad, Sir Hubert Young. His second book, *West Indian Summer*, was an amalgam of the history of Trinidad and his own life there. These early books were a compact of historical sensibility and of good writing. James regarded himself as an artist, in the rather old-fashioned way that writers in the 1920s and 1930s had been prone to do. He was unintellectual, not in the sense of being unintelligent (he was indeed extremely clever), but of being uninterested in criticism or in ideas. Most of my friends were my own contemporaries; most of his were much older or younger than himself. Already in the 1950s it worried me that his life seemed to be built around people he was likely to outlive. The determining influence on his career as a writer was a wise woman of extraordinary intuition, Lady Crewe, who recognized that his gift was biographical and that to realize it he required original material. Lord Crewe, as a result, gave him free access to the papers of his father, Lord Houghton, who, as Richard Monckton Milnes, was a center of cultural life in London in the middle of the nineteenth century and wrote the first biography of Keats. Originally intended as a short memoir, the book grew into a two-volume biography. This was not his most popular but is to my mind his most accomplished and most durable book. The payoff was a volume on Lord Crewe. Hardly was this off the press when the telephone rang on my desk, and I heard James's voice saying, rather contemptuously, that he had been asked to write the official life of Queen Mary and was turning the proposal down. I asked him to come to see me, and told him why I thought that he should write the book. Royalty, I explained, were an endangered species, and this was an occasion to establish, through close inspection of a single life, the nature of the phenomenon. The resulting book, one of the best and most sympathetic of all royal biographies, appeared in 1960. In life James was a poor judge of character and had very little understanding of the motives even of people he knew well, but in dealing with the past his understanding of the human personality was next door to infallible. It was this that made him an exceptional biographer. The book was largely written in Germany, and it confirmed his belief that he must live in isolation if he was to write. After it was published he wished to write on Balzac, but the appearance of Félicien Marceau's *Balzac* put paid to that, and I suggested that he might do a short book about our grandfather, Sir John Pope Hennessy, and Victorian colonial administration. The short book turned into a longer one, *Verandah: Some Episodes in the Crown Colonies 1867–1889*. It took three years to write and involved repeated journeys to West Africa and the Far East, so by the time that it appeared the profits from *Queen Mary* had been dissipated. "The new installment of the book," I wrote to him, "is enormously enjoyable, but I am a little alarmed at the time it is all taking. I do not see that you can afford to go on working exclusively at this for the next eighteen months. Would it not be possible to combine it with something more remunerative, or alternatively to reduce the scale? I have about forty thousand words here, so if the rest is proportionate it will be a two hundred thousand word book." Skillful as it is (and many people look on it as his best book), it seems to me to suffer from being two-dimensional; it reduces colonial policy to the interaction of discongruous personalities. By 1964 when it appeared, James had no regular income, and the death of Lady Crewe had deprived him of his main moral support. Most writers bridge the gap between one book and the next with book reviewing or some other form of journalism. This he could not or would not do. He accepted instead a proposal from George Weidenfeld that he should write a book about the slave trade, and this appeared in 1967. It has passages of extremely clever writing, but is overemotional and was insufficiently researched. It was followed by a commission for what resulted in a miserable little book about Hong Kong, called *Half-Crown Colony*. At this point I suggested that he should write a life of Anthony Trollope. I had a double motive in making the suggestion: first, I admired Trollope, and second, since *Queen Mary* had been followed by a phase of royal snobbishness, Trollope might be followed by one of sober industry. What resulted was a very good book, strong on biography but less so in its critical handling of the novels. The attraction of distance, however, remained strong. The next proposal, made by James himself, was for a book about Lafcadio Hearn, but no publisher would give a significant advance on it, and he fell back on Robert Louis Stevenson. I advised him against this subject, since the quint-essential Scottishness of Stevenson seemed to me outside his scope. But the book was finished when he died—it appeared posthumously with an excellent introduction by Nigel Nicolson—and it now seems to me a far richer and more sympathetic piece of work than *Anthony Trollope*.

James was incurably extravagant (this he inherited from my father), and from 1964 on his life was clouded by insolvency. When insolvency degenerated into a threat of bankruptcy, some of his friends, headed by that good Samaritan John Cholmondeley, stepped in and jointly guaranteed his overdraft. His last contract was lucrative; it was for a life of Noël Coward, with whom he had stayed in Jamaica. He knew very little about the theatrical world, but he went off, fortified by alcohol and Librium, to New York to interview a number of old actresses who had been Coward's friends. Perhaps it was as well the book was never written. "Surely," he wrote to me, "there has never been a more ephemeral world than that of the stage, and surely no more boring reading matter than accounts of the rehearsal, success or failure, of a succession of plays and musical comedies. I do hope I have not made a mistake." I have a portrait of him painted, in the last years of his life, in a style derived from Tchelitchew, by Cecil Beaton, who had photographed him often from the 1930s on. In it his haunted face registers despair.

In my three years at Ladbroke Grove I got to know James's responses very well. He was warm and life-enhancing but intolerant of advice. He had, as he wrote later, "a neurosis connected with years ago, when I was always convinced that M. and you disapproved of and despised me; I know it sounds, is indeed, insane, but I am morbidly sensitive at this one point and shall never be anything else." The saving grace was his *fidus Achates*, Len Adams, who controlled him much more effectively than I could. Sometimes in life one gets to know people best when one is not in their immediate vicinity, and when, in 1953, I bought my own house on Campden Hill, our attachment became deeper than it had been before. He was abroad for long periods of time, at Kronberg-im-Taunus and Hagenau and in Malaysia and the West Indies and Mauritius and West Africa, and from each place there came back brilliantly vivid letters describing his experiences. He had a gift for intimacy which endeared him to countless women friends in London—he read their responses as though they were the pages of a book—and he applied the same gift to any society in which he found himself, whether at Hagenau or Kronberg or Singapore. When I met him at London airport, I never knew whom he was bringing back, sometimes a minuscule policeman from Mauritius, sometimes a Malay. Control of his finances was handed over at one point to a taxi driver from the Frankfurt airport, who in a misguided effort to balance his finances sold his portrait by Lucian Freud for much less than it was worth. So far as I could judge, these relationships were not, or not primarily, physical; they were one facet of a gift for friendship which breached every social, linguistic, and color barrier.

Lest this account suggest that I was always on the giving, not on the receiving, end, I should make it clear that what I owed to James was an enrichment of my whole imaginative life. He was a romantic, a French romantic rather than an English one, and he turned life into romance. On his fifty-fifth birthday when he was starting work on Stevenson, he wrote to me from Edinburgh:

The sunny, brisk afternoon of the day I arrived (powdered snow lying in the square gardens) I walked downhill to 17 Heriot Row, the house in which the Stevensons lived from 1857 to 1887. It is a part of the symmetrical lay-out of the New Town, with a slightly formidable architectural quality. There are area railings, each with a slender but stalwart lamp stand at the summit. I looked hopelessly at the house, which has an oblong plaque stating that Robert Louis Stevenson had lived there, and another highly polished brass plate above the highly polished brass doorbell: "Private House NOT a museum!" Heavy knocker, heavy door-handles, a general sensation, it gives, of the implacable and the unapproachable. I have been there to gaze at it three times since. My most recent information was that it now belongs to an old Mr. Mackenzie, cross, with a sham leg and a wife who was his secretary. I was dispirited and felt shy about ringing the bell. This afternoon, after a solitary birthday lunch of oysters (one bad) at the Café Royal, I took a taxi driven by a boy with pre-Raphaelite floating hair (hair in Edinburgh is worn far longer than it is in London; the students have it to their haunches almost)—anyway driven in a taxi to 8 Howard Place where RLS was born, a small, forlorn, really mean house in a stunted two floor terrace with unpleasant, amorphous commercial premises and a minor factory just opposite. I trudged back up a very steep hill and reaching the junction of Dundas Street and Heriot Row, I thought I would go and have another look at the house in Heriot Row. This time, in the snow-light, I could see clearly two illuminated chandeliers hanging from the drawing room ceiling. I stepped across the road, and leant back against the iron railings of the garden opposite, wishing. As though in an opera scene or a stage melodrama, the heavy door of number Seventeen opened slowly, very slowly, swung open inwards, and a youngish woman with red-gold hair came out and began hunting for something in the back of a parked car. I darted across the road:

"Excuse me, madam, but do you think Mr. Mackenzie would see me? I'm writing a life of Robert Louis Stevenson for Simon & Schuster."

"Well, Mr. Mackenzie's gone, and I am the new shatterlaine." I assumed her to be American. "May I ask who you are?" I gave my name.

"Why it's genuflecting to you I ought to be." I realised then she was a compatriot. "Of all things Simon & Schuster are great, and so are you."

She explained to me that she would ask me to do her a good turn, to step right into the house, look over it and join "two dear old girls" whom she was entertaining to hot kirsch in the drawing room. We whisked through the house, and then went into the drawing room, where were seated a very old, very stumpy lady wearing a purple tweed toque, one grey curl thrust downward upon her forehead; and a rather ethereal-looking middle-aged woman, with a drawn, clever, intuitive face, who turned out to be Shane Leslie's sister-in-law, Mrs. Lionel Leslie. To welcome me to 17 Heriot Row, and even more when she learned it was my birthday, Catlyn MacAfee (our hostess) gave me a bumper of 1958 whiskey from the Outer Isles. Careful though I have been, I felt it would be slapping RLS in his thin, wan, vivid face to mention health or doctors on my first visit, so I accepted it without demur.

The currency in which I repaid him was not accounts of my own work, in which he was not interested, but gossip. About Lady Berkeley at the Palazzo Ravizza in Siena, with the little Neapolitan boy genius she had adopted after the war. "I asked what the child was a genius at. 'Anything artistic or mechanical,' she replied. She talks of nothing else. 'Molly, they said to me when I took him, you'll never do anything with a child with so coarse a skin. And look at him now.' " Or Leslie Hartley's exasperated arrival at dinner after a party at the American Embassy, where he was accosted at half past seven by a manservant who said, "Mrs. Whitney is waiting to say goodbye to you." Or Riette Lamington's fascination with the pianist Fou Ts'ong. " 'I am told his tone is small,' said Riette, but in that little room it sounded like a cannonade. He makes noises through his nose like a Pekinese while playing, turning his head back to bare his huge white teeth at one and saying, 'I play horrible.' 'Sometimes I don't feel I am talking to an Oriental,' said Riette. But I did."

The address to which I moved in 1953 was a small Georgian house in Bedford Gardens, where I lived for longer than I have lived anywhere else, twenty-three years. It had two gardens, one in front filled with hamamelis and ceanothus and the other at the back with a magnolia and tree peonies and a *Buddleia alternifolia*. The rooms were small but well proportioned, and the furniture and pictures were partly inherited from my mother and partly bought. The bought pictures mattered most.

Through work on the Domenichino drawings at Windsor, I had gained some familiarity with the work of Bolognese artists of the late sixteenth and early seventeenth centuries. Their paintings were still generally despised—in England, Denis Mahon was the agent by whom they were rehabilitated—and when it was decided, in 1946, to empty Bridgewater House, which had been bombed, most of the Bolognese paintings were consigned to Christie's, then installed at Spencer House. Very unpromising they looked, but they included a number of works from the Orléans collection which had for generations been looked upon as masterpieces. I had almost no money at the time apart from my exiguous salary, but I succeeded in buying three paintings. One was a small Annibale Carracci, the *Vision of St. Francis*, with in the background a ruin based on the Palazzo Farnese; another was a Domenichino *Christ Carrying the Cross*, for which a number of drawings were in the Royal Library; and the third was a Pier Francesco Mola of the *Baptism of Christ*. The paintings cost, respectively, £28, £38, and £43. Two of them I was eventually compelled to sell: the Annibale Carracci is now in the National Gallery of Canada, and the Domenichino is in the J. Paul Getty Museum. The sale prices were, respectively, £100,000 and $750,000. If I had had just a little more money—or if I had learned earlier than I did that works of art were bought from capital not income—I could have had an important collection. But when I found, at a dealer's in London in about 1947, a set of six inexpensive oil sketches by Giordano for the Palazzo Medici-Riccardi frescoes, I could not buy them, and I passed them to Mahon. As it was, I had thirty years of pleasure from the Annibale Carracci and forty from the Domenichino.

No comparable opportunity to buy major works of art for less than their true value occurred till 1950, when the collection of Henry Harris was sold at Sotheby's. I had known the collection for many years, first in a very distinguished Georgian house on the east side of Bedford Square. Bogey Harris's taste as a collector had been formed in Florence before the First World War by Herbert Horne, the biographer of Botticelli, and like Horne's it embraced Italian primitives and Renaissance applied art and furniture. I was invited when he had German art historians to lunch. After the war he moved to Cheyne Row, and I got to know him and his collection more intimately. He had important bronzes, and when he died, he left me a gilt bronze *Baptist*, which was at one time considered Sienese but is related to the early Jacopo Sansovino. (A second, rather less good example is in the Cleveland Museum of Art.) The remainder of the collection was auctioned. A number of the paintings were quite well known but were miscatalogued, and the prices they fetched were risible. I bought a panel of the *Veil of Veronica* by Paolo Veneziano, which had been published by Fiocco, and a *Lamentation over the Dead Christ* ascribed to an artist called the Pseudo-Bocaccino. Most of the Renaissance furniture was knocked down to the London dealer Alfred Spero, and some of this I also bought. These works of art, along with a number of paintings left to me by my mother, formed the setting of my house in London, were later moved to New York, and are now (without the Domenichino or the Annibale Carracci but with the addition of a fragmentary Ducciesque panel I bought for very little money at Christie's) in my apartment in Florence. My belief has always been that you cannot know about works of art unless you live with them, and this, in a modest fashion, I have done.

My first two books, *Giovanni di Paolo* and *Sassetta*, were published by Chatto & Windus. Chatto was not an art-book publisher, and both volumes required a subsidy, which I supplied. During the war, however, I had the good fortune to meet Bela Horovitz, the chairman of the Phaidon Press, which had initiated an impressive program of art-book publishing in Vienna in the 1930s. A number of the Phaidon books were issued in translation by Allen & Unwin, among them what was then the standard edition of Burckhardt's *Civilization of the Renaissance in Italy*. Transferred to London, the press continued its earlier policy of producing large, relatively inexpensive books with a short text and blurry photogravure illustrations made from what were often excellent photographs. Typical of these wartime products were volumes on Raphael with an introduction by Wilhelm Suida and on Donatello with a text by Ludwig Goldscheider, both of which appeared in 1941. These books look rather out of date today, but they were useful at the time. Bela Horovitz was a wonder-worker. He was anxious that the content and quality of the books he issued should improve, and when the war ended he embarked on a massive publishing program which put the Phaidon Press in the forefront of art-book publishers. At our first meeting he commissioned from me a book that later appeared as *Sienese Quattrocento Painting*. It was published in 1947 and conformed to the pattern prescribed in earlier Phaidon books: a short introduction, a quantity of plates, many of them details, and brief notes on the artists and the works illustrated. I look back on the book without great pleasure—its standpoint seems to me impermissibly old-fashioned—but it taught me a great deal about book production. Initially I proposed a larger number of plates, but this Horovitz turned down. "By giving less, we give more," he said, and he was perfectly correct. He agreed, altruistically, to undertake without subsidy the publication of my book on the Yates-Thompson codex of the *Divine Comedy*, for which no more than a very small sale could be expected, and invited me to edit an India-paper edition of Cellini's autobiography. This was the beginning of my interest in Benvenuto Cellini. The introduction contained the first serious account of Cellini's importance as a sculptor. It had already been agreed that the Phaidon Press should assume responsibility for publishing the catalogues of drawings in the Royal Library at Windsor, and my volume on the Domenichino drawings therefore appeared under their auspices. I was then invited by Horovitz to prepare a book about Uccello, which appeared in 1950, and this was followed, at my suggestion, by a monograph on Fra Angelico, on whom I had been working for some time. This book appeared in 1952. Both these books went into much revised second editions, *Paolo Uccello* in 1969 and *Fra Angelico* in 1974. It seemed to me when I first prepared them that the essential concomitant in any monograph was not the text or the plates but the notes, and that continued usefulness could be ensured only through a system of annotation that was lucid, objective, and complete. With both artists there were many contentious areas. With Uccello the most important arose from the authorship of the frescoes in what used to be known as the Cappella Bocchineri in the Duomo at Prato (whose attribution to Uccello by Longhi has enjoyed a certain success) and the dates of the famous battle scenes from the Palazzo Medici now in the Uffizi and the Louvre and the National Gallery in London. I have had no further thoughts on Prato since the revised edition of the book appeared, but one painting, a *Madonna* in the National Gallery of Ireland, has been cleaned and is evidently the work of Uccello. I think it now more probable than I thought it then that the battle scenes were painted not for Michelozzo's Palazzo Medici but for the Medici palace that preceded it, and they may therefore be somewhat earlier than is generally supposed. I have not changed my views on Fra Angelico in any significant respect since the second edition of the book (which is less restrictive than the first), and the cleaning of the cell frescoes at San Marco seems to me to confirm the distinctions I drew in both editions of the book.

Horovitz also agreed to publish the three volumes of my *Introduction to Italian Sculpture*, of which the first volume appeared in 1955. Insofar as a publisher can be disinterested, Horovitz was. My books were each written for a stipulated fee, but were later placed on a royalty basis. After his early death he was succeeded by his son-in-law, Harvey Miller, and this happy relationship continued with *Essays on Italian Sculpture*, the catalogue of plaquettes and bronzes in the Kress collection in the National Gallery of Art, and the *Yearbook of the Victoria and Albert Museum*. When Miller left the Phaidon Press to found a new firm of his own, my relations with the Press became less intimate. My connection with Bela Horovitz lasted little more than a decade, but it was singularly fruitful, and I owe much to his generosity and his advice. Today, as I watch the convulsions of American scholars endeavoring to get their books printed by university presses, I am deeply grateful to have enjoyed the facilities offered in its missionary period by the Phaidon Press.

The reviews my books received in the general press were flattering but incompetent, and the reviews received by other art books were flattering but incompetent as well. In 1949 I wrote to Alan Pryce-Jones, the editor of the *Times Literary Supplement*, explaining that people who wrote serious books about art history would prefer reviews that were better informed even if they were more critical. The result was an invitation to undertake book reviewing for the paper. For twenty-three years I reviewed there fairly often, and intermittently I do so still. I see that in one year, 1951, I reviewed Kenneth Clark's disappointing *Piero della Francesca*, Martin Davies's good but ungainly catalogue of the Early Italian paintings in the National Gallery, Sydney Freedberg's excellent *Parmigianino*, a collected volume of old lectures by Roger Fry, George Kaftal on the iconography of St. Francis, and William Valentiner's problematic *Studies of Italian Renaissance Sculpture*. The reviews were anonymous, but there was no doubt who had written them. No doubt, save perhaps in the mind of the author being reviewed, for I myself have always been unable to identify the writers of anonymous reviews of my own books. Since reviews in the *TLS* had some influence on the purchasing of books by local libraries, it seemed to me important that the truth be told not just about the text but also about the quality of the color plates. I may say that the reviewing of art books there and in a number of other daily and weekly papers is now on a level of efficiency which would have seemed inconceivable forty years ago.

6

SEARCH FOR TRUTH

THE STUDY OF ITALIAN SCULPTURE IS THE ASPECT OF MY SCHOLARLY work by which I would wish to be judged.

The magnet that drew me back to the Victoria and Albert Museum in 1945 was that it possessed a greater collection of Italian sculpture than any other museum outside Italy. It was very fine and very large, and if there was one center from which the whole span of Italian sculpture could be studied, it was there. The odd thing is that it should ever have been made at all. The Museum of Ornamental Art at Marlborough House, in which it started, was directed to manufacturers and artisans, and its purpose was to inculcate "principles of design among the manufacturing population of the country." The first curator, J. C. Robinson, however, from the beginning opposed this limited view of the museum's scope. He was determined that it should purchase works of art, and was indeed responsible for buying many of the greatest works of art that the museum owns today. When he took charge, in 1852, at the age of twenty-eight, he was self-trained. In the middle of the nineteenth century there was nothing peculiar in that; he was one of those strange people who learn about works of art pragmatically from buying them. He had a skeptical mind and a retentive memory, and he was clever (so clever that he earned the suspicion of his colleagues) and dogmatic (justifiably so since he was so often right) and purposeful.

One of Robinson's first purchases (and retrospectively it seems eccentric) was a relief by the Milanese sculptor Bambaia, *Two Warriors Shooting at the Sun*. It had a historical halo—it was supposed to come from the tomb of Gaston de Foix in Milan—and it was accompanied by two other reliefs. But, to quote Robinson, "the formation of a methodic sculpture collection not being then contemplated, they were rejected, but not lost sight of." Thanks to Robinson's pertinacity, six years later they were also secured. In May 1854 there occurred at Christie's the sale of the Woodburn collection, and at it he bought two works, both of which turned out trumps. One was a wax model for the *Rape of the Sabines* of Giovanni Bologna. It had belonged to Sir Thomas Lawrence, who thought it a bona fide model for the statue in the Loggia dei Lanzi, but it went extremely cheap. It was bought after the sale for one pound. It is now generally regarded as exactly what Lawrence supposed it to be, "a preparatory study for the famous group in Florence." The second work was bought for ten shillings. It was a figure of Neptune, and here there was no bungling. It was not sold as a Giovanni Bologna, but Robinson saw what it was, "the first idea of the celebrated fountain which stands in the market-place at Bologna."

At the time models were thought to have more use for schools of design than finished sculptures, and they were one of the means by which Robinson infiltrated Italian sculpture into the museum. The catalyst was the purchase, also in 1854, of the Gherardini collection of wax sketch models. It was offered to the Tuscan government, who turned it down because they thought the price too high, and was then transported to Paris, but the French government also refused to purchase it. So the models were brought from Paris to London and were offered to the British government for the sum of £3,000. When they arrived they were installed for a month at Marlborough House "with a view to eliciting from the public and the artists of this country such an expression of opinion as to the value and authenticity of the models, as will justify the purchase or the rejection of the collection by Her Majesty's Government." The catalogue contained a report on the models by a number of academicians nominated by the Chancellor of the Exchequer. Sometimes the views of the academicians were favorable and sometimes not. One of the points at which they struck was "a cow lying down, a highly finished model by Donatello." But they accepted another sketch model as by Raphael and concurred in thinking that almost all the arms and legs and quite a number of the figures were by Michelangelo. Providentially the collection was bought, for though the assessors' views were asinine, the collection is of unique and exceptional interest. It did really include a model by

Michelangelo—for the *Young Slave* in the Accademia in Florence, which shows how the back of the unfinished marble might eventually have looked—and those models which were not by Michelangelo include most of the surviving models by Giovanni Bologna. There was one for the great group of *Florence Triumphant over Pisa*, which Giovanni Bologna made as a pair to the *Victory* group of Michelangelo; there was another for the *Rape of the Sabines*; there was a third, wonderfully delicate model for the last great marble Giovanni Bologna carved, the *Hercules and the Centaur*; and there was a clay mask which mystified everyone—it was supposed to have been made by Michelangelo for the Medici Chapel—until it too was identified as by Giovanni Bologna. It occurs on his most important secular building, the Palazzo Vecchietti in Florence.

Fortified by this success, Robinson turned his attention to the Soulages collection at Toulouse. It was formed in the 1830s, and contained a few sculptures and a large quantity of majolica and Renaissance furniture. It was estimated above the price the museum was ready to pay—£15,000 was the asking sum—so a public subscription was opened. The list of subscribers is still preserved; there were collectors like Holford and Miles, artists like Mulready, commercial firms like Minton and Elkington, and dealers and auctioneers. So great was the enthusiasm that more money was raised than was required; the subscriptions came to £23,000. But the only sculptures that passed to the museum were works from the della Robbia studio, which were intended to stimulate the manufacture of enameled terracotta by the Minton firm. One of the most beautiful fifteenth-century terracotta sketch models, the *Virgin with the Laughing Child*, was bought in Paris in 1858 for the risible sum of £28. It was, said Robinson, by Antonio Rossellino, and though it has since been attributed to other artists (among them Leonardo), Robinson's judgment was perfectly correct. It was correct on earlier works as well, for in 1859 he secured in Florence for £10 two marble figures of St. Michael and the Archangel Gabriel, from the shop of Nicola Pisano. He believed them, from hearsay, to come "from a church in the neighbourhood of Pisa," but a century later two of them proved to have been supports of Nicola Pisano's Shrine of St. Dominic in San Domenico Maggiore at Bologna.

Scarcely ever was Robinson guilty of self-deception. The Italian sculptures he bought in 1869 included one masterpiece, Rossellino's bust of Giovanni Chellini. It was very well known; it is recorded in guidebooks to Florence in the Casa Pazzi in Borgo degli Albizzi, always as Donatello, and the correct ascription is again due to Robinson, who found Antonio Rossellino's name incised under the base. But in quality, as he recognized, some of the purchases fell short. When, for example, Robinson bought a relief by the Master of the Marble Madonnas in Arezzo in 1860, he went out of his way to point out that it was the work "of a second-rate Florentine sculptor having considerable leaning to the style of Mino da Fiesole." So it was with special energy that in 1858 he pursued the greatest prize of all, the Gigli and Campana collections. It was a far from easy negotiation, partly because of the turbulence of the Risorgimento ("One might suppose Rome," said Robinson, "to be a second Lucknow") and partly because the papal authorities were involved. In December 1860 matters came to a head, Robinson left Naples "with an escort of papal dragoons and with our revolvers ready in our hands," and in Rome he concluded the purchase. It was of eighty-four sculptures for just under £6,000. Gladstone (who had a stronger cultural sense than his successors in later British governments) was instrumental in authorizing it.

The collection was desirable because it included an almost indecent number of great sculptures. There was a beautiful Arnolfo di Cambio *Annunciation*. There were two *Angels* by Tino di Camaino, which originally formed part of the Orso monument in the Duomo in Florence. And at the other end of the spectrum there were a wax sketch model of the *Deposition* made by Jacopo Sansovino for the painter Perugino and a marble statue which was regarded at the time and for long afterwards as a *Cupid* by Michelangelo. But the weight of the collection fell in the fifteenth century, and truly astonishing it was. First of all there was a low relief in marble by Donatello, the *Ascension with Christ Giving the Keys to St. Peter*. In the late fifteenth century it was in the Palazzo Medici, and is still indeed in the frame in which it was when Lorenzo il Magnifico died. There is no relief by Donatello in which his unique combination of imaginative urgency and intellectual control can be so clearly read. There was another Donatello, the marble *Lamentation over the Dead Christ*, and a splendid cassone front from the Duomo in Florence with glazed and gilded terracotta scenes from Genesis, possibly by Vittorio Ghiberti, the son of Lorenzo. In addition, the collection boasted a little terracotta *Madonna*, also connected with Ghiberti, in which the Child embraces the Virgin with a tenderness worthy of Masolino, and a terracotta cast from a

wax sketch model, of the *Flagellation and Crucifixion*, which Robinson
(and a great many scholars after him) gave to Donatello. Irrespective
of the attribution, it is one of the few true sketch models of this date
that survive. Alongside these were twelve roundels of *Labors of the
Months* by Luca della Robbia. Once more Robinson recognized them
for what they were, part of the ceiling of a small room in the Palazzo
Medici used by Piero de'Medici as a study which is described by
Filarete and Vasari and which had an enameled terracotta floor, also
by Luca della Robbia, that was destroyed. The figures are drawn with
marvelous assurance and expressiveness, like silverpoint drawings
which have been glazed. Last but by no means least was a little sketch
model by Verrocchio for the masterly Forteguerri monument in Pistoia Cathedral, one of those rare works where an artist is caught in
the creative act.

Never was Robinson deterred by size. That is important for the
simple reason that much Renaissance sculpture was conceived within
an architectural context, and no collection is truly representative in
which the relationship is not emphasized. The extent to which that
affected Robinson's purchases and thinking was already evident in
1859, when four very remarkable purchases were made. The first was
from Santa Maria Novella in Florence, a thirteenth-century church
that had suffered a number of later alterations. In 1859 a well-to-do
member of the Dominican community, Fra Damiano Beni, decided
that the additions should be removed. He was inspired by the innocent
purism one sometimes finds among Italian superintendents of monuments today, and it led him first to dismantle the additions made
by Vasari and then to remove a work Vasari described, the organ and
cantoria by Baccio d'Agnolo. What was required, said Fra Damiano,
was a Gothic cantoria (an ugly one made in black stone, for which he
paid, is still in the church), and to make way for it the original *cantoria*
was torn down and left on the floor of the nave. In March, Robinson
turned up in Florence, obtained admission to the church (which was
closed for restoration), and bought the cantoria for less than the price
of the marble.

On the same visit to Florence, Robinson secured a second very large
work of the same date, an altar carved by Andrea Ferrucci in about
1495 for the church of San Girolamo at Fiesole. The church and the
adjacent convent were owned by the Ricasoli, who in 1854 removed
the contents of the church. The altar and a tabernacle adjoining it

were placed for sale in the studio of a Florentine sculptor, and they were bought by Robinson. The whole transaction was perfectly legal, and the altar is notable not just for its quality (another, slightly inferior altar by Andrea Ferrucci is in the Duomo at Fiesole) but for its completeness; the predella, the red marble backgrounds to the niches, even the surface gilding are preserved, and the elaborately ornamented wooden halos of the Virgin and St. John and the halos of the figures on top are all original.

In May 1859 in Florence, Robinson came upon a major work. This time it was a chimneypiece, housed in a villa outside the city but previously in the Palazzo Boni. No one who looked at it then, and no one who has seen it since, has doubted that it is the finest chimneypiece surviving from the middle of the fifteenth century. In Florence it was inevitably given to Donatello, but Robinson knew better; it was, he said, by Donatello and Desiderio da Settignano "working together as master and pupil," and since then it has been almost universally accepted that the fireplace is by Desiderio. The putti on it are marvelously animated and expressive, and still more sensitive are the portrait reliefs.

A year later, in 1860, Robinson focused his attention on one of the biggest works that Luca della Robbia ever made, a roundel with the arms of René of Anjou. It was commissioned by Jacopo de' Pazzi for the Pazzi loggia at Montughi, where René of Anjou was entertained in 1442. The stemma was built into an external wall at a great height from the ground, hence its size; it measures eleven feet across. The heraldry, as one might expect, is French with Pazzi emblems embodied in it, but it was Luca della Robbia who invested the purple flames rising from the braziers and the dragon wings of the helmet with the sense of movement that is one of the great glories of its design. Another of them is the border, with its colossal pinecones and figs and cucumbers, modeled and fired in fourteen pieces; it is by far the finest border of its kind in the whole of Luca della Robbia's work.

A year went by, and then in 1861 Robinson addressed himself to the most ambitious of all these projects, the purchase of the Cappella Maggiore or choir of the Florentine church of Santa Chiara. The church was rebuilt about 1493 by Giuliano da San Gallo, in precisely the same style as Santa Maria delle Carceri at Prato, which had been finished two years earlier, and as in Santa Maria delle Carceri, its gray stone surface was relieved with a frieze by Andrea della Robbia. The

convent was suppressed in 1808, but the church continued in intermittent use until 1842, when it became a sculptor's studio, and those
parts of it which remained intact were bought by a speculator. They
were offered for purchase to the city of Florence, which turned them
down, and they were then offered for sale piecemeal ("fortunately,"
says Robinson, "without success"), and the "right of removing all such
portions of the edifice as might be deemed desirable" was acquired
by the South Kensington Museum.

Posthumously, deep gratitude is due to Robinson for this achievement, but that was not the official reaction at the time. Indeed, the
more great sculptures that arrived, the more evident did it become
that there was a conflict between his view of the role of the South
Kensington Museum (as the Victoria and Albert was then called) and
that of Sir Henry Cole, who was in overall charge. In 1863, he bought
another outright masterpiece, an autograph bronze relief of the *Lamentation over the Dead Christ* of Donatello, but in June of that year he
was, in effect, told to stop buying Renaissance sculptures, and at the
Piot sale in Paris in 1864 he was allowed to purchase only one work
of significance, the Donatello *Putto with a Fish*, as "a specimen of
bronze casting." Thereafter matters went from bad to worse. Robinson
said that people were tampering with his correspondence (no doubt
they were) and offered to "weed the art collection" (that is, to dispose
of the unworthy purchases made by people other than himself). Finally, in 1867 the authorities abolished his post.

With Robinson's disappearance major purchases came, temporarily,
to an end, but in 1881 his breach with the museum was healed, and
the occasion was marked by the purchase of a very large piece of
Venetian fifteenth-century sculpture. It was by Bartolommeo Buon,
and it came from the Misericordia in Venice. Its story was discred-
itable—to the Venetians, not the purchasers. It was carved to go over
the principal door of the old Scuola della Misercordia and was moved
thence to the new hall, where it remained till the early nineteenth
century. After protracted litigation a member of the Moro family
secured a legal title to it and immediately sold it to a Venetian dealer,
who in turn sold it to Robinson. Robinson bought it with regret. It
was, he said, "a work of high merit and importance, but it had infinitely greater significance in its original place. It is indeed a page torn
from the record of Venetian art."

Wherever one looked in Italy in the middle of the nineteenth century some act of vandalism, for profit but only for a modest profit, was under way. No case is worse than that of Gubbio, which boasted a Montefeltro palace with many of the features of the Ducal Palace at Urbino. When James Dennistoun went there in 1843, he found it in use as a wax candle manufactury, and nineteen years later Anthony Trollope's brother Thomas Adolphus Trollope reported precisely the same thing. Unless the carved doorframes were removed, he wrote, before long they would disappear. The sole difficulty was the cost; they were expensive to remove, and their price was therefore relatively high. But by 1886 three of them had found their way into the hands of a Florentine dealer, and two (one of the three disintegrated) are now at South Kensington.

After Robinson's dismissal the buying of Italian sculpture became less confident. There was no one on the museum staff in the late 1860s and 1870s who could compete with Bode, who was buying in Florence for the Kaiser Friedrich Museum with great decisiveness, but a few interesting purchases were made. One, in 1879, was of three wax Passion scenes by Giovanni Bologna, models for the splendid bronze Passion scenes at Genoa. They had quite a long English history. In the eighteenth century they belonged to Locke of Norbury, and in the nineteenth century they were owned by the sculptor Joseph Nollekens. There were four of them then—the missing subject is the Flagellation—and I lived for years in the hope that in some antique shop the fourth would eventually turn up. But then, to my disappointment, I was visited by an Australian colleague with a photograph that proved it had emigrated to Australia. One of the troubles in the last decade of the nineteenth century was that prices had started to rise, and the authorities of the museum were riddled by doubts as to whether the objects they were offered were really worth the prices that were asked for them. Quite a lot of purchases must have escaped on that account. One which almost did so was that of three terracotta models for the Santa Croce pulpit by Benedetto da Maiano. They surfaced about 1880 in the possession of Marchesa Bianchi-Bandinelli, who was said to have "an exaggerated idea of their pecuniary value," and it took nine years to get the price down to the £437 the museum was prepared to pay. But in 1876 the museum snapped up a bargain in the *Allegory of Discord* by Francesco di Giorgio, which was supposed to be by Leonardo but cost only £51.

By the first decade of this century the acquisition of Italian sculpture had greatly slowed down, save for those which came with the bequest of George Salting in 1910. From this time on, however, the acquisitions of sculpture start to reflect the presence on the staff of a sculpture specialist of true sensibility and acumen, Eric Maclagan. His first significant purchase, in 1921, was Bernini's bust of Thomas Baker, which was sold at auction by Lord Anglesey. In the 1920s in England, Bernini was a far from fashionable artist; the references to the bust in the museum files are strangely apologetic in tone. But its importance was undeniable. It was the only bust by Bernini of an English sitter; its history went back to 1682, when it was owned by Lely; it was mentioned in Domenico Bernini's list of his father's works; it was carved at the same time as Bernini's lost bust of Charles I; and it is a brilliant portrait. Baker looks out at us smugly, like a traveler in a crowded train who has reserved a first-class seat. This was the first work by Bernini to enter the collection.

The Bernini bust was followed by a great Early Renaissance relief. It was by Agostino di Duccio, the sculptor of the Tempio Malatestiano at Rimini; it was carved at the same time as the Rimini sculptures; and it must indeed have been made for Sigismondo Malatesta, since it displays Malatesta roses all round the niche. In 1927 another very distinguished purchase was made. It was a little relief by Desiderio da Settignano, which was discovered, bound like a book in a tooled-leather case, in Lord Dudley's library at Himley Hall. In the fifteenth century this was a very well known composition—it was even copied in a drawing by Leonardo—but none of the other versions has the miraculous delicacy of this relief. The best of them I secured many years later as a gift from Audrey Pleydell-Bouverie.

Another purchase of Maclagan's was a little relief of *Philoctetes* by the Venetian sculptor Antonio Lombardo. It seems to have been carved for Ferrara, and depends from a classical cameo, and it forms part of a widely distributed series of reliefs of heroes and heroines of antiquity. For a long time this stood alone, but some forty years later I managed to acquire another relief from the same series, a little *Venus Anadyomene*, which was in the stables at Wilton along with some second-grade classical sculpture, and was unknown and unique. On its base it has a quotation from Ovid's *Art of Love*. At auction the museum was outbid, but the dealer who bought it, Daniel Wildenstein, when he learned the facts, generously offered it for purchase at the price he had paid.

The first catalogue of the collection was written by Robinson and appeared in 1862. In the 1860s the study of Italian sculpture was in its infancy—outside Vasari and other printed sources almost the only volume alluded to by Robinson was the general history of Cicognara—and the mainstays of the catalogue, therefore, were the writer's powers of observation and his innate sense of quality. On both counts the book is a remarkable achievement, detached, admirably formulated, and filled with qualitative judgments which are no less valid now than at the time when they were made. On Robinson's vision, persuasiveness, and energy, the sculptures he acquired speak for themselves. By 1910, when the Salting Bequest was received by the museum, the collection was almost four times as large as when Robinson's catalogue appeared. Preparations for a new catalogue, by Eric Maclagan, were therefore begun. Work on it was interrupted by the First World War, and was cut short in 1924 when Maclagan became director of the museum. Thereafter it was continued by his successor as keeper of sculpture, Margaret Longhurst, and it eventually appeared in 1932 as a joint work. Between 1862 and 1932 the whole study of Italian sculpture had been revolutionized. The main agent of change was Wilhelm von Bode, all of whose published work falls within that term. Other factors were the researches of Cornelius von Fabriczy, the issue of Allan Marquand's volumes on the Della Robbia, the lifework of Frieda Schottmüller at the Kaiser Friedrich Museum in Berlin, the publication of all but the concluding volumes of Adolfo Venturi's *Storia dell'arte italiana*, and the investigation of Venetian sculpture by Pietro Paoletti and Leo Planiscig. The cataloguing of the collection against the background of this bibliography was a much more complex task than it had been in 1862, and the volume that resulted made a serious contribution to the study of Italian sculpture. By 1939 the new catalogue had been sold out, so after the war the museum was confronted with the choice of reprinting it with some revision or preparing a new catalogue. Maclagan himself was an advocate of the second course, and it was with his insistent encouragement that I started work on the new catalogue.

The taking-off point, it appeared to me, was to establish guiding principles. In a celebrated scene in Mozart's *Zauberflöte* Papageno asks Pamina what story they should invent to tell Sarastro, and Pamina replies, *"Die Wahrheit! Die Wahrheit!"* ("The truth! The truth!"). Most people nowadays would agree that the business of a catalogue is to do precisely that. But cataloguing has not always been treated in that way. In the 1932 catalogue of the London sculptures, for example, there were thirteen works attributed to Michelangelo, which were so catalogued because the compilers looked upon it as their duty to defend the good name of the objects in their charge. One of the main tasks of a museum is conservation, but myths are not among the things it is expected to conserve. Before truth can be told, however, it must be ascertained, and it is here that the cataloguer's task begins. What is the physical status of the object he is dealing with? That sounds like a simple-minded question, till we look at great catalogues like those of the Italian sculptures in Berlin. The condition of objects is mentioned, but never is it properly described. The marble *Pazzi Madonna* of Donatello is broken into more than fifteen pieces and quite heavily made up, yet never is this mentioned in a catalogue. Investigating the physical condition of a sculpture is not always a very pleasant task, and sometimes it results in disappointment. In London, for example, there is a terracotta relief of the Crucifixion which has often been associated with Ghiberti. But those features which were Ghibertesque proved, on investigation, to be plaster additions superimposed in the middle of the nineteenth century on a coarse Veronese relief. Sometimes technical examination leads to nothing more than doubt. Especially with marble sculpture there is no technique by which it can be established with total confidence whether the broken parts are original pieces that have been replaced or additions of some later time.

But occasionally physical investigation paid unexpected dividends. It did so with a wooden Annunciatory Angel from the shop of Nino Pisano, which had walked through art literature clad in a gray dressing gown. Under the gray paint was a coat of coarse pigmentation of some age, which extended at the sides and back over three places where the surface was covered with canvas. When the canvas in turn was removed, it transpired that beneath it there survived quite substantial traces of the original paint surface, which was copied from a Lucchese patterned silk. The same search revealed traces of porphyry in the robe and of dark green in the lining of the cloak, which made it possible for the figure, despite its planed-down face, to be reconstituted as a work of art. Something of the same sort occurred with a beautiful wax model that Sansovino made about 1510 for the use of the painter Perugino. It was described by Vasari, who knew it in Florence, and

only in the 1920s was the attribution questioned by specialists. The
trouble was physical, that the whole group had been regilded over a
thick size. This incrustation was removed, and beneath was a coat of
old gilding contemporary with the model. There were some later
restorations and one or two additions which could be either restorations or additions by the artist. But more important was the change
in the whole character of the modeling. It affected not only the Ra-
phaelesque Christ but the other figures too; their block-like backs
revived one's faith in the continuity of creative processes and proved
that the problem that confronted Sansovino was not significantly different from the problem that confronts a figurative sculptor now. With
reliefs in stucco, under the toned surface a whole fifteenth-century
pigmented surface sometimes came to light, as it did in a Medicean
mirror frame with Mars and Venus which for about a hundred years
had been associated with Antonio Pollaiuolo. In its cleaned state it
proved a fascinating piece of applied art of about 1465, and neither
the complex treatment of the space nor the modeling of the Mars was
incompatible with an origin in Pollaiuolo's shop. One useful investi-
gative tool, thermoluminescence testing of terracotta, was not available
when the catalogue was made, but its later development and use have
not made substantial changes necessary, though they have shown that
one or two works whose authenticity I tentatively questioned are older
than I supposed.

There remained the problem of what kind of catalogue one should
produce. The most admired catalogue at the time was one by Martin
Davies of the fourteenth- and fifteenth-century Italian paintings in the
National Gallery. It was based on decades of research by Davies and
earlier members of the National Gallery staff, and was an impeccably
objective, honest-minded piece of work, setting a new standard on
that account. But it seemed to me a skeleton, lacking in historical
dimension, clumsily written and occasionally inarticulate, and based
on a sometimes defective sense of quality. It was essential in my view
that the entries in the new sculpture catalogue should give exhaustive
and precise accounts of the physical condition of the sculptures. They
should provide a balanced review of the whole literature of every
sculpture and should define the range of problems to which each work
gave rise. Above all, they should do justice to the historical context
in which each work was produced. On this, the historical aspect of
the catalogue, I had the benefit of a talented member of the library

staff, Ronald Lightbown, who succeeded in unearthing, in Italian libraries and archives, a wealth of new material and whose name joined mine on the title page of the catalogue.

One of the practical differences between sculpture and painting is that sculpture is less portable. For that reason the whole area of provenance and history is more important in a catalogue of sculptures than in a catalogue of paintings. I give one example of the kind of collaboration that was involved. It relates to a well-known work, the chimneypiece in *pietra serena* ascribed to Desiderio da Settignano. We know, from a passage in Filarete's *Treatise on Architecture*, that Desiderio undertook decorative carving, and the chimneypiece is almost the only piece of decorative carving for which an attribution to the sculptor can be seriously entertained. Not for the lateral supports, which are by two different hands, one, on the left, closely related to Desiderio, and the other, on the right, heavier and less elegant, but for the frieze which shows two putti and two portrait heads and was probably carved by the master himself. The chimneypiece belonged in the 1840s to an elusive figure called Pietro Masi, who had a villa at Arcetri outside Florence. While in his hands, it was published by the antiquary Filippo Moisè in a pamphlet, of which it took upwards of three years to trace a copy. Moisè was aware that the chimneypiece had been brought to Masi's villa from a house owned by the Boni family, but he interpreted the arms in the center of the frieze as those of Acciaiuoli, not Boni, and explained that it came into Boni possession through a marriage between the two families in 1563. But he was wrong; a fleur-de-lys was added to the Acciaiuoli arms only at the beginning of the sixteenth century but was included in the closely similar Boni coat of arms at a much earlier date. The chimneypiece must therefore have been commissioned by a member of the Boni family. The two portraits in the frieze showed that it was probably connected with a marriage, not of Bono de' Boni, who was born in 1404, but of one of his four sons. One of them, Smeraldo, could be ruled out at once because he never married, and another, Andrea, the youngest, because he married only in 1475. The marriage of the second son, Giovanni, however, took place in 1463, and the name of his bride was significant, for she was Camilla Marsuppini, a member of the family for whom Desiderio carved the Marsuppini tomb slab and the Marsuppini monument in Santa Croce. So the chimneypiece must have formed part of the same series of commissions.

The new catalogue covered acquisitions through 1960, but was not published till 1964, in three large red volumes, which have since served me, and I hope other people too, as a platform for the further study of Italian sculptures. In the preface I wrote:

> The principal difference between the study of sculpture in 1961 and its study in 1932 is not that a large quantity of further information has come to light (though in some respects knowledge has made a significant advance) but that today we know more clearly what we do not know. In 1932 Donatello was a mythical figure traditionally credited with a quantity of heterogeneous and mutually exclusive works; today our image of Donatello's personality is firmer, more restricted and more factual. This is true also of Verrocchio and many other Italian sculptors. But when an artistic personality becomes more sharply defined, the vague penumbra of works that are unattributable or unattributed necessarily increases in extent. If, therefore, what was uncertain in 1932 has in some cases been translated into certainty, in others what was certain then seems much less certain now. The duty of a cataloguer is to define degrees of doubt. There is some speculation in the present catalogue—speculation is, after all, one of the propellants without which the study of art history cannot advance—but an effort has been made throughout to distinguish between what is possible, what is probable and what is fact.
>
> In scarcely any case does an entry, however elaborate it may be, represent the last word on the work that is discussed. It will indeed be a source of disillusionment, not least to the compiler of this catalogue, if in 1990 there is no demand for a fourth catalogue of the Italian sculpture in the Victoria and Albert Museum.

There was no reason to suppose that by 1990 the Victoria and Albert would, as a scholarly institution, have collapsed and that its staff would include no specialist in Italian sculpture. If I were redoing the book, there are some entries I would change. It has been shown, for example, that a thirteenth-century *Virgin and Child* that was supposed to be Tridentine really comes from Cremona, and that two carved pillars which I gave to the Pisan sculptor Giovanni di Balduccio really formed part of Tino di Camaino's monument to the Emperor Henry VII in the Pisa Cathedral.

All scholars are indebted to other scholars, and I was no exception. I was, to my regret, too young to have known Bode. Initially I was critical of a good deal that he had published, but with the passage of time skepticism gave way to admiration, first of his achievement as a collector and then of the content of the *Denkmäler der Renaissance Skulptur Toskanas*, in which his results were synthesized. Friedrich Kriegbaum, who wrote admirably on Florentine Cinquecento sculpture, I never knew, but I called on the presiding Quattrocento specialist, Leo Planiscig, in Florence, where he lived in retirement in the Via Masaccio. I found him seated at his desk with the Italian translation of a poor little book he had written on Ghiberti open in front of him. "I am astonished to have written so excellent a book," he said, and the ensuing conversation was on the same level of unreality. I took his major books, on the bronze sculptor Riccio and on Venetian Renaissance sculpture, more seriously then than I do now. The only work by him that has stood the test of time is a long essay on Venetian Gothic sculpture. I learned during our talk that he had never been to London, though he had written extensively about the bronzes and the other sculpture there. The reason for this was that he could not travel without his wife and his wife could not travel without her dog, so the quarantine regulations in England precluded his crossing the Channel. It is unfair to judge any scholar by the effect he makes on strangers in old age, but the effect made by Planiscig on me was one of senile frivolity, and lack of seriousness seems to me today to vitiate even his earliest work.

The scholar to whom I was most deeply indebted through the whole period of research was the director of the Kunsthistorisches Institut in Florence, Ulrich Middeldorf. His life had been dedicated to the study of sculpture, and he was inspired by a disinterested and self-effacing determination that knowledge should advance. He was generous in encouragement and frank in criticism, and the friendship between us was firm and deep. One of the qualities in which many art historians are deficient is a sense of probability; it is the intellectual equivalent of a sense of balance in daily life. Middeldorf had this essential gift, and since it was linked to generosity and open-mindedness, he was, for a large number of younger scholars, a positive, persuasive, and highly beneficial influence. One of the problems of old age is that one's mentors fall away. All mine have done so, and there is none whose death I regret more than Ulrich Middeldorf's.

I enjoyed cataloguing sculptures, but I enjoyed buying sculptures even more. Robinson's bust stood in my office on the windowsill, and a great many works of whose purchase he would have approved were added to the collection. The quarter century between 1945 and 1970 was a buyers' market. Neither of the two great auction rooms had serious specialists on sculpture—at Sotheby's I remember one morning buying the Houdon bust of Miromesnil, the date on which had been mistranscribed, and a bronze bust by Pigalle and a terracotta by Pajou for a few hundred pounds, and at Christie's we were equally fortunate with Falconet. There were no well-informed dealers in Italian sculpture as there are today. The principle in the museum was that the knowledge of members of the staff was available to any member of the public who asked for it, whether or not he was engaged in trade, and the result was a nexus of warm relationships with dealers which proved highly beneficial to the museum. At the dealer Crowther's at Syon anything might turn up. One day at Syon I was shown a tabletop, leaning against a wall, that was inlaid with colored marble from the Cook collection at Doughty House. It interested me because it had the arms of the Sienese family of Chigi incised on the edges of the marble slab. Though it was a heavy object something prompted me to look behind it and there I found part of the thirteenth-century choir screen of Siena Cathedral. The screen, which separated the presbytery from the choir, was carved soon after 1270 by three pupils of Nicola Pisano, and other parts of it are in the Museo dell'Opera del Duomo in Siena. The tabletop, which was so heavy as to be virtually unsalable, was priced at £25, and Crowther gave it to the museum. Some fifteen years later it was possible to associate this relief with another sculpture from Siena Cathedral, a head of a male prophet, Haggai, from the façade, which appeared in London in 1962 in the hands of Colnaghi's. This was a more expensive purchase, and it involved a visit to Siena to establish first that it had not been recently smuggled out of Italy, second that it had at one time been in the possession of the Opera del Duomo in Siena, and third that the drill holes in it were of the same dimensions as the drill holes in the statues from the façade still preserved in the Museo dell'Opera del Duomo. Thanks to the cooperation of my friend Enzo Carli, then Superintendent in Siena and a specialist in the work of Giovanni Pisano, and of the then rector of the Cathedral, these points could be established, and this splendid and moving work was secured for the museum.

When Robinson's purchases were made, baroque sculpture was unfashionable, and looking at the Italian sculpture collection in 1945, one was very, very conscious of the weakness of its seventeenth-century sculpture. The greatest Roman baroque sculpture in England was a *Neptune and Triton* by Bernini at Brocklesby. It had been carved in 1622 for Cardinal Montalto to decorate a pool in the Villa Montalto designed by Domenico Fontana, and there were numerous paintings and engravings of it in its original position. The Villa Montalto occupied a site near the present Stazione Termini, and was maintained intact till 1784, when it was bought by a speculator, who sold Bernini's group to a dealer in antiquities named Jenkins. Jenkins in turn sold it to Sir Joshua Reynolds. Reynolds seems not greatly to have liked it—he kept it in his coach house—and after his death his executors sold it to Lord Yarborough, who moved it to Brocklesby. One evening in 1950 I was dining with an old friend, Paul Wallraf, who was then employed by Wildenstein. To my surprise he asked me some questions about Lincoln and its cathedral, and when I got home I took a map and drew a circle with a thirty-mile radius round Lincoln. One major house fell within it, and that was Brocklesby. So we at once opened up negotiations with Lord Yarborough to forestall a bid by Wildenstein. Molesworth and I went down to see it, and found it standing desolately in an untidy garden. "Since we can't keep up the rose garden," said Lady Yarborough, "the statue seems to have lost its point." Shown out of doors for so long, it had lost not its point but its surface (the only part that was perfectly preserved was the inside of the thigh) and Molesworth was on that account reluctant to buy it. But I persuaded him that as a work of art the sculpture was unimpaired, and we succeeded in buying it for £15,000.

In England there was another large group of comparable importance: *Samson Slaying a Philistine* was the only large-scale marble group by Giovanni Bologna outside Italy. Its history was even stranger than that of the *Neptune*, for until it was bought by the museum, it had, time after time, been given away. It was a Medici commission—almost all Giovanni Bologna's great works were—and it was placed by the Grand Duke Francesco I on a fountain in the Giardino de' Semplici (the herb garden that is passed by Florentine buses when they leave the Piazza San Marco). Francesco de' Medici and his successor, Ferdinand I, were half Spanish, and in 1601 the entire fountain was dispatched as a gift to the Duke of Lerma, the chief minister of King Philip III. The Duke of Lerma gave the fountain to the King, who installed it at Valladolid and then in 1623 gave the group but not the basin to Charles, Prince of Wales, the future Charles I. Hardly had the Prince returned to London when he gave it away to his favorite, the Duke of Buckingham. By this time the subject of the group had been misconstrued as Cain and Abel, and as Cain and Abel it was set up by Buckingham in the gardens of York House. From York House it was moved in the early eighteenth century to Buckingham House, and in 1762, when Buckingham House became Buckingham Palace, it passed to King George III. George III again gave it away, this time to Thomas Worsley, his Surveyor-General of Works, and Worsley transported it to his Yorkshire house of Hovingham. In the 1950s the director of the Metropolitan Museum, Francis Taylor, took up the trail, asking the director of my own museum, Leigh Ashton, whether export would be blocked if it were bought. Ashton, who knew nothing whatever about the statue, replied that it would not, so negotiations were opened by Taylor for its purchase. One day, to my horror, there appeared on my desk the application for an export license, which I immediately turned down, and after a difficult exercise in saving my director's face the statue was bought for the Victoria and Albert for £25,000. The surface of the group was protected with a cement wash, which was removed comparatively easily, but the legs of Samson proved to be broken through the ankles, and in what in the field of sculpture was the equivalent of a bypass operation, stainless-steel bars were inserted to ensure its stability. Anyone who tries to move it in the future will be in trouble.

Italian Mannerist and baroque sculptures streamed into the museum. Baroque in Florence was still generally undervalued, despite the publication of Klaus Lankheit's *Florentinische Barockplastik*, and it was possible to secure excellent portrait busts, like Foggini's bust of Cardinal Gian Carlo de' Medici and a bust by him of the Grand Duke Cosimo III, commissioned by Alexander, second Duke of Gordon, in memory of the favors granted to him by the Grand Duke. In the eighteenth century Florentine bronze sculptures, and especially the work of Soldani, enjoyed great popularity in England. Here again acquisitions could be made—of two magnificent bronze ewers which I bought in New York for something less than £5,000, and wax sketch models for two of the beautiful gilt bronze reliefs with scenes from the life of the Beato Ambrogio Sansedoni made for the chapel of the Palazzo Sansedoni in Siena.

The museum owned one bust attributed to Bernini's rival Algardi, but its attribution had long been doubted and was in fact wrong. Fortunately in 1970 it was possible to buy (far from cheaply by the standards prevailing at the time) the greatest of the full-scale sketch models made by Algardi for his portrait sculptures. A work of extraordinary directness and virtuosity, it represented Cardinal Paolo Emilio Zacchia, and was made in preparation for a marble bust then owned by the executors of Ugo Ojetti and now in Florence in the Bargello. Few works have given me such pleasure when they were in my office as did this bust. In 1985 it was seriously damaged through negligence and has been reconstructed. A second work by Algardi ought properly to have gone to the museum. It was a superb sketch model for the relief on a fountain in the Vatican. I was shown it by a dealer in Rome and agreed to buy it if a legal export license could be obtained. Not long afterwards I was told that it was in Switzerland but that it had no export license, so I bought another, inferior relief instead. The Vatican model was bought by the Minneapolis Institute of Arts and published for them by Wittkower, and never was there a word of protest from the Italian side. There was a moral obligation scrupulously to observe the Italian regulations, but it was self-defeating to have done so.

The capricious Italian licensing system made it hard to buy in Italy, but in the middle of the 1960s a dealer in Rome took me to see the residue of the collection of Baron Lazzaroni. The palace was extremely dark, but it contained, in addition to some forgeries, two marble busts which seemed to me of conspicuously good quality; I thought they might be early works by Giovanni Caccini. We agreed to buy them, and only when they reached London and were unpacked did they prove to have inscriptions on the back which identified them as the lost busts of his parents made by the Florentine sculptor Ridolfo Sirigatti, which are described in Borghini's *Riposo*. At about the same time my friend David Carritt mentioned to me that he had seen an interesting bust of Christ in an Irish collection. I pretended to more enthusiasm than I felt, but when I wrote to the owner, an old friend, Anita Leslie, I received a photograph, not of the bust, but of an entirely different work, a *Virgin and Child* in the style of the late-sixteenth-century Venetian sculptor Girolamo Campagna. When it was sent to London it proved to be a lost *Madonna* by Campagna carved for an oratory by the entrance to the Arsenale in Venice which had been untraced since the occupation of Venice by Napoleon's troops. I should also have pursued the bust of Christ which later surfaced in the sale room and proved to be by Giovanni Caccini.

An important collection of Venetian sculpture owned by the Cavendish-Bentincks was preserved in a house in Harley Street. In 1948 the owner offered to give the museum any of the works that could be removed. But the resulting negotiations were long and difficult, since the house, after bombing, was structurally unsound and the new owners required to be indemnified against the possibility of further damage. To my regret some of the sculptures were abandoned, but we succeeded in securing a number of important pieces, including some terracotta Vittoria busts, a fifteenth-century Istrian stone lunette, and a splendid Paduan portrait of the lawyer Leone de Lazara, who commissioned a celebrated Squarcione altarpiece for the Carmine in Padua. There was nothing in the collection relating to the work of the Venetian sixteenth-century sculptor I most admire, Jacopo Sansovino, but from a different source, at a later date, we secured a marble bust of a bearded man by or from the circle of Sansovino, for which the terracotta model is in the Rhode Island School of Design. More significant, because indubitably autograph, was a stucco relief, the *Story of Susannah*, which I first saw outside Pistoia in the ugly villa of Dino Philipson. Philipson had diplomatic privileges, and I managed, when he brought it to London en route for New York, to detain it and buy it for the museum. It may have formed part of the temporary decorations made for the arrival of Leo X in Florence in 1515.

A number of other important sixteenth-century sculptures were secured. In the collection of Henry Harris there was what seemed to me one of the finest sixteenth-century papal gilt bronze busts. It represented Sixtus V and was by Bastiano Torrigiano. The owner had bequeathed it to the Vatican, but I told him that this was carrying coals to Newcastle and he left it in his will to the museum. The museum ought properly to have bought a large number of undervalued objects at his sale, but it did not do so. One work of genuine interest, however, was secured, a fragmentary trial cast by Vincenzo Danti of the relief of Trajan burning the tax returns made for the door of the private safe of the Grand Duke Cosimo I of Florence. The most exciting of the smaller High Renaissance acquisitions was an accident. One day a woman dealer in ceramics from Brighton came to see me bringing a small bronze head which at first sight looked like a reduction from the head of Medusa in Cellini's *Perseus*. Initially I was skeptical but the differences of detail were so many that I felt bound to admit it as a possible Cellini model. A bronze model for the whole statue exists in Florence in the Museo Nazionale, and when the two were compared their facture proved to be identical. Nowadays the Medusa model is universally accepted as Cellini's. To the best of my belief it is the only sculpture that was first published in an article in *The Times*.

The first Italian sculpture secured for the museum was a Bambaia, and the last sculpture to be purchased before the publication of the new catalogue was a Bambaia too. Lombard Renaissance sculpture is a specialized taste, and nowhere more so than in reliefs of humanist themes. To my mind one of the most beautiful is a relief on the Pusterla monument in San Marco in Milan showing a recumbent figure on a tomb chest beneath a spreading tree. It is by a slightly inferior collaborator of Bambaia, Cristoforo Lombardo, and when a relief by or related to Bambaia became available for purchase I was determined it should be bought. It showed in the background a tree like that in the relief in Milan and beneath it a youth in classical dress reclining on a classical couch or sarcophagus addressed by three girls, representing Hope (pointing upwards to a star), Faith (carrying a chalice), and at the back Charity (holding a bag full of money). I do not think that since it was acquired it can have given many people the acute pleasure it gives me, and I can only say in its defense that it illustrates a kind of Lombard sculpture that cannot be seen outside Milan. And anyway, it cost only £2,500.

By far the most important of the Quattrocento sculptures I promoted was the last; the purchase was consummated by my successor. While I was working on the catalogue of the Italian sculpture at South Kensington, I was baffled by Antonio Rossellino's bust of Giovanni Chellini. The trouble was not the authorship of the bust—it was signed—nor the identity of the sitter—his name was inscribed on it. It was that we knew next to nothing about Chellini. I arranged for Ronald Lightbown, my collaborator on the catalogue, to go to Florence, and there he discovered a *memoriale* written by Chellini in old age for his descendants. Among much else it recorded that Chellini was the doctor of the sculptor Donatello and that in 1456 Donatello suffered a serious illness and was saved from death by Chellini. In gratitude Donatello gave Chellini a bronze roundel the size of a plate with a Virgin and Child and four angels. On the back of the roundel was a mold, casts from which were identical with the relief on the front face. I inferred that the composition was probably identical with one recorded in a bronze relief in Washington, in two coarse stucco reliefs in churches near Florence, in a plaster relief in the Sir John Soane Museum, and in an engraving by Sherwin, but of the original there was no trace. Late one evening, leaving a dinner party for the Queen Mother at the American Embassy, I ran into David Carritt, who told me that he had found a circular fifteenth-century bronze relief in use as an ashtray. I asked him to let me see it, and he brought it round the following day. Its front face corresponded with that of the other reliefs. But what mattered was the reverse, and when I turned it over I found the mold described by Chellini. So this was a new and exactly datable relief by Donatello. Initially the owner did not wish to sell it and would not allow it to be published. Her reluctance was eventually overcome by the Artemis firm, who bought it with the intention of reselling it in the United States. But the Victoria and Albert was clearly the museum in which it belonged, and after a rather undignified public appeal in the subway it was secured.

The collection of bronze statuettes in the Victoria and Albert is especially fine. They were not included in my sculpture catalogue for the same reason that they are omitted from the sculpture catalogues of other museums: they constitute a study apart. The criteria of judgment before the 1970s were experiential and wholly qualitative. Attempts have been made since then to develop them on scientific lines, by thermoluminescence testing of the core of the bronze (if indeed there is a core) and by infrared photography. A certain amount of new information has been assembled in this way, but the subject is still beset by doubt. One learns about bronzes only by handling them, and most of the great collections of bronze statuettes formed in the late nineteenth and early twentieth centuries were put together under the advice of specialists like Bode, who was responsible for the Beit and Wernher and Morgan collections as well as for a number of collections in Berlin, or Planiscig, who formed the Lederer collection and other collections in Vienna. In the Victoria and Albert the collection was uneven—it included, that is to say, a large number of inferior bronzes—but it contained a quantity of works of absolutely first-rate quality. To live for over a quarter of a century in the vicinity of Riccio's *Warrior on Horseback* leaves one with a sense of the magic of these mysterious works. Bronzes of the second quality could be

acquired comparatively easily, sometimes with useful results. I became interested in the 1940s in a number of interrelated models of
equestrian figures, a *Turk on Horseback* and a *St. George and the Dragon*
among them, and when good versions of them appeared they were
acquired for quite small sums. Looking through Vertue's *Notebooks*
one day, I came across an account of the work of an Italian bronze
sculptor named Francesco Fanelli, who worked in England in the first
half of the seventeenth century. The subject of the Fanelli bronzes
described by Vertue corresponded exactly with those of the bronzes
that the museum had been buying. This was the first stage in the
reintegration of Fanelli's artistic personality, and bronzes by him
which then fetched twenty or thirty pounds are now sold for quite
large sums.

What mattered, however, was to add great bronzes to the collection.
Very seldom was this possible. I remember with special pleasure one
afternoon when there landed on my desk from nowhere in particular
the *Satyr and Satyress* by the Paduan bronze sculptor Riccio. Inferior
versions of both figures were known, but this group was autograph,
in the sense that it seemed to have been chased by the artist. The
subject was aggressively physical (in Padua the satyr was an embodiment of sensuality), and the bronze, as an allegory of attraction,
represents one of those rare points at which modern and Renaissance
responses coincide. On another occasion a dealer in furniture with a
small shop in the Fulham Road visited my office. He had been part
of a ring of dealers at an auction in Sussex, and had, when the objects
were knocked down, been left with a parcel-gilt bronze figure of
Meleager which was thought to have come from a neo-classical clock.
It was in fact a Mantuan bronze of about 1500 by the Gonzaga bronze
sculptor known as Antico, and seemed to my eyes to be the equal of
the very best Anticos in the Kunsthistorisches Museum. After I had
examined it, I explained to the owner what it was and made an offer
for it, suggesting that he should get a counter-offer from Sotheby's.
Sotheby's estimate was marginally higher than our own, but because
he had been treated decently he sold it to the museum for the smaller
sum. With its silver eyes and gilded cloak and gilded sandals it has
been a source of acute pleasure to discriminating visitors ever since it
was acquired. "Quite a modern hairstyle," said the Queen appositely,
looking at its unruly gilded locks.

Looking back through this period of specialized purchasing, I think three factors were conducive to its success. The first was that the Victoria and Albert Museum in those days had no trustees. Purchasing rested in the hands of the director of the museum, who would consult the Department of Education and Science if a substantial sum of money was involved. Had there been trustees, the process of acquisition would have been slowed down and it would have been necessary to convince a reluctant amateur board of the need to purchase works the acquisition of which one knew to be desirable. The second was the National Art-Collections Fund. All the large purchases made in my time were generously aided by the Fund. The then chairman, Lord Crawford, had a thorough, highly professional knowledge of Italian art, and without his enthusiastic support much less would have been achieved. The third was a donor, Dr. W. L. Hildburgh, whom I think of to this day as one of the few wholly disinterested people I have ever met. He had an erratic, indeed rather a poor eye, and for that reason before the war was put onto collecting English alabasters, one of the few art forms of which there are no forgeries. He formed a magnificent collection of them, which he gave to the museum. Though not a rich man—he lived in indigent conditions in a basement flat not far from the museum—whenever a relatively inexpensive purchase presented itself he was ready and willing to help. Looking through the catalogue of Italian sculptures, I see that in this field alone he presented no less than sixty-four works.

I spent summer after summer in Italy while I was working on the catalogue. Sculptures cannot be looked at rapidly; they must be recorded slowly and seen repeatedly. They convey a message to the eye, but it is a message that must be confirmed by touch. The longer I looked at them, the more vital did it seem to regard them as things made and to reconstruct the process by which they were produced. In the post-war years the study of sculpture in the original was often difficult. At Sant'Angelo a Nilo in Naples, before one was allowed to study Donatello's relief on the Brancacci Monument, one had to sign an affidavit precluding legal action if one were hit by falling masonry. With the Angevin monuments in San Giovanni a Carbonara, there was the same formality. In Pisa, on the other hand, study was easier than it is now, for most of the great monuments had been disassembled and for two years were shown together in a superb exhibition that offered ideal facilities for detailed study. Pisa was then a very different place from the university town that it had been and has once more become. Copulating soldiers lay in the long grass round the Cathedral, and at the railway station you had to get a porter to jump onto the train as it approached if you were to get a seat. Elsewhere a high proportion of the greatest Trecento and Quattrocento sculptures were readily accessible, but in conditions that made study difficult. However frequently you looked through field glasses at the triumphal arch of the Castelnuovo in Naples, you simply could not see the differences of execution which became self-evident from scaffolding a few years ago when it was cleaned. The façade of San Petronio at Bologna and the sculptures of the Baptistry at Parma then read very differently from the way in which they read today. Berenson called me a pilgrim, and I was indeed a pilgrim in the months I could get off from the museum. I learned two things of importance, that no knowledge was absolute and that there were no shortcuts. What was required was to return again and again to the same monuments in the hope that one's understanding of them would gradually increase.

In the 1940s there was next to no interest in Italian sculpture. In Florence the Bargello was destitute of visitors. One reason for this was that there was no book that would explain to educated people how Italian sculpture developed and why it took the course it did. So, with what I now look on as an act of courage, I embarked in 1950 on a three-volume *Introduction to Italian Sculpture*. I use the word "courage" since in any such book value judgments are necessarily involved. The scheme, which had the blessing of the Phaidon Press, was quite a simple one. Each volume would illustrate what I conceived to be the most representative or important sculptures, with detailed notes on the sculptors and the works reproduced which could be used by students, but with a text conceived in broader terms. The first volume was written as a book, and it seemed to me after it appeared that the notes were rather thin and the introduction was a little dry. I tried to correct this in later editions. The text of the second volume originated in lectures—they were given at Oxford, where I was Slade Professor in 1956—and so did that of the third. The *Introduction* has been through three editions (four if one includes an Italian translation), and is, I am told, a work on which two generations of students have been brought up. The most reassuring moment was an encounter with Kenneth Clark at a Royal Academy banquet soon after the volume on Michelangelo appeared. "You really have got the old man," he said. It was, not unnaturally, the third volume, dealing with Michelangelo and Bernini, that gave me the most trouble. I received the proof in 1962 when I was teaching in Massachusetts, and I remember reading it in the train from Albany to New York with relief at finding that it said just what I wished to say. I discussed the book frequently with Berenson, who lived to read the first two volumes. This was beneficial because no book of the kind can succeed as history if it does not succeed as criticism. I pray that in this book the critical criteria are valid and correct.

Since bronze is a reproductive medium and the study of bronze statuettes is a treacherous field, a good deal can be achieved through careful analysis of the bronzes in one large collection, but ideally it is essential to juxtapose bronzes from different collections with one another. An occasion to do so occurred in 1961 when, through the agency of the Arts Council, a joint exhibition of bronze sculptures was organized by the Direzione Generale delle Antichità e Belle Arti in Rome, the Rijksmuseum, and the Victoria and Albert Museum. This was the first occasion on which I worked closely with that paragon of exhibition organizers, Gabriel White, the art director of the Arts Council. The practical difficulties were considerable, because the Italian nominee on the committee, Antonino Santangelo, the director of the Museo di Palazzo Venezia in Rome, knew very little about bronze statuettes. But a creditable list of works in bronze from Italian collections was eventually approved—it included major works from the Bargello, like the Pollaiuolo *Hercules and Antaeus* and the Bertoldo *Battle Relief* and some of the bronzes from the Studiolo of the Palazzo Vecchio; the Giovanni Bologna *Neptune* and *Mercury* from Bologna; the Bertoldo *Hercules on Horseback* from Modena; and the Francesco di Giorgio *Flagellation* from Perugia—and these were correlated with bronzes from English museums and collections and from the Kunsthistorisches Museum and the Louvre. The exhibition that resulted was an anthology, but an anthology of amazingly high quality.

On two later occasions I was able to indulge what had become a passion for bronze sculptures. One was in 1966, when I was invited to prepare a catalogue of the sculpture in the Frick Collection. This task covered a good deal of marble sculpture, much of it of cardinal importance like the great Laurana bust, but the bulk of the collection consisted of bronze statuettes, and never shall I forget the pleasure of handling the individual components of one of the greatest collections of small bronzes in the world. The dazzling Pollaiuolo *Hercules*, the

Bertoldos, the Francesco da Sangallo *Baptist* from Pistoia, and the marvelous series of Riccios and Severo da Ravennas were placed one by one on my desk, and when I go now to the Frick Collection, I struggle to restrain myself from touching them as I was once allowed to do. The other occasion was in 1964, when I was asked to catalogue the bronzes and bronze plaquettes in the Samuel H. Kress collection. The bronzes, with the single exception of a splendid statuette by Vecchietta, were not of the highest quality, and my reason for undertaking the book was that Kress had purchased from Duveen's the collection of more than four hundred and fifty bronze plaquettes formed in Paris by Gustave Dreyfus. In quantity and quality it was by far the finest collection of Italian Renaissance plaquettes. To me its appeal was not that it would lead to many new discoveries—a privately printed catalogue had been prepared by that excellent scholar Seymour de Ricci—but that plaquettes were part of the framework of Renaissance life; they occurred on inkstands and on boxes and on weapons, and were one of the main means by which style and imagery were diffused. A great part of the catalogue would necessarily be conventional, but it would inevitably leave me with a wider and deeper understanding of Renaissance art. This proved to be the case. After the completion of the *Introduction* I published two more books about Italian sculpture. They were intended as essays in method. The first—it had the rather unimaginative title *Essays on Italian Sculpture*—explained, among other things, why the so-called Michelangelo *Cupid* in London was a restored antique and why the *Palestrina Pietà* in the Accademia in Florence could not be by Michelangelo. The second had a Berensonian title, *The Study and Criticism of Italian Sculpture*. Among much else it corrected Krautheimer's account of the style development of Ghiberti's *Gate of Paradise*, it dealt with a subject ignored by Janson, the Madonna reliefs of Donatello, and it included lectures on the Italian plaquette and the forging of Italian sculpture.

In 1970 I signed a contract with the Phaidon Press for what I had long wanted to write, a monograph on Luca della Robbia. It sprang from a meeting many years earlier, at Vallombrosa, where I was staying, when a former Prime Minister of Italy, Vittorio Emanuele Orlando, came to visit Berenson. As he was leaving—in his country clothes he looked a little like Lloyd George at Chirt—he started talking about La Verna and the della Robbia altarpieces there. They were composed, he said, of sky and snow. This empty political rhetoric brought back old memories of Pater's apostrophe of Luca della Robbia and stirred my interest in writing on him. I became free to do so only after I left London for New York, and even then the book proved an immensely exacting, time-consuming task. I remember a scorching summer in Florence when I lived in a flat looking over the car park in front of the Palazzo Pitti, with the proofs spread out on the dining-room table. It was an agonizing experience (fortunately my research assistant Larry Kanter was there to share it), because the simplest artists are the hardest to discuss in print. I rewrote the proofs—to this date both I and the Press are out of pocket on it—determined that this coolest, most intimate of sculptors should receive a painless book.

7

THE
SPOKEN WORD

NOT EVERY ART HISTORIAN WISHES TO COMMUNICATE, BUT THOSE who do are bound to give some thought first to the kind of audience they will be addressing and second to the means by which their points can best be made. Broadly there are only two alternatives, writing and lecturing. In Germany and in the United States, solid reputations are, by tradition, based on solid articles buttressed by solid footnotes. In England, on the other hand, emphasis has lain on lecturing. Between the two world wars Roger Fry explained to packed audiences in Queen's Hall why he liked French and disliked British painting, and after Fry's death in 1934 his mantle was inherited by Kenneth Clark. At Oxford in my day Clark delivered the lectures which formed the core of his superb book on Leonardo, and when he returned there in 1946 his lectures on landscape painting gave rise to another work of synthesis, *Landscape into Art*. In London, when he talked at the Royal Institution on Alberti or Piero della Francesca, a line of smartly dressed ladies would be found walking up Albemarle Street, and inside the lecture theater voices were lowered as Emerald Cunard and Sibyl Colefax and Hannah Gubbay were shown to their seats in the front row.

From quite an early time I recognized the need to master the technique of lecturing, but it was some years before I was able to speak with anything approaching clarity or ease. My earliest lectures, in the big, tiered lecture theater at the Victoria and Albert, were stiff and clogged with fact, and I look back on them with some embarrassment. But gradually I gained control of the rhetoric of lecturing. Spoken prose differs from written prose, and a satisfactory lecture about art depends upon the form in which the material is disposed—the only useful guide to this aspect of lecturing is the *De Institutione Oratoria* of Quintilian—and upon establishing a counterpoint between the text and slides which will keep the audience visually alert. Lecturers, like musical performers, prefer some halls to others, and I have always felt happiest addressing a small, ferociously clever audience in the Frick Collection.

In the winter and spring of 1955 I paid my first postwar visit to the United States, where I replaced Charles Seymour at Yale, teaching an undergraduate course on Tuscan Early Renaissance painting and sculpture and a graduate seminar on the Quattrocento in Siena. I was met at the dock by an old friend, Stuart Preston, with whom I spent a week before moving to New Haven. I knew nothing of New York— as a boy I had been packed straight into a train to Washington—and if any individual can be held responsible for my affection for it, it is he.

I had never taught in London, but at Yale I found that I liked teaching. I had a graduate assistant, Ted Coe, who had been brought up in Cleveland with a major collection of nineteenth-century paintings and who became a close friend; he was later director of the Nelson-Atkins Museum at Kansas City. He read the roll call before classes began, and filled in the multitude of forms the educational machine required. One undergraduate was markedly superior to the rest (I had indeed to stop his answering questions), a swimmer called Edgar Munhall who is now at the Frick Collection, and one of the graduate students, Robert Herbert, already known as a specialist on Seurat, was a model of cleverness. The Art History Department was dominated, from the grave, by Henri Focillon, who had lived a revered life in the Taft Hotel and whose *Vie des Formes*, in an overexplicit English translation, was required undergraduate reading. When I arrived examinations were in progress. Students were required to compare any two of the miscellaneous objects in a vitrine in the corridor in terms of Focillon's categories. I was curious about this, and taking up the topmost of a pile of papers, I read: "The cylix and the predella panel are both made of matter, but the predella panel does not hold water." This was my first encounter with conceptual art history.

The Yale art history faculty at the time was distinguished. It included George Kubler, a man of extraordinary niceness and real profundity whose mind I did not fully understand, and Vincent Scully, an inspired orator, lecturing on architecture to enormous audiences, and George Heard Hamilton, whom I still think of as the most perceptive teacher on nineteenth-century French painting I have ever listened to. Social life was agreeable, and I look back with special pleasure on dinners with a friend of Paul Oppé's, Mrs. Troxall, who owned a superlative collection of Rossetti drawings and the Millais illustrations to Trollope's *Small House at Allington*. With her I met Chauncey Tinker, the curator of rare books in the Sterling Library and the dean of English literary studies, and William Ivins, who had been in the Metropolitan Museum as curator of prints and had written a number of brilliant polemical articles.

At the weekends I explored America. In zero-degree weather I visited Providence and Hartford, and paid the first of many visits to the Pope house at Farmington, the only place in which one can look from a Monet *Haystack* at one end of the drawing room to a Monet *Haystack* at the other. I got to know the Cleveland Museum of Art, at its zenith under that great director William Milliken, and the Detroit Institute of Arts, then directed in the wake of Valentiner by Ted Richardson, and the museums at Toledo and Indianapolis and the Walters Art Gallery at Baltimore. In Cambridge I was put up by my old friends W. G. and Olivia Constable (their house became a home away from home on later visits to the United States), and in Philadelphia I stayed (as I was to do often in later years) with Henry McIlhenny, who lived in Rittenhouse Square in one of the most welcoming and most sheerly beautiful houses I have ever visited. It was exhilarating when one woke up to see Bonington's *Death of Titian* on the bedroom wall. Everywhere I learned something of museum policy and problems. I looked not only at works of art but at museum services as well, and I brought back with me to London a much clearer notion than I had had before of the functions museums could and could not perform.

Nowhere did I learn more than at the National Gallery of Art in Washington, where I was welcomed by John Walker, an old friend, Perry Cott, the chief curator who rapidly became a new one, and Huntington Cairns. Most of the Kress paintings were in storage in the gallery pending a division between those which would be retained and those which would be sent elsewhere. The assembly and distribution of the Kress collection was one of the most imaginative cultural projects of its time, and though the quality of the paintings was uneven, they included quite a large quota of masterpieces and a quantity of second-grade paintings of great interest. One or two major paintings slipped off the hook—among them was the Peruzzi polyptych of Giotto, which should now be in the National Gallery of Art but escaped to Raleigh—but the ratio of great paintings was extraordinarily high: they embraced the Goldman *Madonna* of Giotto, a panel from the Duccio *Maestà*, a great triptych by Nardo di Cione, two splendid Gentile da Fabrianos, the magnificent Cook tondo of Fra Filippo Lippi, a fine group of Ferrarese panels, and very important Venetian High Renaissance paintings. The negotiations were handled by John Walker with incomparable skill. In Washington, the permanent collection, of which these paintings form part, is now overshadowed in the public mind by the exhibition area in the East Wing, but it was Walker who was responsible for the formation of the gallery, perhaps the greatest museological achievement of this century.

There were still many people in Washington who had known my parents in the 1920s, chief among them that paragon of patronesses Mildred Bliss. My memory of her as a boy was of a figure who moved so lightly that, as in some Sienese predella panel, her feet seemed scarcely to touch the ground, and till the onset of old age she still moved in the same way. During the war she sent monthly parcels to my mother—among the multitude of parcels hers alone were always carefully considered and contained things of which we really were in need—and no sooner was the war ended than she herself arrived in London in uniform. Subsequently she came there every year, bringing with her new Byzantine artifacts in tissue paper crumpled by countless royal hands. Her drawing room in Washington was a mecca of civilized society. She was sharp and amusing and sensitive, and when I first went back to Washington she was engaged in building the exquisite tempietto planned by Philip Johnson for her husband's splendid pre-Columbian collection—of all pre-Columbian collections this is the one which has least to do with archaeology and most to do with art—and the creation of her great gardening library. I remember her with regret each time I return to Washington.

In 1955 Ezra Pound was still incarcerated in a Washington asylum, St. Elizabeth's. Since my mother had been a friend of his in the distant past, Huntington Cairns asked me to go there. The hospital had the dilapidated look of any run-down Anglo-Saxon institution, its walls covered with peeling dark green and cream-colored paint. The long ward in which Pound was housed was filled with drooling inmates. Halfway down it was a bay protected by a screen and there, seated in a deck chair, Pound was closeted with a man whom I assumed to be another inmate till it transpired that he was a former member of some Polish government. I was startled by the nobility of Pound's appearance; with his exceptional height, his domed forehead, and his beard he looked like Delacroix's *Le Tasse dans la Maison des Fous*. He talked with great freedom, first about the corporate state on which he was unregenerate, and then about the distinction of the lawyer Blackstone as a stylist. I had never read Blackstone (I believe his work is better known in the United States than it is in England), but so contagious was Pound's praise that when I returned to Yale I took out a volume of the *Commentaries* from the library. It was ponderous, lucid, and unreadable, and Pound's admiration (though obviously sincere) seemed to me as perverse as Eliot's praise for the prose of Lancelot Andrewes.

Only one cloud cast its shadows over my months at Yale. The Yale University Art Gallery, like so many university and college art museums at the time, was ostensibly an autonomous institution with its own director and staff, but the director was weak, and members of the faculty of the Art History Department had, or claimed to have, rights of intervention in the museum. This system was unsound; it meant that the faculty members had power without responsibility. On no part of the museum did this have more unfortunate effect than in the treatment of the great collection of Italian primitives known as the Jarves collection. James Jackson Jarves who is the subject of an excellent book by Francis Steegmuller, had settled in Florence in 1852, and there, under the influence of the Christian art movement and of the books of Rio and Lord Lindsay, he built up a collection of some hundred and twenty Italian primitives. In 1860 it was shipped to the United States. The pictures were first installed in the Institute of Fine Arts on Broadway, where they elicited little interest, and were then stored by the New-York Historical Society. In 1867, however, Jarves was short of funds, and the paintings were made over to Yale University in return for a loan. The loan was not repaid, and in 1871 the pictures were sold at auction, for a risible sum, to the university. Jarves had an exceptionally discriminating eye (much more so than Bryan, whose collection of Italian paintings was formed at the same time and was till recently preserved at the New-York Historical Society), and the Jarves collection was the earliest major collection of

Italian primitives on exhibition in America. In 1916 it was catalogued by Osvald Sirén, not particularly well, and in 1927 it was the subject of a book by Richard Offner.

The Jarves pictures were in much the same condition as those in other collections of primitives formed in the middle of the nineteenth century. They were dirty, many of them were damaged, and some had been consolidated while they were in Italy. At Yale the principal Italian art historian in the 1950s was Charles Seymour, who, though a serious scholar, had no proper curatorial training. Seymour made up his mind to have the Jarves pictures cleaned. The restorer selected was inexperienced—he had not been to Europe—and Seymour was a fundamentalist; he believed that repainting was not only unsightly but ethically wrong. Work started with the finest of the pictures, a half-length *Madonna* by Gentile da Fabriano. Gentile's technique presents special difficulty to restorers (there are indeed only two living restorers to whom I would entrust one of his works), and the painting emerged in a pitiable state. It looked flat and textureless, and when I first saw it, it was shown in the dark with a small electric bulb under it to simulate the candlelight in which it was supposed originally to have been seen. If ever a picture had been gratuitously ruined, it was this. One of the most famous of the Jarves pictures was a lunette of the *Annunciation* by the Sienese painter Neroccio. Its condition had one fault, that the azurite of the Virgin's cloak had been replaced with more recent (but not modern) dark blue paint. In 1954 the dark blue paint was removed and the vacant area was painted an inharmonious light blue. The effect of this operation was to wreck the panel as a work of art. A third piece of restoration, of the Pollaiuolo *Hercules and Deianira*, was no less culpable. The paint, which had an oil component, had contracted all over the panel, leaving a number of little white spots. Shortly before I left London I had seen the *Martyrdom of St. Sebastian* of Pollaiuolo under restoration at the National Gallery, and there the same change had occurred. It seemed to me it would be helpful if the restorer at New Haven were sent to London to discuss this problem, but this was disallowed on the grounds that the independence of what was called the Yale Experiment would be compromised if outside professional assistance were solicited. As a result, work continued, with the blind, as in Brueghel's painting, leading the blind, and a great part of the collection suffered damage that was irreversible.

When I returned to London in June 1955 I wrote to Seymour

expressing my concern over what was being done. The paramount obligation of a curator, I suggested, was to ensure that the objects for which he was responsible did not suffer while under his temporary control. He was a delegate acting on behalf of others who, now and in the future, might be interested in his field, and the only permissible policy was one of enlightened conservatism. Not unexpectedly, there was no reply. Some years later a new catalogue of the collection by Seymour was published, from which it transpired that no significant addition to knowledge had resulted from this disastrous enterprise.

On my return from America I was elected Slade Professor at Oxford. The normal tenure of the Slade Professorship was for three years, but it was proposed that thereafter Slade Professors should be appointed for one year only, and I accepted the appointment on the understanding that I could resign after one year. The Slade Professor was required to lecture weekly in the Michaelmas and Lent terms, and if he was not resident in Oxford and had a full-time post elsewhere, the task of delivering a well-prepared weekly lecture was onerous. When I looked at the lists of lectures delivered by my predecessors, it seemed to me that most of them had run out of steam in the middle of the second year. There was indeed one term in which the most distinguished recent Slade Professor, Kenneth Clark, had delivered only one lecture, called "Taste." Another practical consideration was that for some years Oxford had had a regular professor of art history in the person of Edgar Wind. Wind was not only a scholar of great distinction but, from a technical standpoint, one of the most brilliant lecturers I have ever listened to. The sense of form throughout his lectures was impeccable, and at the lectern he was a magician. Using the same lectern, I found that when one pressed the button for a change of slide the movement of one's hand was imperceptible to the audience. His range was very great—it extended from Michelangelo to Matisse—and his manner was intimate and confidential; one's mind moved forward alongside his own. It was Wind's subtle account of the Matisse chapel at Vence that established the level on which art historians visiting Oxford had to speak. Wind's reputation in London was checkered, since he had arrived there with the Warburg Institute and had, when war broke out, urged the transfer of the Institute to New York. In America he had held a succession of chairs, returning to England only when a chair of art history was created at Oxford to entice him back. He was not credited with possessing the evil eye, but he had strange extrasensory perceptions which filled one with alarm. Years later, when I had not seen him for some months, I was sitting one evening in my study in London writing a mildly disobliging footnote about him in my book on Raphael. The telephone rang and I heard his gentle voice. "John, this is Edgar," he said. This made him an unnerving colleague. His English was excellent, but in Oxford he seemed very foreign, and I remember the embarrassment of being taken by him to lunch at his college, Trinity, and being punctiliously introduced to dons with whom I had grown up. The Slade Professor had a room at All Souls, where the warden, John Sparrow, was an old friend. In 1955 the first volume of my *Introduction to Italian Sculpture* had appeared, and it seemed reasonable to devote the Slade Lectures over two terms to Early and High Renaissance sculpture. They adhered to the scheme I had drawn up for the second and third volumes of my book, and whatever fluency and liveliness the book may have is due to the fact that it was first directed to an audience.

In 1961 I was asked to inaugurate an annual professorship endowed by the trustees of Robert Sterling Clark at Williams College in Massachusetts. Clark, had been an omnivorous collector, and his original intention was to found a museum in New York in the vicinity of the Frick Collection. In the late 1950s, however, the threat of an atomic war took on a hideous actuality, and Clark was determined, whatever the outcome, that his museum and collection should survive. On the edge of Williamstown, therefore, he constructed a low-lying, not undistinguished neoclassical fortress with a deep basement in which his collection could in emergency be housed. Though it abutted on Williams College, the Clark Art Institute was an independent foundation with its own trustees. I paid a preliminary visit to Williamstown on the invitation of the president and was enchanted by what I saw. The art history faculty was congenial; the chairman was an old acquaintance, now an old friend, Lane Faison, who had originally written articles on Sienese Trecento painting and had then moved on to Bavarian rococo sculpture and contemporary art. There was an excellent medievalist in Whitney Stoddard, and a good young architectural historian in Richard Pommer; and a friend of mine from Florence, Fred Licht, was also on the staff. I hoped that when I went to Williamstown I should find a small white house with a maid to look after me, but this was impracticable (there were plenty of little white houses but no maids), so for nine months I lived in the Williams Inn with a handful of drawings I brought over from London. I taught for one term on the Early Renaissance and for the other on the High Renaissance and held a seminar on Michelangelo. I found the students intelligent and interesting. They were clever boys without vocations, and a number of those I taught went into the museum field. They include the director of the Art Institute of Chicago, the deputy director of the National Gallery of Art in Washington, and a former deputy director of the Metropolitan Museum. As always, one of the pleasures of teaching American undergraduates was their naturalness. One of them failed to understand some point, and I explained it to him a second time. I then asked him if he understood. "No, but I think it will dig into my head," he said. Another "seemed to get the mediums all messed up." But they were keener than equivalent English students by far.

The only difficulty at Williams, apart from the inadequacy of the library in the areas in which I was teaching, was its size. It was smaller than Smith College, which was not far away, and it had a correspondingly smaller faculty. One lived in a glass box, and all one's movements were known. I stayed in Williamstown for two weekends when I arrived, and always thereafter went elsewhere. The gate to freedom was the Albany airport, and since the students for the most part were well off and were therefore interested in earning money, student drivers took me on Friday afternoons to Albany and collected me there on Monday mornings. After Christmas there was also the problem of snow. When Brueghel painted snow, the shadows in it were gray, but the Impressionists had taught one that they were really purple or mauve, and this was how they looked. Four months of snow at Williams—the last snowfall occurred in the middle of April—convinced me that, whatever his other achievements, Monet had spoiled snow.

Two social contacts were of importance. When I arrived in September two close friends from London, Arthur and Ethel Salter, were still settled in a wooden house of Ethel's set in five hundred acres of woodland at Tyringham. Primitive but not barbaric, Arthur called the house, as he drove me to see the Mission Inn at Stockbridge and the music shed at Tanglewood, and very congenial it was. The second contact was due to Harold Nicolson, who had said before I left London: "Williamstown is a small place and is very remote, and you will need someone within two hours' driving distance to whom you can say the first thing that comes into your head with no risk of being misunderstood." The result was an introduction to Mina Curtiss, who lived near Northampton and became a central figure in my life from that time on. Our first assignation was in the sun, on the steps of the Clark Art Institute. She was a big, confident woman (if she had been younger, "strapping" is the word that would have come to mind) and as we strode round the gallery I found to my surprise that we were looking at the paintings (and therefore the world) with the same eyes.

I later stayed with Mina in other houses (she used to send her red Rolls-Royce to pick me up at Kennedy and transport me straight to the country; it gave me a sense of never having left America), but the first house I knew, at Ashfield, was the one that I preferred. It was a succession of linked single-story buildings which was entered through a pigeon tower; most of its rooms were paneled and the floors were covered with colonial rugs; outside, an orchard sloped down from the terrace to a pool and a dammed stream, and beyond were woods in which the maples, on my first visit, were turning scarlet and gold. Mina had an uncompromising and exceptionally well-filled mind and life consisted of continuous conversation, as she lay on a chaise longue surrounded by guests. A posse of editors from the then new *Massachusetts Review* came over to lunch one Sunday and stayed all afternoon. "I am glad they were not abashed by my legend," Mina said. She was Lincoln Kirstein's sister, and she had as a result a deep commitment to the New York City Ballet and the performing arts. But the main focus of her interest was Proust, and research on Proust is the subject of *Other People's Letters*, her best and most personal book. She was herself a first-rate letter writer—she is indeed the only person in my life other than my brother with whom I have maintained a cogitated two-sided correspondence—and I hope that her letters (which are at Smith College) will someday be treated as serious literature, as they deserve. Her proximity (if one can call a two-hour drive proximity) was one of the things that made my academic year at Williams the enjoyable experience that it proved to be.

Inevitably I became involved, in a peripheral fashion, in the affairs of the Clark Art Institute. Unlike his brother, Stephen Clark, most of whose splendid nineteenth-century French paintings are now in the Metropolitan Museum or at Yale, Robert Sterling Clark was an untalented collector. The best-known feature of the Clark Art Institute was a series of thirty-two Renoirs, most of them dry paintings from the early 1880s of secondary quality. Once, when the guards in the gallery struck, it was warded by men from Pinkerton's armed with revolvers. The presence of a gun in a gallery always leads me to think what I would choose to steal; among the Renoirs there was only one work, a little picture of onions painted in Naples, for which I would have taken any serious risk. The strength of the collection (though this was not recognized by the administration at the time) lay in its American paintings. They were of first-rate quality, and it was from one of them, *The Bridal Path*, that I first learned what a great painter Winslow Homer was. The collection also contained a number of Italian paintings, among them a fascinating, damaged Piero della Francesca *Madonna and Child with Four Angels*, a beautiful Perugino *Pietà*, a Signorelli predella panel, and one or two other, less important works. One of Clark's interests was English silver, and the director of the museum was a former dealer in English silver, Peter Guille. The controlling body was the board of the foundation, which in my time consisted of self-appointing members of the firm of New York lawyers who had handled Clark's affairs. The capital sum, whose income could theoretically be applied to buying paintings, was very large, but the board was slow-moving and indecisive, and in my year at Williamstown I could persuade them to buy only one work, a seven-panel altarpiece by Ugolino da Siena. There were countless other possibilities but none of them did they accept. I explained repeatedly that the value of works of art was escalating, that a number of great works of art were at that time available for purchase at prices that would, in the near future, seem very low, and that the character of the museum could be transformed if they acted sensibly and soon. But all to no effect. With the silver collection ample funds were earmarked for purchases, and I tried to check their obsession with teapots and milk jugs by proposing the acquisition of the beautiful French silver doors from the Peshcherskaya Lavra at Kiev, which were then on the market. But by the time the trustees made up their minds to negotiate for the doors, they had been sold. The museum owned a small but good collection of drawings and prints, and I suggested that they should appoint a specialist in prints to the staff and authorize him to make purchases for the collection. But this too was aborted; they interviewed a suitable candidate and then offered him a smaller salary than he received in Washington. After my time there it was decided to build a library and to establish a graduate program. The timing of both decisions was wrong. At the end of nine months the only practical outcome was the purchase of the Ugolino, and when I left Williams in the early summer of 1962 I was given an inscribed silver inkstand, with my name misspelled, in gratitude for my advice.

My program at Williams was so arranged that it left time for other lecturing. I gave six lectures on Michelangelo in seven days at Cleveland. In the Wade Park Manor Hotel (which is now an old people's home), as I was preparing the lectures, I could hear Clifford Curzon on the floor above practicing the Brahms D-minor concerto. The stunning performance he and George Szell gave of it is now perpetuated on compact disc. The following weekend I lectured in Toronto and lunched with Vincent Massey, whose sons were my contemporaries in Washington. During the spring recess I spoke in Chicago and was taken up to the Saarinen law school, flew on to San Francisco, where I lectured at Berkeley and the De Young Museum, and Los Angeles, where I spoke at UCLA and the Huntington Library, and Riverside and Claremont and Pomona. I also spoke at Harvard and Columbia and Baltimore and Raleigh, to the New England Renaissance Society, and to a hundred and sixty-five little Lolitas at Miss Hall's School at Pittsfield. In my office at Williams I was busy starting work on the Mellon Lectures, which would eventually become *The Portrait in the Renaissance*.

My last outside lecture was given at Raleigh, where I was followed round the museum by two students from the University of Virginia and their instructor. I signed two books for them and thought no more about it. In Italy that summer I went first to Milan, to see an exhibition of French portraits in the Palazzo Reale. There, a boy came up to me and said: "I was introduced to you at Raleigh—in America." His name, he explained, was Everett Fahy, and when he came later to Florence I thought him the most gifted young student I had ever met. We made firm friends and have traveled together to more places than I can count. After a period as director of the Frick Collection, he eventually succeeded me as chairman of European Paintings in the Metropolitan Museum.

From the time it was initiated in 1952 one lecture series exceeded all others in importance. This was the A. W. Mellon Lectures in the Fine Arts at the National Gallery in Washington. They had been inaugurated, on the highest possible level, with Maritain's *Creative Intuition in Art and Poetry*, and had given rise to a number of major books: Gilson's *Painting and Reality*, Gombrich's *Art and Illusion: A*

Study in the Psychology of Pictorial Representation, Blunt's *Nicolas Poussin*, and Grabar's *Beginnings of Christian Iconography*. By prescription they dealt with broad problems, and when I accepted the invitation to deliver them in 1963, I decided to talk on a subject that I had always found of compelling interest, portraiture. For some months I played with a scheme that would cover the problems of the portrait from the antique to the present day, but it seemed to me that though a review of this type might have been fun to listen to, it would not have yielded a book of more than transient interest. So I narrowed the subject of the lectures down to "The Artist and the Individual: Some Aspects of the Renaissance Portraits," and the title of the finished book became *The Portrait in the Renaissance*. I have never enjoyed preparing lectures or a book more than I did these.

In 1964, a year after they were delivered, I was elected Slade Professor at Cambridge, where the post was combined with a fellowship at Peterhouse. To anyone educated at Oxford or Cambridge the gulf between the two seems bewilderingly wide. You know by sight only a few of the major colleges and scarcely any of the streets. Though the haven of Peterhouse was agreeable, I felt something of an intruder in an unfamiliar academic society, and I was surprised to find myself dressing up repeatedly in a white tie and decorations for some college feast. From my standpoint the election felt awkward in that I had just delivered the Mellon Lectures and was preparing, under pressure, the Wrightsman Lectures for delivery in New York. There was therefore no alternative but to repeat the Mellon Lectures in my first term and to deliver a preliminary version of the Wrightsman Lectures in the second. The lecture theater was badly situated and attendances in the second term were patchy, since Raphael, was already on the teaching curriculum. By and large the whole experience was less rewarding than my tenure at Oxford, save for the fact that I worked closely with the head of the Art History Department, Michael Jaffé. At the time, art-history teaching at Cambridge was in many respects the best in England, and only as my acquaintance with Jaffé developed into friendship did I realize the personal qualities that contributed to this result. He was resilient and confident (qualities he shared with the main focus of his interests, Rubens), and his buoyancy was transmitted to the undergraduates he trained. As Carl Winter's successor at the Fitzwilliam Museum, Jaffé developed into the most distinguished English museum director of his day.

In some respects the Wrightsman Lectures in New York were a more taxing assignment than the Mellon Lectures in Washington. They were given under the auspices of the Institute of Fine Arts of New York University but were delivered at the Metropolitan Museum, and were addressed therefore to a dual audience consisting in part of sophisticated academics from New York University, Columbia, and other teaching bodies and in part of a general public of great intelligence. It was important not to bore the second and not to disappoint the first. It was agreed at an early stage that the first series of Wrightsman Lectures should be delivered by Kenneth Clark, and should deal with Rembrandt. He had given some inspiring talks on Rembrandt on the BBC in London, but for the New York lectures he chose a narrower subject, Rembrandt and the Italian Renaissance. In New York a small number of specialists on Dutch painting regarded him as a poacher, and it was evident from the beginning that he was looking at Rembrandt with different eyes from theirs. This was, however, no bad thing. When they were delivered, the lectures—I attended only the first three—seemed a little thin, though in their printed form they read well. But to one key area they failed to do anything like justice—Rembrandt's technical indebtedness to Titian. One lecture was indeed entitled "Rembrandt and the Venetians," but it was limited to formal or iconographical comparisons and gave no account of what Rembrandt's pictorial language owed to the facture and glazing of Titian's mature paintings.

The second set of Wrightsman Lectures was a more substantial piece of work. Entrusted to the masterly hands of Erwin Panofsky, it dealt with Titian. The resulting book, *Problems in Titian, Mainly Iconographic*, was one of Panofsky's last publications. It comprised five specialized lectures, of great brilliance and depth. The introductory lecture contains one of the most moving short accounts ever produced of the career of a great artist. Without the stimulus of the Wrightsman Lectures, Panofsky's work on Titian might, when he died in 1968, have gone with him to the grave.

When I was invited to give the third set of lectures, my mind turned, not unnaturally, to sculpture. But the last volume of my *Introduction to Italian Sculpture* had been published in 1963, and I was not anxious to traverse this field again so soon. Sitting with Craig Smyth, then the director of the Institute of Fine Arts, in a gloomy restaurant called Paoli in Florence, I talked over the possibility of lecturing on the

medium of bronze, but finally decided to treat a subject I had wanted
to write on ever since I was an undergraduate, Raphael. From the
seventeenth to the mid-nineteenth century there was a view that two
classical painters were supreme and irreproachable. One was Domenichino, whom I had attempted to rescue from oblivion in the
catalogue of the drawings at Windsor Castle, and the other was Raphael. Only when the choice was made did I realize the full hazards
of the enterprise. I did not wish to offer, in lecture form, a ragbag of
new facts and theories about Raphael, and the lectures, if they were
to be of use, must be addressed to a cultivated general public, not,
like Panofsky's *Problems in Titian*, to specialists. But how was this to
be achieved? Not, obviously, by a conventional chronological review
of Raphael's work. It was necessary to explain his creative processes,
which could be in large part deduced from drawings, the structure
of his frescoes, their poetic content, and their influence. For this reason
the series was planned as a sequence of six lectures, five of which
reviewed one of these themes through the whole span of Raphael's
career. The lectures were dense, though less so than in their printed
form, and they endeavored to explain why Raphael remains one of
the greatest and most rewarding of all artists. The pleasure of delivering them was very great, and since they took place twice a week,
not weekly like the Mellon Lectures in Washington, one had a sense
of audience continuity. The lectures were a good deal expanded in
the ensuing book, but not to a point at which their impetus was lost.

8

THE LURE OF TUSCANY

IN THE 1950S AND 1960S LIFE IN LONDON PURSUED ITS NORMAL course. The house I went to most often belonged to the Salters in Glebe Place. Ethel Salter had become a friend of my mother's in Washington when she was married to her first husband, Arthur Bullard, who was in the State Department. She seemed at that time to be hard up—when other people had Packards, she drove a little Chevrolet—but when their mother died she and her sister found, unexpectedly, that they were very rich. She had a warm, expansive, generous personality, and when, at the beginning of the war, she married Arthur Salter, he too became a friend. She was musical—she left me her Steinway, on which I play today—and was a belligerent supporter of American orchestral playing. "It's just the way we like it," she replied when, after a Beethoven concert by Ormandy in London, I said that the timbre of the Philadelphia Symphony Orchestra seemed rather inflated and thick. The chain of dry martinis one was compelled to drink was the only drawback to her hospitality. She was clever—"Ethel is of much better quality than Arthur," said the mischievous Ava Waverley, who disliked Lord Salter—and the guests I remember most clearly at her house were Americans in public life. In Glebe Place one felt that Washington was over the garden wall.

One of the focal points in the art life of London both before and after the war was the *Burlington Magazine*. From 1933 till 1939 it was edited by that universally respected figure Herbert Read. A man of great personal courage (he won the DSO in the First World War), he was best known to the world at large as a poet and literary critic and for two vivid accounts of his experiences at the front. In no sense was he an art historian but he was visually sensitive and he was fair-minded to a fault. On his suggestion in 1937 I wrote the first of a series of articles, called "Recent Research," summarizing the findings in articles in the current periodical literature. I continued them under other editors till 1953. During the war the paper was taken over by Tancred Borenius, to whom credit is due for its survival, and later the post of editor passed to Benedict Nicolson, whom I first knew as an undergraduate at Balliol. At Oxford I was much attached to him, but when the war was over he aged more rapidly than I did. He wrote a good book on Wright of Derby, a subject that requires no great acuteness of visual perception, and a less good book on Georges de La Tour, in which his own unhappy marriage is recorded in his interpretation of the painting of *Job and His Wife* at Epinal. I remember a weekend at Maud Russell's at Mottisfont at which he spent the time giving interviews on the telephone in which he claimed that a newly purchased La Tour in New York was a modern forgery. It was nothing of the kind—he arrived at the result through mulish adherence to misconceived principles—but his irresponsible interviews caused a good deal of trouble for the staff that had bought the painting. Ben was that Bloomsbury phenomenon: an anti-hedonist. He collected what are loosely called Caravaggesque paintings, and he equated their brown surfaces and yellow highlights with moral uplift and seriousness. We slowly drifted apart, and when publication in the *Burlington* became intolerably slow, I transferred my allegiance to Denys Sutton's swifter and more lively *Apollo*.

Of the figures in the postwar art world the most life-enhancing was Douglas Cooper. I met him soon after the war, during which he too had been in the RAF, but as an interrogation officer. He was already a collector on a substantial scale, and his judgment of quality in Picasso and Braque and Léger was impeccable. I liked his outré clothes and his malignant and extremely funny sense of humor, and I admired his written work. However mendacious he might be in life, his concern as an art historian lay with truth. Addiction to truth can make one many enemies, especially if it is combined, as it was in Douglas, with a witty and exceptionally astringent tongue. It was to his enemies and not to him that preferment invariably went. The exhibitions of nineteenth-century French painting he organized in the 1950s for the Arts Council were exceptionally good, and I am thankful that he did not live to see fourth-rate Monets and Gauguins and Cézannes fetching the vast prices that they do today. I have a weakness for people who are intolerant—there are not enough of them about—and we had no disagreements, though, for fear of trouble, I never went to stay at his house in France. He was embarrassingly unpredictable. I once asked him to give two lectures at the Victoria and Albert on Picasso and the theater. For the first he wore an orange shirt, and since he spoke with his coat unbuttoned and his trousers were cut very low, the whole audience watched in fascination as, in the light of the lectern, his pregnant orange stomach moved in and out as he spoke. At the second lecture he appeared in my office in a shirt that looked more respectable, but once the lights were lowered the embarrassing truth was revealed, that it was a then fashionable see-through shirt, so for an hour one watched not his shirt but his naked stomach as he spoke. An excellent linguist, he was less quarrelsome in Italian or German than in English or French. Difficult as he was, in his own field he represented standards—not only visual standards but intellectual standards too—and in a world peopled with limp critics and sequacious art historians the ruthlessness with which he used the battering ram of talent invariably earned my admiration and almost invariably my support. How many true friends he had was revealed when a posthumous exhibition of Cubist works on paper from his collection opened in the Öffentliche Kunstmuseum at Basel, and a party for it was given by his heir at the Drei Könige. Why am I going there? I wondered as I looked out from the train window at the low clouds covering the mountains round Lucerne. Because I respected him, I said to myself, and at Basel one learned how many highly discriminating, deeply affectionate friends had respected him too.

During the 1950s the Courtauld Institute of Art went from strength to strength. The deputy director, Johannes Wilde, was a great scholar and a remarkable teacher, but much of the credit for this success is due to the director, that now disparaged figure Anthony Blunt. Our relationship before the war had been uneasy. To me the Marxist view of contemporary art propagated in his articles in the *Spectator* seemed more than a little naive. They followed the orthodox Party line, whereby third-rate paintings were credited (on social grounds) with first-rate importance. His first book, *Artistic Theory in Italy, 1450–1600*, was also queered, as I implied in a review, by the stratified social thinking beneath it. After the outbreak of the war he first reduced and then discontinued his art-critical articles. He did this not, as one of the journalists who have written on him claims, on the instructions of his Moscow control, but because Fritz Saxl warned him that they would impede his acceptance as a serious art historian. And a serious art historian he unquestionably was. Already before the war he was associated, at the Warburg Institute, with the first volume of Walter Friedlaender's *Drawings of Nicolas Poussin*, and during the war he was recruited by the Royal Librarian, that charming and civilized man Owen Morshead, to take charge of the cataloguing of the Old Master drawings in the Royal Library. The project had started under poor auspices but in Anthony's hands it became totally professional, yielding volumes which form an invaluable tool for scholars in many different fields. During the years in which I was working on my catalogue I frequently saw Anthony. We were both in uniform, he as a captain and I as a flight lieutenant, and since the days we spent there and our periods of leave sometimes coincided, a close friendship might have been expected to result. But in some mysterious fashion it never did. He was supportive and helpful, but again and again one had the sense of coming up against a barred door in his personality.

After the war, for almost thirty years, we worked together on the same committees. I saw him regularly at the Courtauld Institute, where I lectured from time to time and became a member of the board of studies; at the Victoria and Albert, where he was a cooperative member of the Advisory Council; and at the British Academy. Occasional clashes were inevitable, and I remember one with special vividness. In 1960 Blunt was responsible for the magnificent Poussin exhibition at the Louvre. Before it closed a number of criticisms of the catalogue (and therefore, by implication, of the connoisseurship on which the catalogue was based) were made by Denis Mahon in the *Burlington Magazine*. They were repeated and elaborated in 1962 in an article in the *Gazette des Beaux-Arts*. I took Mahon's English article to Paris, and concluded that his views were substantially correct. Fundamentally the disagreement was over method, whether Poussin's work should be approached from an essentially cerebral standpoint or through meticulous visual analysis. Mahon held no official post, but he had been, over a long period, single-handedly responsible for rehabilitating the work of the Carracci and their pupils and had thereby exercised a worldwide influence on taste. In 1964, therefore, I proposed his name for election to the British Academy. Blunt pressed me to withdraw the nomination, since Mahon's presence

at meetings would, he claimed, make his own position very difficult.
I refused, and Mahon was very properly elected. I was left with the
impression that Blunt's besetting sin was vanity.

In 1972 allegations appeared in _Private Eye_ impugning Blunt's loyalty. I remember at the time running into Denys Sutton, then editor
of _Apollo_, on the stairs leading up to the Victoria and Albert library.
"One would put one's hand in the fire," he said, "for Anthony's
integrity." I replied that I would put only one finger in. My reason
was that I knew him less well than anyone I saw so frequently. When
the allegations were repeated in 1979, I nonetheless sent Anthony
from New York a letter in which I said that though we had known
each other for many years we had not known each other very well,
and that I hoped he would not think it intrusive if I expressed sympathy over his persecution by the press. By return of post I received
an emotional reply saying that never had he so greatly needed the
support of all his friends. There followed his denunciation by the
Prime Minister in the House of Commons and his disgrace. In retrospect I should have put two and two together and realized that
something was deeply wrong. I knew, from my brother, who was a
friend of Burgess, a good deal about his private life, and I heard from
other sources, some of them in the Institute, of the homosexual parties
he gave in his official flat (there was no objection to his giving homosexual parties, but there were strong objections to his giving them in
the building in which he was in charge). Yet, evening after evening,
I continued to meet him, a model of propriety in white tie and decorations, at some official city dinner or at the Royal Academy. If a
wise man like Lionel Robbins accepted him at his face value, how
could I refrain from doing so? The less so when his own ethical
standards (they formed part of his cover, no doubt) appeared to be so
high. "So-and-so behaved disgracefully," I often heard him say of
people whose conduct did not to my eyes seem reprehensible.

Blunt was an excellent teacher and an exceptionally able art historian. Like all cerebrotonic art historians, he was soundest on architecture: his work on Borromini and Mansart is remarkable for its
imagination and lucidity, and a quarter of a century after they appeared his volumes on that most architectural of painters, Poussin,
remain unsurpassed. With art historians the subconscious is generally
very near the surface, and character flaws are prone to be reflected in
their printed work. With Blunt this did not occur. There were mis-

takes but they were due to a defective eye, not to concealment or evasiveness. He was, moreover, an admirable Surveyor of the paintings in the Royal Collection. To his initiative we owe the cleaning of the Mantegna *Triumph of Caesar* by John Brealey at Hampton Court, as well as the opening of a public gallery in which works of art from the Queen's collection could be shown. Neither scholarly nor organizational accomplishment can be balanced against treachery, but as a scholar and organizer the art world owes him a great debt.

Three of many journeys made in the 1950s stand out in my mind. The first was to Spain, where I had never previously been. In Madrid the greatest pleasure was naturally the Prado, where I was given every help by the director, Francisco Sánchez-Cantón—like the directors of many Spanish museums at the time, he was well beyond retirement age—and in which I spent the best part of a week. The revelation of the journey was not El Greco or Velázquez but Goya, whose quality one could not gauge from reproductions or from most of the paintings outside Spain. Where one had no introductions, there was nothing to be done. I wished to see some bronzes in the Archaeological Museum. "The director is in conference," was the reply. Is the assistant director available? "No, he is also in conference." When will he be free? "The conference will last all day." Are there any other officials? "Yes, a secretary, but he is away." At what time will the director or assistant director be free tomorrow? "They will not be here tomorrow; they are going to Ávila." And the next day? "The following day they are going to Toledo." At the Romantic Museum, with its pretty stenciled blinds, the director, to whom I had an introduction, was only in his office between half past one and two three days a week. My dislike of Spain was only quenched years later by the hospitality of Xavier and Carmen De Salas.

Outside Madrid and Toledo my concern was to see as many Italian works of art as possible, especially the exquisite Botticelli *Agony in the Garden* in the Capilla Real at Granada and the Italian paintings and monuments at Salamanca. In the church of the convent of Santa Ursula, I met a young Dutchman negotiating through a grille with one of the nuns. He was a pupil of Van Regteren Altena at Amsterdam and was engaged on a dissertation on Juan de Flandes. One little panel after another was handed through the grille until he was supplied with the painting, by an imitator of Juan de Flandes, that he wished to see. This was the beginning of a long friendship with Egbert Haverkamp-Begemann, whom I next knew as the organizer of a fascinating exhibition of Rubens oil sketches at Rotterdam and who is now my colleague at the Institute of Fine Arts in New York.

Later in the year I rashly accepted an invitation to lecture in German on Matteo di Giovanni at the Zentralinstitut für Kunstgeschichte in Munich. I was the guest of the Leonardo specialist Ludwig Heydenreich, whom I had met often in Florence and greatly liked. This was my first postwar visit to Germany and I still recall the ruined streets of Munich in the prosperous Munich of today. There was a compensating factor in the presence, in the Prinz-Carl-Palais, of what I still think of as the most enriching exhibition I have ever visited. Under the title *Ars Sacra*, it comprised works of art from the sixth century to the thirteenth century. The manuscripts especially made a truly overwhelming impression. Starting with the purple pages and silver lettering of the Vienna Genesis, open at the depiction of the Flood, they continued with a magnificent series of Carolingian and Ottonian manuscripts, the Soissons Evangelary of Louis the Pious, the Fulda Evangelary from Würzburg, with its sublime miniatures of the Evangelists, the Evangelary of the Emperor Lothair from Paris, the greatest of the surviving manuscripts from Tours, the Codex Aureus from St. Emmeram, with its visionary page of Christ and the Evangelists, and the Pericope Book of Henry II, open at the double page showing the three Maries with their pale green, pale yellow, and violet halos, looking suspiciously at the majestic angel, with gray wings unfurled, guarding the sepulcher. There were the Echternach Codex Aureus from Coburg, and the St. Gereon Sacramentary from Paris, and the Gunold Evangelary from Stuttgart. The loans from Paris were especially rich, but rather shamefully there were no British loans. One was used to seeing manuscripts singly in the exhibition areas of libraries, but never before was there a display so rich that the essential character of each of the main schools of illumination was properly defined. The power of their imagery, their contrasts in tonality, the tension of their line emerged as I have never seen it since. The display was important from an academic point of view, but it was important also as an aesthetic experience. Set in the disorder of the present, it represented an appeal to the common culture of the past. Of all the exhibitions I have seen it was this that taught me most about the communicative power of art.

In 1958 a group of British museum officials was for the first time invited to the Soviet Union. It was headed by the director of the National Gallery, Philip Hendy, and included Mary Woodall, the director of the Birmingham City Art Gallery, David Baxandall, the director of the National Gallery of Scotland, and myself. The visit was a short one, but it served to break the ice and paved the way for later visits. Jet aircraft at the time were a new experience, and as the Russian jet took off from Brussels, I watched beads of perspiration gathering on Baxandall's anxious face. In Moscow we were shown what I now think of as the conventional sights—the Lenin Mausoleum, the Kremlin Museum, the Pushkin Fine Arts Museum, and the State Tretyakov Gallery—and outside Moscow the visit followed conventional lines as well, with visits to Zagorsk and to the Tiepolos at Arkhangelskoye. I had always supposed that to eyes trained on Duccio even the best icons would look as dead as they do in color photographs, but in the original the effect they made was very great. More revealing than the works of art was the sense of Moscow as a world capital. When the elevator doors opened in the Ukraina Hotel, they admitted parties of every nationality and color, and the hall of the hotel, with its ceiling painted by a Soviet Tiepolo, was stridently international. If the visit was conventional, so were my responses, for no one who is impregnated with Russian literature can visit the countryside round Moscow without emotion. I have never been back to Arkhangelskoye, but its memory stayed with me, not least that of the theater where Rossini's *Barbiere di Siviglia* used to be sung. Years later, when I was in Leningrad, I went out one freezing evening to a small theater to hear how the coloratura of the *Barbiere* sounded in translation sung by Russians.

Not unnaturally, Leningrad proved on every level more exciting than Moscow. The initial rewards were urbanistic and architectural—Venice apart, it is the most agreeable city to walk about in the world—and at the Hermitage Loewinson-Lessing was a warm and understanding host. I had hoped to meet Lazarev, the great Byzantine art historian, but this proved impossible, since I was on museum not on academic rails and the two tracks did not converge. A first experience of the Hermitage is unforgettable, and for long afterwards I was haunted by memories of Titian's visionary *St. Sebastian*, Giorgione's *Judith*, and Rembrandt's voluptuous *Danaë*. The human contacts established through this visit were no less important. It was thereafter possible to write personally to individuals when one wanted information and conversely for them to write to one. Most impressive to visitors from a country where the past is perpetually threatened by the present, was the universal concern for the preservation of every relic of a socially alien society. At Pushkin we listened to a long harangue which, knowing no Russian, I assumed to be political, only to find when it was translated that its content was that of an enthusiastic member of the National Trust. Great strides had been made with the repair and reconditioning of monuments, especially of the neo-classical interior of Pavlovsk. Of the performances we were taken to at the Kirov Theater the most memorable was of *Prince Igor*. I had seen it only once before, in London, where it was conducted by Beecham, and I have since urged one opera house after another to revive it.

From Leningrad we flew to Kiev. The museum was in course of restoration, but we were taken through the Peshcherskaya Lavra and its catacombs. Half the Russians who accompanied us through the shrine proved to be believers and genuflected at the tombs, and half were skeptics who stood ironically to one side. As a city Kiev proved less evocative than I expected, save for the eleventh-century mosaics and paintings from St. Sophia and what remained of those from St. Michael and the beautiful centralized Rastrelli church of St. Andrew with its view over the Dnieper. One night was once more devoted to opera, on this occasion Prokofiev's *War and Peace*, which had not at that time been performed in London. It made a deep impression (as it continued to do later when given in English at the Coliseum), mitigated by the fact that it was sung in Ukrainian and was therefore accompanied by a buzz of whispering as Ukrainian members of the audience explained the dialogue to companions who knew only Russian.

The constant factor in each year that passed was two months in Italy. Initially I spent more time in Siena than in Florence, then in a second phase I split my time equally between the two, and finally, when Siena became overfamiliar and I remembered every scratch on every painting there, I deserted it and based myself in Florence. The Palazzo Ravizza in Siena then was not the tourist-oriented place that it is now, and for some years it provided an ideal base for study. Communications with the rest of Italy may have been poor, but with a little effort every village in the Sienese *contado* could be reached, and there was not a pallid altarpiece by Cozzarelli nor any desiccated panel by a follower of Bartolo di Fredi that I did not know in the original. The Sienese countryside enjoys a magic of its own, and when today I return to Sant'Anna in Camprena with its crystalline frescoes by Sodoma and its view over the gray brown hills known as the *crete* or go from Asciano to the Badia a Rufeno or bump up the dirt track to San Leonardo al Lago, with its innocent frescoes by Lippo Vanni, the spell it cast on me so long ago still works. My personal pleasure in living in Siena was due largely to the presence of three people. The first was Dario Neri, the founder of the publishing firm in Milan known as Electa. A friend of Berenson, he was a man of wide imagination and quite extraordinary helpfulness. He was an enthusiast, and the focus of his enthusiasm was Siena, where he lived, until his early death, in Peruzzi's Palazzo Pollini opposite the Carmine. The books about Siena that he sponsored are still on my shelves, and each time I look at them the memory of expeditions made in his voluble company through the Senese comes to mind. The second was Raffaello Niccoli, the Superintendent of Fine Arts, who was infinitely helpful and with whom one could chart the progress of restoration throughout the countryside. The third and most important was his successor as Superintendent, Enzo Carli, the focus of whose interest was Gothic sculpture. When he retired after a highly successful tenure of the Superintendency, he became rector of the Opera del Duomo and took charge of the great sculptures by Giovanni Pisano from the façade of the Cathedral. There is no aspect of art in the Senese on which Carli has not written and written well, and his bibliography must be one of the longest on record. When he was working on Goro di Gregorio's Arca di San Cerbone at Massa Marittima, I went there with him, as I did to San Lucchese at Poggibonsi and Montalcino and San Gimignano, and as we ate grapes with the priest at the Abbadia ad Isola or spent an afternoon picking wild raspberries on the slopes of Monte Amiata, I slowly learned something of the network of personal relations on which protection of the Italian patrimony in the last resort depends. The honor that I most value is to have been awarded the prize of the Mangia d'Oro and, at a ceremony in the Teatro degli Rossi on the Feast of the Assumption 1982, to have been invested as a member of the Contrada della Tartuca and an honorary citizen of Siena.

One of the pleasures in the decades after the war was the openness of all relationships. Italian scholars had been confined to Italy as I had been in England, and on both sides there was a sense of reaching out. Most of my professional Italian friends date from that time. Some of them are dead, like Francesco Arcangeli, a brilliant critic rather than an art historian who took me in Bologna to the studio of Morandi to see the pepper pots and bottles that Morandi painted and the table on which he painted them. That Morandi was a genius no one in Italy had any doubt, and the competition for his work is now worldwide. There was an obvious parallel to be drawn with painters in the fourteenth and fifteenth centuries whose merits were the outcome of narrow, dedicated lives lived without interruption in the place in which they were at home. Or Giovanni Paccagnini, who seemed a timid and complaining figure until, as Superintendent at Mantua, he discovered the frescoes and sinopie of Pisanello, the most important addition made to the corpus of Italian painting in the last half century. Or Franco Russoli, whom I first met as a bewilderingly charming student at Pisa University in 1946 and who became a highly successful director of the Brera. Or Cesare Gnudi, whom I admired not only for his sensibility and seriousness, but because he operated simultaneously, as I have tried to do, on the two tracks of administration and art history. Of all the Superintendents of Fine Arts I have known, he was the most creative and purposeful. The construction of the new Bologna gallery, the cleaning of the façade of San Petronio, the saving of the Mezzarata frescoes, for all these he was responsible. He was responsible also for a succession of great exhibitions which changed the course of taste. If people nowadays, when they visit some museum, look at Reni and the Carracci and Guercino and Domenichino with the attention they would have received in the first half of the nineteenth century, they are reflecting the long-term influence of the exhibitions Gnudi planned. Or Luisa Becherucci, an extremely capable directress of the Uffizi and a woman of extraordinary refinement, who is now remembered for an admirable catalogue of the Museo dell'Opera del Duomo and the only sensible book that has been written on the Donatello pulpits in San Lorenzo.

The debt one owed to exhibitions organized in Italy throughout these years was immense. Most of what I know about Bolognese Trecento painting I learned from an exhibition at Bologna in 1950, where I saw for the first time that miracle of Gothic painting, the altarpiece by Andrea da Bologna from Fermo. I thought then, and have thought whenever I have seen it since, that its gilt ground is the most beautiful of any fourteenth-century Italian painting. I spent two days at the exhibition of Veronese Gothic painting at Verona with Evelyn Vavalà, the only scholar whose conclusions did not require to be revised as a result of the display, and two more at the exhibition of Gothic art in Milan. I paid repeated, but less remunerative visits to the rather quirky exhibitions of Sienese painting and sculpture organized by Previtali and Bellosi in Siena, and to successive exhibitions of Sienese wooden sculpture, in which attribution replaced attribution like a kaleidoscope. I spent a week at the Lotto exhibition in Venice ("not the longest exhibition but the Longhiest," said B.B. kindly) and went with Berenson round the Giorgione exhibition. I went to exhibitions of Tommaso da Modena in Treviso, Rutilio Manetti in Siena, and Cigoli at San Miniato al Tedesco, to crowded Cremonese exhibitions at Cremona, to Moroni at Bergamo, to Lombard exhibitions at Varese, to Luini at Como, and to Romanino at Brescia. I went to Batoni at Lucca (where the great portraits of English grand-tourists were unwisely shown without their frames), and Hayez in Milan, and Lotto at Ancona (one of the only wholly bad exhibitions I can recall), and spent an enormously rewarding week in 1951 at the revolutionary Caravaggio exhibition in Milan, and a much shorter time at a Caravaggio exhibition at Syracuse, where the dark paintings, through some misunderstanding, were shown in a blacked-out room with a beam of light focused on each of them.

These exhibitions and the traveling they involved were, however, incidental to my main task. Florence meant work, and work meant hours spent in the German Art-Historical Institute, first in the Palazzo Guadagni in Piazza Santo Spirito and then, thanks to the foresight of Ulrich Middeldorf, in more spacious premises in Via Giusti. I go there still, and though it is now more bureaucratic than it was then, it is still the most productive and most stimulating art-historical library in the world. It is the seedbed from which most of my own published writings spring.

Gradually through these years Florence became a center for the study of sculpture. Max Seidel and Gert Kreytenberg were rewriting the history of the Pisani, Detlev Heikamp was preparing what became an invaluable book on Florentine baroque sculpture, and Hanno-Walter Kruft was working on Renaissance sculpture in Sicily and Naples. The most brilliant and most stimulating, though not the most productive, of these younger students was James Holderbaum.

In Florence in the summers I lived in rented flats, first in one in Via Romana belonging to a friend of B.B.'s, Guglielmo Alberti, and then in one in Piazza Pitti belonging to an Englishwoman, Noel Sheldon, who became quite a close friend. In the last year of her life she entrusted the preparation of the apartment to Contessa Elneth Capponi. I found a note from her when I arrived and, to my astonishment, a snapshot of my uncle Hugh, who was killed in the first war and to whom my financial start in life was due. In the photograph he was in Canadian uniform. Contessa Capponi introduced me to her son Neri and his wife, Flavia, whose apartment I later rented for a number of summers and who are now my landlords and some of my closest Florentine friends.

Most native Florentines leave Florence for the country when summer begins, so one depended for relaxation on foreign centers of hospitality. One of them was at La Pietra, where Harold Acton, after his mother's death, continued to maintain the standards she had set. Whether at lunch or dinner, the huge villa—it had been built for the Medici banker Francesco Sassetti in the fifteenth century, and redecorated in Tuscan rococo style for Cardinal Capponi—was a cool oasis, in which orderly life, of a kind that had become uncommon with the passage of time, was still observed. Your taxi was greeted by a white-coated footman waiting at the door, and skirting the Susini in the stairwell you found Harold and one or two guests seated by red lacquer tables with dark green rubber vine leaves on which to place your drink. Circular tables make for better conversation than oblong tables, and when on the dining-room walls there are excellent fifteenth-century reliefs and splendid primitives, a contagious feeling of well-being asserts itself. I went to birthday party after birthday party there—the most recent was the eighty-fifth—surprised that at an age when most people's faculties deteriorate, Harold's incisiveness and wit were unimpaired.

The Villa Capponi at Pian di Giullari, which was owned by Henry Clifford, was regularly rented in the summer. The most stimulating of the tenants were Ronnie and Marietta Tree and the guests they assembled there. The house had the mysterious faculty of making one like people one had not registered properly before, and it was there that my friendship with Pamela Hartwell began. She became a member of my Advisory Council at the Victoria and Albert and later a trustee of the British Museum, and she and her husband, Michael, used often afterwards to come to Florence for a few days' intensive sightseeing. From time to time the house was also taken by the sister of Adlai Stevenson, Buffy Ives, and her gentle, blind husband who showed one views from the garden that he was all but unable to see. Sometimes small things that people do count more than big ones, and I remember that late one August Mrs. Ives asked me the date of my first Mellon Lecture in Washington. I told her when it was. "I shall be there," she said, and sure enough she was. On the way up to Fiesole, at San Domenico, was Le Palazzine, the house of George Gronau, best known for his work on Titian and on the documents relating to Urbino. A capacious, totally Tuscan house filled with beautiful drawings and with a terrace overlooking Florence, it was lived in by his daughter-in-law, Carmen Gronau, the widow of his son Hans, whom I had much admired. She was an old friend and had been, with Peter Wilson, one of the architects of modern auction-eering, but no one would have guessed it from the warmth she generated.

The most stimulating contact was with Hugh Honour and John Fleming, who lived, and still live, in an enchanting villa at Tofori, midway between Pescia and Lucca. For many years we have given a day of our lives to one another, sitting beside their lotus pool (a water garden in Italy is a possession of great rarity) and talking about art history and art historians and life and books. Of all of my contemporaries Hugh and John have constructed for themselves the most enviable lives, opting for civilized values, not for competition, but working nonetheless, with iron discipline, at their chosen tasks. One of the blessings of life in Florence is that I now see them more frequently.

Two exclusive centers were Pratolino, where Prince Paul of Yugoslavia and Princess Olga lived during the summer, and the Villa Sparta, which belonged to Queen Helen of Romania. I wrote to my brother James in 1958 describing a lunch *en famille* at Pratolino, with Princess Olga's sisters, the Duchess of Aosta, and Princess Marina, Duchess of Kent: "I found Princess Olga's guttural manner rather disconcerting, but Prince Paul I liked from the beginning. A daughter was there too who thought you were my nephew. That barrage of royal questions is so difficult. How old is your brother? Topic then changed. How much older are you than your brother? Another change of subject. Then more questions. I do not understand why they cannot

ask everything they want to know at once." James replied: "I can
easily give you a simile for royal questions. I see their minds like
conveyer belts for luggage at London airport. First comes one's own
suitcase, then someone else's typewriter, then *drei Stücke*, later another
piece of one's own luggage. They usually forget what they have asked
you when you are in the midst of a reply, and you find they have
moved on to a discussion of flying-saucers or drinking habits in Zan-
zibar." When I last went to Pratolino, Giovanni Bologna's great statue
the *Appennino* had been repaired, but the dodecagonal chapel near it
by Buontalenti was in the same derelict condition as when I visited
it with Prince Paul, and the house (it consists of the outbuildings of
the demolished villa constructed for the Gran Principe Francesco de'
Medici) was converted to an artist's colony. It was difficult to reconstruct where the splendid Napoleonic furniture and the Schubin busts
had stood.

Prince Paul and Princess Olga had suffered political vicissitudes,
but vicissitudes less grave than those overcome by that heroic figure
Queen Helen of Romania. She once described to me how, after the
Communist takeover in Bucharest, she and her son had been confined
in the palace at Sinaia not knowing what their fate would be. "It was
no use twiddling our thumbs," she said, so she arranged for local
carpenters to construct cases of double thickness for the royal pictures,
in which the great El Grecos could be hidden behind secondary paintings. She took them with her when she was eventually allowed to
leave the country. One of them, a magnificent male portrait, is now
in the Kimball Art Museum at Fort Worth, and another, a tiny *Visitation*, was in a box by her bed. On one strange occasion she invited
me to lunch to meet my brother at a time when he was in Germany.
I explained this, but Queen Helen knew better, since she had had a
telegram signed "Jamie." Looking at it again, she saw that the writer
was going to Porto Ercole, so she rang up the Queen of the Neth-
erlands at Porto Ercole to ask if she had seen my brother. Queen
Juliana (who did not know him) said that she had not, but offered to
ring up the police. Mercifully Queen Helen said this was unnecessary.
So we waited patiently for the unknown guest, who proved to be the
publisher Jamie Hamilton. But it was an extremely enjoyable lunch.
"They were very musical," said Queen Helen of the Romanian royal
family. "There were thirteen pianos in the palace, and it was only a
little palace."

The high points of each summer from the late 1940s on were visits to the simple house to which Berenson retreated for the summer at Vallombrosa. Sometimes there were other guests, Umberto Morra or William Milliken or Jamie and Yvonne Hamilton or Daisy Barr or that enchanting woman Clotilde Marghieri. "Take care, or she will steal your heart," said B.B. as Clotilde and I walked off together through the pine wood. I learned much during these weekends about looking, but at nature rather than at art.

The rhythm of each day was planned by Berenson's secretary, Nicky Mariano, the angelic architect of his apotheosis, with unfaltering skill. One had the morning to oneself till, at midday, B.B. appeared, and one sat with him on what had once been a tennis court, listening to Nicky rapidly reading through the newspaper. At lunch each day there was a fresh bowl of wildflowers in the middle of the table, picked and arranged, with great imagination, by Vittorio, the butler, who came from Terranuova Bracciolini. After coffee in a little hut beside the house there was a compulsory siesta, and at five we met again for tea, which was followed by a drive uphill and a fast walk back. On these walks B.B. talked with great freedom and brilliance. In 1953 I was alone at Vallombrosa, and B.B., as we walked downhill over the slippery pinecones, gave me a talk on the need to marry. "Unless you marry soon," he said, "your children will have a grandfather and not a father." I explained that I was intended to be celibate, that marriage seemed to me a precarious and unhappy state, and that it would involve putting in pawn everything I wished to do.

In the summer of 1955 B.B.'s faculties were unimpaired. He still stood on the balcony at Vallombrosa to doff his nightcap to the new moon. He was (I quote from a letter) "entirely charming, sitting up talking last night till half past eleven and so far as one could see not aged in any way." I could scarcely remember him so animated and so funny. He remained so through 1957, when I was present at his leave-taking with Richard Offner. Offner and I drove up together, lunched with Nicky, and then went upstairs, where B.B. was lying on a sofa covered with a plaid rug. Offner, bending over him, told him that he had recently reread his book on Lotto, and what a model of method he thought it. This gave no more than qualified pleasure, and B.B., turning up to him, said: "But you, Richard, you have also made discoveries. Think of the Master of San Martino alla Palma." The Master of San Martino alla Palma was a follower of Bernardo

Daddi who was for long confused with Daddi. Blushing slightly, Offner took this as a compliment, not a joke. As the door closed behind him, B.B. exclaimed: "*S'invecchia male.*"

By the following summer B.B.'s decline was very marked. At I Tatti he was "brought down to the music room to work and deal with correspondence before lunch. You lunch in the French library. His brain works perfectly, and he hears almost everything one says, but he makes for the first time an impression of great passivity, and is propelled about by a trained nurse, who collects him after lunch and supports him upstairs." There followed two horrific weekends at Vallombrosa: "B.B. seems to me to be going downhill very fast, and can hardly walk. He insists on eating with one, and you wait in your room until you are told he has been settled at table. When you go upstairs, you find him at a tiny table with four places at it, very close together. He is fed by the nurse standing behind his chair, and opens and shuts his mouth like a fish. He is in a good deal of pain and moans quietly from time to time. The nurse kisses him on the top of his head, and says '*Coraggio.*' " I went up once more later in the summer, not because it would give pleasure to B.B. but because it provided a respite for Nicky. When B.B. died, she gave me two Sienese walnut angels from his study (I later returned them to I Tatti), and when she in turn died, Willy Mostyn-Owen and I arranged a Mass at the Brompton Oratory at which the choir sang the Vittoria Requiem.

It is hard to define exactly what it was one gained from all these visits. I made no notes of the conversation—it would have seemed rather indecent to do so—but slowly one was permeated by B.B.'s personality. One felt protective and affectionate and uncritical. The main thing I learned from him was honest-mindedness. It affected points of attribution—whether one thought in one's heart of hearts that a portrait at St. Louis was or was not by Titian—but it affected value judgments too. His thinking, as it had never been in earlier days, was of one piece. In that revealing book, the diaries published as *Sunset and Twilight*, he writes: "It is a pity that owing to my age and worse still to my manners younger men are seldom natural with me." To me, in the twelve years I knew him well, our relationship seemed entirely natural; there was no faking on either side. It is to this that my devotion to his memory is due.

Bernard Berenson died in October 1959, and his house, I Tatti, was accepted, after some delay, by Harvard University, as the Harvard Center for Renaissance Studies. In the United States in 1961 I became involved in the new institution, first at dinner with Nathan Pusey, the president of the university, who seemed to have no very clear idea as to the future role of the Renaissance Center, and then at a fund-raising luncheon in New York which was addressed by the first director of I Tatti, Kenneth Murdock. Murdock was a specialist in Cotton Mather, with no evident qualifications for his post, and as his speech at lunch continued, one could hear prospective contributors pushing their checkbooks back into their pockets. Fortunately, before long Murdock was succeeded by a distinguished historian, Myron Gilmore, who had close contacts with the Italian university world and enjoyed the confidence of everyone who knew him. The only relic of the first director is a little book by his wife, Eleanor Murdock, called *My Years at I Tatti*, written in the style of Daisy Ashford's *Young Visitors*, with the names of guests at I Tatti misspelled and their posts wrongly described.

In the summer of 1956 when I went up to Vallombrosa, John Walker and his daughter were fellow guests. At tea one day he produced a set of stereoscopic slides of the Palm Beach house of a collector whom he had met recently, Charles Wrightsman. As I held the slides up to the light, they showed him and his wife, Jayne (who is now one of my closest and most valued friends), against a background of Meissen birds. What paintings, asked John Walker, should the Wrightsmans buy? I said that on my last visit to New York I had been impressed by two excellent conversation pieces by Jean François de Troy which I had seen with Rosenberg and Stiebel, and Johnny went off to the post office at Vallombrosa to send a telegram drawing the Wrightsmans' attention to them. That winter in New York, at a party given by Alfred Frankfurter, the editor of *Art News*, I met the Wrightsmans. At first I was disconcerted at the contrast between Wrightsman's suave manner and his overpoweringly strong personality, but I was asked to lunch. Never before had I encountered, in a modern setting, works of such uniform distinction. The paintings were dominated by the Arenberg Vermeer, and the French furniture was of the highest possible quality. The gift one looks for in collectors is discrimination, and here it was present in a high degree. Many earlier American collectors had differentiated, on the basis of business acumen, between the average and the good. Charles Wrightsman distinguished between the very good and the superlative, and it was only the superlative that he would buy. With the applied arts the process was intelligible; he had practical experience of cabinetmaking, and looked at the French eighteenth century with a technically sophisticated eye. With paintings the process was more mysterious. Over the years I learned to predict his responses without fully understanding them; he was not prepared, for example, to buy a top-class Claude, because it was no more than an ordinary Claude raised to a higher power. But if the content of a first-rate painting spoke, he would purchase it at once.

Charles Wrightsman was a perfectionist. As a trustee of the Metropolitan Museum his concern lay with standards, and on these he was uncompromising. The Wrightsman galleries at the Metropolitan Museum were revised again and again till they exhaled the "general sense of glory" Henry James found in the French eighteenth century to which Wrightsman responded with such warmth and which he wished the public to respond to too. He was determined that the catalogue of his collection should be the *ne plus ultra* of catalogues, and in the skilled hands of Francis Watson and Everett Fahy it became what he intended, not just an expensive record of his acquisitions but a work of fundamental value for the study of furniture and painting.

Charlie regarded money as a lubricant. One of the things that it made possible was traveling. A number of the guests on the yacht he and Jayne rented each summer were museum officials or art historians. I refused his invitations on more than one occasion. If you go on yachts, you surrender free will as soon as you step up the gangway. But once I was kidnapped. I was going with the Wrightsmans to Istanbul, where they would board the yacht, when a student revolt in Turkey aborted the journey, and instead we flew to Athens, got onto the yacht at the Piraeus, and sailed northward to Athos, landing at three separate points and seeing every steatite in the monasteries we visited. Thence we sailed on to Samothrace, spending a magical day looking at the excavations, and to Kaválla.

But the occasion for which I have most reason to be grateful to Charles Wrightsman was a domestic one. It arose in the summer of 1966 when I was giving a luncheon party at my house in Bedford Gardens for him and Jayne. During the morning Jayne rang up to ask if they might come a little early. When they arrived Charles asked abruptly whether I would become his candidate for the vacant directorship of the Metropolitan Museum. I demurred at this, first because at the time I had never directed a museum and second because I felt

I knew too little about the legal and social context in which the Metropolitan Museum operated. But he continued to press. There would, he insisted, be a fallback position in a professorship at the Institute of Fine Arts. The only person with whom I discussed this was Arthur Salter, who said he was convinced that I would end up in America but that I should make some contribution in London first. So I refused. But something fundamental had nonetheless occurred. I had looked upon myself till then as a scholar immured in a museum. I was an ambitious scholar, but I was not ambitious in a wider sense. With the knowledge that I commanded the respect of a man of exceptional shrewdness and experience, who had seen something in my character of which I previously was unaware, my view underwent a change. I realized that what I had hitherto regarded as an occupation was a career.

In Florence that summer the weather was unsettled, and there was constant rain. One of the last things I did was to drive over with Everett Fahy to see Roberto Longhi at his seaside house at Ronchi. During the drive torrential rain bounced off the asphalt and made little streams on both sides of the road. While I was talking to Longhi, about a painting wrongly ascribed to Duccio that had been bought by the National Gallery in London, the downpour continued, and when I left it was still raining hard. The following day I returned to London. Two months later, on November 5, there appeared in the press the shocking news of the Florentine flood. A relief committee, the Italian Art and Archives Rescue Fund, was at once set up in London under the chairmanship of the recently retired ambassador in Rome, Sir Ashley Clarke, and a fortnight later I was asked by the committee to visit Florence, jointly with Nicolai Rubinstein, to report on conditions there. Rubinstein was concerned with libraries and archives and I with monuments and works of art. The first indications of disaster appeared on the road from Bologna, where lorry after lorry loaded with rusty cars was climbing slowly northward up the Futa Pass. Scarcely did we leave the highway than in the western suburbs of the town, far from the river, oil stains started to appear along the streets at shoulder height and piles of rotting woodwork could be seen standing outside each door. Inside the town parties of soldiers were at work clearing the slime, but more than two weeks after the flood the mud in the Piazza Santa Croce was still ankle deep, and the Via de' Bardi at the south end of the Ponte Vecchio was a morass of mud and oil.

Grave as the damage was, it was nothing to what might have been; it was as though providence had decreed that the city and all its monuments should be effaced, and then relented at the eleventh hour. But the devastating consequences of the flood for works of art in Florence could scarcely be imagined by anyone who did not see them at first hand. Though few great works of art were totally destroyed, the numbers damaged ran into thousands, and the campaign of restoration (of buildings as well as paintings) seemed likely to engage all the available resources for many years to come.

Particularly startling, even to someone used to wartime bombing, was the violence of the inundation that had occurred. Parts of the north side of the Lungarno crumbled away under the impact of the water, and the Lungarno Acciauoli was eroded almost to the level of the houses on the far side of the street; in building after building flooded basements filled with heating plants discharged their oil into the streets, and a kind of tidal wave tore at the Ponte Vecchio and then overflowed the banks, running, at a great distance from the river, northward as far as the Annunziata and the university. The water buffeted the Duomo and the Baptistry, and further to the west the cloisters of Santa Maria Novella and the Ognissanti were submerged. Looking at the scene, I was reminded of the images of supernatural disasters that punctuate Florentine Quattrocento painting—Botticelli's *Mystic Crucifixion* in the Fogg Art Museum, where divine anger, in the form of a storm cloud, descends on Florence; Leonardo's terrifying drawings of tempests; and Uccello's brutal fresco of the *Flood*.

The Biblioteca Nazionale on the north side of the Arno faced the full force of the flood. Behind it the tide spread to Santa Croce, where, in the cloister and refectory and Pazzi Chapel, it rose to between fifteen and eighteen feet. The first cloister, the one by which you enter when you visit the museum or the Pazzi Chapel, presented a picture of desolation—it was a sea of mud—and a nineteenth-century monument on the right wall was stained with oil to its full height. There was, of course, nothing particularly tragic about damage to this monument, but it presented a graphic picture of the danger to which the great works of art in the same area were exposed. The most important were in the refectory, which was incorporated in the Museo dell'Opera di Santa Croce. On the end wall was the great fresco of the Last Supper by Taddeo Gaddi, and to the right of the entrance was the painted Cross by Cimabue. A strip along the base of Taddeo Gaddi's *Last Supper* had been blackened and was being restored. But the painted Cross by Cimabue, which was supported by a wooden scaffolding free of the wall, was submerged and had become an all but total loss.

To my mind, however, the horror of the situation was not so much the violation of single art works as the unreasoning disorder that had overwhelmed a fully rational building like Brunelleschi's Pazzi Chapel. The grille of one window was wrenched out, and inside the water rose to about two-thirds of the height of the *pietra serena* arcading on the walls and over the level of the bottom molding of the high window behind the altar. In the adjacent church of Santa Croce a margin of inches saved the Giotto frescoes in the Bardi and Peruzzi chapels and the Maso and Daddi frescoes in the north transept of the church. On the right wall of the nave Donatello's *Cavalcanti Annunciation* was soaked with oil to the level of the Virgin's knees.

North of Santa Croce the water had poured down Via Ghibellina and broken the windows of the Casa Buonarroti, which was flooded to a point above the level of the entrance door. The oil line stopped just short of the bust of Michelangelo. Luckily there were no works by Michelangelo in the severely damaged ground-floor rooms, where devastation was complete. The Horne Museum in Via de' Benci was in precisely the same state and the Museum of the History of Science in the Piazza dei Giudici was likewise flooded; in the basement and on the ground floor the collections were pulverized. At the center of the maelstrom was the Baptistry, where the bronze doors, as was customary when the church was shut, were closed. Two gilt bronze quadrilobe reliefs were knocked out of the bronze door by Andrea Pisano on the south side—the force of the water could be judged from the fact that a horizontal split ran across the whole width of the right-hand wing—and part of the frieze by Ghiberti surrounding it was sucked into the mud. The *Gate of Paradise* was more gravely damaged still. Five of its ten large bronze reliefs were detached, but were eventually recovered. It was not only the reliefs at the bottom of the door that were affected; it was the reliefs above as well, and particularly the miraculous panel with the Creation of Adam and the Expulsion, and the scene beside it with the story of Cain and Abel, the climax of Ghiberti's achievement as a narrative artist. The head of Cain plowing was almost, but fortunately not entirely severed—if it had been severed, the chances of its recovery would have been very small. The undulating surface of all of the reliefs was stained with oil.

The Archaeological Museum near the Annunziata had suffered more gravely than any other Florentine museum. The confusion in the long series of Etruscan galleries on the ground floor was indescribable. The vitrines were coated inside with oil and mud, and a vast number of fragile objects had been fragmented or displaced. A complicating factor was that hardly any of them were of intrinsic interest. They owed what little value they possessed to the sites in which they had been found, and to their connection with other unimportant objects which had been disinterred at the same place at the same time. The need was for re-excavation. To recover a great part of the collection it was necessary to filter the deposits of slime in the basement and on the ground floor. The strangest spectacle was the Bargello, where the water had the effect of cleaning part of the colossal marble sculptures of Giovanni Bologna and Bandinelli in the cortile while at the same time of impregnating them with dense patches of black oil. There I found the director, in rubber boots, engaged, not in removing oil, but in dirtying down the newly cleaned parts of the statues with water from a bucket to simulate the state in which they were before.

This was a situation in which sympathy was of no use; the need was for practical help. At the time Florence fortunately had, in Piero Bargellini, a *sindaco* of great distinction and ability, and, in Ugo Procacci, a Superintendent of Fine Arts whose consistency and dedication and disinterest had won him, in England and in the United States, a host of professional admirers and personal friends. When I arrived, assistance was already being given by the American fund CRIA and other national committees. Rows of restorers, some of them of great distinction, could be seen on scaffolding giving first aid to frescoes. But there were two areas in which the salvage operations were notably deficient; one was the restoration of sculpture and the other that of the applied arts. The Conservation Department of the Victoria and Albert was in a state of high efficiency at the time. Its head, Norman Brommelle, had been trained as a painting restorer at the National Gallery and had reorganized the entire Conservation Department, and was married to Joyce Plesters, the head of the Research Laboratory at the National Gallery. I had, moreover, for some years been working with a specialist in sculpture restoration, Kenneth Hempel, who, when the flood occurred, was the most accomplished restorer of Italian sculpture in the world. The Conservation Department naturally had much experience in the purchase of equipment and materials (fields in which the Soprintendenza in Florence seemed to be woefully unpractical) and a first-rate administrator named Gorton, who was himself an experienced restorer of furniture and woodwork. Help in these areas could be given to the Florentine authorities, provided that the Ministry of Education allowed members of the museum to work in Italy without formality and provided that funds, for travel, subsistence, and the purchase of materials, were made available by the London committee. When I returned to London both conditions were met. The Italian Art and Archives Rescue Fund, under the vigorous chairmanship of Ashley Clarke, gave the project full support, and the attitude of the Establishment Division of the Ministry of Education was also cooperative and liberal. In Florence I explained, with the Bargello in mind, that when disasters occur, it is best to accept them as portents, and to adopt the target, not of restoring the status quo, but of improving on it. Hempel therefore inaugurated a broadly based campaign for cleaning marble sculpture, and a young man called Galli (who is now in charge of sculpture restoration in Florence) was brought over by the British Council for training in London. The results achieved were impressive and positive. With the invaluable help of Kirsten Aschengren-Piacenti, a restoration studio was set up in the Palazzo Davanzati, and it was there that Hempel and Joyce Plesters jointly discovered the first traces of gilding in the hair of Donatello's wooden Magdalen.

It is difficult today to visualize the worldwide sense of sympathy and compassion that the flood aroused. Numbers of students found their way to Florence anxious to help. As one looks back over the lists of contributions, especially small contributions from the student bodies of colleges and schools of art, the enterprise reads like an affirmation of faith. I went myself to Edinburgh and Glasgow universities to speak on the appeal and experienced at first hand the astonishing warmth of the response.

The situation in Venice after the November flood was very different from that in Florence. Whereas the flood in Florence was an almost unique emergency—floods had occurred before, but in the distant past—Venice had suffered high tides which flooded the Piazza San Marco, the basilica, and shops and hotels from time immemorial. The level of conservation was deplorable, but the prime cause was negligence. At one time effective conservation measures were adopted to replace disintegrating Verona marble, and from the eighteenth century on copies were made of the capitals of the Palazzo Ducale in substitution for the eroded originals. In the recent past, however, conservation had been neglected, and deterioration from capillary damp and chemical pollution had proceeded unchecked. I visited Venice on behalf of the British Fund in the last week of March 1967, met the principal officials, and visited twenty-three churches and most of the museums. Both in churches and in museums it was difficult to distinguish damage due to negligence from damage attributable to the flood. It was repeatedly urged on me that this distinction was academic, and in a sense that was correct. But it was not academic from the standpoint of the Fund, and I had to insist throughout that unless buildings and works of art had suffered demonstrable flood damage they were not eligible for assistance. Some of the requests were frivolous. The head of the Ca' d'Oro proposed that we should fund the relaying of a tessellated pavement on the ground floor, but since this was of no historical interest (it was laid down personally by Baron Franchetti, the composer of *Germania*) there was no case for intervention. It was also suggested that the Fund should pay for the cleaning of the Ca' d'Oro sculpture; but dirty as this was, it had suffered no damage in the flood. In the Soprintendenza itself emphasis rested on the restoration of paintings, part of which was financed by CRIA. It seemed to me that this should not be the main area of concern. In churches the flood level (as distinct from the salt level) varied from twelve inches to about four feet, and though the damp was steadily extending, almost no efforts had been made to stop it. Inside Santa Maria dei Miracoli the walls were covered with a salt deposit to about five feet, in the Madonna dell'Orto and Sant'Alvise the damp level was about eight feet, and in San Nicolò dei Mendicoli and the adjacent Oratorio delle Terese the altars and altar cloths were wringing wet. Owing to a shortage of staff there was no inspection system. I had more than once drawn attention to the fact that the very important bronze altar frontal by Roccatagliata in San Moisè and the bronze relief by Francesco di Giorgio in the Carmini had developed patches of bronze disease. As I went round the churches by boat with Eugenio Riccomini, then a junior official, later Superintendant at Parma, and now professor at the University of Messina, it was impressed on me that a policy of patching was of no use. The most valuable course would be to take one church which presented every possible problem and restore it totally. In this way alone could conservation sights be raised. The strongest candidate seemed to me to be the Madonna dell'Orto, since it presented a clear-cut structural problem that necessitated the introduction of damp courses, the damp-proofing of walls, and the replacement of sodden intonaco. It had important Trecento sculptures on the façade which required treatment and protection, and contained great paintings which either (like the Cima altarpiece) had suffered from the flood or (like the great Tintorettos) were threatened by its consequences. In making this choice I had a second point in mind, that in Venice the parish is still a social unit and that the restoration of a parish church was therefore important from a social as well as an artistic point of view. This recommendation was accepted, and the Madonna dell'Orto was restored with great success. In due course, after the Italian Art and Archives Fund was wound up, a new body, Venice in Peril, came into existence. Along with a parallel committee in America, Save Venice Inc., it has done invaluable work. From the Madonna dell'Orto it moved on to San Nicolò dei Mendicoli (which presented damp problems of special urgency) and thence to the cleaning of the Sansovino Loggetta (where the polychrome marble was restored to something approaching its original color and the bronzes were also treated) and of the Porta della Carta of the Palazzo Ducale. The protagonist in these two projects was Kenneth Hempel, working under the supervision of both Superintendents. The momentum of the program was due to Ashley Clarke, who was then living in Venice. He followed all the work and checked every detail of expenditure. Both he and I developed a warm friendship with Francesco Valcanover, the Soprintendente ai Beni Culturali in Venice, a man of great energy and imagination, who realized, as did no Florentine official, that without some measure of foreign intervention and foreign money the situation that confronted him could not conceivably be rectified.

It could be argued that the Italian cultural heritage is so rich and the problems of its preservation so complex as to constitute, in a moral sense, an international responsibility. Thinking of this kind at UNESCO led in 1968 to the creation of two international committees, one for Florence and the other for Venice. The appropriate British member of the Venice Committee would have been Ashley Clarke and the appropriate member of the Florentine Committee myself, but instead I was appointed to Venice and he to Florence. The notion of international intervention by UNESCO was unwelcome in Florence, and the committee met only once. The Venice Committee, on the other hand, continued to meet for a number of years; one was put up at an expensive hotel in Venice and sat on a little gold chair at the Fondazione Cini as UNESCO appointees gave their views on flood prevention, population problems, slum clearance, pollution, and other topics. After a time I could bear this no more, and in conjunction with the Egyptian representative, I resigned. When René Maheu, who was responsible for creating the committee, was replaced as Secretary General of UNESCO by Amadou-Mahtar M'Bow, such activity as there was petered out. On the committee I achieved only one thing, a recommendation that for the future the responsibilities of the Soprintendenza in Venice should be confined to Venice and should not extend to the *terra firma* as they then did. This was accepted, and a new Superintendency for the *terra firma* was instituted, leaving the Venetian Superintendency to cope with problems that were peculiar to Venice.

9

ART FOR
PEOPLE

EACH OF THE THREE DIRECTORS UNDER WHOM I WORKED AT THE
Victoria and Albert Museum made a personal contribution to its development. The first, Eric Maclagan, was a highly civilized man of
impeccable propriety. A distinguished scholar and an excellent linguist, he maintained, till his retirement in 1945, the elitist standards
observed by great European museums in the nineteenth and early
twentieth centuries. His successor, Leigh Ashton, was an Orientalist
who brought with him a very different sense of the function of a
museum. Cutting across old departmental boundaries, he created a
series of what were known as primary galleries, in which the greatest
works of art in all media were shown side by side. The public he
addressed was not the specialized public of the past but a postwar
public that could be expected to respond to the aesthetic message of
works of art when they were skillfully exhibited and to learn, by
observation rather than precept, the cultural lessons they spelled out.
It was a cardinal principle that objects should be so displayed as to
attract the notice of visitors whose interests lay elsewhere. In the
European museum field Leigh Ashton was a highly innovative figure,
and I count myself fortunate to have worked with him. He made a
late marriage. "Sir Leigh," warned Queen Mary, with royal prescience
when she came to the museum, "don't let it spoil your work." But it
did precisely that, and he succumbed to drink. I first noticed what
was wrong when, one day after lunch, I was arranging a wall case of
medieval objects. I was dissatisfied with it, and when Ashton came
through the gallery I asked him to put it right. "My dear, take all the
objects out, and I will do it," he replied, so all the objects were removed

from the case, and he slowly put them back in exactly the same positions they were in before. The weight of supporting him in his decline fell on my colleague Terence Hodgkinson, but despite his efforts the situation became untenable and Ashton was retired.

He was succeeded by the director of the Birmingham City Art Gallery, Trenchard Cox, a neurotically modest man of extraordinary niceness and of considerable moral weight. He was not by temperament an innovator, but he was an excellent and supportive director. He brought with him, from his years in Birmingham, a concern with provincial museums and their relation to the Victoria and Albert from which I learned much. When he retired in 1966, it was recommended that I should succeed him, but slips may occur between the cup and the lip, and it was with some relief that I learned, at the Hotel Sacher in Vienna, by telegram from the Secretary of State for Education, Anthony Crosland, of my appointment.

Of all the museum constitutions I have encountered, that of the Victoria and Albert at the time I took it over seems to me to have been the happiest. The director was nominated by the Secretary of State for Education and Science. He was a member of the staff of the Ministry of Education, and was responsible to the Secretary of State through whatever junior minister might be designated for the task. In 1967 the junior minister responsible for the arts, initially as Parliamentary Secretary and later as Minister of State, was Jennie Lee, with whom I had from the first a close working relationship and whom I continue to regard as the most principled Minister of Arts in my experience. She gave directions on policy (and very sensible directions they were) but did not interfere in their implementation. The only case I can recall in which she intervened directly was one in which injustice to some warder was involved. I believed that museums were places in which works of art were put to use, and so did she. I shared many of her social and educational convictions, and they were the more valuable in that they could be adopted as the basis of a coherent, active, outward-looking policy which affected the whole country and was accepted by the entire staff of the museum. When in 1970 she was succeeded by Lord Eccles, the situation changed. The small office responsible for the arts was expanded into a mini-ministry (staffed, like Arts Ministries in other countries, by dead-end civil servants with no promotion prospects), and the obstinate, egocentric personality of a minister with cultural pretensions impinged more heavily on the

Victoria and Albert than it did on trustee-controlled museums. Instead of trustees, the Victoria and Albert had an Advisory Council, which met four times a year, with no defined area of authority. It seemed to me from the first that any institution disposing of so large a budget should have a strong board representing public opinion and the public interest, and I did what I could to strengthen it. At the end of my seven years there it consisted (with one exception nominated by Eccles on a "You must let me do something for my friends" basis) of people for whose cleverness, judgment, and experience I felt genuine respect. Head for head, its members were of far higher quality than the body of trustees with which the museum was later saddled under the chairmanship of Lord Carrington. In practice members of the Advisory Council were treated as trustees, and I owed much to their criticism and support.

The museum constitution did, however, have one serious weakness: the maintenance of the fabric of the building was in the hands of the then Ministry of Works, the taste of whose architects was defective, and which preferred radical and wrong solutions (such as covering the mosaic floors of the large halls with concrete) to laborious yet far-sighted ones (such as spending their limited funds to train mosaicists by whom the floors could have been repaired).

The Secretary of State to whom I was answerable in my last three years at the Victoria and Albert was Mrs. Margaret Thatcher. In the week of her appointment I was lunching at the Mansion House when she was announced, and a figure dressed in vivid green came into the room. Since she was alone, I went over to speak to her. I said: "You know, Mrs. Thatcher, you are responsible for me." "I don't think so," she replied. "I think you belong to David." When I told her she was wrong, she looked up at me and said: "Anyway it's so nice for us to have someone really distinguished to deal with, instead of all those dreary schoolteachers." For a newly appointed Secretary of Education speaking to someone she had never met before, this seemed to me improvident. No future for you, my good woman, I said to myself. How wrong I was! One day I was asked to a drink party in her office before lunch. I realized why when I saw two empty bookcases lined in pale green silk. "What are you going to put in them, Secretary of State?" I asked. "I was hoping for some ceramics," she replied. She came down to the museum, where three services were arranged for her to choose from. Going round the galleries, she registered nothing;

she might indeed have been blind. But in the Conservation Department I took her to the textile conservation room, where a plastic fixative was being used. It was as though she were stuck with plastic fixative to the room. Faced with the ceramics for which she had asked, she opted, predictably, for a Chelsea service covered with pastel-colored fruit. I vividly remember a further meeting, at the annual dinner of the British Academy, where she sat at the right of the president, Isaiah Berlin, and I sat on her right. As soon as we sat down, she turned to the president and explained her difficulties in reading Karl Popper. I asked him afterwards if she really had read Popper, and if her difficulties were serious difficulties, and his answer to both questions was affirmative.

People often talk about museums as though they were just containers for the works of art they display. They are a good deal more than that. Any museum that is long-established is a highly individual organism, and the options open to it are circumscribed by its history and by the function it was originally intended to perform. The motive with which the Museum of Ornamental Art was founded was commercial. When it was opened at Marlborough House in 1852, it was directed to manufacturers and artisans, and it resulted from the application to problems of industrial design of the eclectic theory which was common in fine-arts training at the time. But the director, J. C. Robinson, was from the first determined that the museum should contain works bought for intrinsic quality, however inapplicable they might be to industry, and thanks to his genius and enthusiasm, the collection had, by 1868, when he was relegated to a less influential post, acquired an astounding number of great works. Only two years after his dismissal, it paradoxically secured the greatest works of all, when the Raphael tapestry cartoons were deposited on loan by Queen Victoria. Their significance for industry was nil, but they had an impact upon public taste that was analogous to that of the Elgin marbles rather more than a generation earlier. They established the course the museum was to follow, as an institution that paid lip service to trade through the study of techniques, ignored archaeology, and concentrated upon works of art.

It is a little difficult to guess what manufacturers and artisans can conceivably have made of the original display at Marlborough House, even if we assume, as I think we are justified in doing, that Victorian minds were more selective, more critical, and more sharply focused than our own. The purpose for which it was founded was not idealistic, it was practical. In 1835 a select committee of the House of Commons was set up to investigate the means of inculcating "principles of design among the manufacturing population of the country," and the new museum came into existence after ten years of agitated effort to establish what in effect were schools of industrial design. This was not an English problem—there were precedents in Berlin and Steglitz for museums of the kind—but what distinguished the English variant was that the policy behind it was illogical and ill defined. The point was best put by Palmerston. He visited Marlborough House in 1856, looked at vitrines piled with majolica and Palissy and Hispano-Moresque ware, and exclaimed: "Of what use is this rubbish to our manufacturers?" But when, in 1857, the museum was transferred to its new site at South Kensington, some degree of order was introduced into the display. For that, and for the whole development of the South Kensington scheme, we have to thank that inspired administrator Sir Henry Cole. The people who crossed the grass to visit the new museum in 1857 must have been even more conscious of that than modern visitors, for whom Cole's achievement is masked by Aston Webb's façade of 1909.

The fabric of the buildings illustrates very clearly the forces through which the institution evolved. The first attempt by Aston Webb to synthesize the buildings put up in the 1860s was not particularly enterprising, but by the time that it was carried out, a sense of history had supervened. The laying of the foundation stone in 1899 was one of Queen Victoria's last public appearances, and in the building as it was executed provision was made for a whole series of sculptures that gave it the character of a great national monument. As you walked along the Cromwell Road, the lantern, in the form of an imperial crown, came into view, and with it the statue of Fame set on the top. Below it, in tabernacles, were figures of Sculpture and Architecture, the two arts on which Fame was held to rest. In the middle of the lower part of the façade was a statue of Queen Victoria, and then in the center of the doorway immediately beneath stood the Prince Consort, to whose initiative after the Great Exhibition the establishment of the museum was largely due. Flanking Prince Albert were statues of Knowledge on the right and Inspiration on the left, and above them were spandrel reliefs showing the poles between which art could oscillate—above Inspiration, Beauty, and above Knowledge, Truth. Immediately over the doorway was a quotation from Sir Joshua Reynolds's *Discourses*: "The excellence of every art consists in the complete accomplishment of its purpose." It related to the fine, not the applied, arts, and so did the rest of the façade. Statues of British sculptors, painters, and architects punctuated the front, while statues of craftsmen were relegated to the obscurity of the Exhibition Road.

Within the building, for better or worse, generations of purists had been at work. The early decoration was conceived as a kind of gloss on the works of art that were exhibited. How odd the collection of ceramics must have looked when it was housed in a gallery plastered with enameled terracotta, and how odd the early medieval objects must have seemed when they were shown beneath a mosaic of the Prince Consort, on a bridge which was known as the Prince Consort's Gallery. No museum can allow itself the luxury of a rigidly archaeological approach toward its own galleries, and for that reason almost nothing of the South Court, the main decorative project of the late 1860s, was visible. But it was planned as a sort of pantheon, with mosaic portrait roundels of men connected with the arts (most of them were presidents of the Board of Trade) and mosaic figures of artists. The whole project was planned by Cole. It culminated in two frescoes by Leighton at the ends of the Court, *The Industrial Arts Applied to War* and *The Industrial Arts Applied to Peace*. Like most of the artists employed in the building, Leighton was allowed a great measure of latitude in subject matter. The *Arts of War* he set in Renaissance Italy, and the *Arts of Peace* he "transported to Greece, partly out of sympathy and partly on account of the special beauty of the Greek ceramic and jewel work." In the arch above were some frescoes executed in the 1890s, with Leighton's approval, by W. E. F. Britten, which mark the close of a long, erratic search for a means of investing High Renaissance iconography with contemporary significance. There, Britten tells us, we shall find Plutus, the little god of Wealth, playing at the side of Irene, or Industry, and next comes Fortuna, or Fortune, directing the disposal of wealth, without the conventional blindfold which would have impeded her ability to do so. I believe this is the only painted exposition of the economic theory of laissez-faire. It would be easy to ridicule this program, and many of the earlier programs too, but as director I derived much satisfaction from the sense of how confident and how convinced, how extroverted and how optimistic my predecessors were.

During the early days of Robinson's administration, medieval objects were collected with almost the same vigor as Renaissance sculptures. Only a year after the museum opened on its present site, there appeared at the Shrewsbury sale that great example of Mosan twelfth-century enameling, the Alton Towers Triptych, and it was bought for the museum for £450. I have always felt a frisson of excitement when a major sale catalogue comes onto my desk, and how much more exciting it must have been in 1861 when what arrived was the sale catalogue of the Soltikoff collection, the richest private collection ever formed of medieval works of art. Opening it, one would have come at once to the description of the twelfth-century Gloucester Candlestick, aesthetically one of the most powerful and historically one of the most suggestive objects of its time. It fetched 15,000 francs, and was bought on behalf of the museum by John Webb. The sterling equivalent of the price was £650. The most sensational price paid at the sale was for that marvelous work, the Eltenberg Reliquary; it was bought by Webb, again on behalf of the museum, for 51,000 francs— that is, about £2,000. From the records, it becomes clear that the museum owed John Webb for a great deal more than his assistance on this occasion. He made many private purchases at the Soltikoff sale, and passed them on to the museum without profit, as the money to buy them became available. In this way the Lorsch Book Cover, one of the greatest Carolingian ivory reliefs, was secured for the museum; it was bought from Webb in 1866 for £588; in 1971, when it was lent to the Council of Europe exhibition at Aachen and reunited with the companion relief from the back of the cover in the Vatican and the parts of the manuscript that survive, its value was conservatively estimated at a quarter of a million pounds, and it would be ten times higher today. The works bought from Webb in 1865 included a wing of the fifth-century Symmachi Diptych and that paragon of Gothic ivories, the Soissons Diptych. So long as Robinson remained as art referee, purchases from Webb continued on a generous scale—£4,000 in one year, £2,000 in the next. But when he left, cheeseparing began. One can still read the exasperating minutes of one of his successors, Sir Matthew Digby Wyatt: "Very pretty late-thirteenth-century altorilievo—French no doubt—worth I think from ten to fifteen pounds. Very desirable at the former price." When Sir Matthew came down in favor of a purchase, as of "four early chess-men," he did so in the hearty language that was typical of the time.

"Good," he exclaimed, "cheap, genuine. And full of life and spirits."
And the spirited chessmen were, of course, bought for the museum.
But Webb was undeterred; he continued to sell to the museum, and
indeed remained an active force through a purchasing fund set up by
his daughter, the John Webb Trust. This was the great period of
medieval buying for the museum, and nothing like it occurred again
until the time of Eric Maclagan, who was instrumental in securing
the gift in 1926 of what is now called the Andrews Diptych, the
earliest-known ivory with a Christian subject, and in buying the Ba-
silewsky Situla (an ivory holy-water bucket) from the Hermitage.

At the time the museum was making its purchases from the Soltikoff
collection, there were laid the foundations of what many people would
think of as its most distinctive group of medieval works, the English
embroideries, or *opus anglicanum*. Effectively the collection dates back
to 1863–64, with the purchase in a single year of the Syon Cope and
the Clare Chasuble. They are still two of the most important and
most beautiful surviving English vestments, and together they cost
just over £130. No comparable opportunity arose for another fifteen
years, and then, in 1889, they were joined by the second of the great
English copes, the fragmentary Jesse Cope, bought at the modest
figure of £190. This pattern of major acquisitions for low prices continued till 1955, when the finest English vestment in private hands,
the Butler-Bowden Cope, was sold to the Metropolitan Museum in
New York. It was manifestly of national importance, and an export
license was withheld. The price, £33,000, appeared a large one at the
time, though it seems less so in the perspective of today, and with
support from the National Art-Collections Fund and city companies
and the indispensable backing of the Treasury, the cope was secured
for the collection. If the Butler-Bowden Cope is excluded from the
calculation, the whole of what is incomparably the finest collection
of English medieval embroideries was assembled over one hundred
and six years at a price of just under £5,000.

Even Robinson, great man as he was, had his blind spot, and it lay
in the area of English silver. He disliked the notion of utility, and
prized silver in the ratio of its ornament. When the beautiful cup
presented by Charles II to the Lord Almoner, Archbishop Sterne,
was offered for sale to the museum in 1865, it was turned down.
"From its boldness of style and paucity of ornamentation," said Robinson, "I do not think that it can be considered as coming within

the category of works of art." Sixty years elapsed before the Sterne
Cup was actually secured for the museum at a much increased sum.
Nonetheless, in the early years of the museum's history a certain
amount of first-rate, highly ornamented silver was bought for the
collection. One of the finest pieces was the Dyneley Casket, a London
work of about 1620, which was connected with the kind of continental
art that Robinson admired. Though bought on a wrong premise—
that it was Flemish and was datable to about 1580—it was one of the
cases where Robinson's almost infallible sense of quality paid off.

The administrative structure of the museum was modified in 1909,
when a system of technical departments was introduced, and with
the creation of a Department of Metalwork, with specific responsibility
for forming a collection of English silver, the acquisition policy became
better focused. As almost always happens when that occurs, the gifts
to the department improved in quality. One of the most notable was
the late-fourteenth-century Studley Bowl, a major piece of English
medieval secular silver, which a private donor bought for the museum.
In 1925 when the Elizabethan Vyvyan Salt, of 1592, came on the
market, a third of the purchase price was supplied by the National
Art-Collections Fund and a third by another great benefactor of the
museum, the Goldsmiths' Company. The National Art-Collections
Fund were also contributors to an outstanding piece of eighteenth-
century silver, the engraved Walpole Salver, made by Paul de Lamerie
for Sir Robert Walpole from the silver of an Exchequer seal.

The oldest part of the museum collection, the India Section, went
back to the very end of the eighteenth century, when a number of
historical relics and curiosities were presented by serving officers to
the private museum of the East India Company. In 1858, when the
East India Company was wound up, the museum was taken over by
the Secretary of State for India, and though it was independent of
the museums at Marlborough House and at South Kensington, it took
on rather the same focus, concentrating on arts and crafts. Most of
the collection of Indian textiles was acquired at this time. The museum
had two contradictory roles: to foster respect for Indian craftsmanship
and to supply British manufacturers with the intelligence they needed
to compete with and defeat the Indian textile industry. When shortage
of space in Whitehall made it impossible for the museum to continue
there, it was split into three parts: the India Office Library received
the books and manuscripts, the British Museum received the objects

classified as archaeology or natural history, and everything else was placed in an Indian Museum in South Kensington. Initially it was autonomous, but in the 1930s it became in effect a department of the main museum. The relationship was consummated in 1955 by a shotgun marriage, when at short notice the lease of the India Museum premises in Prince Consort Road was ended, and such parts of the collection as could be shown were transferred to the main museum. This was described as a temporary solution, which would be in force for no more than ten years, but the loss of exhibition space was not made good. When I took over, a great part of this very rich collection was in store, where it was available to students but not to casual visitors. Despite this, the visible collections, in the Primary Gallery of Indian Art, were progressively enriched, mainly with paintings, and by far the most distinguished postwar Indian acquisition—it was effected under the directorship of Sir Trenchard Cox—was that of the jade wine cup of Shah Jehan. The cup itself had been known for a long time in various private collections, and had always been supposed to be Chinese, but when the very faint inscription on it was deciphered by an officer of the museum, Robert Skelton, it proved to have been made for Shah Jehan and to be dated 1657. So it is a central point of reference for the study of Islamic jades, as well as an artifact of the utmost elegance and of fantastically high quality.

The Department of Woodwork was one of the last of the main museum departments to get off the ground. Initially the concept of fostering design resulted in the purchase of specimens of paneling and carving that had almost no value for exhibition purposes. When contemporary furniture was bought, the objects chosen were generally selected for their opulence. The application of this test led to one fortunate anomaly, that at an extraordinarily early date, in 1858, an excellent German baroque bureau was bought for the museum; it ran counter to the general trend of taste, but it conformed to current standards of elaboration and finesse. A good deal of Renaissance furniture (some of it of real distinction) was also purchased at this time. But the first substantial change occurred in 1882, with the arrival of the Jones collection. A tailor and army clothier, John Jones was born in 1800 and by 1850 had made a fortune that enabled him to retire from business and concentrate upon collecting. When he died in 1882, his collection, then housed at 95 Piccadilly, was of the first rank. His taste drew him to the French eighteenth century, and though he occasionally strayed from the narrow path of orthodoxy—to buy masterpieces like a *Virgin and Child* of Carlo Crivelli or Isaac Oliver's magnificent miniature of the *Earl of Dorset* or, more regrettably, contemporary English narrative paintings—his collection was remarkably coherent. It had been seen to advantage only once, when it was redisplayed, with great skill, by Leigh Ashton in 1939. Unhappily that installation was not reinstated in 1946, and for the next twenty years the collection was miserably shown not far from the main entrance.

The museum had been in existence for almost forty years before it came to be accepted that the collection ought properly to include period rooms. Whether they are still necessary, at a time when so many great houses are open to the public, is a matter for debate. The collection of English furniture was at the time relatively weak. A very high proportion of the furniture in the present English primary galleries was acquired after 1930, when the Department of Woodwork was fortunate enough to be in the charge of a keeper who raised the whole level of the study of English furniture. Through many decades there was an intimate relationship between research and purchasing. One example is the superb coin cabinet made by the royal cabinetmaker William Vile for Frederick Prince of Wales in about 1750. The museum was instrumental in reintegrating the work not only of Vile but of another eighteenth-century cabinetmaker, John Channon, who in the 1730s and 1740s was the leading exponent of brass-inlaid furniture. A fine bureau cabinet by Channon was acquired in 1953 and it was followed in 1956 by a splendid library desk with ormolu mounts, which is one of the finest surviving pieces of English eighteenth-century furniture. In 1959 these were joined by an armchair by Channon, and in 1964 a magnificent mahogany cabinet with ormolu mounts and engraved brass inlay from the same workshop was secured. Together the group presented an unrivaled survey of the activity over twenty years of a great and till recently forgotten English cabinetmaker. In 1973 a French-looking commode on sale in Paris proved to have been made in London in about 1760 by an immigrant cabinetmaker, Pierre Langlois, who settled in London in the late 1750s to produce furniture in the French style at a time when it was difficult to obtain the genuine article from France. One of the things that visitors to the museum expected and indeed had the right to find there was an anthology of all that is best in English furniture.

The development of the ceramic collection had been much more consistent, in that from comparatively early times its aim had never deviated. It was to create a completely representative collection, a kind of encyclopedia of ceramic art of every kind. A great scholar, Bernard Rackham, in forty years of devoted service gave the department its present character. There was a core of masterpieces, of course, in almost every field—among the majolica which was bought at the Bernal sale in 1855 (on this occasion the museum made more than four hundred purchases); among the Limoges enamels, where the Bernal sale was once more a major source; among the French porcelain, where the Jones collection held pride of place; in the Salting bequest, which brought to the museum more majolica of the first rank, more Hispano-Moresque ware, more Venetian glass, and a rich display of Isnik pottery; and in the Buckley collection, which came to the museum in 1936 and contained over 750 pieces illustrating the whole history of glass manufacture. The principal donor of English ceramics was Lady Charlotte Schreiber. Her gift consisted of 807 pieces of English porcelain, 574 pieces of English pottery, and 444 examples of English enamels and glass. Her intention was completeness, her goal a catalogue. A recent writer declared that "to examine the great collection, displayed in serried ranks in an upper gallery of the Museum, is a labour of love," and there is some justice in that view. But it was hoped that when more space became available the Schreiber collection would eventually be shown in its entirety in a less unworthy way. The collection of Chinese ceramics was formed much later, between the two wars. There the climactic point was the acquisition in the 1930s of a large number of works from the Eumorfopoulos collection.

The Department of Textiles had rather the same reference character as the Department of Ceramics. At first it was concerned mainly with medieval and Renaissance textiles, then at the end of the nineteenth century it was widened out in the direction of Islamic and Coptic textiles, and special attention was paid to English post-medieval textiles and to textiles from the Far East. The study collection, which was extremely important for technical reasons, was increasing at the rate of about four hundred pieces a year. Historically one of the most interesting aspects of this department was its connection with William Morris. When he gave evidence to the Royal Commission of 1882, Morris declared he had used the museum "as much as any man living," and he repaid the debt by supplying the museum with advice. Sometimes it was bad advice—he tried, for example, to dissuade the museum from accepting the Jones bequest and its degrading French collections—but sometimes he was more provident, as when, in 1893, he supported the decision to buy the great carpet from the mosque at Ardabil, which was offered to the museum for what then seemed the sizable sum of £2,000. One of the works of which he specially approved was a late-fifteenth-century Tournai tapestry of the War of Troy, which was bought in 1887, and he seems also to have supported the purchase of the still more important Brussels Triumph tapestries in 1883. If he approved of the Troy tapestry, how much more enthusiastically would he have promoted the acquisition in 1963 of the far more distinguished Hunting tapestries from Chatsworth, which were made at Tournai in the second quarter of the fifteenth century, perhaps in connection with the marriage in 1445 of Henry VI and Margaret of Anjou.

Oil paintings no longer fell within the scope of the museum so far as acquisitions were concerned, but they were originally meant to do so. No sooner was the museum opened at South Kensington, in 1857, than it received the gift of the Sheepshanks collection. It was a collection of contemporary British paintings, and was intended by the donor as the nucleus of a National Gallery of British Art. Sheepshanks was a forward-looking man—he insisted that "the public, and especially the working classes, shall have the advantage of seeing the collection on Sunday afternoons," and he required that a special building should be put up to house the paintings. This wish was met so promptly that the first catalogue, with an introduction by Richard Redgrave, appeared in 1857; it made the curious claim that English subject painting in the middle of the nineteenth century was morally superior to Dutch subject painting in the seventeenth.

The terms of the Sheepshanks bequest in turn formed a pattern for the bequest in 1869 of the Reverend Alexander Dyce, which included a number of paintings as well as a very important collection of books, mainly theatrical literature, and drawings and prints. The implementation of Dyce's will was supervised by his friend John Forster, the biographer of Dickens and Landor and a friend of Browning. When Forster died in 1876, he too left his effects to the South Kensington Museum. In this case it was not the paintings that were important, though some of them are interesting, but the manuscripts and the Dickensiana. One extraneous item in the Forster bequest was a group of three little manuscript notebooks of Leonardo da Vinci, which were given to Forster by Lord Lytton, who had bought them in Vienna. There is something rather incongruous in the fact that they were so long preserved cheek by jowl with the Dickens and other manuscripts in Forster's library in Palace Gate.

The most exciting event in the field of oil paintings occurred eleven years after Forster's death. It was the arrival of a letter from Miss Isabel Constable, the painter's daughter, offering to present to the museum "some landscape sketches by J. Constable RA." The gift brought 390 drawings, oil sketches, and paintings by Constable to the museum. The full-scale sketches for the *Hay Wain* and the *Leaping Horse* were already there on loan, and became the property of the museum in 1900. Despite the presence of the Constables, the practical emphasis in the Department of Paintings lay in the areas of portrait miniatures and watercolors. Very inspiring these collections were, the miniatures headed by Holbein's *Mrs. Pemberton* and the watercolors by magnificent Cozenses and Girtins and Cotmans and by Palmers which had worldwide currency.

The most familiar criticism of museums is that they continue to make acquisitions while their basements are bulging with surplus works of art. At the Victoria and Albert that simply was not true. A number of the departments had, in addition to their primary function, a reference character. One of them was the Department of Textiles, where the study material was freely accessible and was exceptionally rich, and another was the Department of Engraving, Illustration, and Design, with its comprehensive collection of engraved ornament. But with the Department of Ceramics about 90 percent of the works held were actually on display, and with most other departments the volume of nonexhibited material that was worth looking at was very small. The exception was the India collection, the greater part of which was still stored, and would remain so until the provision of space compensating for the loss of the old India Museum enabled it to be displayed.

When I became director, I had a fairly thorough knowledge of museums in the United States, and especially of the Metropolitan Museum of Art, and this left me in no doubt that the traditional division of departments by medium and technique should be preserved. At the Metropolitan Museum a single department dealt with post-medieval sculpture, metalwork, ceramics, furniture, and textiles, and my experience of its operation suggested that this was not an efficient system. Only one structural change seemed to me to be desirable, the creation of an Oriental Department. Chinese and Japanese artifacts were distributed through the technical departments, and in hardly any case (in none indeed save the Department of Ceramics) was there a specialist on whose advice purchases could be made. It seemed to me imperative that this should be put right, and in due course an Oriental Department was created, to which holdings of the technical departments were transferred. The transfer was phased over two years. It also seemed to me essential that the India Section, which was confined to one primary gallery, should receive adequate study galleries of its own. This became possible only some years later, when the museum took over adjacent premises known as the Huxley Building. I left the museum, however, at that point, and the available space was made over by my successor, not to the Indian and Oriental study collections, as I had intended, but to the Departments of Prints and Drawings and Paintings.

Before the creation of the primary galleries in 1946, there had been a general tendency toward timid departmental purchasing. Major purchases were made, but they were the exception rather than the rule. On Saturday mornings the heads of the various departments set out on a table in the boardroom the odds and ends they wished to purchase, and purchases were sanctioned for £20 or £30 or £40. Often the objects purchased were bargains in the sense that they would have fetched three or four times as much if they had been recognized for what they were, but since they could not again be sold, that was irrelevant. They may have been worth more than was given for them but they were often nonetheless superfluous. From the standpoint of the 1960s, what was bought in the period between the wars appeared to have been less important than what slipped by—the furniture and bronzes and silver, the porcelain and vestments and tapestries sold for derisory sums, which are now for the most part in the United States. How was it possible, I used to wonder, that at a time when prices were depressed, works of high intrinsic quality and often of great historical importance were not pursued in a more energetic and decisive way?

After the war the purchasing policy of the museum became more purposive. For documentary reasons a few inexpensive objects were still acquired—especially in areas like textiles, where storage presented

15. Domenichino: *Christ Carrying the Cross* (*J. Paul Getty Museum, Malibu*)

16. Gian Lorenzo Bernini: *Neptune and Triton* (*Victoria and Albert Museum, London*)

17. Giovanni Bologna: *Samson Slaying a Philistine (Victoria and Albert Museum, London)*

18. In the director's office at the Victoria and Albert Museum, London
(*photograph by Anthony Crickmay, 1968*)

19. Donatello: *Chellini Madonna*, obverse (*Victoria and Albert Museum, London*)

20. Antico: *Meleager* (*Victoria and Albert Museum, London*)

21. Louis François Roubiliac: *George Frederick Handel* (*Victoria and Albert Museum, London*)

22. Charles Wrightsman at Palm Beach (*photograph by Cecil Beaton, 1956*)

23. Jacques-Louis David: *Antoine Laurent Lavoisier and His Wife* (*Metropolitan Museum of Art, New York, Gift of Mr. and Mrs. Charles Wrightsman*)

24. Georges de La Tour: *The Penitent Magdalen* (*Metropolitan Museum of Art, New York, Gift of Mr. and Mrs. Charles Wrightsman*)

little difficulty—but the quantity of acquisitions was drastically reduced. Unless a large sum was involved the decision in every case
was taken by the director jointly with the keeper concerned, and
purchases were made and gifts accepted only in the light of strong
conviction that the work in question really was required for the museum, and that, if it cost more than a few hundred pounds, it ought
ideally to appeal to members of the public and not just to specialists.

Two other factors contributed to a revision of purchasing policy.
The first was the introduction, at the very beginning of the war, of
export control of works of art. It started as a casual measure (works
of art were listed with jute sacking as a commodity whose export must
be stopped), but later it was rationalized under what were known as
the Waverley criteria. The heads of most departments in the Victoria
and Albert, like their counterparts in the British Museum, were appointed individually as advisers to the Board of Trade on export
licensing. There could be no objection to this practice if a uniform
standard were applied, but different advisers applied different criteria.
Before I took over (and indeed for some time afterwards) the Metalwork Department was under the control of an unregenerate keeper
who believed, in his heart of hearts, that English silver should not be
sold to foreigners. No matter if the purchaser were an American
museum with a strong and representative collection, like the Boston
Museum of Fine Arts or the Clark Art Institute, export would be
prohibited for as long as possible. It was essential that this should not
develop into a situation in which the museum incurred the hostility
of dealers or was required to buy the silver which had been blocked.
But with other departments, and especially in the contentious area of
furniture, the system worked well. A number of provincial museums
pressed that the criteria should be interpreted in such a way as to
facilitate their purchases, but the distinction between nationally important works covered by the Waverley rules and works of art that
museums would like to add to their collections was self-evident, and
it was generally accepted, both by the expert advisers and by the
Reviewing Committee on the Export of Works of Art, that the two
categories were not synonymous.

The second factor favoring major acquisitions was the level of death
duties. When works of art from heavily taxed estates were sold to
national museums, the purchase price was exempt from duty, and
they could therefore pass from private to public ownership at a rel-

atively low figure which was nonetheless advantageous to the estate. This accounted for the presence, in the tapestry court of the Victoria and Albert, of the finest medieval tapestries in England, the Hunting tapestries from Chatsworth, as well as of the thirteenth-century Syrian glass beaker known as the Luck of Edinhall, which was bought for the museum in 1959 at an agreed figure below its estimated auction value. Another work secured in this way was Isaac Oliver's *Countess of Suffolk*, one of the greatest English portrait miniatures.

If a more ambitious purchasing policy were to be pursued it was essential that there should be no duplication, in relation not only to the existing collections in the Victoria and Albert but also to those of other national museums. The principle was therefore laid down that so far as the Victoria and Albert was concerned the collections in national museums, including the Wallace Collection, should be regarded as one. A number of crass cases of duplication had occurred in other institutions in the past; one of the most conspicuous was that the National Gallery, which owned no altarpiece by Philippe de Champaigne, had bought a not quite first-rate Champaigne altarpiece when a much finer altarpiece was exhibited at the Wallace Collection. In the medieval field particularly, it was important that the collections of the Victoria and Albert and the British Museum should be looked on as complementary.

The purchasing policy of a museum is never wholly logical. It responds to the availability of potential acquisitions and to the specialized knowledge of the staff. The Victoria and Albert, however, had an overriding obligation toward British art. In sculpture this had been very well discharged. Under Maclagan the eighteenth-century collection was greatly enriched—busts by Roubiliac and Wilton were then quite inexpensive, though they cost $200,000 to $300,000 apiece today; and when I was myself in charge of sculpture it had been possible to secure perhaps the finest English eighteenth-century sculpture, the statue of Handel commissioned from Roubiliac for one of the main places of entertainment in London, Vauxhall Gardens. Over and above its interest as sculpture, it had an important place in the iconography of Handel, who was shown seated with a harp and with the score of *Alexander's Feast*. When Vauxhall Gardens closed down, the statue passed to the Sacred Music Society, and when the society was in turn wound up, it became the property of the music publisher Novello, and stood on a landing outside their London showroom. One day I read in small print in the newspaper that Novello had sold their premises in Dean Street and were moving to a smaller building. My only contact with the firm was through the then editor of the *Musical Times* and at my request he put me in touch with the board. As a result, the statue was sold to the museum. The collecting of modern English sculpture was the responsibility not of the Victoria and Albert but of the Tate Gallery, but in both collections there was a paucity of unfashionable nineteenth-century academic sculpture. This was a field where discrimination was called for, but a good many of the gaps were filled before prices began to rise.

When I first joined the museum staff, it was contrary to practice for the main departments to buy works of art less than a hundred years old. This precluded a large number of desirable purchases, and the period was first reduced to fifty and then to twenty-five years. The reason for the avoidance of current purchasing was that the basis of selection of works at the time that they were new would almost always be wrong. Only when they had matured for twenty or thirty years did the legitimacy of a purchase become evident. But it was clearly essential that the primary galleries should culminate in a twentieth-century gallery. Twentieth-century glass had been bought in small quantities but extremely well by the Department of Ceramics, and in the Department of Circulation much thought had been given to early-twentieth-century furniture and metalwork. Two of my last acquisitions as director were of a Calder wall hanging and of a very distinguished period room by Frank Lloyd Wright. The room, which was presented with extraordinary generosity by Edgar Kauffmann, had been his father's office and was complete with Wright-designed furniture. When I left the museum, it was on exhibition, but it was later dismantled and stored, and never since has it been shown.

Some members of the staff in each department were concerned, as they should properly have been, with aspects of research. But research is inhibited if it can be published only in overcrowded commercial periodicals. Before I became director I initiated, in 1965, a quarterly *Bulletin*, through which the results obtained by the museum staff could be communicated, and in 1969 this became an annual volume, the *Victoria and Albert Museum Yearbook*, issued by the Phaidon Press. In this way it was possible to direct the attention of individual members of the staff to problems which deserved investigation, and to support from the travel grant the study their research required. To take no more than a few examples, a donor bequeathed to the museum "my metal fire guard and the figures on the mantelpiece." The fire guard and figures proved to have formed part of an altar commissioned from Hubert Gerhard for the Dominican church in Augsburg. Arrangements were therefore made for the monument and the related documents to be investigated by Michael Baxandall, who produced an excellent article for the *Bulletin*. Two large sculptural complexes familiar to every visitor to the museum, an altar from Troyes and the rood screen from 's Hertogenbosch, had never been seriously studied, and successive articles on these were written by Charles Avery. The greatest piece of Indian figure sculpture in the museum, the Sanchi torso, was restudied in India by John Irwin with important original results, and another article in the same issue of the *Yearbook*, by Anthony Radcliffe, dealt with the bronze oil lamps of Riccio, one of the most notable of which is in the museum. Substantial articles were also contributed by specialists who were not members of the staff, like Hugh Honour (on Canova) and Mirella Levi d'Ancona (on Girolamo dai Libri). When I moved from the Victoria and Albert to the British Museum, both these publications and the activity they represented came to an end.

I had from the beginning been associated with the arrangement of the primary galleries, and this work continued after 1967. A revised series of Italian Renaissance galleries was opened in November 1966, and a new installation of the Early Christian Byzantine and Romanesque collections in April of the following year. An enterprising gallery of music instruments opened in the second half of 1967, and the continental eighteenth-century primary gallery (which was in the charge of the keeper of furniture and woodwork) opened in 1971. It presented practical difficulties since the terms of the gift of the Jones bequest of eighteenth-century furniture provided that it should be segregated, so the Jones collection was arranged on one side of the suite of galleries and the related material from the main collection on the other. This was followed by a good display of jewelry in a new Jewelry Gallery. In the course of 1973, agreement was reached on a new Indian Primary Gallery, but this scheme was never implemented. The most popular of the study collections in the museum was that of the Department of Ceramics. It was heavily visited despite the fact that the ceramics were shown densely in old cases, and it seemed to me that this could be remedied if one-quarter of the galleries were modernized each year. This plan was not followed up by my successor.

Acquisition and display, however, were only two of the museum's responsibilities. It was also a service institution whose efficient functioning was fundamental for a whole series of educational and other extramural activities. It housed the National Art Library, a prime center of art-historical and other research. Libraries are mysterious things; unless they are stimulated, they become torpid and slow. Their purchasing policy must be comprehensive, the registration of books must be completed in the shortest possible time, and the service they offer must be speedy and willing. Libraries work best under pressure, and the efficiency of the National Art Library could be assured only if constant pressure was applied to it by the director and the heads of the individual departments. Some years after I left a librarian was appointed whose main interest lay in research. As a result, standards slumped, and—for this the librarian was not personally responsible—the ceiling of the library fell in. A second important service area was the Slide Department. I had been asked to reorganize it by my predecessor, and I took the unpopular step of closing it for six months, so that the entire slide collection could be transferred to 35 mm slides and the filing of slides modernized. It required constant restocking and renewal, but it seemed to me in 1967 to be very well run.

A third aspect was education. In museums the term "education" means many different things. It embraces child education as well as the education of adults, and it can be directed to giving pleasure, to imparting knowledge, or to encouraging the development of visual concentration and of a discriminatory faculty. In the United States I had, over a period of years, looked carefully at the educational techniques employed in the museums that I visited. In the 1960s the most progressive museum was Chicago, where I once spent an hour watching how children were persuaded to enter that most impenetrable of great paintings, Seurat's *Grande Jatte*. They were asked questions. What day of the week was represented? Sunday, they replied. They were asked to count the curved forms, which were all women, and the straight forms, which were all men and trees. Why was the picture important? Because of its perspective. But at this point they were asked an unexpected question. How far can you see? There was silence for a moment, and then one little girl got up and, in a voice trembling with emotion, replied: "Real far." This exercise seemed to me of value;

a succession of parties of children had been persuaded to spend five or ten minutes walking about inside the painting. It is often argued that American experience is not applicable to conditions in Great Britain, but I saw no reason why the Raphael cartoons or the Constable paintings should not be treated in the same way. Over the years substantial improvements were made to the educational services, but looking back, I believe more could have been done through an innovative system of labeling. Of educational aids for schools outside London, by far the most important were not conventional color postcards (which were in the sluggish hands of the Stationery Office) but color slides, and a total of 450 was reached comparatively soon.

Still more important were touring exhibitions. It had long been recognized that there was a grave imbalance between the collections held in national museums in London and the works of art that could be studied in regional museums. Never in England was there the systematic distribution of military loot that took place in France under Napoleon, to which we owe the fact that Mantegnas that might have been in Paris are actually at Tours, and that first-rate paintings are distributed on a fairly equitable basis through the French provinces. It seemed to me incumbent on anyone in charge of one of the great national collections to give careful thought to the means by which its resources could be made more widely available. The South Kensington Museum had had a department whose sole responsibility was that of organizing circulating exhibitions. The Circulation Department indeed came into existence a couple of years before the museum. At first, exhibitions were distributed in railway vans. Their purpose was to aid exports by improving standards of design in manufacture, and they were extremely popular; the first two exhibitions are said to have attracted 800,000 visitors. The museum had circulated exhibitions ever since. In the early days of the present century the standard declined, but by the time I took over as director it had been run for some years by its keeper, Hugh Wakefield, with great enthusiasm and efficiency. In the early 1970s over seventy circulating exhibitions were available. Half of them were simple two-dimensional exhibitions designed for schools or libraries, and half were more substantial. The works they made available were increasingly important to the bodies that received them, since in a period corrupted by television no provincial museum visitor could be expected to pay recurrent visits to an unchanging permanent display.

The exhibitions covered a vast variety of subjects, but had the disadvantage that even the largest of them were comparatively small and failed for that reason to offer an in-depth experience. For that there was only one remedy—to circulate bigger, richer exhibitions. A first step was taken with a large exhibition of Chinese ceramics lent by the Mount Trust, and a second in 1971 with a major exhibition of Indian sculpture from the primary and study collections of the museum. But for the determination of the Department of Circulation and the keen support of the India Section such an exhibition would have been impossible. The sculptures were in the main freestanding, and some of them were very large. The biggest proved to weigh half a ton. But the view was taken that any exhibition of Indian sculpture must contain a quota of large works, however difficult they were to move. The catalogue not only was academically correct but tried to anticipate the kind of questions nonspecialists might ask themselves before the sculptures and to offer a framework within which the individual pieces could be seen. The subject was selected because there was for the first time in living memory a lively popular interest in Indian art. The best analysis of its appeal is that of Roger Fry. "The Indian," writes Fry, "is one of the most completely anti-rationalist civilisations that has ever existed. . . . what we should regard as gross sensuality may be to them a constituent of the highest spiritual condition, and it is not surprising therefore that their art is difficult to the Western mind in most respects." However alien it seemed to the rational intelligence of the 1930s, the evidence was that in the 1970s Indian art was something at which people wished to look. And look they did, not only in the Manchester City Art Gallery but at Bristol and Cardiff and Dorchester and Sheffield and Birmingham and Bradford.

In the seven years in which I observed its operation, the Circulation Department went from strength to strength. It developed into a kind of regional liaison group, and if, in 1973, there was a more general understanding of regional problems in national museums and of national problems in the regions, that was due to the work of this department. It was also responsible for administering the grant-in-aid that was made available by the Exchequer for purchases by regional museums. This was popularly, though mistakenly, known as the Victoria and Albert Museum Fund. In administering it, the museum was acting on behalf of the national museums as a whole, and applications for grants were immediately referred to the body to which they pertained—the British Museum, the National Gallery, or the Tate Gallery as the case might be. A good deal of the expertise was, however, supplied domestically. Before 1960, when the grant was raised to a figure of £25,000 a year, it was not a factor of much significance, and even at the higher figure, spread over the whole country it represented encouragement rather than help. In 1963–64 things started to look up, and contributions were made to a spectacularly pretty Seurat sketch for Bristol, to a small Barberini Claude bought for Cambridge, and to a Koninck for the Southampton Art Gallery. The following year the sum was doubled, but pressure on it mounted in such a fashion that four months after the beginning of the financial year there was no money left. Again, however, it had been instrumental in securing for museums throughout England a number of really notable works. In 1965–66 the sum was doubled once more, and it was at the level of £100,000 when I assumed control. Prices by then had risen, but it was possible in one year to help to buy one of Baron Gros's best portraits for Bristol, and an excellent figure painting by Guardi for Hull, and a Ferneley hunting scene for Leicester, and a Verzelini goblet for the Fitzwilliam Museum. Looking over the whole field, I felt no doubt that the range of works of art on public exhibition was greatly enriched through the action of the Fund.

The Fund was subject to the reasonable demand that 50 percent of the price of any object should be raised locally. Otherwise policy was permissive; it was based on the belief that in regional museums the only acquisitions that pay off are those that are initiated locally. The question sometimes presented itself: "Why exactly do they want that?" But in nine cases out of ten the fact that an object was wanted was a sufficient answer, and provided that the work was genuine and was on offer at a reasonable price, a grant was made. Perhaps the most exciting proposal for the acquisition of a modern work of art to which the Fund contributed was that of a Schwitters *Merzbau* for the University Gallery at Newcastle. The *Merzbau* was in fact a gift, and the money was required for its dismantling, transport, and re-erection. I am not a Schwitters addict, but the *Merzbau* is probably his most important surviving work; he can now be better seen in Newcastle than in New York.

An interest in regional museums was by no means universal among London museum directors at the time. In January 1970 I received a copy of a paper called *On View* with an article headed "Museum Muddle." It represented the reactionary, London-based thinking from which I hoped we had escaped. Museum directors, said the article, "spend their time divided between moans and groans and mutual self-congratulation." Never did they reflect on "how very recent the whole museum industry in fact is." The whole museum structure must be rationalized, the article went on, in order to "eradicate for ever those dispiriting accumulations of broken Roman pots and Aunt Maud's earrings." But great works of art absolutely must be housed in London, because it was so easily accessible and because the aims of the regional collections "had never been defined." The writer knew, however, what they should be. They were there "primarily to reflect the history and culture of the localities of Britain. They are not there to demonstrate in full the history of Seicento Italian painting or the vagaries of the French Impressionists." Let museums in London be metropolitan and let museums in the regions be provincial, was the moral of the article. That doctrine (if it can be called a doctrine) is provincial and narrow and wrong. I should add that the writer of the article was Dr. Roy Strong, and that when he succeeded me at the Victoria and Albert Museum he acquiesced in the abolition of the Circulation Department.

Almost at once I was involved in exhibition projects. The first was for an Anglo-Soviet exhibition to be opened in February by Kosygin. The proposal was made by the Russians at Christmas 1966, and the time of preparation was therefore very short. Its theme was historical—it was to illustrate relations between Britain and Russia from the late sixteenth century down to the present day, with half the contents to be provided by the Russian side and half to be raised from British sources.

Much of the finest English sixteenth- and early-seventeenth-century silver is in the Kremlin, and a representative cross section of it was made available. But as every visitor to the Kremlin knows, it is contrary to Russian practice to clean silver—this prejudice must go back to a time when abrasives were used—and the silver when it arrived was almost indistinguishable from the reproductions of it in the museum. Pressed by telegram to agree to at least some cleaning, the Russian authorities refused, so it was shown in the depressing state in which it arrived. This apart, the Russian contribution consisted principally of documents. But in England a certain amount of interesting material came to light. The Empress Catherine II had been vaccinated by an English doctor called Dimsdale, on whom she had conferred a Russian barony. The barony was retained by his descendants, and the present Baron Dimsdale proved to have a number of gifts from the Empress which could be shown. A wealth of Fabergé was also available. There was, however, one central difficulty—that only during the Napoleonic wars was there in England anything that could be construed as popular interest in Russia. For the Russians, on the other hand, the Napoleonic wars had never taken place. Hostilities with France had ended at the Treaty of Tilsit in 1807, and no material that was even marginally anti-French could be allowed into the exhibition. The head of the Russian National Archives arrived bringing with him one unlisted item that he thought would specially please us, a packet of unpublished letters from Queen Alexandra to her sister, the Tsarina. One Fabergé Easter egg caused endless trouble. It had a gold-enameled imperial monogram and was lent by Her Majesty the Queen. It must be withdrawn, the Russians said. I explained that since it belonged to the Queen this was not possible. For the opening by Kosygin, however, it was reversed so that only the white back was visible. It was reversed once more, exposing the imperial monogram, when the Queen visited the exhibition.

The opening was a bizarre occasion. A formal luncheon was given for Kosygin at the Guildhall, and the inauguration of the exhibition was scheduled for four o'clock. I left the lunch early and was taken down with a police escort to the museum to receive the guests. They were timed to arrive at the museum in ascending sequence—first the mayor and mayoress of the local borough, Kensington, then Jennie Lee, the Parliamentary Secretary, then Crosland, the Secretary of State for Education, then the Prime Minister, and finally Kosygin with his enormous suite. The mayor and mayoress were punctual, but the next to arrive was Kosygin, followed closely by the Prime Minister, who ran up the steps after him. Once inside the entrance the only situation for which I was entirely unprepared occurred when the Prime Minister said: "I think the Premier would like to use the lavatory." So the dense crowd between us and the lavatory had to be pushed aside, two policemen inspected it to see that it was free of bombs, and I then sent Kosygin down with a chief superintendent to look after him. The thought crossed my mind that the Prime Minister might want to use the lavatory as well. "Not at all," he said, "but I suppose it would be civil," and hurried down the stairs. When they

both returned, I led Kosygin to the Raphael Cartoon Court, where
the ceremony was to take place. On the far side of a rope were members
of the public, one of whom, a woman, waved at Kosygin with out-
stretched arms. He interpreted her gesture as one of protest and,
seizing her hand, did not release it till she was pulled almost off her
feet. The remainder of the opening went well, and the speeches were
translated in extenso into Russian for Soviet television. The exhibition
looked quite smart, and for the duration of its run had an undeserved
success.

A serious exhibition program slowly got into its stride. The Anglo-
Soviet exhibition was followed at the end of June by a large exhibition
of Persian miniatures, selected and arranged by a member of the staff,
Basil Robinson. It seemed to me one of the most sensitive and sheerly
beautiful exhibitions that had ever been held in the museum. This
was followed in October by an exhibition of Hungarian religious art,
in connection with which I visited Budapest. Its strength lay in paintings—they included a good many of the Danubian panels I had seen
at Esztergom thirty years before—illuminations, vestments, and
metalwork, and very opulent they looked. The ostensible purpose of
my visit to Hungary was to open relations between the British Academy in London and the Magyar Tudomanyos Akademie. I was met
at the airport by a specialist in Dante iconography, and among the
new friends I made during the journey were Klára Garas, the director
of the Széptmüvészeti Múzeum, Jolán Balogh, the historian of Mathias
Corvinus, and Miklós Boskovits, with whom I saw the fascinating
excavations of the Angevin palace beside the Danube at Visegrád. It
was also possible to work through the much overrated collection of
Italian sculpture which was collected in haste in two years in the 1890s
before the opening of the Széptmüvészeti Múzeum in 1895. The merit
of this and other Central European exhibitions was not bound up
exclusively with the quality of the works lent. They enabled warm
and lasting relationships to be built up between the beleaguered staffs
of the museums involved and the free world.

This was also true of Czechoslovakia and an exhibition called *Baroque in Bohemia*. It started in the exhilarating Dubček period, and
when I first went to Prague in connection with it the atmosphere was
one of buoyancy and hope. But by the time that it took place all this
had changed. It resulted, however, in a cordial and lasting friendship
with Jiří Kotalík, the director of the admirably run Národní Gallery,

and with members of his staff. At the Prague airport I was asked what I most wanted to see in Czechoslovakia. I replied Kroměříž (Kremsier). It was a difficult request because of the distance involved (Kroměříž is near Olmütz, almost on the Polish frontier), but I was driven there to see the late Titian *Flaying of Marsyas* under cleaning and spent a day with the restorer and the X-ray photographs. The painting has since come to London and Washington and is now accepted as one of the most profound and most emotive of Titian's late paintings. But when I was shown it, it was relatively little known. Bohemian seventeenth- and eighteenth-century painting, with its Piazzetta palette, has always seemed to me a little stodgy, but the equivalent sculpture, and especially the work of Braun, was of startlingly high quality. The best of Braun's work—the big marble figures of Virtues which stand on the terrace at Kuks and the statues carved from living rock in the park—was not transportable, but the exhibition nonetheless contrived to show what a great and underrated sculptor Braun was. In Prague there were also three fascinating exhibitions of the work of Kupka.

In 1969, on behalf of the British Council, I spent an enthralling fortnight in Japan. The purpose of the visit was to negotiate a Constable exhibition in Tokyo and Kyoto, but it afforded an occasion to see museums in Tokyo and the shrines at Kyoto and Nara. For the beauty of Japanese ceramics, I was fully prepared. Japanese sculpture, however, proved a constant surprise, in the case of bronze sculpture for its majestic scale and in the case of wooden sculpture for its expressive quality. The problem of wood statuary, wherever it is carved, is uniform, to change a tree trunk into a simulacrum of the human form, and in Kamakura sculpture, as one sees it in Kyoto, the impulse toward doing so is the same impulse that inspired the wood sculptures of Donatello. When I arrived in Tokyo an exhibition of Rembrandts, from the German Democratic Republic and the U.S.S.R., was on show in the National Museum. It was very popular, and when I went there I was puzzled by the effect made by the Rembrandts, which seemed overemotional in the impassive context of Japanese art, and by the lack of contact between the Japanese public, milling about in the galleries, and the works of art they had queued up to see. But when a fortnight later I returned to the National Museum for an exhibition of copies of the burned Horyuji frescoes, the Japanese visitors were looking respectfully at the frescoes, and the figures in the frescoes seemed to be looking back.

In the 1970s a great deal of pioneering work was being done in the Victoria and Albert on Victorian art and artifacts. This led, after four years of work (not on my side but on that of the specialists concerned), to a large exhibition of Victorian church art, which opened in December 1971. My own interest in this topic was of recent growth. I had been brought up to despise Comper at Downside and Butterfield at Balliol, and scorn cannot become admiration overnight. Nonetheless it seemed to me that in an anti-ritualist period it would be interesting to examine the Victorian thirst for ritual, and this the exhibition did.

One of the most satisfactory exhibitions was of jade; it was organized by the Oriental Ceramic Society, with which the museum had had a long relationship. It opened in June 1971 and I spoke on the same event at a dinner to celebrate the fiftieth anniversary of the founding of the society:

> Generally I speak as a specialist to amateurs. Tonight the position is reversed; I am an amateur addressing a formidable body of professionals. When I was invited by your president to propose the toast of this society, I accepted with great diffidence. I accepted for two reasons, first that my father was a founder member of the society, one of the little group that met to form it at the Winkworths' house in January fifty years ago. I still indeed cohabit with two large, coarse vases which were discussed at one of the first meetings. Teas with Eumorfopoulos, visits to Oscar Raphael, formed part of the fabric of my childhood, and when I looked down the list of the first members, there was scarcely one whose physical presence I did not recall. Those experiences did not, I am ashamed to say, produce an Orientalist, but they left me with a kind of homing instinct, so that today I catch myself sneaking out of the National Gallery of Art to visit the Freer Gallery or taking time off from the Frick Collection to visit Asia House, in search of works of art which address one in the timeless language of color and texture and form. One suspects that the founder members would feel frank incredulity could they be here tonight. There were twelve members then; there are nine hundred now. And what started as a tentative provincial body has become a name to conjure with wherever Far Eastern ceramics are valued and displayed.
>
> What was envisaged from the first was a partnership between collectors and museums, and speaking from the museum side of the fence, I must say frankly that museums in this country have derived

incomparable benefits from that. In no area of collecting, none at all, has there been greater public spirit or a more general determination that the aesthetic enjoyment which collectors derive from their possessions should be widely shared.

There were, naturally, other exhibitions, many of them devoted to contemporary design and contemporary artifacts. The single criterion applied was that exhibitions should be of merit in themselves, and should not be directed solely at increasing attendances at the museum. Some of them, however, did precisely this, especially an exhibition of contemporary dresses chosen by Cecil Beaton. It originated in 1969 when I was in New York and found myself after dinner sitting next to Cecil. It was a moment when Balenciaga dresses were in vogue, and looking round the room, I said to him I could not understand why clothes were not collected by museums by the same criteria of quality as other works of art. He volunteered to form a collection on our behalf and he did so with spectacular results, producing wonderful dresses from Mrs. Loel Guinness, and Pauline de Rothschild, and Jayne Wrightsman. Lee Radziwill complained after his visit that she had nothing left to wear. To my mind the prettiest thing in the exhibition was a hat of flamingo feathers from Sibyl Cholmondeley. The only problem from my standpoint was that of resisting all the ladies who wished to be but were not included in the exhibition, which was in a silver tent with twenty-four revolving turntables. More dresses were accepted than could be shown in a first installment. Only Lord Mountbatten protested angrily at the omission from the first showing of his wife's wedding dress.

The museum had had for many years a declared responsibility for the theater and for theatrical design, and this was covered from time to time by exhibitions. One of them was devoted to Gordon Craig (about whose talent I feel some reserve). It was opened by John Gielgud, and since I received a number of letters from Craig's many illegitimate sons who wished to be present at the opening, only two chairs were placed on the platform, one for Gielgud and the other for myself. Of much greater interest was a survey of the work of Appia, whose talent seems to me far superior to Craig's (his productions were conceived on a large scale, not for the small stages to which Craig was confined). There was much to be learned from it, though there was no evidence at the time that its lesson had been taken seriously.

I still believe that any opera house which, through indigence or from some other motive, returned to Appia's stagecraft would earn a reputation for contemporaneity. I was at the time a director of the Royal Opera House at Covent Garden, and its centenary was celebrated with a large and very successful retrospective exhibition.

I was convinced that general museums must serve a single constituency of culture that involves music and literature as well as art, and provision was therefore made for occasional musical and literary exhibitions. The cult of Berlioz had for many years been fostered more carefully in England than in France, and when it became evident that there would be no substantial French tribute on the centenary of his death in 1969, plans were made for a large exhibition under the title *Berlioz and the Romantic Imagination*. It was a highly evocative display with sophisticated sound equipment, conceived by a number of Berlioz specialists headed by David Cairns. It was opened by Georges Auric on behalf of the Paris Opéra—it seemed strange that the staid old gentleman who arrived from Paris had been a member of Les Six and a lightweight composer of some distinction—and by Jacques Barzun from Columbia University. The first of the large literary exhibitions dealt with Dickens, the centenary of whose death fell in 1970. I promoted it for three reasons—first that a vast quantity of Dickens material had been bequeathed to the museum by his first biographer, John Forster, second that my mother had written a standard life of Dickens and that I therefore knew his novels well, and third that the depiction of social conscience in nineteenth-century England deserved closer study than it had received. The exhibition was organized by Graham Reynolds and seemed to me an unqualified success. The second literary exhibition was devoted to Byron. It was generously supported by the descendant of his publisher, Jock Murray, but I had left the museum by the time that it took place and the result, though informative, had a Madame Tussaud-like quality I did not find congenial.

In size and intrinsic importance one exhibition, *The Age of Neo-Classicism*, surpassed all the rest. It was undertaken on the invitation of the Council of Europe, and was the fourteenth of a great series of exhibitions which had opened in Brussels in 1954 with the exhibition *Humanism in Europe* and had continued with *Romanticism* in London, *The Triumph of Mannerism* at Amsterdam, *The Age of Rococo* in Munich, *Byzantine Art* in Athens, *Charlemagne* at Aachen, *Sources of Twentieth-*

Century Art in Paris, and *Gothic Art* in Vienna. The invitation reached me in 1970, and I accepted it on condition that Gabriel White, who had recently retired as director of art at the Arts Council, should be appointed as director. We had worked closely together for some years, and I thought him then, as I still do today, the wisest and ablest exhibition organizer I had ever known. David Roell, the director of the Rijksmuseum, once told me that when he was searching for a title for the Council of Europe Mannerist exhibition in Holland, he opened a newspaper with an article headed "The Triumph of Stupidity" and decided to name his exhibition *The Triumph of Mannerism*. With the neo-classical exhibition the title was of greater consequence, since it would define the scope and purpose of the whole display. I felt strongly that the exhibition should deal not with the academic subject of neo-classical style but with the moral and philosophical ideas and the political events that lent it force, and it was therefore entitled *The Age of Neo-Classicism*. Lord Eccles had the effrontery to tell me publicly I should have called it "Napoleon and His Marshals or something like that," but it was not that sort of exhibition. I have always believed in cleverness, and the steering committee appointed for the exhibition was an exceptionally clever one. It included Isaiah Berlin, and Kenneth Clark, and Roger Mynors, and Mario Praz, and Anthony Blunt, and Edgar Wind, in addition to specialists like Francis Haskell and Hugh Honour and Robert Rosenblum. Some of the elements were not easily compatible. Blunt told me he would not have agreed to serve on the committee if he had known that it included Edgar Wind, but since Wind was responsible for the only intelligent articles that had ever been written on English eighteenth-century portraiture, I did not take his objection seriously.

The defect of some of the earlier Council of Europe exhibitions had been that they were planned by a national committee to which a few foreigners were added at a late stage. This had prejudiced *The Age of Rococo* in Munich, which was a German exhibition with minimal French participation. The French component would be specially important for a neo-classical exhibition, and before taking any other step Gabriel White and I went over to Paris to have preliminary conversations with my friend Michel Laclotte, who gave the exhibition wholehearted support. The display was from the first planned internationally, and French, German, and Italian representatives were associated with it from a time when its design was still unformed and malleable. I cannot recall any exhibition in which so many minds were actively engaged. Nothing could have exceeded the generosity of the Louvre and of provincial museums in France, which volunteered to lend some of the largest and least portable of the great masterpieces of French painting, such as the Ingres *Dream of Ossian* from Montauban and the Girodet *Riots in Cairo* from Versailles. Over and above the member states of the Council of Europe there were three sources which made notable contributions to the exhibition. The first was the Vatican, which contributed the heaviest single work, a great table of bronze and Egyptian granite, celebrating events in the pontificate of Pius VI, which is generally regarded as the finest piece of late-eighteenth-century Roman furniture. The second was the German Democratic Republic, whose contribution was indispensable if the work of Schinkel was adequately to be shown. We had no diplomatic relations with East Germany at the time, but I visited East Berlin and secured a number of important loans from the Altes Museum, Potsdam, and other sources. Third was the United States, headed by loans of furniture from the Metropolitan Museum and a group of Jefferson drawings from the University of Virginia.

The subject of the exhibition was historically one of the most stirring and intellectually one of the most adventurous periods in our past, and the exhibition had therefore to be constructed round ideas and to reach its climax in the years in which Neo-Classicism became first a revolutionary and then an official style. Moreover, Neo-Classicism still affected our environment, so architecture, and particularly town planning, had to be more fully treated than in any previous exhibition. Its concepts impinged on daily life, in interior decoration, furniture, and the applied arts, and it was agreed that these should be the subject of a separate interrelated exhibition.

People nowadays talk about "blockbuster exhibitions." At the time that it took place *The Age of Neo-Classicism* was in fact the largest art exhibition organized since the last war. It contained 1,900 separate objects, and it did so because this was the minimum with which justice could be done to one of the greatest creative periods in European art. The paintings and sculpture and a section dealing with theatrical design were displayed at the Royal Academy, the Diploma Gallery on the second floor of Burlington House housed the section on architecture, the decorative arts were shown at the Victoria and Albert Museum, and a further exhibition was arranged at Osterley, an out-station of the Victoria and Albert and the most important Adam house within easy reach of central London. The selection of applied arts was supervised by a very strong committee, under the chairmanship of Francis Watson, the director of the Wallace Collection, which included among its members Svend Erickson of Copenhagen and Alvar Gonzáles-Palacios, who was responsible for the selection of the Italian neo-classical furniture, and the architectural committee was headed by Wend von Kalnein. At an early stage I found it necessary to replace two of the original committee members. One of them was Roy Strong, who demanded an independent budget and personal recognition for everything that he arranged. When Strong told me that there was no such thing as neo-classical stage design, he was succeeded by Manfred Boetzkes of the Institut für Theaterwissenschaft at Cologne. The exhibition and its mammoth catalogue were the result of months of devoted and disinterested work by a group of extremely gifted individuals. On September 7, 1972, the exhibition was opened by the Prime Minister.

In 1968, a year after I took over the Victoria and Albert, I became a member of the Arts Council and chairman of its Art Panel. The Art Panel was concerned principally with contemporary art. Its members were in large part critics and artists; they included in the five years in which I served Lawrence Gowing, David Sylvester, Alan Bowness, Richard Hamilton, Bryan Robertson, Sheridan Dufferin, Theo Crosby, and David Hockney. Art historians sometimes refer to artists of the past as "hands." What hand is this by? they ask. I found it stimulating to be confronted by live artists, who in addition to hands were endowed with brains, convictions, and principles. I had always believed that for the art historian contact with live art was a prophylactic against academicism, and so it proved. There were two subcommittees of the panel dealing with the allocation of grants and with exhibitions, and thanks to the wise guidance of the permanent staff (headed first by Gabriel White and then by Robin Campbell, himself an artist, whom I had first known in 1937 in Berlin and for whose highly principled character I had the warmest admiration) no disagreement in either area arose. The sums available for grants were widely and fairly distributed, with a bias toward experiment, and the establishment of the Serpentine Gallery in Kensington Gardens provided young artists with a forum for the exhibition of their work.

For upwards of twenty years there had been agitation for a large-scale gallery in London for public exhibitions, and in the late 1950s the London County Council agreed to build a substantial exhibition gallery that would be rented to the Arts Council. The site selected was on the south bank of the Thames near the Royal Festival Hall. The Hayward Gallery was an ugly, ill-designed building that was difficult of access for the public and offered a succession of ungrateful exhibition spaces. From the time of its inauguration in 1972 its exhibition policy was determined by the Arts Council Art Department and by the Art Panel. What artists could dominate its awkward rooms was anybody's guess. Matisse naturally did so (in a splendid initial exhibition organized by Robin Campbell), and so did Anthony Caro and Rothko and Bridget Riley. At the Riley exhibition the guards demanded eyeshades, complaining of vertigo. Claude unexpectedly stood up to the clinical conditions of the gallery with great resilience, and so did Millet, the subject of a formidable exhibition planned by Robert Herbert. One of the most popular painting exhibitions held there was devoted to Burne-Jones. I, almost alone, had predicted its success. I had long believed Burne-Jones to be a much greater painter than Rossetti or Millais or Ford Madox Brown. Soon after I joined the staff of the Victoria and Albert I had gone with Mrs. Mackail, Burne-Jones's daughter, round the Burne-Jones collection there, and I had looked, as intently as manners allowed, at the fine Burne-Joneses in Lady Horner's dining room in Fitzharding Street. A cartoon for a stained-glass window by Burne-Jones of the Good Shepherd had been acquired not long before by the Victoria and Albert, and the figure, with its silky, over-shampooed hair, its sensual lips, and its glassy, introspective eyes, corresponded very closely with the models for male fashions shown in the window of Harrods in the Brompton Road. If this was what the young wanted to look like, they would, it seemed to me, be ripe for Burne-Jones. This proved to be the case.

One of the most gratifying exhibitions was *Frescoes from Florence*, which had already been shown in New York at the Metropolitan Museum. At the Hayward Gallery it was entrusted to an Italian designer of great distinction, Carlo Scarpa, and now that its components have been put back where they belong, in the Capponi Chapel in Santa Felicita in Florence and the Museo dell'Opera di Santa Croce and elsewhere, I still see them as they were shown by Scarpa at the Hayward Gallery.

It had long been planned to hold an exhibition called *Art in Revo-*

lution, which would illustrate first the use of visual propaganda in the early stages of the Russian Revolution and second the work of Tatlin and Malevitch and other progressive Russian artists, which was then officially proscribed. At quite a late stage relations with Moscow improved, and much of the space had therefore to be given over to worthless Soviet loans, which embarrassed even the officials who accompanied them. Despite my urging, one of them, a sculpture called *Fly, Little Swallow*, was not even unpacked.

I had for long been an addict of Pop Art—Leo Castelli said that this was an extension of my interest in Sienese fifteenth-century painting—and a large Pop Art exhibition was held at the Hayward Gallery. There was a dichotomy between the setting and the contents of the exhibition—squashed beer cans do not look their best when shown formally in vitrines—and the result seemed to me to be more rigid and museum-like than it should properly have been. Inevitably there were controversies. Paying a pre-inaugural visit to an exhibition of the work of Southern California artists, I was startled to be told that a disaster had occurred; the fish had died. What fish? I asked. Catfish, they replied, and sure enough one of the exhibits was a large metal tank for the display of catfish, which were in due course to be electrocuted and eaten by young British artists. The catfish were easily replaced, but their electrocution, on humanitarian grounds, had to be stopped, so they swam about purposelessly in their tank for the duration of the exhibition.

The spaces in the Hayward Gallery lent themselves more readily to the showing of other objects than paintings. I remember with special pleasure an exhibition of Near Eastern rugs arranged with exemplary skill by David Sylvester, and an American bicentennial exhibition with the title *Sacred Circles* covering two millennia of North American Indian artifacts, selected with great visual acumen by a specialist I had first known as a graduate student at Yale twenty years before, Ralph T. Coe. But the greatest source of pleasure in my association with the Arts Council arose not from its exhibitions, fine as many of these were, but from repeated contacts with its chairman, Arnold Goodman, to whose mixture of principle and pragmatism the success of the Council at that time was so largely due.

When my period at the Arts Council ended, I was invited by Lord Drogheda to become a director of the Royal Opera House at Covent Garden. I served on the board, under his chairmanship and that of his successor, Claus Moser, from January 1971 till December 1976. The board was an extremely strong one—among its members were Lionel Robbins, Arnold Goodman, and John Sainsbury—and performances were monitored by two subcommittees, one dealing with opera under the admirable chairmanship of Burnet Pavitt and the other, under Mark Bonham-Carter, with ballet. My own interests lay in opera rather than ballet, and I became a member of the Opera Subcommittee. Both subcommittees had the dual task of laying down the parameters of policy and of representing informed public opinion as a kind of opera house users' association. Each new production or revival was discussed frankly and critically as it occurred with the general administrator, John Tooley, and sometimes with the musical director, Colin Davis.

At the close of 1970 a great period in the history of the opera house was at an end. Its success had been due first to Garrett Drogheda, who exercised farsighted, authoritative, and meticulous control over the opera house and its activities, and then to Georg Solti, who, with a series of often superlative performances, transformed it from a provincial opera house, which occasionally gave remarkable performances, into an international house of the first rank. It was a difficult succession, and more than once when I was a member of the board I found myself wishing that Solti's successor had been a conductor with greater experience of the operatic repertory than Colin Davis. It seemed to me hazardous that a new *Ring* should be entrusted to a conductor who had never directed it before. There were creditable performances (especially of *La Clemenza di Tito*), but the ratio of second-rate performances manifestly was too high. The Royal Opera was in competition with the English National Opera at the Coliseum, and in the last three years that I was on the board I had the sense that public opinion was sliding toward the Coliseum, where the repertory was more enterprising, policy was less elitist, and the official subsidy seemed to be more wisely used.

Opera is a mysterious, highly irrational art form, and the success of any new production is determined by the quality of the conductor and the singers on the one hand and on that of the producer and designer on the other. The staple of the Covent Garden repertory was a number of very distinguished, long-lasting productions by Luchino Visconti and Franco Zeffirelli commissioned by John Tooley's predecessor, David Webster. Zeffirelli's productions had been expensive, but they were successful (with *Lucia di Lammermoor* and *Falstaff* and *Tosca* miraculously so), and they retained their freshness each time they were revived. They established the appropriate style context of each work, and their rich, broadly realistic detail commended them to people who were only fairly musical. The productions of Visconti were more erratic. At their best, in *Don Carlo*, they were definitive. But Visconti could not be relied on to resist the sin, one to which so many modern operatic producers are prone, of imposing a false style on some repertory work. From a purely visual standpoint the result in a black-and-white *Traviata* and an *art nouveau Rosenkavalier* was tasteful and amusing, but it was inimical to the nature of both operas as works of art. No further productions of the quality of Zeffirelli's and Visconti's were commissioned in the six years I was on the board.

The first thing I learned at Covent Garden was that there is a substantial difference between unified productions springing from one mind (as Zeffirelli's and Visconti's did) and productions in which the producer nominates a tame designer of his choice. The production team of Peter Hall and John Bury, for example, yielded poor results in London as it did also in New York. The second thing was the importance of preventing conductors from meddling in production and design. Davis was sometimes guilty of doing so, and so was Solti, who turned down some good designs by Koltai for a new *Carmen*. There had in the past been an ineffective design subcommittee at Covent Garden, but I did not think that this could be usefully revived. The general administrator was directly responsible for what went on on the stage, and the running of the opera house would have been impossible if he had been tied down by a design committee insisting that the interior of Don Pasquale's house should not look like a hotel in California. Supervision of design would, I concluded, become feasible only if a new post were created, whose occupant would be responsible for determining, jointly with a committee, the type of production that was required and for selecting, on the basis of a broad knowledge of stage design at the present time and in the past, an artist by whom it could be executed. Had such a post existed, the opera house would have been spared atrocious and unpractical productions of *Nabucco* and *Tannhäuser* and *Don Giovanni* and *Ariadne auf Naxos*. As one ugly new production followed another, one recalled with envy the sense of historicity that had inspired the great operatic productions of Nicola Benois in the 1950s and 1960s in Milan. With the formal appointment of that contentious figure Götz Friedrich as a regular producer at the Royal Opera House, any such solution became impossible, and the principal achievement of the first half of the 1970s was a new *Ring*, with Friedrich as producer, which contained some exciting scenic effects, but at many key points ran counter to Wagner's intentions. In fairness it should be added that nowadays operatic productions elsewhere are sometimes even worse. I have since seen a *Rigoletto* in Florence (Corbelli) in which Gilda, shut up in a little white house like a villa at Boca Raton, represented the soul of Rigoletto; a *Fliegende Holländer* in New York (Ponnelle) in which the narrative was interpreted as the sleeping Steersman's dream; a *Tosca* in Florence (Miller), fileted of its religious element, in which Tosca emptied the contents of a filing cabinet over Scarpia's body; a *Guglielmo Tell* in Milan (Ronconi) in which the stage was blocked with wooden choir stalls and the action, in a tiny space in the center, was dwarfed by a film of Swiss mountain scenery; a *Boris Godunov* in Florence (Frigerio) in which the Pretender, in the inn scene, had to escape from a platform without walls; and a *Peter Grimes* (Ponnelle) in which the indoor scenes were played against a curtain of marshland and the body of the dead apprentice was carried in by Grimes as the curtain fell. All this is vandalism, not legitimate reinterpretation.

It is often argued in the press that national opera houses have a duty to sponsor or commission new operas. Their obligation to contemporary opera is self-evident, and at Covent Garden, in relation both to Benjamin Britten and to Michael Tippett, it was well discharged. Both in London and New York, Britten's operas speak to a vast public. The appeal of Tippett's operas is more restricted, owing to the weakness of their libretti, but this was fortunately no deterrent to Colin Davis, who seemed to understand whatever it might be that Tippett was endeavoring to say. Walton's dull *Troilus and Cressida* was, rather grudgingly, revived; by some unfortunate miscalculation the spotlight turned on the composer in the director's box at the end was green, so that he looked like Banquo's ghost. John Tooley had an imaginative plan for commissioning collaborative operas, in which foreign composers would be furnished with libretti by English dramatists. The only commission to get off the ground had a libretto by Edward Bond and music by Hans Werner Henze. It started life as an opera on that treacherous subject King Edward II and ended as a pacifist manifesto called *The River*. It was an impressive work of great complexity, and to my mind, though not to that of the general public or most of the board members, it did credit to the opera house. But how much less expensive it would have been to put on Henze's *Prinz von Homburg*, a little-known opera of proved viability.

At board meetings I sat opposite the secretary, a temporizing civil servant called Robert Armstrong. Little did I anticipate the harm that he would later do or the notoriety that he would earn in my own field.

THE MOTHER OF MUSEUMS

10

AT CHRISTMAS 1972 I WENT, AS I HAD OFTEN DONE BEFORE, TO A party at the Department of Education and Science. When I arrived, I was taken aside by the Permanent Secretary, Sir William Pile, who said that he had that morning received a letter soliciting his advice on the directorship of the British Museum, from which Sir John Wolfenden would be retiring in twelve months' time. In reply he had recommended that I be appointed. This was a situation I had not envisaged. The idea of exchanging a museum I understood for one covering areas in which I had no special competence was disconcerting, and I asked Pile to inform the chairman of the British Museum trustees that in no circumstances would I accept the appointment. In the spring I received two more informal proposals, which I again turned down. I thought at this point that I was safe from further pressure, but in the summer, at the annual dinner of the British Academy, I found myself seated next to Lord Boyd, a long-standing trustee of the museum. Halfway through the meal he gave me a list of the candidates being considered for the post. It was so weak that I agreed to reconsider my decision. Next morning at ten o'clock the chairman of the trustees, Humphrey Trevelyan, and Alan Boyd came down to my office and offered me the post, promising their support in modernizing the museum and its procedures. I asked for a week to think over the proposal, and at the end of the week I accepted it. I insisted only on one condition, that I should continue to live in my own house in Bedford Gardens and not in the director's rather forbidding house in the museum compound.

It is always difficult to reconstruct why, at some turning point in life, one reached the decision that one did. From my standpoint the move involved a very real sacrifice. After thirty-five years at the Victoria and Albert I felt a sense of vicarious ownership of parts of the collection and personal affection for many members of a clever and unfailingly cooperative staff. At the British Museum I might feel pride in the post and the scale of the collections, but they would (the Department of Prints and Drawings apart) be alien to my true areas of concern. I would be exchanging a flexible, modern museum for an inbred institution where staff problems were of notorious difficulty. Nonetheless, I saw no responsible alternative but to accept. Three considerations were uppermost in my mind. The first was my admiration for Trevelyan, a dynamic man of great personal courage with a long record of public service, who recognized that fundamental changes were required. The second was the fact that the museum had been separated from the library. The separation was administrative only. The British Library retained its reading rooms, its stacks, and the gallery space it previously occupied, but it had an independent staff, an independent chairman, and an independent board. In the future the museum would have to function not as a group of scholarly departments ranged round a library but as a museum in the modern sense. The third consideration (and I am embarrassed to admit it) was curiosity. The British Museum was an inward-looking institution, and again and again in Bloomsbury one had wondered exactly what went on behind that imposing Ionic façade.

No sooner was my appointment to the British Museum announced on May 15 than I received a letter sent up by hand from the National Portrait Gallery to my house in Bedford Gardens. It was from Roy Strong, who wanted to know whether he dared think of applying for the vacant directorship of the Victoria and Albert. When he was a child, he said, his mother had had just enough money to give him the fare to spend the day there with a packet of sandwiches. He was anxious, he explained, that his interest in the post should be concealed from the chairman of his own trustees. I answered that the appointment was not in my hands, and that he was clearly free to apply for it if he so wished. I had another letter from him asking advice on a number of possible referees; I did not reply. In the middle of September he was appointed director by a Civil Service board. He wrote to give me "the amazing news. I feel numbed and overwhelmed but desperately happy because one feels it is the right thing to happen at the right time." It soon transpired, however, that it was not the right thing or the right time at all. My devoted and extremely able secretary, who had also worked with my predecessor, was cursorily dismissed, and Dr. Strong's own secretary came down to announce that my office would be redecorated by Supertheatricals Ltd. When asked why this was necessary, she replied: "Because Dr. Strong will be receiving members of the aristocracy." This was the beginning of a thirteen-year regime that reduced the museum and its staff to a level from which it will not recover for many years.

The tone of the letters of congratulation that started to pour in differed from those I had received at the Victoria and Albert. Many expressed satisfaction at the appointment of a professional director, but most were based on the belief that the museum needed reform. "No one," said Bernard Ashmole, "could be better fitted to be at the helm at this most critical moment." "The British Museum," wrote one correspondent, "is in great good luck to have you willing to take on such a tremendous job." "Your decision will give hope to all those who were distressed by the state of affairs in the British Museum," said another. "The whole archaeological and art-historical world is delighted and deeply grateful to you for accepting this post." The most perceptive letter came from my old mentor Dom David Knowles: "The British Museum and the National Gallery are, I suppose, the twin summits of your profession in this country, and of the two the British Museum certainly demands a greater and more varied set of qualities than the other, though I am not sure you might not have chosen the Gallery had the choice been given. But at the British Museum you certainly have the challenge of a great national institution that has not been immune from justified criticism in the recent past." An indiscreet letter came from the dean of medievalists, Joan Evans: "I am not sure that I congratulate you, but I do very warmly congratulate the British Museum. You will find it in the most frightful mess, as I am sure you are well aware. I was a Trustee from 1959 till 1967. When I began it was the old Board of Trustees, mostly over eighty, with that horrid Archbishop Fisher in the Chair. Lord Valentia and his son-in-law, our nice Thompson, who were Harleian and Cottonian Trustees, and I were kept waiting in the Ante-room until business was over, seething with rage. We were then admitted and the Council's decisions reported to us. You will find there was then quite a reasonable Board of Trustees under the admirable chairmanship of Lord Radcliffe. Eccles had not the distinction of Radcliffe, but did get things done. I have heard about the British Museum all my life and can even remember Wollaston Franks. The best Director, I would say, since him was George Hill." It was encouraging to feel not only that one enjoyed the support of many well-wishers but that there was a widespread, if inchoate, understanding of the difficulties of the job.

At the time I accepted the directorship I suffered from one especially serious liability: I knew nothing at first hand of the Near and Middle East. So I accepted with great enthusiasm and some relief a suggestion of the Wrightsmans that we should visit Iran in September 1975. There was nothing at the time to suggest that in the foreseeable future the Iranian frontier would become impassable. I had met the Shahbanah in London—she was the only royalty in the world with whom one could discuss the music of Stockhausen—and in Iran iconic photographs of her and of the Shahanshah were displayed in every shop. From Teheran we flew down to Shiraz, spending two days at Persepolis, and four nights in Isfahan, and a day driving to Passagardae and Naq-i-Rustam. This was a mind-opening journey. Apart from the intense visual pleasure that it afforded, to see the Persian wars not from the standpoint of Herodotus but from the Persian side alters one's view of history. I have always regretted that it was not possible to repeat or extend this extraordinary experience.

The omens when I took over my new post on January 2, 1974, could not have been worse. The Conservative government was on its last legs. Its policies had been divisive from the start, and had led not simply to industrial opposition, but to a universal lethargy which was pervasive and in the long term more serious. As the result of a successful miners' strike, heat and light were rationed and a three-day working week had been imposed. The three-day week was accepted with depressing docility, and a number of commodities were slowly disappearing from the shops. At four o'clock the public poured out of the museum—I could see them from the window of my office hurrying down the steps—and in the offices the lights went on and off in a seemingly capricious way. On two days a week, Thursdays and Fridays, there was no lighting in the offices at all, so, like the rest of the staff, I was forced to leave at dusk.

One of the measures imposed by the Heath government provided for admission charges at the national museums. This seemed to me ill-advised, but per se to involve no issue of principle. The resistance it aroused was due in the main to the intransigence of the Minister of Arts, to whom the term "consultation" was unknown, and to the ham-fistedness of his staff. I had had difficulty over this at the Victoria and Albert, in relation not to the main museum but to the Bethnal Green Museum, which had been created to offer educational facilities in a deprived area; I saw no reason why children should be expected to pay even a small sum to visit a museum they did not particularly wish to see. The British Museum trustees had agreed to impose an admission charge, and it was inaugurated on my first day in the museum. The weather was cold, and when I went round to the main entrance to see what was going on, I found that the dispensers for the tickets had been attached to the backs of the columns in the open air. The rolls of tickets were locked up in the museum, so at each dispenser there was a queue of freezing visitors. I arranged for their admission without charge till the tickets turned up. This idiotic procedure continued till March, when the government collapsed. It was very agreeable, at the Hartwells' election party, to see top politicians confronted by well-deserved defeat.

As director one had a heavy bunch of keys, like a jailer, which were needed to unlock even the lavatory, and I found the members of the staff, who spent their time writing letters to one another as though in a government office at the end of the last century, far more congenial than I had expected. The whole building gave the impression of being smothered with paper—minutes of working parties and subcommittees, redrafts of minutes, endless memoranda. In the drawers under two ugly bookcases in the director's office were directorial papers dating back to the 1930s. There seemed no point in sorting through them, since none of my predecessors—not Wolfenden, nor Francis, nor Kendrick, nor Forsdyke, nor Hill—had attempted to do so, so I had the bookcases and their contents removed and imported a better-looking Regency bookcase in their place.

I started with three advantages. The first was that my predecessor, Sir John Wolfenden, spared no pains to introduce me to the administrative background of the institution. A professional administrator, he had been successively headmaster of Uppingham and Shrewsbury and vice-chancellor of Reading University. When conversation with him or his wife ran dry, one could discuss the merits and demerits of the many official houses in which they had lived. He was tolerated but not liked by the heads of the museum departments, who complained that his office was like a headmaster's study, and he was disliked by his personal staff, especially by his secretary, Enid Roberts, who became my secretary and friend. The second was the conduct of Trevelyan, who mistrusted Wolfenden, and worked regularly in his own office along the corridor. When I arrived, he assured me that he would discontinue doing this but would be available on the telephone at any time. I did not at first suppose that he could break the habit of interference, but he was as good as his word and left me on my own. The third was the presence of an extremely talented deputy director, Maysie Webb. She not only was a woman of great cleverness and personal ability—for ten years she had been in charge of the administrative staff and controlled the museum's financial estimates—but had sensitive antennae and an intuitive sense of how changes could best be made. Our relationship was, from the first, one of great warmth and total confidence.

The Victoria and Albert Museum was a post-Industrial Revolution museum; it was designed, that is to say, for a world not entirely unlike our own. The British Museum, on the other hand, was a pre-Industrial Revolution museum, whose roots went back to the seventeenth-century tradition of antiquarianism. From the time that curiosities were first assembled, it was accepted that the purpose of collecting them was to augment knowledge. When John Tradescant, one of the founders of the Ashmolean Museum, published the catalogue of his own and his father's collection in 1656, the collection was described as a "benefit to such ingenious persons as would become further enquirers into the various modes of Nature's admirable works, and the curious Imitators thereof." It enumerated first what were described as "Naturall" materials, and then the "Artificialls, as Utensils, Housoldstuffe, Babits, rare curiosities of Art etc." The museum of Nicholas Chevalier that opened at Utrecht in the very early eighteenth century was arranged in the same way. There were fish in any quantity—among them a Zwaard-Visch and a *Piscis cornutus*—two roses of Jericho, some classical vases, a figure of Vespasian, some Egyptian odds and ends, and a bronze Baptist. To get into the museum one paid twopence if one was in company "and a single person a schilling." In the eighteenth century in most substantial towns, and in major university towns almost without exception, there were private museums of the kind. So general were they that in 1727 there appeared the first book on museology. Entitled *Museographia*, it was printed in Leipzig, and it contained an account of museums open to the public—"*Raritäten kabinetten*" they were called—a bibliography of published guides and catalogues (of Aldrovandi's Museum Metallicum at Bologna, the Museo Moscardo at Padua, the collection of insects at Gotha, and so on), and, most interesting of all, advice about their use. One's hands must be clean, so that one left no dirty marks upon the specimens. One must be decently dressed (on the principle "*Vestis ornat virum*"—I wonder how many modern visitors to the British Museum would qualify). And one need not feel ashamed at asking questions—what the objects were, whether they were natural or artificial, and if they were works of art, by whom they were made, and for what purpose, and exactly why they were to be admired. It was useful to carry a magnifying glass, a "*gutes Microscopium*," and one should if possible make notes.

The British Museum evolved directly from this antiquarian tradition. The original collection, that of Sir Hans Sloane, included a vast variety of exhibits, ranging from natural history at one pole to coins and drawings and objects of curiosity at the other, and on that there were superimposed the acquisition of (to take no more than a few examples) Sir William Hamilton's collection of vases and antiquities, of Egyptian antiquities (at the very beginning of the nineteenth century), of the Elgin marbles, and of the great Assyrian sculptures. To display these collections there was constructed (1823–47) the building in which the museum is now housed; it is claimed to be, and no doubt is, the largest neo-classical building in the British Isles. For the first century or more of its existence it was the only great museum that conformed to the precepts laid down by Diderot in the middle of the eighteenth century for a central museum which covered the whole range of knowledge, which housed a great national library, and which formed a living embodiment or re-creation of the classical *mouseion* where works of interest or merit, and books, and scholars were all housed side by side. That did not happen in Paris, or in Berlin, or in Vienna, or in any other large city in the world.

Nowadays the term "antiquarian" sounds derogatory, but Sir Hans Sloane as a collector was, by the standards of his time, aggressively professional. Credulous perhaps—the limits of permissible credulity in the first half of the eighteenth century were less clearly defined than they were at later times—but inspired by one central belief, that the basis of knowledge must be a really comprehensive collection of the data on which knowledge rested. That was the principle behind Sloane's early *Catalogue of Jamaica Plants* and his *Natural History of Jamaica*, and it dictated his attitude to the related area of conchology. He bought up collection after collection of shells and fossils—the famous collection formed by James Petiver, who died in 1718 (it consisted of East and West Indian shells), the Charlton collection, which John Evelyn, the diarist, visited in the Middle Temple and described as "such a collection as I had never seen in all my travels abroad, either of private gentlemen or princes," the collection of Engelbert Kaempfer, who was in Japan between 1690 and 1692 and wrote a history of Japan that Sloane published in translation in 1727, the collection formed by Mark Catesby in Carolina and the Bahamas (this was the source of Catesby's own *Natural History of Carolina, Florida, and the Bahama Islands*)—and he secured an immense number of individual gifts, from visitors to Maryland and China and the Philippines. From that it was no sharp transition to carved nautilus shells (whose interest lay in their workmanship) and mounted pearls (one of which was given to him by Sir Robert Walpole). In 1753, when Sloane died and his collection was taken over by the nation, it contained a total of almost six thousand shells. One of the trustees appointed under Sloane's will was Horace Walpole, whose taste was biased toward objects that were artificial and not natural and who was openly contemptuous of the enterprise. "You will scarcely guess how I employ my time," he wrote, "chiefly at present in the guardianship of embryos and cockleshells."

Sloane's benefaction to the nation was linked up at once with two other, wholly dissimilar gifts, the Cotton and Harley libraries, so the museum had from the beginning an ambivalent character. But in the early days it was dominated by natural historians and scientists. In its first home at Montague House the main upper rooms were allotted to minerals and geology, birds and mammals, and when the King's Library was built by Sir Robert Smirke, and the Montague House premises were abandoned, the long gallery over the King's Library was again occupied by the natural not the artificial collections. As late as 1843 there were four principal departments: Geology and Mineralogy, Zoology, Egyptian Antiquities, and Greek and Roman Antiquities. The conflict between the two pairs of departments was not tacit, it was overt, and in 1846 it was proposed, by Lord Francis

Egerton, that the museum should be "relieved of the burden of natural history in all its branches." What precipitated (or at least lent force) to this view was the arrival of the sculptures from the Mausoleum of Halicarnassus. The fight continued through the 1850s, when the museum was under the innovative control of the Principal Librarian, Antonio Panizzi, who objected to the current arrangement not only in principle but on the practical grounds that the zoological specimens attracted a lower type of public than the antiquities, and "the fewer persons of this class that are attracted as visitors the better." Finally, in 1883 there took place the first of the two major changes imposed on the museum since its creation, the separation of the natural history collection from the main museum. Ruskin discusses it in a letter of 1880 on the functions and formation of a museum or picture gallery. "I am heartily sorry for the break-up of it," he wrote, "and augur no good from any changes of arrangement likely to take place in concurrence with Kensington." But the creation of a physically separate Natural History Museum was of benefit to the natural history collections, to education and to research, and it was of benefit also to the British Museum. The second great change was more recent—the administrative separation of the museum from the library. Libraries and museums make uneasy bedfellows, and my own belief was that the divorce would eventually prove beneficial, since the museum would be free in isolation to develop along lines which had not been open to it in the past.

The museum building reflected this encyclopedic heritage. In the front, projecting on either side, were houses for the distinguished scholars on its staff. One of them had been inhabited till 1971, but in my day they were all of them turned over to warders' quarters and offices. Was the neo-classical idea of a group of administrator-scholars living round a library and a museum still viable at the present day? I questioned if it was. There are places like the Institute for Advanced Study where scholars still live together in fruitful harmony, but I did not feel myself that the collegiate conception of the British Museum would contribute very much if it could be revived.

In the eighteenth century the concept of museums as temples of the muses was a not uncommon one. A section was dedicated to them in the Council of Europe exhibition *The Age of Neo-Classicism*. It showed the plans made by Simonetti in the 1770s for the museum designed to house the Vatican antiquities, the Museo Pio-Clementino, and

Klenze's designs for the Glyptothek in Munich and Schinkel's for the Altes Museum in Berlin. The British Museum was a structure of that kind. It was not an art museum, but the museum itself was a work of art. Inside and out it was in a state of deplorable neglect, and it seemed to me that one of the duties of an incoming director was to ensure that its grimy façade was cleaned and that Smirke's front hall was repristinated, so that it looked once more like the entrance to a great museum, not a railway station waiting room.

Many of the letters I received on my appointment complained of the installation of the museum galleries. But the fact was that one set of galleries, that of the Greek and Roman Antiquities, had been reinstalled extremely well. When these rooms opened in 1969 they were the best-designed galleries in any London museum and the best-designed galleries of classical sculpture in the world. They set a standard so high as to underline the deficiencies of the rest of the museum. The galleries of Assyrian sculpture had also been reinstalled, but much less skillfully. The reliefs did not sit easily in the confined space to which they were consigned, and they were shown against panels of contrasting colors that came within touching distance of vulgarity. The adjacent galleries of Egyptian sculpture were the large, depressing places they had always been, and their arrangement, as it seems to have been from the beginning, was anti-chronological. Nine-tenths of the visitors approached them from the south, encountering first the Ptolemaic and Roman period sculptures and ending up at the north end of the gallery with the earliest sculptures. The upstairs galleries of all three departments were deplorable. The mummy cases, some of the few museum objects which were best seen by artificial light, were jammed together in a top-lit gallery. The upper Greek and Roman galleries led to a dreadful Greek and Roman life room, evidently designed by some architect in the Ministry of Works, and the subsidiary Western Asiatic galleries, including the marvelous Sumerian and Babylonian antiquities, were old-fashioned and uncommunicative.

The first task, it was clear, was to bring the Egyptian sculpture galleries up to a level commensurate with those of the Greek and Roman sculpture. This was a big and extremely expensive task, but I secured agreement in principle that it should be begun. It was entrusted to Robin Wade, who had also worked on the earlier galleries, and I presented his designs to the trustees. But it was some years before work started, and the galleries were opened only in 1979, three years after I had left the museum. Not long after taking over, I went round the subsidiary Western Asiatic galleries with Max Mallowan. He explained to me that he had never wished his Nimrud ivories to come to the museum, since he knew they would be shown as badly as they were. Some of the Nimrud ivories are great works of art and the collection as a whole is of the utmost interest. I gave an undertaking that the quite small room in which they were housed would be given priority in the reinstallation program. It did indeed receive priority, but only in 1976, after a three-year delay, were the new cases supplied. I found it exasperating that simple installations of this kind could not be pushed through more rapidly. When I arrived work was already in progress on three of the Medieval and Later Antiquities galleries. Two of them, the Clock Room (where the display was efficient, didactic, and technical) and the Tile Room, were well conceived and executed, but the third, containing the Waddesdon bequest, looked when it was finished like a congested temporary exhibition. Only one department, that of Oriental Antiquities on the north side of the building, was arranged, on conventional lines, with great sensibility. The cases bore the stamp of the former keeper, Basil Gray, who looked on Oriental artifacts as works of art.

In only one area could relatively rapid results be obtained. This was the Department of Prints and Drawings, which had excellent modern exhibition space and a keeper whom I knew well and whose work I had long admired. Plans had already been laid for an exhibition to commemorate the centenary of the birth of Turner in 1975. It was arranged by a Turner specialist from the limitless resources of the Turner bequest and was admirably shown. But two other important centenaries were coming up in the immediate future, the first that of the birth of Michelangelo in 1976 and the second that of the birth of Rubens in the following year. Nothing, I was told, had been planned to commemorate either event, and two large exhibitions were therefore scheduled. I did not myself see the Rubens exhibition, but the display of drawings by Michelangelo, mostly from British sources, with a few additional sheets from New York and Paris, was among the most exciting exhibitions I have ever seen. It was very well arranged and impeccably catalogued, and when I go to the Print Room today I still recall the surge of emotion with which the late Crucifixion drawings, in a case on one side of the doorway, filled so many visitors.

As a regular attendant at the exhibitions of drawings held by the department, I had, before moving to the museum, been disconcerted by the lack of twentieth-century material. At a relatively recent exhibition of portrait drawings, the display had petered out with a handful of drawings made during the First World War by Eric Kennington. It seemed to me that purchasing in this area should be extended, and that the new policy should be established with a contemporary exhibition. I put the problem to my friend Vera Russell, who came up with the excellent suggestion that the exhibition should be of the Auden-inspired lithographs of Henry Moore. This ensured that, briefly, a breath of fresh air blew through the galleries. The museum later appointed an assistant keeper empowered to develop the collection in the contemporary field.

The central problem of the museum was that the collections were too big. As I went round one department after another looking first at the exhibited and then, in the labyrinthine basement, at the unexhibited collections, I was horrified by what I saw. Dame Kathleen Kenyon once said to me at lunch: "I can't understand why you dislike archaeology. After all it is only a way of finding things out." I explained to her that it was not archaeology I disapproved of, but the passive, undiscriminating state of mind it generated. Departments like Prints and Drawings or Coins and Medals were reference departments, whose value resided not just in their best objects but in their comprehensiveness. But there were other departments of which that was untrue, but which rested on the fallacy that knowledge was increased by aggregation. Before the invention of photography that view may have been defensible, but it could have few defenders today. Any archaeological museum, even a small one, is liable to contain a quantity of objects which are present only because they happen to have been dug up in the same place at the same time. The result at Bloomsbury was basement after basement bursting with material which was in part redundant and in part of very little interest. The exhibited collections were big enough; the unexhibited collections defeated all imagining.

The cure was not what is now called deaccessioning. For a variety of reasons no disposals procedure was desirable. But wealth in resources carries with it certain obligations, and it seemed to me it would be highly reprehensible if the museum were not generous in making loans. In the past the loan policies in individual departments had been restrictive, but while I was there I did everything I could to facilitate short-term loans to temporary exhibitions and long-term loans to other institutions. The aggregate number of loans did indeed reach a point where it imposed quite a serious strain on some departments, but it was not for that reason cut back. Any regional museum which was organizing a serious loan exhibition could feel pretty confident that the trustees would accede to almost all of their requests.

Of much greater consequence was the fact that the museum had in storage a great deal of cumbersome material which could be put to use elsewhere. The Department of Prehistoric and Romano-British Antiquities had a fascinating group of what were generally regarded as prehistoric canoes. There was no possibility that in the foreseeable future they could be shown in the museum, and they were therefore transferred on long loan to the Museum of London and the National Maritime Museum. Part of the large reserve of classical sculptures was already scheduled to be put on exhibition. The Townseley marbles were to be installed in a new basement exhibition gallery, and a gallery of classical inscriptions and a third new classical gallery were also planned. But even when the objects destined for those rooms were set aside, there was a substantial residue, and the logical policy was that at least part of it should be shown elsewhere. Why should the Greek Museum at Newcastle depend exclusively on purchases when their collection could be so easily reinforced by loans? A start was indeed made. Some excellent statues from Cyrene were sent to the National Museum of Wales, and Roman sculptures were lent to the National Gallery in London and to the Royal Scottish Museum. They were deposited for a ten-year renewable loan period, but I hoped that they would never be recalled. Museums in Great Britain which maintained the necessary standard of security were encouraged to solicit long-term loans. It was clearly preferable that some of the surplus Indian sculptures be shown at the Gulbenkian Museum in Durham than that they remain in store at Bloomsbury. I was especially keen to find museums which had the floor or wall space to show Roman floor mosaics. There they were, in storage, cut up into big squares and placed one behind the other, so that they could not possibly be studied and, subject to security provisos, the only sensible course was to deposit some of them in places where they could be seen.

The early 1970s were a period of rampant trade unionism. Decaying institutions like the British Museum had been infiltrated by agitators, the more easily in that responsible members of the staff by and large refused to vote or play any active part in the union to which they all belonged. I hoped initially that the union would participate in improving working conditions for the staff. But their interest lay in making trouble elsewhere. They had been handled skillfully for some years by the deputy director, who had promoted a dialogue between active unionists and the administrative staff. It became a kind of game, and it consumed an immense amount of time. On one occasion she was convinced that her office had been bugged by the union, but when it was stripped by the security authorities no trace of any bug was found. One Communist agitator operated from a darkroom in the Photographic Department. When heads of state paid official visits to Great Britain, they frequently, in the free half day they had available, expressed a wish to visit the museum. One of these was the President of Brazil, a nice old German who had eyes for nothing but the notice "*Nicht rauchen*" at the museum entrance. I did not inform the union of his visit for fear that some agitation might ensue. After it was over, there was a protest, on the ground that trade unions were suppressed in Brazil. I explained that since the President was a guest of the Queen it was incumbent on me to treat him with civility. "That was not accepted as a defense at the Nuremberg trials," the chairman of the association, a dim little clerical officer, replied. Incidents of this sort were repeated week by week. Never could one anticipate what the next subject of agitation would be or where the next strike threat might occur.

When I took over, I inspected each of the museum departments. In a number of them I was horrified by the conditions in which the staff was required to work. In a corridor leading to the offices of the Department of Medieval and Later Antiquities, I noticed a cupboard which might have contained cleaning materials. I pushed open the door and inside was a research assistant. This kind of discovery was repeated throughout the building. Before I became director of the museum, I used, like other outsiders, to feel exasperated that it seemed to contribute so much less in the museum field than other institutions. Its stock-in-trade was research, and to people like myself, who had always taken scholarship for granted and for whom knowledge was not a value but a currency, it all seemed very odd. My first discovery was that the museum seemed to contribute relatively little because it was so organized that it could not possibly contribute more. It was a federation of semi-autonomous departments, not a museum in a unitary sense. The central services that were taken for granted elsewhere—transit, packing, conservation—were absent or were operated departmentally. Indeed, the only effective central service was the excellent Research Laboratory. Each department had its conservation unit, and very wasteful of time and skill that seemed to be. Bronze was treated in five different departments, in each according to slightly different criteria. After an interminable series of discussions, conservation was unified, in the autumn of 1975, in a single Conservation Department. But in one department, that of Ethnography, the conservation requirements were so heterodox—they might involve the preservation of mummies of Peruvian children or the cleaning of feather cloaks—that a separate conservation unit was preserved.

I learned gradually to read the minds or share the interests of members of the staff. The Department of Ethnography and the Department of Prehistoric and Romano-British Antiquities presented little difficulty; the value of their work spoke for itself. In other cases I was suprised at what seemed an imbalance of activity. I was puzzled that the Department of Western Asiatic Antiquities, whose exhibition galleries on the first floor were manifestly so much inferior to the galleries of comparable material in Philadelphia, should appear to devote most of its effort to the transcription of cuneiform tablets. In 1973 the computerization of the collections had begun and the quite large computer was producing excellent results in reconciling the conflicting systems of numbering throughout the collection. It was engaged on other tasks as well, and one of these arose out of the quarry known as Grimes Graves. The computer, to my surprise, was analyzing soil samples in the hope of establishing human habitation on the site. The results, not unexpectedly, were negative, and it was then suggested that the whole elaborate investigation should be repeated in the hope of obtaining a positive result. I vetoed a second test, wondering whether the inquiry had not at the beginning been wrongly framed. A number of the interests of the Department of Medieval and Later Antiquities overlapped with those of the Victoria and Albert, and it seemed to me that these would eventually need to be rationalized.

One of the things that puzzled me was the psychology of middle members of the staff. They felt loyalty to their departments and to the concept of the British Museum, but not to the administration or to the trustees. A number of them seemed to be in constant contact with the press, and again and again one was rung up by some newspaper (generally the *Guardian*, but sometimes the *Evening Standard* or the *Evening News*) with a canard planted by an unnamed museum officer. At first I found this infuriating, but I do not hear criticism easily, and latterly, when some newspaper asked me on the telephone: "Do you realize that there is an insurrection in such-and-such a department at the decision to do something or other?" I found myself replying: "I don't know and I don't care."

Somewhat to my surprise, I found when I inspected them that most departments were slightly understaffed in relation to their commitment. This was rectified. A good scholar is not necessarily a good administrator, and I was anxious that promotion on scholarly grounds should be divorced from administrative promotion. A number of new deputy keeper posts were created as reward for scholars who were poor administrators. I was also anxious that gaps in knowledge in major areas should be filled. The Department of Coins and Medals contained a number of first-rate specialists on coins but no one who was thoroughly familiar with the medallic field. The reason for this was that Sir George Hill, the great medallic scholar who had been head of the department and was later director of the museum, had never transmitted his knowledge to a junior member of the staff. Similarly the Department of Prints and Drawings had a number of world-respected specialists on drawings but no specialist on prints. These and other voids were gradually made good by the recruitment of young staff. I made it a practice to be present at all appointments boards in order to ensure that new members of the staff were selected not simply by the criteria of training and knowledge but also by that of real ability. Most of the assistant keepers who were appointed in my time have remained with the museum.

With senior vacancies it seemed to me important that there should be no automatic promotion at the keeper level, and that a system of open competition should be generally applied. The test case occurred in 1974 with the death of the keeper of the Department of Ethnography. This department had been moved from a building formerly used by the Civil Service Commission to a new museum in the center of London in Burlington Gardens. Despite its advantageous position close to Bond Street, Regent Street, and Piccadilly, the galleries had few visitors, and the museum, which was named the Museum of

Mankind (on the grounds that there would have been feminist opposition had it been named, like its French counterpart, the Museum
of Man), had never succeeded in getting off the ground. The scope
of the department was worldwide, but its West African holdings
were of particular importance, and I thought it was essential that the
new keeper should be free of the least taint of colonialism. One of the
external applicants, Malcolm McLeod, an assistant curator at the Museum of Archaeology and Ethnography at Cambridge, was appointed
though he was only thirty-four. The appointment paid off extremely
well. Excellent relations were established with the Asantahene and
other African rulers and officials, and the exhibition policy at the
museum not only attracted a large public but was of real educational
significance. More important still, the vast reserves of stored material
were put in order and study facilities were improved.

After my appointment was announced, I had a number of conversations with those members of the staff whom I knew well. What, I
asked, could I do that would be welcome from their point of view? I
received one invariable answer: "Save us from the weight of the trustees." After two trustee meetings, however, I saw the problem rather
differently. There were twenty-five trustees, fifteen of whom were
appointed by the Prime Minister, four nominated by other institutions
(the Royal Society, the Royal Academy, the British Academy, and
the Society of Antiquaries), and five co-opted by the trustees themselves. In addition there was a royal trustee, the Duke of Gloucester.
Royal trustees had in the past been passive members of the board,
but the Duke of Gloucester was a specialist in architecture who made
in his own area an invaluable contribution to the trustees' delibera-
tions. Individually the trustees were of great distinction. In addition
to Trevelyan, they included Lord Boyd, a former Secretary of State
for the Dominions and Colonies; Lord Trend, a former Secretary of
the Cabinet; Lord Boyle, a former Minister of Education then serving
as vice-chancellor of the University of Leeds; Lord Annan, the vice-
chancellor of London University; Sir Arthur Drew, a former Permanent Under Secretary of State at the Ministry of Defense; Professor
Gower, the vice-chancellor of Southampton University; Lord Clark;
Sir Denis Hamilton, chairman of *The Times*; Professor Hall, the head
of the Research Laboratory for Archaeology at Oxford; Sir John Ken-
drew, the son of my old friend Evelyn Vavalà and a Nobel Prize
winner with a special interest in the Research Laboratory; Professor

Graham Clark, the master of Peterhouse, Cambridge; Sir Edmund Leach, the anthropologist; Lord Fletcher, a former Minister of State with a lively interest in British archaeology; Sir Max Mallowan, the excavator of Nimrud; and Dame Kathleen Kenyon. All in all this was an exceptionally intelligent and exceptionally experienced board. The trouble was structural; there was no means whereby the experience of its members could be brought to bear on the problems of the museum. A subcommittee dealt with the building and another with finance, and in addition each department had its own trustee committee, to which decisions that would in other museums be the prerogative of the keeper were referred. The trustees were dedicated and extremely diligent—an average of twenty-three regularly attended the nine meetings that took place on Saturday mornings throughout the year—and their level of distinction greatly exceeded the distinction of the staff. The trustee committee system, I concluded, needed to be revised. The vertical departmental committees should be abolished, giving greater freedom to the staff, and should be replaced by a system of horizontal committees, dealing with staff, scholarship and publications, education, and fieldwork throughout all those fields covered by the museum. In this way only would it be possible to take rational decisions on the recruitment and promotion of staff, on the vast backlog of unpublished research, on the relative claims of the areas that should be investigated, and on display priorities. Humphrey Trevelyan, who was open-minded to a fault, agreed with this analysis, and so indeed did the members of the board, who welcomed the possibility of closer association with the work of the museum. From my standpoint (and I hope from that of my successor) the arrangement had another practical advantage. Earlier directors, up to and including Wolfenden, had protested at the fact that in cases of dispute keepers could appeal over the head of the director to the full board. It was the departmental committee system that had made this possible, and with its abolition the right of appeal automatically disappeared. I was concerned also with a further point, that the trustees as a whole had an imperfect knowledge of the museum and its departments. To rectify this it was arranged that one informal visit be made to each department every year, under the direction of a nominated member of the board, which any interested trustee would be able to attend. I hoped that after a couple of years the individual board members would build up knowledge of the working conditions in each department, would see with their own eyes the tasks that it was undertaking, and would meet, down to research assistant level, the members of the staff who were responsible. This system worked well, and the discussion of departmental problems at board level and in the trustee committees rapidly became less theoretical.

Acquisitions were determined not by a subcommittee but by the full board of trustees. This system was satisfactory, and in my three years at the museum a number of notable purchases were made. One was of the Savernake Horn, a great English medieval work that I knew well, since it had been on loan at the Victoria and Albert. This was both a welcome and, in view of its historical importance, an inevitable purchase. A second was of an extremely fine group of medieval ivories from the collection of Sir Harold Wernher at Luton Hoo, which were taken over in lieu of death duties. These represented a substantial enrichment of the medieval collection. Acquisitions for the Department of Prints and Drawings included a famous Holbein drawing that once formed a part of the Holbein collection at Windsor and was owned by Lord Bradford, and a well-known study by Mantegna for the Ovetari Chapel at Padua. The Mantegna was pasted to its mount, but when one held it up to the light a drawing on the back, for one of the colossal heads in the spandrels of the Ovetari Chapel, was visible. I have asked repeatedly since whether the sheet has been removed from its mount and whether the back has been photographed, but the answer is always negative. The museum tended to be secretive about its acquisitions as about so much else, and I arranged that they should be displayed in the entrance so that the public could see how its money had been spent.

One important initiative had been taken by the trustees before I was appointed director. This was the creation of an autonomous body, the British Museum Publications Company. It had its own directors and was independently financed, working in office space in one of the British Museum houses on the east side of Bedford Square. The office space was rented from the museum and so were the sales areas. The company owed its creation and its success to the exertions of Sir Denis Hamilton, and since it was conspicuously well run it played from the first a significant role in the museum's educational thinking. In addition to museum catalogues, it commissioned books and ensured that useful earlier publications, like Roger Hinks's *Greek and Roman Portraiture*, were once more put in circulation. For reasons I never understood, the company incurred the hostility of a group of self-important MPs, the Public Accounts Committee, who would, it appeared, have preferred no publication company to a company whose activities they could not oversee.

Another initiative was the creation of the British Museum Society, which under its first chairman, Sir Richard Thompson, enjoyed quite substantial public support. I had joined it when it came into existence in 1970, but on only one occasion did I participate in its activities. This was at a private view of the Tutankhamen exhibition, when the members were received in the gallery housing the Elgin marbles and for half an hour were given acid red wine to drink because the exhibition was still full of visitors. After an interval we were told that we might move slowly toward the exhibition gallery. In the stampede that ensued the victors were Jennie Lee, Paul Getty, and myself. The rooms were stuffy and very full, and I spent my time extricating Getty from the exhibition. When the chairman of the society retired, I urged that his successor should be a woman, since women in my experience manage such things better than men. I proposed the appointment of an old and admired friend, Pamela Hartwell, who directed the society with great skill and was eventually appointed a trustee of the museum.

If you stood in the entrance hall, one thing was very plain, that casual or infrequent visitors to the museum (and these must have comprised the bulk of the two million visitors) were lost once they went through the portico. To visit the galleries of Greek and Roman or Egyptian or Western Asiatic Antiquities was easy enough: you turned to the left on the same floor on which you entered, and you could find what you were looking for. But if your interests lay in the objects excavated at Sutton Hoo or in Celtic art or in Ur or in Egyptian mummies, you went up the main staircase from the information desk and then fended for yourself, asking some generally unhelpful warder where to go. The task of getting to the Department of Prints and Drawings on the north side of the building would have daunted even a professional explorer. Palpably, there was need for some form of signposting, and a guide system by which visitors were directed to the principal collections was in fact introduced. I did not care greatly for its appearance—it was designed professionally but not particularly well—but it made visits to the museum less penitential than they might otherwise have been.

More important was the matter of a museum guide. The standard publication of the time, *Treasures of the British Museum*, had the merit of including photographs of many of the most important objects, but its text dealt principally with the archaeologists who had discovered them or the individuals from whom they had been acquired. The history of the British Museum is a fascinating subject and has been treated many times, but the area in which visitors needed help was in looking at the works displayed and in establishing the context in which they were produced. An excellent guide to the collections of the Metropolitan Museum in New York had recently been issued by Tom Hoving (it has now been replaced, however, by a less imaginative publication), and at the British Museum something of the same sort was required. The new guide contained plans of the museum, squared off and colored like a Mondrian, so that the galleries looked less intimidating than they really were, and followed the sequence of the galleries, with outline maps of each of the areas discussed. Its preparation was a slow job, and it was not published till the year of my retirement, 1976.

A great deal of time at trustee meetings was devoted to discussing education, and as the result of a new series of appointments the education service was markedly improved. But my own view had always been that the prime duty of museums was not to educate the public but to assist them in a process of self-education. Labeling that was directed to the specialist seemed to me anti-educational. Once when I was going round the galleries with Lord Drogheda, a newly appointed trustee, I was stopped by a lady who inquired: "What is a penannular ring?"—a term used on the label she was reading. I told her that, on the analogy of the word "peninsular," I thought it meant an ornament which just failed to be a ring but that I was far from certain if this were so. Experimentally a post was created in each department to be filled by a research assistant whose duties were to produce labels and other educational material that would be generally intelligible. The result was improvement, but less marked improvement than I had hoped.

In 1976 two major exhibitions took place. The first, which was cultural and historical, and had no artistic implications, commemorated the American bicentennial and was sent over as a package from the United States. It was shown at the British Museum rather than in a more appropriate setting like the Hayward Gallery because no prior arrangements for its display had been made. The opening by

the Vice President, Nelson Rockefeller, was something of an embarrassment, since he brought with him as part of the jamboree two
airplanes filled with representative Americans in various walks of life.
The only member of the party who seemed ever to have visited the
British Museum (other than Rockefeller and his family and Tom Hoving, the director of the Metropolitan Museum) was the singer Pearl
Bailey. The second exhibition enjoyed greater success, and consisted
of Thracian gold and silver excavated mainly in Sofia and dispatched
to London by the Bulgarian government. The level of quality was
very high, and the exhibition was admirably arranged by the British
Museum designing staff.

Attendances at the museum were already so high that there was no
obligation to plan an exhibition program of the kind that was necessary
in New York at the Metropolitan Museum or at the Victoria and
Albert. By 1976 they had reached a total of just over three million
visitors. Before I took over arrangements had been made to create a
temporary exhibition space in the large room in which trustee meetings
were held and to build a new meeting place for the trustees. I regretted
this on historical grounds. But if a new exhibition hall were to be
opened it should open with a worthy exhibition, and it would, it
seemed to me, be best inaugurated with an exhibition of Scythian
objects from the Hermitage. In March 1976, therefore, I went to
Leningrad to enlist the support of the director of the Hermitage, Boris
Piotrovsky, who had once lunched with me in London. I look back
with the utmost pleasure on this visit. Though I had been to Russia
on three previous occasions, I had never seen it under snow, and
beautiful as Leningrad is at other times of the year, it is at its best
when the Neva is frozen and the spire of SS. Peter and Paul is reflected
in the ice. In the Hermitage I was allowed briefly to return to my
curatorial role and go over the very rich collection of stored sculpture.
I tried also to establish a relationship between the Ethnographic Museum in Leningrad and the Museum of Mankind.

In New York in October 1974 I was invited by the president of
the American Assembly to attend a symposium at Harriman dealing
with art museums in America. Planned by Sherman Lee and attended
by senior American museum directors, the conference covered a large
number of topics of general interest: the concept of artistic quality
and its applicability to art museums; the duty of art museums toward
living artists; the social responsibilities of museums and the parameters

of their activity; their educational responsibilities; their function as centers of research; trustee responsibility and public representation on governing boards; and the advantages and disadvantages of government subsidies. The discussions were stimulating, though they led to a somewhat disappointing report. It was recognized that the position of American museums differed widely from that of their European counterparts, many or most of which were government-subsidized, and it was suggested that a further meeting should be held in Europe at which these differences could be discussed. I agreed to chair this meeting, which took place under the auspices of the trustees of the British Museum at Ditchley in October 1975. The agenda were more practical than those of the Harriman meetings. They dealt with the effects of economic recession on art museum activities; the differences in the constitution of controlling boards and the type of structure to be preferred; the dual responsibility of museums to scholarship and to the general public, and how far this influenced the recruitment of museum staffs; the contribution of museums to society and the educational means by which this could be discharged; acquisition policies and the extent to which they should be coordinated; and the criteria governing the disposal of surplus acquisitions in museums of contemporary art. In addition to the principal American museum directors, the three-day meeting was attended by Ernst Gombrich, who gave the opening address; Herman Fillitz (later director of the Kunsthistorisches Museum, Vienna); Xavier de Salas, the director of the Prado; Marco Chiarini from the Palazzo Pitti; Baudouin from the Museum of the City of Antwerp; Dahlbäck, the director of the National Museum in Stockholm; Erik Fischer from the Statens Museum for Kunst in Copenhagen; Werner Hoffmann from the Kunsthalle in Hamburg; Hubert Landais; Erich Steingräber, the director of the Alte Pinakothek in Munich; Wend von Kalnein from Düsseldorf; Germain Bazin; Pierre Rosenberg of the Louvre; Matthias Winner, the head of the Print Room in the Staatliche Museen in West Berlin; and Stephan Waetzoldt, the director of the Staatliche Museen. The report of the meeting once more was anodyne, but the formal discussions were stimulating, and the opportunity offered for informal discussion of common problems proved of great value. The participants were selected on a personal, not a national or institutional, basis, and at the end of the last session I greatly hoped that it would be possible to arrange further meetings of the kind. No further meeting has, however, been held. I was pleased that the British Museum (which was often described in letters to me as the mother of all museums) could for once exercise an initiative in the museum field.

At Christmas 1975 I drew up a balance sheet of what had been achieved. The new trustee committee structure had had highly beneficial consequences throughout the whole museum. Thanks to the willingness of the trustees to involve themselves more deeply in its affairs, rational policies had been, or were in the course of being, worked out in the main areas with which the museum was concerned. Steady progress had been made with the policy of replacing older by younger keepers. With two departments, that of Prehistoric and Romano-British Antiquities and that of Ethnography, the consequences were already manifest, and it was likely that the Department of Medieval and Later Antiquities under its new keeper would likewise develop along more active lines. Only two departments gave cause for concern: Oriental Antiquities, which had an old-fashioned keeper and a talented but discontented staff, and Prints and Drawings, where the keeper was a first-rate scholar but a secretive administrator. The policy of applying criteria of ability as well as knowledge in the recruitment of staff at the assistant keeper and research assistant level was also paying dividends. Improvement in the educational services was potential rather than actual, and the record was one of good intentions rather than achievement. There was, however, greater curatorial interest in the educational use of the collections in its broadest sense than I would have anticipated. Evidence of increased public interest spoke for itself. Attendances in the calendar year 1975 were roughly 850,000 greater than in 1974, and the increase in the popularity of the Museum of Mankind was particularly marked; it was attracting 200,000 visitors a year. The prime factor in the latter increase had been its exhibition policy, and the increase would accelerate if exhibitions continued to be geared to areas of general interest suitable for visual presentation, and not to subjects of specialized appeal best dealt with in print. There had been some improvement in public relations in terms of press coverage, but the situation was still unsatisfactory. The full advantages arising from the establishment of an independent Conservation Department would emerge as soon as the department was provided with central premises. A number of serious and useful catalogues were in course of preparation, but work on them was still impeded by a prevailing lack of urgency. After a thirty-year delay, the publication of a report on the Sutton Hoo excavation had begun. There was an almost universal inability to distinguish between topics which were important and topics which were not, and in some departments major holdings were still unstudied and uncatalogued. I was continually conscious of a prevailing malaise through the whole museum. Its symptoms were apathy, lack of initiative, and intellectual sluggishness. I could not but contrast this situation with the museum as I knew it before the war, when it dealt in ideas and not simply in knowledge and had many brilliant, intellectually ambitious curators on its staff. A number of new assistant keepers were, however, of real potential excellence, and it was important that steps be taken to ensure that they did not sink to the prevailing norm.

In the light of this balance sheet I thought over my position with some care. It seemed to me (and to Kenneth Clark, with whom I discussed it) that I had two alternatives, either to remain on in my post and accept an extension of it if it was offered, going to City dinner after City dinner and ending up with some further decoration or a peerage like my predecessor, or to resign and return to scholarly life. The second seemed to me the more useful course. Resigning is a difficult skill. I wrote, with great personal regret for the trouble it would cause, a letter to the chairman, to whose support I owed so much, and when he and a delegation from the board came to my office and asked me to continue in my post, I explained the reasons for my decision. I told them I would remain for a further twelve months provided that neither collectively nor individually did they attempt to make me change my mind. If they did so, I would leave my post at once. This was understood, and at the end of 1976, at a ceremony like that at which Wolfenden three years before had been presented with a painting, I was given a bronze bust of myself by Elizabeth Frink (a very beautiful bust; versions of it are in the British Museum and the National Portrait Gallery). The sittings for it were an exhilarating experience. Used as I was to reconstructing sculptural processes, I still recall with something of a shock the moment, at the end of the first sitting, when I looked at what had been a lump of clay and found that a third person was in the room.

In my farewell speech on that occasion I said:

> I find it very hard to judge what has been achieved during the last three years, and still harder to believe that whatever gains were

made are durable. Certainly no regime could possibly have started under worse auspices. There can be few people today who feel more confident about what the future holds than they did then. Those doubts are, of course, reflected in every walk of life, and in a rather special sense in this museum. When I was appointed, I felt from outside (and the outside image of the museum is, as you know, a very curious one—the only thing the two Bloomsburys seem to have in common is the appearance of self-sufficiency) that what was needed was not a director but a thaumaturge, and after the first year I asked myself whether what was required was not a wonder-worker but an analyst. I suspect that my successor will ask himself that question too.

The focal point of this neurosis is the conviction, which is entertained in every department of every large museum in the world, in the Metropolitan Museum and at the Louvre, in Vienna and no doubt in Dahlem too, that museums can run themselves, or rather that they can be run by a sort of consortium of departments. I call it a conviction, but like so many convictions it is a fallacy. There is, everywhere, a compelling need to determine how far the expensive luxuries we call museums are measuring up to their responsibilities, and what they are contributing not just to learning (important as that is) but to the national well-being as a whole. Nowhere is that more necessary than here. For crude as was the act of amputation by which the museum was severed from the library, it undeniably offered the museum a new challenge and new opportunities. No longer could it peer out at the world beyond the railings from behind an ambuscade of books. It was compelled to operate as a public museum in the full sense, as the educational institution it should from the start have been. For that reason it was incumbent upon somebody to decide in broad terms what it could do, what was its future role, and how the gulf between its actual performance and its potential could best be bridged.

Even in the physical darkness of three years ago, one or two points seemed to me pretty clear. The antiquities departments as a whole were understaffed, and promotion prospects were inadequate. Something, just a little, was done about both points. It was not a question of increasing staff for the sake of staff increase; the objective was to reduce pressure, and to ensure that coverage, in terms of knowledge, for the areas for which the museum was responsible, was less inadequate. There was, moreover, a recoil against the whole concept of central services. The standards of the education service had therefore to be raised to a level at which they did not incur the scorn of the antiquities departments, and the departments themselves had to become involved, at least peripherally, with educational activities. The Design Office seemed to be mistrusted and, most surprisingly, the development which was of the greatest potential usefulness, the Publications Company, was a target for suspicion and misplaced ridicule. I must confess to a certain impatience over that. After all, the company is a kind of public-address system, through which, in the future, museum departments will speak to the whole world. Whatever its temporary defects, they are as nothing to the opportunities that it affords.

When I arrived here, from another, lower planet, and went round the offices, I am bound to say I was appalled by the working conditions imposed upon the staff. Slowly one learned that they were a symptom of something worse, archaic managerial practices. It was this that provided one of the compelling arguments for transforming into reality what had hitherto existed only as a concept, external appointments to the upper reaches of the staff. I hope that my successor and the trustees will continue to stand firmly behind that policy. Merit and merit only, a fresh mind, not long assiduous service, entitles people to top jobs, and if that had been acknowledged a generation earlier than it was, many of the problems that confront us would not have arisen in their present form.

I would urge the staff on every level to think more about the future and how it should be shaped, and less about the small exacerbations of the present or the legendary glories of the past. Whether we like it or not, public interest in museums is here to stay, and there is not the smallest possibility of turning the museum back into a scholarly cloister protected from the outer world. The problem is how traditions we value in the past are to be reconciled with the exigencies of the world in which we are. In one sense the British Museum is and has always been a confidence trick. The perpetrator of it was Smirke, who made what has always been a federation of departments look like a single institution. The main task of the future is, it seems to me, to give the message of the architecture some reality, to develop the sense of the museum as a unitary organism, with common goals and common policies, and to speed up the recognition that loyalty to an institution is something more than the sum of loyalties to its constituent parts.

11

THE PLEASURE OF THE MULTITUDE

I HAVE DESCRIBED MY YEARS IN THE BRITISH MUSEUM AS THOUGH they were a period of uninterrupted administration. But they were nothing of the kind. Three weeks after I had taken over as director, on January 24, I found on my return from lunch a message asking me to ring up the police station at Ladbroke Grove. I did so, and was told that at eleven o'clock that morning my brother had been killed in his flat on the opposite side of the road. The murder, for murder it was, was of particular brutality. He had been tied to a chair, and beaten, and had died from swallowing his own blood. I was taken down to identify his body in a morgue at the Chelsea Coroner's Court, and when the trolley was wheeled out of the refrigerator and the sheet over his face had been turned down, I was appalled at the dissolute, almost evil expression on his face. It was as though one were participating in some unwritten Jacobean tragedy.

Since he was a well-known writer, the murder was reported in headlines in the evening papers, and when I got back to my own house in Bedford Gardens a group of curious spectators stood outside. The telephone began to ring, and rang almost uninterruptedly into the night, and the next day hasty obituaries and reports on the crime started to appear. I was helped through these harrowing days by the support of a close friend, Andrew Porter, who was at All Souls and came up to stay with me, and by that saintly figure Arnold Goodman, who rang up next day to ask what he could do. Only one thing, I said, would help, to stop the daily papers' continuous reporting on the crime. He was chairman of the Newspaper Publishers' Association at the time, and the reporting, in all save small print at the bottom of a column, ceased. As our conversation ended, he added one injunction: "Remember, this is nothing to do with you."

But it was to do with me in a more fundamental sense than I supposed even at that time. It was as though part of one had been cut away. Our relationship was not the common compound of shared experience; it was rather that we had complementary characters. I believed in his talent, and my job was, and had always been, to save him from himself. I experienced after his death (as I still experience when I remember it today) a sense of failure and of isolation I had never known before. A decent Latin Mass was arranged at St. Mary's, Cadogan Street—there could be no catafalque because with murders the body is impounded till the case is tried—and after it was over I left with Andrew Porter for Italy. That evening, walking in Milan down Via Manzoni, we found the Museo Poldi-Pezzoli lit up with an exhibition of early medieval church artifacts from the area between the Rhine and Meuse. Never before have I been so conscious of the therapeutic value of works of art. As one looked at the great silver chasses from Liège and Tournai, the awful present shriveled into insignificance. After a peaceful recuperative week I returned to the backlog of work on my desk in London. I had been in the habit of dining out at most three times a week, but I see from my diary that after I got back I started to dine out almost every evening, and I continued to do so for the next three years. Activity, however, was no more than a superficial remedy, and I longed, at first subconsciously, then consciously, to be released from the ghost-haunted atmosphere.

When I resigned, my plan was to move to Florence to work there on Italian sculpture. I had a book on Luca della Robbia to complete, and I had long had it in mind to produce a sculptural equivalent for Berenson's *Italian Pictures of the Renaissance*. The trustees were anxious that no early announcement of my resignation should be made, but I warned them that if rumors of it circulated to the press and I were asked to comment on them, I should be forced to tell the truth. My resignation was therefore announced. I at once received a number of offers of employment from the United States. Though they were not part of my life plan, it seemed to me that two of them should be considered seriously on account of the research facilities they offered, one from Carter Brown in Washington and the other from Tom Hoving in New York. I spent a doubt-ridden week in April in Palm

Beach—the weather was unsettled, and the palm fronds banged against each other through the night—and arranged on my way home to lunch at the National Gallery of Art and to spend a morning at the Metropolitan Museum. "Tell me about the *casus belli*," said Carter as we sat down to lunch, and I explained that there had been no disagreement of any kind with my trustees. The post he offered was a new one, and was bound up with the promotion of scholarship in the National Gallery and with the eventual development of the Center for Advanced Study in the Visual Arts. The East Wing was not yet open, and as I walked round it with him the temptation to accept was very strong. But when I reached New York I was glad I had refrained. If you are used to interviewing people, you become hypercritical when you are interviewed, and Hoving's performance seemed to me one of incomparable skill. Years later, when he was editing the *Connoisseur*, for which I had refused to write some article, he said: "Won't you do this for the guy who brought you over here?" I replied: "No, not even for the guy who baited the hook." What I found captivating was not so much the nature of the package he proposed—it was a combination of the consultative chairmanship of the Department of European Paintings at the museum and a professorship at the Institute of Fine Arts— as the shrewdness with which he read my mind. I asked him to put his proposals on paper, and when I got back to London I accepted them.

The arrangement was a generous one, but not so generous as to be embarrassing. I was anxious that the period of uncertainty should be as short as possible, to deter journalists from ringing up to ask if I were accepting a chair at Princeton and the *Boston Globe* from announcing that I was to take over the Museum of Fine Arts. Lionel Robbins, in an interval at Covent Garden, described my move as a "cultural catastrophe." "Won't you miss us?" people asked, and thinking back over lunch after lunch, dinner after dinner, party after party, I was often tempted to give an honest answer: "No, I don't believe I shall." I wanted a new life, and a new life was what I got. Foreign and particularly British participation in the running of the Metropolitan Museum had an unhappy history—Roger Fry, largely through his own fault, had had a disastrous period there—and I recognized that success would be possible only if the cable with London were cut and one were able to identify totally with New York cultural life.

The directorship of the Metropolitan Museum is not an enviable job. It is a post whose occupant is open to pressures that have no equivalent in London, from his own trustees, from a critical, not wholly reliable staff, from press exposure, and from the city of New York. It requires administrative steadiness, intelligence, and grasp of principle. I met the creator of the modern Metropolitan Museum, Francis Henry Taylor, only once in London, when he lectured at the Victoria and Albert and I dined afterwards with him and his wife and Trenchard Cox. His lecture was very poor; it was snobbish and conceited, and had I not met him afterwards I would have written him off then and there as an inflated fake. But when one talked to him, the effect left by the lecture proved totally misleading. He was warm and natural and cultivated in ways in which one might expect the author of *The Taste of Angels* to have been. His successor, James Rorimer, I had known for many years. As curator of the medieval collections at the Cloisters he maintained close contact with the Department of Sculpture at the Victoria and Albert, first with my predecessor and then with myself. He came from Cleveland and was a brother-in-law of the violinist Samuel Dushkin, for whom the Stravinsky violin concerto was first written, and he had an excellent sense of quality for French, German, and Spanish medieval art. The Cloisters at the time he took it over was a picturesque assembly of not quite first-rate artifacts in a genuine medieval setting. When I first went there, in 1955, Rorimer's contribution was at once apparent in every room. Through the years, by exclusive concentration on the areas of his specialty, he transformed it into one of the great museums of the world. Following Taylor's resignation he became director, not at once but after a protracted interval in which other candidates were interviewed, and the outside world was left with the impression that he was appointed *faute de mieux* and did not enjoy the trustees' full confidence. He took over the job with zest, but could not delegate. I remember my surprise one wet Sunday afternoon to find him by the cloakroom investigating how the intake and output of umbrellas could be speeded up. He was anxious as director to be associated in the public mind with brilliant discoveries, and this led, inevitably, to mistakes. Not long after his appointment he and Jack Phillips (who was in charge of sculpture and the decorative arts) bought for a small sum at auction a pigmented copy of the Verrocchio *Lady with the Primroses* in the Bargello. It was hustled onto television before they had had time even to examine it, and the claims they made for it were treated with general derision. Similarly at Spero's in London he bought a reliquary bust on an enameled base which he claimed, in an unwise article in the museum bulletin, to be a documented bust commissioned from Donatello by Poggio Bracciolini for a church in his native village of the same name. The bust was a copy of a reliquary bust in Belgium, set on a base which indeed dated from the fifteenth century. His personality seemed not to inspire great confidence in his staff, but I liked him very much and found him considerate and imaginative. When I told him that the works of art in private hands I most wanted to see in New York were John D. Rockefeller's busts by Verrocchio and Laurana, he took me to the Rockefeller apartment himself. Our views on the place of research in museums ran parallel, and he invited me to speak on it at a meeting of ICOM (the International Council of Museums) in New York. Distinguished as Rorimer was, he was treated with indulgence rather than liking by his trustees. I remember an uncomfortable dinner in his apartment with three or four pairs of trustees (one of them was that difficult man Robert Lehman and his wife) conducted in an atmosphere of artificial joviality. When Rorimer died of a heart attack in 1965, there was widespread regret that a man of such capacity and distinction had been impaled on museum administration.

I was among the vast number of people consulted on the succession, and I had no doubt that the appropriate appointment was that of Rorimer's successor at the Cloisters, Tom Hoving. Hoving was an excellent medievalist with a compulsive, highly articulate enthusiasm for works of art. He became director of the Metropolitan Museum in 1966, a year before I became director of the Victoria and Albert. The Metropolitan Museum was a far from dormant institution when he took it over, but he made it in ten years into the liveliest museum in the world. He was an effective director—unlike most directors, he exercised control over all of its departments and over its whole staff— he was a far from negligible scholar, and he had an instinctive sense of what the relation of the museum to its public ought to be. He organized creative exhibitions, not simply what are now called "blockbusters" but exhibitions with an intellectual spine in which new statements were made, and though some of them were the object of well-grounded criticism, the credit balance of his exhibition policy was very large. He was confident, overconfident indeed, and he imposed his own personality on the museum.

The most important of Rorimer's medieval purchases was his last, the whalebone Bury St. Edmund's Cross. The cross was owned by a Yugoslavian, Topic Mimara, and was kept in a bank vault in Zurich, where I went to see it. I spent two days there in 1966 sitting at a little table behind the safe door as Mimara placed one object after another in front of me. Many of the objects were forgeries. He was not prepared to sell the cross alone, but would agree to part with it if it were included in a group of reputedly English objects he wished to sell. When the negotiation reached a dead end, I passed the matter over to the British Museum, who succeeded where I had failed in persuading Mimara to sell the cross alone. It was an English work of unique importance, and arrangements were made for the voting of a special grant to cover the purchase. At this point, however, the Treasury minister responsible asked what evidence there was of Mimara's title to the cross. The answer was that there was none, and the deal was therefore abandoned. The Metropolitan Museum held the second option on the purchase, and on Rorimer's instructions Hoving forthwith collected the cross. In a book on the cross, published after Rorimer's death, Hoving claimed responsibility for the purchase, but he was an agent, not the prime mover in the negotiations.

Hoving had the reputation of being difficult to work with. I was confident, however, that we could cooperate constructively, and I was disappointed when the telephone rang one day in my office in London and he told me that he had resigned. His relations with his trustees were unhappy (he had indeed subjected them on more than one occasion to gratuitous embarrassment), but in the museum field he was a kind of genius, and during the years I was in New York the Metropolitan Museum lived initially on the overspill from his regime. Hoving remained at the Metropolitan through my first year there. I was asked by the trustee committee appointed to select the new director whether I wished to be considered for the post. I replied that if it were offered to me I should accept it, but with reluctance since I had come to New York to put the then discredited Department of European Paintings in order, and if I were to become director they would forfeit the prospect of my doing this. This reasoning was respected, and I remained on in my department.

Not only was I anxious to administer a large collection of paintings, but I believed that if this could be done successfully it would have implications far outside the Metropolitan Museum. In London since

1945 the National Gallery had been the target of ceaseless criticism. There had been intermittent controversies in the press over the cleaning of the paintings, but successive directors had enjoyed the support of a passive, compliant board. The policy of radical cleaning had been espoused by Philip Hendy (who must have suffered from some retinal defect which made him see pictures as flat areas of color) and had continued under his successors for so long that proof of the damage done to the collection over thirty years could be seen in almost every room. The gallery was badly and insensitively hung, and under the then director, Michael Levey, this had reached a crisis point, where those walls which were painted were covered with dirty fingerprints and the standard of cleanliness was that of a museum in the French provinces. Levey's strength lay in his purchases; they were made at great cost but were undeniably of distinguished paintings. He later wrote, in an invidious obituary notice of his predecessor Kenneth Clark in the *Proceedings of the British Academy*, that at the National Gallery Clark's "own strongest concerns probably lay in exercising his taste through hanging of paintings." Had later directors shared this interest, had they indeed had any taste to exercise, the gallery would have appeared less uninviting and less run down. It was my belief (and this was borne out by events) that if the Department of European Paintings in the Metropolitan Museum could be reformed, this would lead to reformation at the National Gallery.

For anyone who has not experienced it at first hand, it is difficult to describe the excitement generated by the Metropolitan Museum. From the moment you enter the main hall it conveys a sense of animation which is totally unlike that of any large museum in Europe. This is due in the first instance to its public. They are enthusiastic, inquisitive, and critical, and they throng round the central information desk with a zest that has sometimes reminded me of the spectators in Leonardo's *Adoration of the Magi* thronging round the Holy Family. The need to satisfy, or at least to live up to, their expectations permeates the entire staff. They put you on your mettle to produce not just results but results of superior quality. In 1976 the most recently arranged of the main galleries were those housing the Egyptian collection. They were far from perfect (to my mind they were inferior to the Egyptian galleries at Brooklyn), but they were vivid and interesting, and were in total contrast to the inanimate galleries of small sculpture and material relating to Egyptian life in the British Museum.

Also new were the Islamic galleries, which had been brilliantly arranged by Richard Ettinghausen.

American visitors are more open-minded than their European counterparts. Many of them are prepared to look, and look attentively, both from a historical and an aesthetic perspective, at Early Christian silver, or Chinese sculpture, or medieval works of art. But when there was no major temporary exhibition, a high proportion of them, up to a third perhaps, come to the Metropolitan with one intention, to visit the galleries of European painting. As I went round them in 1976, I found to my concern that they were among the most unattractive, unregenerate galleries in the whole museum. The pictures were abominably hung, some of them had in the past been grossly overcleaned, some of them were very dirty, some of them were well, some badly framed, and some of them were not what they were supposed to be. In no gallery was there the least attempt at visual emphasis, and the assistance given to the visitor was minimal. For forty years the department had had an unhappy history, which was bound up with the personality of Theodore Rousseau. Rousseau had joined the staff in 1947, and had been successively curator and chairman of European Paintings till 1973, when he became vice-director. He was agreeable and had good manners, and was a personal friend of many of the trustees. But he had a defective sense of quality, he did not believe in knowledge, and he was a poor administrator. Rorimer as director mistrusted him, and on one occasion, in Florence, had asked me if I would be willing to take over his job. The years after the war were a great buying period, but at the Metropolitan Museum very few paintings were bought. Attention was focused on spectacular purchases that could be publicized—the magnificent Rembrandt *Aristotle*, the Georges de La Tour *Card Sharpers*, the deplorably damaged El Greco *Seventh Seal*, and the great Velázquez *Juan de Pareja*, which was bought at auction for a record price. When the Velázquez was bought and cleaned, it was discovered that a section on the right was fully painted but had been folded in. This was a common practice of Velázquez—the contemporary portrait of Cardinal Massimi at Kingston Lacey is treated in precisely the same way—but after cleaning the canvas was not folded back as it should properly have been but was left fully exposed, with the result that Pareja's head is off-center and the effect made by the image is less dynamic than it used to be. It was lack of funds to cover the purchase of the Velázquez portrait, a

Greek vase, and a contemporary sculpture that caused the scandal of deaccessioning from the collection in which Hoving and Rousseau were both deeply involved. The principal pictures concerned were a Douanier Rousseau which was sold privately to a dealer at a comparatively modest figure, and was then resold, at a proper Rousseau valuation, to a collector in Japan; a van Gogh sold without permission of the donors, the Bernhard family; and a Modigliani, sold for a third of its true value subject to a clause that the price would be refunded if it proved not to be genuine. A number of other pictures were sold at auction at the same time.

Rousseau's successor was a German, who after a few months reverted to his natural habitat as a picture dealer, and supervision of the department was entrusted to Everett Fahy, who successfully resisted the sale of other paintings. When Fahy after a short time became director of the Frick Collection, the former director of the Minneapolis Institute of Arts, Anthony Clark, a specialist in eighteenth-century Rome, who was also a proficient Byzantinist, was put in charge. Tony Clark was one of the nicest human beings I have ever known; his taste was discriminating and refined, and his personal relationships (he had a host of friends) were likewise delicate and sensitive. But he had a skin too few for the post he occupied, and before long he clashed with Hoving. One morning when I was staying briefly in New York I met him beside the information desk. His hair was ruffled, and he told me that he had just handed a letter of resignation to the director's secretary. It was intended as a torpedo, but no torpedo primed by Clark was likely to sink Hoving. Not long afterwards he had a heart attack in Rome and died. I was happy that later it was possible to propitiate his ghost with the purchase of the most beautiful of all the mythological pictures produced by the artist whom he most admired, Pompeo Batoni.

American museum collections are very different from their European counterparts. Most of them have been formed by donation or bequest, and they consist in large part of collections of collections or of groups of paintings that have been given in lieu of tax. It is therefore tempting to do as Rousseau did—that is, to deposit a very large number of pictures in storage, and endeavor, from time to time, to secure a masterpiece. But if the Department of European Paintings was to become, as I hoped, a serious center of study and research, and if its collections were to form a rounded whole, this option was impermissible. It was necessary first to establish what the museum owned, which pictures were not what they were supposed to be, which over-cleaned paintings were ruined and which were salvageable, and then to concentrate purchasing in areas that were conspicuously weak. Before this could be done, however, it was necessary to assemble an efficient staff. The thing that struck me most when I took over was the discrepancy between the public image of the Metropolitan Museum as a progressive, forward-looking, modern institution and the archaic character of the Paintings Department. The files on individual paintings were contained in white envelopes—archive envelopes they were called—which were far from up to date and to which no mind seemed ever to have been applied, and these had to be used in conjunction with an index in which groups of dirty cards were tied together with string.

Before taking over I discussed the problem of departmental staffing, and I was told that the beneficial move from the standpoint of the museum would be to persuade John Walsh, who had resigned with Tony Clark, to return from Columbia, where he was teaching, and take up his old post in charge of Dutch and Flemish paintings. During a morning together in my office in the British Museum he explained to me the principle that had led him to resign. I did not understand precisely what it was, but when people think they have resigned on principle one cannot admit to this, so I said I understood the principle and hoped he would return. He decided to remain on at Columbia, so at the beginning of 1977, the staff consisted of one specialist in nineteenth-century French painting, Charles Moffett, who proved a valuable colleague, a capable woman administrator, and a little group of jumped-up secretaries. Some three years earlier, when I was lecturing at the Fogg, I was taken round the paintings there by a group of students, one of whom seemed to me in every way exceptional. He knew which parts of every picture had been X-rayed and what the X rays showed. So perfect was his information that I felt a little skeptical, but when next day I visited the Conservation Department and looked at the X rays everything he told me proved to be correct. There was a compelling need at the Metropolitan for an Italian specialist, and since his dissertation topic was Gentile da Fabriano, I determined to recruit him. His name was Keith Christiansen, and he has since, in exhibition after exhibition and with painting after painting, made major discoveries of a kind that are possible only in museums. The collection of Dutch paintings at the Metropolitan is one of the finest in the world, and the department clearly could not survive without a Dutch specialist, who could speak on equal terms to specialists in Holland and London and Berlin. The vacancy was filled by Walter Liedtke, who had produced an excellent book on the painting of Dutch church interiors. There were two current cataloguing projects. One of them was for a catalogue of later Flemish paintings. It had been worked on for some years by an extremely nice and cultivated scholar who had retired from the museum, but when I read the text it seemed to me, by present-day standards, to be unacceptable. The Flemish paintings were therefore catalogued by Liedtke, in the first creditable catalogue of paintings issued by the museum for some years. A second cataloguing project was a legacy from Rousseau, who recognized that in the Italian field neither he nor his staff could tell who painted what. The result was a commission to a first-rate scholar, Federico Zeri, to take charge of a four-volume catalogue of Italian paintings, in which the attributions would be his and the entries would be worked up by a member of the departmental staff. This is not a way in which serious catalogues can be produced, and I suspect that Zeri, whom I much admire and who was responsible for an impeccably thorough catalogue of the Italian paintings in the Walters Art Gallery at Baltimore, must have regretted undertaking this commitment. The entries in the first two volumes gave no account whatever of the condition of the paintings—Zeri was not to blame for this—and though this was rectified with summary condition reports in the third and fourth volumes, the catalogues made a rather perfunctory impression. It seemed important that they should be completed, but the work on them now requires to be done over again. A number of very good exhibitions of French painting (they included the Manet and Monet exhibitions) were organized by Charles Moffett, and his decision to leave the museum and move to San Francisco would have left a serious void but for the recruitment of Gary Tinterow, who had been responsible for a fine exhibition of Picasso drawings at the Fogg and later undertook a Juan Gris exhibition in Madrid. He was later jointly responsible for the Degas exhibition in the form in which it was presented in New York in which Degas's works were explained in greater depth than that of any other nineteenth-century French artist. The collection of Flemish primitives in the Metropolitan Museum is the finest in the United States, but not for many years had

it been under specialist control. A gifted connoisseur of Flemish painting was recruited from Princeton in the person of Guy Baumann. I
reserved to myself control of the hanging of paintings through all the
galleries.

The linchpin of the operation, however, was the Paintings Conservation Department and its head, John Brealey. I had known Brealey
in London slightly for many years and had boundless admiration for
his work. It was unfailingly sensitive, resourceful, and tenacious, and
in England he had to his credit the cleaning of large numbers of
masterpieces, including the Mantegna cartoons at Hampton Court.
He arrived at the Metropolitan Museum two years before me, and
was in course of turning its Conservation Department into the best
in the world. In the 1930s incompetent restoration had wrecked countless paintings in the Metropolitan Museum. Pictures which seemed
from photographs to have been intact when they arrived at the museum had had their surfaces removed; one of the most notorious cases
was that of a beautiful Benozzo Gozzoli predella. When two celebrated
panels by the Barberini Master came to the United States in 1935,
one of them, the *Presentation of the Virgin in the Temple*, was bought
by the Boston Museum of Fine Arts and was left in the sound condition
in which it had arrived. The other, the *Birth of the Virgin*, was bought
by the Metropolitan Museum and was immediately restored; shadows
were cleaned away, and the fictive marbling in it was reduced to a
flat ground. Things took an upward turn, however, when a first-class
European restorer, Hubert von Sonnenburg, now director of the Alte
Pinakothek in Munich, was persuaded by Rousseau to take charge,
and a number of difficult paintings, among them the Titian *Venus and
the Luteplayer*, were cleaned with very good results. Sonnenburg was
a reclusive figure who consistently avoided press exposure and publicity. Brealey saw his post in very different terms: he was a crusader
whose mission was to reform the restoration of paintings in the United
States. I tried to persuade him that in this context polemics were
counterproductive. What was required was to put selected pictures
of every period in the Metropolitan Museum in optimum condition,
so that people could see with their own eyes the difference between
pictures that had been well cleaned and those that had been mutilated.
In addition Brealey undertook the cleaning of major pictures in museums outside New York—the Kimbell Art Museum at Fort Worth,
the Wadsworth Athenaeum at Hartford, and the Minneapolis Institute

of Arts, for which he cleaned the great Poussin *Death of Germanicus*. He was also responsible for restoring the Turners and the Fragonard decorations at the Frick Collection. His studio was a training ground for young restorers, and he held annual seminars for members of other museum staffs. As a result, not only was restoration in the Metropolitan Museum raised to an unprecedentedly high level, but throughout the United States Brealey's standards came to be accepted as a norm.

One further cog in the administrative machine must be mentioned here, since it was in fact of some importance. Each of the museum departments had a visiting committee, with a trustee chairman, composed of a handful of trustees and trustee-nominated private individuals. With some departments the visiting committee was a negligible factor; it was not consulted and seldom met. But potentially it was of value, as a sounding board rather than a fund-raising device. I explained to my committee, which had a first-rate chairman in Drue Heinz, that it would be told when matters discussed were confidential, but that otherwise its members might talk freely about any topic raised. It played a useful part in publicizing the department's policies.

The decade during which I was at the Metropolitan Museum was a golden age for acquisitions. That it was so was due not to me but to the imagination and the generosity of Charles and Jayne Wrightsman. Never in its history can the Department of European Paintings have received a succession of gifts of such high quality. In 1977 they gave to the museum a notable panel by Gerard David and a Poussin painted for Cassiano del Pozzo, *The Companions of Rinaldo* from the Harrach collection, the brilliant *modello* by Giovanni Battista Tiepolo for the ceiling fresco above the staircase at Würzburg, and the greatest of all neo-classical portrait groups, the large painting of *Lavoisier and His Wife* by Jacques-Louis David, which had hung for many years in Rockefeller University in New York. The year 1978 witnessed the gift of two more masterpieces, the El Greco *Christ Healing the Blind*, which I had seen when it was auctioned in London, and the finest *Penitent Magdalen* by Georges de La Tour. These were followed in 1979 by the Vermeer *Portrait of a Girl* from the Arenberg collection. When it was possible some years later to juxtapose this Vermeer with the Vermeer *Portrait of a Girl* from the Mauritshuis, the Wrightsman portrait proved the subtler and better-preserved painting of the two. A year later there arrived the Giovanni Domenico Tiepolo *Dance in*

25. Peter Paul Rubens: *The Painter with His Wife and Son* (*Metropolitan Museum of Art, New York, Gift of Mr. and Mrs. Charles Wrightsman*)

26. Lorenzo Lotto: *Venus and Cupid* (*Metropolitan Museum of Art, New York, Gift of Mr. and Mrs. Charles Wrightsman*)

27. Juan de Flandes: *Marriage Feast at Cana* (*Metropolitan Museum of Art,
New York, Gift of Mr. and Mrs Jack Linsky*)

28. Andrea Sacchi: *Marcantonio Pasqualini Crowned by Apollo*
(*Metropolitan Museum of Art, New York*)

29. Piero della Francesca: *The Dream of St. Jerome (Galleria Nazionale, Urbino)*

30. Piero della Francesca: *The Meeting of Solomon and the Queen of Sheba* (*San Francesco, Arezzo*)

31. Piero della Francesca: *The Victory of Heraclius over Chosroes* (*San Francesco, Arezzo*)

32. Simon Malgo: *View of Lake Geneva* (*collection of the author*)

33. On my loggia in Florence (*photograph by Massimo Listri, 1987*)

the Country, one of the most effervescent and exhilarating of his canvases, and it was followed in 1981 by the most spectacular of all the Wrightsmans' gifts, the great Rubens portrait of the painter with his wife, Helena Fourment, and their son Peter Paul, which had been given by the city of Brussels to the first Duke of Marlborough and had been preserved at Blenheim until, in the late nineteenth century, it was bought by Baron Alphonse de Rothschild. I learned of the purchase in my bedroom in a hotel in Venice, when Charlie, who always thought I would be kidnapped, rang me early in the morning with the words: "John, I have spent all your ransom money." The last picture Charles Wrightsman bought was a splendid Sweerts of one of the acts of mercy, *Clothing the Naked*, an appropriate symbol of what he had done for the museum. These gifts raised the whole character of the Metropolitan collection. To them in 1986 Jayne Wrightsman added what is probably the finest and undoubtedly the most appealing North Italian painting in the collection. Signed by Lorenzo Lotto and painted in the 1520s in either Bergamo or Venice, it shows a naked Venus lying on a blue cloth spread on the ground. She wears a gold-jeweled diadem and, with her right hand, holds up a laurel wreath through which a naked Cupid playfully urinates. Her face, turned toward the spectator, conveys a message of contentment and intelligence. The urinating Cupid was a decisive factor in the acquisition; it made the painting ineligible for purchase by many galleries, including the National Gallery of Art. The New York trustees, however, were less prudish and more open-minded than trustees elsewhere, and I had a group of them to dinner so that I could explain the superstitious connotations of urine in Renaissance Italy. Almost certainly a marriage portrait, the painting speaks across time with its freshness unimpaired. It is a more sympathetic and less mannered North Italian equivalent of Bronzino's famous *Venus, Cupid, Folly, and Time* in the National Gallery in London. Of all the pictures acquired for the Metropolitan during my time there, this is the one I most admire.

The Wrightsman gifts were not just gifts of important paintings. They were gifts designed to make good some of the inequalities of the collection. Private collectors in the United States had always set more store by Rembrandt than by Rubens. The Metropolitan had in the past had the possibility of buying one great Rubens, an altarpiece now in the Toledo Museum of Art, but the occasion was muffed, through ignorance or through timidity, and the arrival of the great triple portrait was a means of putting the balance right. It showed that Rubens was a far, far greater painter than earlier visitors to the museum might have supposed. The Giovanni Battista Tiepolo was an entrancing work. It had been discovered years earlier by David Carritt in a London suburb at the Hendon Hall Hotel, which had belonged to the actor David Garrick. There was no narrative El Greco in the collection (none, that is, save the abysmal *Seventh Seal of the Apocalypse*), and the *Christ Healing the Blind* was a fit companion for the charismatic Havermeyer *View of Toledo*. There was a great pre-revolutionary Jacques-Louis David in the collection in the *Death of Socrates*, but no pre-revolutionary portrait, and it might indeed be claimed that the *Lavoisier* was the finest French portrait of the eighteenth century.

Naturally there were other gifts and bequests as well. When the missing Jacopino del Conte portrait of Michelangelo was identified in the collection of Clarence Dillon, it was at once, with great generosity, given to the museum. An enchanting Winterhalter portrait of the Empress Eugénie, which I had often seen in the private collection of Germain Seligman, was given by Mr. and Mrs. Claus von Bülow, and a vivid Toulouse-Lautrec portrait of René Grenier was bequeathed by an old and highly discriminating friend, Minnie Fosburgh. Jean Fowles, in memory of her first husband, Langton Douglas, bequeathed an academically distinguished late Trecento panel of *St. Catherine of Alexandria*. One of the finest postwar collections of Old Masters and French furniture in New York was that formed by Jack and Belle Linsky. I had known them in London, and had indeed watched them bidding at the Spencer-Churchill and other sales. The Linskys had a long-standing interest in the Metropolitan Museum and financed the redecoration of the galleries of Flemish primitives. They were down-to-earth—I estimated the cost at about a hundred thousand dollars, and on the telephone I heard Belle Linsky's incisive voice saying: "Jack says seventy-five"—and after her husband's death Belle Linsky gave the museum two full-length saints by Perugino from the high altar of the church of the Annunziata in Florence (pairs to two saints at Altenburg) and a miraculously well-preserved *Head of Christ* ascribed to Niccolò di Tommaso. The fate of the rest of the collection lay in the balance for many months, but eventually twenty-one pictures were given by Belle Linsky to the museum. They included two pictures I had known at Northwick; an enchanting Giovanni di Paolo *Adoration of the Magi*; a *Madonna* by Carlo Crivelli from the Ericson collection, a damaged picture of which two of the wings were already in the museum; the most beautiful of all *Madonnas* by Vittorio Crivelli; an unpublished Andrea del Sarto portrait; an early male portrait by Fra Bartolommeo; a superlative Juan de Flandes *Marriage Feast at Cana* (which the National Gallery of Art had failed to buy at Christie's; they bought a slightly inferior companion panel); the earliest-known Rubens portrait, signed and dated 1598; a better Jan Steen than any in the museum collection; two tiny Cranachs; a first-rate Nattier portrait; a heroic still life by Meléndez; and a landscape by Boucher which formed a pair to a painting in Stockholm. Mrs. Linsky, to my regret, insisted that the paintings should be segregated along with furniture, bronzes, and ceramics from her collection, in a special gallery, where they are hung too thickly to make their full effect.

The strength of the Metropolitan collection lay in the seventeenth century, but there were certain major painters whose work was badly represented or not represented at all. One of these was Claude. On paper one might have thought that all was well, but the condition of most of the paintings was defective, and Claude is a painter who can be properly appreciated only when his work is well preserved. When, therefore, an almost perfectly preserved small Claude appeared for sale, it seemed to me essential to secure it, and it was generously bought for the museum by Walter Annenberg. The ideal donor, however, was his sister Enid Haupt, who was prepared to back acquisitions without interposing her own taste. It was she who enabled the museum to buy the huge Sacchi portrait of *Marcantonio Pasqualini Crowned by Apollo* from Althorp. It is a strange, highly evocative painting produced in Rome in the orbit of Cardinal Antonio Barberini at a time when Sacchi was in daily contact with Poussin. Bellori describes it quite accurately as "not a simple portrait but an extremely beautiful conceit." Another acquisition for which she was responsible was of an altarpiece by the Lombard painter Giulio Cesare Procaccini. Looking at it with her, I said tentatively that the price was rather high. "I don't think so," she replied, "if you count the number of cherub heads." This was indeed the way in which the value of the canvas must originally have been assessed. There was a lack of major seventeenth-century figure paintings, and this was repaired with a great Preti *Pilate Washing His Hands* and a magnificent Guercino *Capture of*

Samson, one of the missing paintings commissioned by the papal legate in Ferrara, Cardinal Serra. It was bought by Charles Wrightsman, but Denis Mahon was responsible for directing it toward the museum.

One hears many horror stories of the irresponsible behavior of the boards of American museums, but my experience was the contrary, that the board was prepared to back the purchase even of paintings they did not, as individuals, greatly like. One of the big gaps in the collection was of German Renaissance painting other than Holbeins. When therefore a splendid Baldung *Vision of St. John the Evangelist* came on the market, it was clearly imperative to buy it. Painted for Strasbourg, it is a figure painting of extraordinary strength with one of the most romantic landscapes in German Renaissance painting. The trustees did not respond to it, but recognized its importance for the museum, and it was bought. The same thing occurred with a painting discarded from Althorp, a sketch model on panel of the *Annunciation* which had been miscatalogued in the Spencer collection and appeared in New York as the work of Mazzola Bedoli. It was indeed the source of a painting by Bedoli at Capodimonte in Naples, but neither I nor my staff felt any doubt that the picture was by Parmigianino. It was a difficult picture for anyone not tuned in to Parmigianino's wavelength, but it too was secured. I do not, for the matter of that, think the trustees can have felt much enthusiasm for the single Roman Counter-Reformation picture bought for the museum by a generous donor, an austere altarpiece of the *Lamentation over the Dead Christ* painted for the altar of the Passion in the Gesù in Rome by Scipione Pulzone. It was given, very appropriately, in memory of Cardinal Cooke. I had got repeated pleasure from Seurat's early *Sous-Bois* from the time I was at Oxford, when it hung in the Clarks' house at Headington. Though the trustees bought it, they did so with reluctance, and were converted to it only after it was cleaned. With its purchase the Metropolitan became the single museum in which the whole span of Seurat's work was visible. Another major nineteenth-century painting, bought on grounds of its intrinsic quality, was the elusive Klimt portrait of Serena Lederer, painted under the influence of Monet in 1895, which I had first seen in Vienna fifty years before.

The most frequented part of the collection was, very naturally, the nineteenth- and early-twentieth-century French paintings. Partly from the Havemeyer collection, partly from the collection of Stephen

Clark, partly from other sources, it was one of the finest groups of Impressionist and Post-Impressionist pictures in the world. It was agreed in principle that for the future they be shown on the upper story of a newly built wing on the south side of the building in which the Rockefeller collection of primitive art would occupy the bottom floor. New top-lit galleries, paid for by the banker André Meyer, to be known as the André Meyer Galleries, were due to be constructed on the roof of the new building. The architect was Kevin Roche, and together we designed the floor plan of the galleries and the installation. Hitherto the paintings had been shown in conventional galleries, but though this was the way in which one had always seen them in rich houses it was not the way in which they could be seen most advantageously. Given the proportions of the galleries and the presence of a glass roof, to construct artificial rooms without ceilings and with walls of normal height would have been impracticable. But the space had a number of undeniable advantages. Impressionist paintings represent a way of looking at the world; they were in great part painted out of doors, and if they were shown as simply and as naturally as possible, with a variable combination of artificial light and daylight, they would, I believed, cease to look like static images (as they do with artificial lighting in conventional galleries) but would in fact appear a little different each time one saw them. I turned down a number of proposals whereby the space would have been divided into corridors like those in the Carnegie Institute at Pittsburgh and approved a scheme providing for a very large central space to be divided by big mobile screens, surrounded on all four sides by narrower galleries. Since nineteenth-century French paintings are related by almost everybody nowadays to the artists who produced them and since the representation of each artist's work was rich enough to enable his development and scope to be fully intelligible, the works of individual painters were grouped together and not mixed. In the large gallery therefore one was confronted in the center and on the right by Manet, on the right lateral wall by Renoir, and on the right side of the west wall by Cézanne. To the left lay Pissarro and the superb series of Monets, dominated by what seems to me his greatest painting, the *Grenouillère*, and culminating in the late works, followed by Toulouse-Lautrec, the Douanier Rousseau, and Gauguin, with on one face of a central screen van Gogh and on its back Seurat. The first of the corridors contained neo-classical paintings, especially David and

Ingres, the second contained romantic nineteenth-century paintings from Goya to Delacroix, Turner and Constable, and the third was devoted to Courbet. The Courbet exhibition held in Paris at the Grand Palais had been rather disappointing, but the Metropolitan Courbets made a considerable effect shown together in one large room. Beyond them lay Daubigny, Rousseau, and a roomful of Corots, and beyond that a miscellaneous room dedicated to Daumier, Millet, and Böcklin. The Degas, which required controlled lighting, were shown with the associated bronzes in the corridor on the opposite side. Within this scheme it was clearly necessary that the labels of the pictures should contain more than the title and the artist's name, and an attempt was made to explain, in a short space, the position each painting occupied in the totality of the artist's work and what its critical importance was. I thought when I arranged the room that I was dealing simply with a gallery installation, but the result was a kind of pleasure palace, at which attendances remained extremely high through the whole of my period in New York. I hoped that when visitors left the gallery, they would have the sense I had after arranging it, that the real world, looked at from the hedonist standpoint of Monet and Manet and Renoir, is a more enjoyable place than one had thought.

The reinstallation of the galleries of Old Masters was a slower process, since it was necessary to obtain private funding for everything that was done. It was determined by the dual principles of ensuring that each painting was shown so that its artistic quality was evident to any visitor and so far as possible was placed in a sequence or grouping that was valid from a historical and therefore an educational point of view. From time immemorial the visitor who climbed the staircase was confronted, in the facing gallery, by the Raphael altarpiece known as the *Madonna of the Nuns of Sant'Antonio*. It was, indeed, one of the most important Italian paintings owned by the museum, and it looked very beautiful when John Brealey had finished cleaning it; the drawing of those heads which were undamaged proved to be far subtler and more delicate than had been supposed. But it was not a painting with great public appeal, and still less so were the High Renaissance pictures by which it was surrounded. But the museum owned a magnificent collection of eighteenth-century Venetian pictures, headed by three huge paintings of scenes from Roman history by Giovanni Battista Tiepolo. They had been painted for the Ca' Dolfin in Venice, and no one who was not blind could fail to respond to their outrageously opulent appeal. Before they could replace the Raphael they needed to be cleaned (with paintings of this size a lengthy business) and to be reframed, since on arrival at the museum they had been put into particularly vulgar frames with white-and-gold moldings. I asked a member of the staff who lived in Venice to go to Ca' Dolfin (which is now part of the university) to see whether molded plaster frames survived in the room from which they had been moved. She reported that they did, and arrangements were made to have them photographed. But when the photographer reached Ca' Dolfin he found they were fictive painted moldings, not stucco frames. Two more paintings from the same series are, however, in Vienna, and when I went there I found that they had been reframed in excellent taste. The frames had been made in the 1930s, and it was reasonable to bet that if their style were acceptable forty years later it would still be acceptable forty years hence. So specimens were taken of the Vienna moldings and they were reproduced. The museum also owned a ceiling painting by Tiepolo from the Palazzo Barbaro and oil sketches for the altarpiece at Este, for the Würzburg ceiling, and for the Royal Palace in Madrid, so the whole room could be devoted to the inventive genius of one artist. That it could be arranged, and arranged really well on specially prepared Fortuny fabric, was due to the generosity of Jack Heinz.

The large gallery behind the Tiepolo room (the only really big gallery available) was devoted to the eighteenth century, with special emphasis on the work of Gainsborough and Reynolds. The English paintings at the Metropolitan had been neglected through the whole period when English portrait painting was unfashionable—if a general exhibition of the portrait in the eighteenth century could be arranged, they would prove artistically and psychologically to be the greatest portraits of their time—and they too were cleaned extremely well. From this room there are two sets of parallel galleries, one, on the left, devoted to Northern and the other to Italian primitives. One of the first collections of Italian primitives in the United States was the Bryan collection, which passed to the New-York Historical Society and was kept in storage there. A number of loans from the Bryan collection were negotiated, to be shown with the museum's paintings. They included an object of great historical as well as artistic importance, the painted tray commissioned by Piero de' Medici for the birth of his son Lorenzo il Magnifico. This became the centerpiece of a room devoted to secular paintings, a field in which the museum collections were especially rich.

The seventeenth-century paintings in the Dutch galleries had been hung in extraordinary confusion: the visitor's eye was constantly defeated by sudden changes of theme as well as by changes of scale. Small Dutch genre paintings (especially paintings of the quality of those in New York) cannot usefully alternate between sea paintings and landscapes, and the various classes of painting were therefore segregated. Once more a good many paintings were reframed. Many of the smaller pictures were in plastic reproductions of Dutch ebony frames, and on masterpieces like Vermeer's *Allegory of the Sacrament* this had a lethal effect. After a number of experiments it was provided with a French seventeenth-century frame, of a type that was frequently used in the late seventeenth century for small Dutch paintings, and it looked extremely good. This was a picture for which I felt a special sympathy, not only as a transcendent work of art but because as a boy I cut photographs of it from the *Boston Globe* when it was bought by Colonel Friedsam. The Dutch landscapes were augmented with a well-preserved late Koninck (since one, the larger, of the two early Konincks was no longer exhibitable on grounds of condition) and by a Brazilian landscape by Frans Post, the first European landscape painter to work in the New World. The great series of Rembrandts in the collection were well able to look after themselves, though a number, and especially the *Aristotle with a Bust of Homer* and the *Saskia as Flora*, were brilliantly cleaned by John Brealey. In the Kaiser Friedrich Museum before the war the early Rembrandt *Rape of Proserpine* was accompanied by another, and in some respects more beautiful, Leyden Rembrandt from a private collection, *The Rape of Europa*. The owner, who was living in the United States, had left it in Europe at Basel, but was anxious to have it closer at hand, and it was therefore transferred from the Öffentliche Kunstmuseum to the Metropolitan. With its figures reflected in the river and its veiled landscape it seems to me one of the most beautiful of all Dutch paintings.

One of the accusations commonly directed against the Metropolitan was that its policies were dictated by expediency and that in relation to past testators it had been less good than its word. Most of the significant benefactions of paintings in this century were distributed through the galleries, and arrangements had been negotiated whereby the Bache and Altman collections should be treated in the same way. Fine as they were, it would have been embarrassing to have to show the Bache pictures together, since they were of widely differing styles and periods, but the nucleus of the Altman collection was a world-famous series of Dutch paintings. Apart from the department store which bore his name, Benjamin Altman's claim to a posthumous identity was as the creator of this collection, and I therefore arranged with the chairman of the Altman board for Altman's paintings (with the exception of two pictures by Velázquez and a Van Dyck) to be reintegrated in the way he had envisaged in the terms of his original bequest. This could be done relatively easily in the new layout of the galleries, since one fell in the normal sequence of the Dutch galleries and another was contiguous to an Italian gallery containing related works. The Dutch gallery, with a wall of Rembrandts and one of the most beautiful Ruysdaels in the world, made an unforgettable effect.

It is commonly said that museums are justified by the quality of the experience they afford. The term "quality of experience" is naturally bound up with the wealth and diversity of their collections, but in practice it means something more than this; it means that members of the public are persuaded to look attentively at least at a few works of art and take away with them mental snapshots of the objects they have seen. Well-educated people have a broad historical sense which enables them to put pictures in their appropriate pigeonholes, but the man in the street is in a totally different position. His sense of the relation between time and style is fallible, and if he watches television he is used to looking at a sequence of rapidly changing images, not a stable image as it was looked at in the past. How was this to be remedied? Not by guide lecturers, valuable as is their work. The answer is rather that museums must afford an occasion for self-education by a type of labeling which will focus the visitor's attention on some specific aspect of each individual painting. The American public is more sophisticated and more highly educable than its English counterpart, and from the time that I arrived there I believed that in the Metropolitan Museum labeling was integral to the whole problem of display. Labeling is a difficult task. If the label contains too much information, it becomes a substitute for looking at the picture, but if its content is judged carefully it can form a taking-off point from which the visitor can edge his way into the painter's world. At the Metropolitan Museum not all the labeling of paintings was equally successful, but it ensured that people with next to no prior information could approach the pictures with less difficulty than they might otherwise have had. The labels were in some cases too large and much too white (this is because they were printed inexpensively), but they were very generally read.

Space in the Metropolitan Museum, as in most museums, is limited, and when I first went round the paintings storage areas I found that they were clogged with pictures. Some of them belonged to private owners, who used the museum for free storage, and these could be returned. But the vast majority had drifted into the museum and were its property, and it seemed to me essential that they should be thinned out. The machinery to do so was available. After the scandal caused by earlier deaccessioning, a set of sensible, foolproof rules governing the disposal of objects from the museum collections was issued. This provided for consultation with any interested party before deaccessioning could be approved, and precluded private sales. Objects disposed of could be sold only at auction, under the name of the museum. Any trade-off between art dealers and museum departments (of the kind in which Rousseau had indulged) was ruled out, and in every case the reasons for deaccessioning had to be presented to the trustees. There were two limiting factors, however, both of which were psychological. The staff of the department claimed to have vivid memories of the director and the chairman walking round the galleries choosing pictures to be sold. For this reason they were frightened at the implications of further selling, and recognized that the public, especially the informed public in the shape of picture dealers, would rightly scrutinize all sales. There were, however, quite a number of large, unwieldy paintings that should, on grounds of condition alone, be disposed of. It seemed to me best to begin with the pictures in the area in which I was, or was supposed to be, a specialist, and the first sales were of a totally repainted altarpiece by Costa (the only genuine area in it was a patch of yellow in one dress) and an irreparably damaged *Assumption* by the Sienese painter Girolamo di Benvenuto. Slowly the tide of deaccessioning mounted. Typical of the pictures sold were a once fine, now battered Alessandro Longhi portrait, which could at no time in the future be shown, and an early Canaletto of the Piazzetta of St. Mark's in which the foreground figures were adequately preserved but the upper three-quarters of the canvas was so damaged as to be irreparable. There were unwieldy pictures which were not badly preserved but were of no merit, and there were paintings that were not what they were supposed to be. Typical of these were two flower paintings from a group of Maltese still lifes at one time ascribed to Francesco Guardi. There were works that had been directed to the museum under the tax system and had never been hung, and never would be. Certain paintings which ought on grounds of condition to have been expelled were retained for fear of criticism (they included two ruined Claudes), and a large number of nineteenth-century academic paintings were also retained on the ground that they might in due course be reappraised by changing taste. The money raised by sales went into purchases, but never was a picture sold in order to raise money, and never was a picture bought in the hope that the cost would be defrayed by deaccessioning. The separation of sales from purchases was absolute. I wish this policy could have been extended to other museum departments. When all this was complete, a very large number of paintings remained in storage. They were available to students, but were in practice inaccessible to ordinary visitors. Since they formed part of the public patrimony, and had been given or bequeathed to the museum in order that they should be seen, I arranged that those which were of interest should be shown in special galleries as a reserve collection. There was space for most of the early Italian and Northern paintings (including some skeletons in the cupboard like a repainted Botticini *St. Sebastian*, which had been bought with much excitement as a Castagno) and for a selection from the secondary Dutch, French, and English paintings, most of which would eventually be shown on a rotating schedule.

After Hoving's resignation, the trustees turned their attention to the administrative structure of the museum. The result was a decision to weaken the director's post by allocating part of his duties to a paid president. The two posts were to have equal status, and disagreements, if they occurred, would be settled by the chairman and the board. The theoretical objections to a system whereby the director was deprived of responsibility for many of the administrative services of the museum were voiced publicly at the time, but at first were of little practical significance since the new president did not preside and the new director did not direct. Only later, when a passive president was succeeded by an energetic one and the director, Philippe de Montebello, had felt his way into his job, did trouble arise, and when it did there was no doubt in the minds of the curatorial staff that the director, not the president, should be in overall control.

The position of a director with no more than partial control over a museum and its staff is not an easy one. In any active museum there is an inbuilt tension between the curatorial staff and the administrative staff, whose concern is to maximize receipts from sales areas, publications, and the renting out of space for social or other activities. A minor donor to the museum who lived on the opposite side of Fifth Avenue once complained to me that he and his wife repeatedly watched guests arriving for black-tie dinners to which they were not invited. I had to explain to him that the black-tie dinners were, for the most part, not the concern of the museum. Obviously curatorial and administrative staffs had a common interest in ensuring the museum's success and solvency, but from time to time arbitrary decisions were made by the administration which were not cleared with the curatorial staff. These would have been far more serious but for the presence of Ashton Hawkins, who, as executive vice president and counsel, commanded the confidence of the whole staff and of the trustees. The debt due to his cleverness and good sense throughout the years that I was there cannot be overstressed.

Philippe de Montebello, whom I had known slightly for a number of years, had worked in the Department of Paintings under Rousseau, had then become director of the Houston Museum of Fine Arts, and on Rousseau's death had been appointed deputy director of the Metropolitan by Hoving, with special responsibility for planning temporary exhibitions. He did this very well, and continued to do it very well after he became director. His first language was French, and so was his whole personality. He inspired liking which did not develop into trust. Posterity is likely to speak well of him as director. It will do so because he believed in the museum as a serious institution and not simply as a place of entertainment. (Though he was not himself a scholar, his heart was where it should have been.) It will do so also because of the excellence of the exhibitions that he sponsored. In the Metropolitan Museum temporary exhibitions are a necessity; without them attendances would decline and receipts fall. During my ten years in New York they were the lifeblood of the Metropolitan Museum. Superior people sometimes speak of mammoth exhibitions with contempt (they see them simply as publicity without regard to the works of art they make available), but when I review my memories of them as a frequent visitor or a participant, I am astounded by the wealth of experiences they supplied. The exhibition *Treasures from Dresden* brought to New York two of the greatest Venetian sixteenth-century portraits, Titian's *Lady in White* and Tintoretto's *Lady in Mourning*, the *Jacob and Rachel* of Palma Vecchio, Tintoretto's *Arsinoë*, Poussin's *Realm of Flora*, major portraits by Holbein and Dürer, a great Vermeer, and Ruysdael's *Jewish Cemetery*, and a number of major bronze sculptures, along with a superb cross section of works from the Green Vaults and the porcelain collection. *The Vatican Collections* brought the *Apollo Belvedere* and the Belvedere torso and with them two Raphael predellas, the Leonardo *St. Jerome*, the Caravaggio *Entombment*, the Poussin *Martyrdom of St. Erasmus*, a splendid group of Bernini bozzetti, and a great relief by Pierino da Vinci. From Vaduz, with *Liechtenstein: The Princely Collections*, came the mysterious Fouquet-like portrait of 1456, the celebrated Massys *Portrait of a Canon*, a beautiful group of small Dutch paintings, a splendid sequence of Van Dyck portraits, and incomparable Rubenses, which reached their climax in the *Decius Mus* paintings and the latest and finest of his altarpieces of the *Assumption of the Virgin*, specially cleaned for the occasion, as well as a treasure trove of bronzes, ivories, firearms, and ceramics. *The Thyssen-Bornemisza Collection* brought superb primitives and the Caravaggio *St. Catherine of Alexandria*, and a labored exhibition of French seventeenth-century paintings in American collections, planned by Pierre Rosenberg, yielded the Poussin *Death of Germanicus* and most of the other Poussins in the United States as well as a very fine series of Claudes.

The most popular exhibitions inevitably were those dealing with the nineteenth century. Two exhibitions covered the late work of van Gogh (which to my shame speaks more clearly to the public than it does to me), and others, organized jointly with the Louvre, reviewed the work of Manet and Monet in brilliant detail. There were in addition numbers of smaller exhibitions; those I remember with most pleasure were of Japanese prints of actuality given by Lincoln Kirstein, of Greek vase painting organized by Dietrich von Bothmer, and of Constable oil sketches planned by my former colleague Graham Reynolds as part of a celebration called *London Salutes New York*. If you put yourself in the position of a relatively indigent New Yorker whose travel possibilities were circumscribed, the debt of gratitude which would be due for all of the experiences these exhibitions offered would be very great.

An agreement was reached with the Italian government providing for a series of joint exhibitions to be held at the Metropolitan Museum and in Italy. This had the advantage of enabling pictures from Italy to be shown more freely in New York and pictures from non-Italian sources to be shown in Italy. It was felt, by Christiansen and by myself, that much might be learned from a jointly planned exhibition of the work of Caravaggio. No major exhibition had been held since the celebrated exhibition held in Milan in 1961, in which Roberto Longhi set Caravaggio in his rightful place as one of the greatest Italian painters. Clearly it would be impossible in New York to secure the almost complete coverage of major paintings that was shown in Milan, but sufficient pictures were available to make the exhibition, from both a public and a scholarly point of view, thoroughly worthwhile. On the Italian side the moving spirit was Raffaello Causa, with whom I had never previously worked, and Mina Gregori.

Through the agency of Causa, I was for the first time converted to Naples, where the committee meetings took place. Unhappily, before the exhibition was held, Causa died, and in the ensuing confusion a number of loans were disallowed. The Soprintendente ai Beni Culturali in Rome said that he had arranged the loan of one of the Doria Caravaggios, but proved never to have done so, and no pictures came from San Luigi dei Francesi or Santa Maria del Popolo. As a final aggravation the loan of the Ambrosiana *Still Life* was, at the last moment, canceled. Nonetheless the exhibition, though less representative than that in Milan, was of real value. It was packed with visitors, and it enabled a large number of problematic attributions to be cleared up in a prize-winning article by Christiansen. From the public standpoint one of the merits of the exhibition was that it covered, in a sketchy fashion, Roman and Bolognese religious painting before the emergence of Caravaggio. The second joint exhibition was devoted to Emilian paintings from Correggio to the Carracci. This time the organizer on the Italian side was an old friend, Andrea Emiliani, and there were no pitfalls and no mistakes. The representation of Parmigianino, with the *St. Roch* from San Petronio at Bologna, the *Conversion of St. Paul* from the Kunsthistorisches Museum at Vienna, and the newly cleaned *Antea* from Naples, was especially fine. But Correggio's appeal is more esoteric than Caravaggio's, and the public response was correspondingly more limited.

When I retired from the British Museum in 1976 I touched in my speech on the current defects and future problems of the institution. My retirement from the Metropolitan Museum in 1986 was very different. I could look back on ten of the happiest and most constructive years that I had ever known. I was presented, in a generous speech by Philippe de Montebello, with a printed bibliography of my writings, edited by Everett Fahy, with an introduction by John Russell, and I was moved to learn that a successful subscription had been organized by my friends and the friends of the museum (there was in practice no difference between them) to ensure that my name would for the future be attached to the chairmanship of the department.

New York produced one last surprise. Not long before my retirement it was proposed by Keith Christiansen that an exhibition should be held of fifteenth-century Sienese paintings. It would have, he explained, two functions, the first and the more positive to resolve some art-historical problems with which we had both been deeply concerned, and the second to celebrate my seventy-fifth birthday. Initially I doubted whether the plan was feasible. The policy of the Metropolitan Museum precluded the loan of panel paintings, and so did the policy of the Ministero dei Beni Culturali in Rome. A number of earlier exhibitions in New York had nonetheless included panel paintings; one of these was that of Old Masters from the Thyssen collection, and another that of masterpieces from the Vatican. While the risks involved in the loan of large panel paintings were considerable, those arising from the loan of small panels could be reduced to a negligible point through the use of climatically controlled boxes and hand transport. The loan negotiations required great pertinacity, but so successful were they that the exhibition in its final form included loans from centers as far-distant as Melbourne and Budapest and Altenburg. It was intended from the first that emphasis should rest on small narrative panels. The reason for this was that in the nineteenth century the predellas of many altarpieces containing narrative scenes were sawn up so that the individual pieces could be sold separately. This was the case with some of the most important Sienese narrative complexes, such as the Arte della Lana predella of Sassetta, the scenes from the life of St. Catherine of Siena by Giovanni di Paolo, and the scenes from the life of St. Anthony the Abbot by a painter known as the Osservanza Master. The hope was that in these three cases (and in a number of others as well) panels which originally belonged together could be reunited for the first time since they were cut up. The Superintendent in Siena, Pietro Torriti, took a benevolent view of the whole enterprise, and other bodies in Siena, especially the Biblioteca Communale, did so too. Siena also yielded a generous sponsor in the oldest active Tuscan bank, the Monte dei Paschi, to whose altruism and good offices the city owes so much.

Some weeks before the opening I received a copy of the catalogue. Written by Keith Christiansen and by two other younger scholars with whom I had long been associated, Carl Strehlke, the curator of the Johnson collection in the Philadelphia Museum of Art, and Larry Kanter, the chairman of the Lehman collection, it was one of the most beautiful as well as one of the most innovative illustrated art books I had ever seen. But it still left me unprepared for the spectacle of the exhibition as I first saw it in the Lehman Wing.

From Sassetta's Arte della Lana predella alone there was the *Institution of the Eucharist* and the scene of St. Anthony the Abbot beaten by emasculated devils, which I had first looked at in the Pinacoteca at Siena in 1935; the scene from the Pinacoteca Vaticana of St. Thomas Aquinas, on his knees before a mystically reanimated crucifix, holding the *Summa Theologica* in his hands; a panel I had first been to Budapest to see half a century before of St. Thomas inspired to compose the liturgy of the Feast of Corpus Christi by a vision of Christ and the Fathers of the Church; the little painting I had so often driven over to see at Barnard Castle of a heretical communicant whose incredulity causes the Host to bleed and whose soul is seized by a devil as he endeavors to receive the sacrament; and the mysterious panel from Melbourne of the burning of a heretic which had been brought to my office at the Victoria and Albert for authentication by the Galerie Sankt Lukas in Vienna. The tally of pictures to which I had some personal attachment continued to the very end, with a scene from the life of St. Clement by Fungai from York which I had enjoyed so often before the war in Peter Lycett-Green's gallery at Goudhurst. A little further on were the two scenes from the life of St. Anthony the Abbot, about whose cleaning and inpainting I had protested when I was at Yale, and a Signorelli predella panel I had looked at week by week in Williamstown, and two Sano di Pietros I had not encountered since I saw them in the 1930s at Altenburg, and the Giovanni di Paolo scenes from the life of St. Catherine of Siena, of which I had first seen eight, in sequence, not juxtaposed, in 1937 in the house of the Stoclets at Tervueren, and Giovanni di Paolo's Lecceto codex from Siena, which I had worked over carefully when I was publishing the Dante codex in the British Museum. I have never adopted a Proustian view of works of art, but to me the exhibition was a relief map in which the topography of my professional and emotional life, with its peaks and its declivities, was exposed.

The general visitor, of course, viewed the exhibition very differently. Most people today have lost the ability to read works of art in the way in which they were originally intended to be read. For them a work of art is something to be looked at briefly, in the hope that it will leave an instantaneous image on the mind. This attitude is a legacy from nineteenth-century French painting. But the New York exhibition, to my surprise, was very popular. People came to it in droves, and they went round it very slowly, assimilating everything there was to learn—about the streets of Siena as they are represented in the panel *St. Anthony Giving Alms* from Washington; about the cool space of Siena Cathedral as it is represented in a recently cleaned panel from Berlin; about the countryside as it appeared to Sassetta and Sano di Pietro and still appears today; about the hermit-filled woods between San Leonardo al Lago and Lecceto, where the Osservanza Master's St. Anthony the Abbot meets a centaur and is accosted by the devil dressed as a seductive, pink-clad girl; about pattern, where landscape becomes geometry; about the repertory of gesture and the human responses it expressed; and, more succinctly, about the nature of works of art. From the standpoint of scholarship a great deal transpired from the exhibition that was genuinely new. It is common for art historians to assess finality in terms of their own work. I have never been tempted to do this. I am content to have made some contribution to an understanding of the field, but I regard the part that I have played in it as no more than the laying of a path which, if it is pursued, may lead to sounder, more exact results. For me the ultimate pleasure of this extraordinary exhibition was the fact that study of the Quattrocento in Siena had now passed to eyes and minds that were younger and in some respects more penetrating than my own.

12

TEACHING
TO LEARN

MY GREAT SATISFACTION IN NEW YORK WAS SUCCESSFULLY TO HAVE reverted from a directorial to a curatorial post. Each day I was in contact with great works of art, and when I looked at them I had the sense (it was, of course, illusion) of understanding a little more about their nature and the creative process through which they were produced. It was an illusion because great works of art are produced in precisely the same fashion as the general run of works of art, but with a concomitant of inspiration that can be apprehended but can never be explained. How was it possible for an imperfect human being to transcend his natural limitations, and through the neutral medium of paint to plumb the emotional depths of Rembrandt's *Aristotle with the Bust of Homer*? How was it possible for a Venetian painter in the sixteenth century to explore the sensuous world of Lotto's *Venus* and to establish, so lucidly, the questioning intelligence of her face? How was it possible, in the stuffy society of Delft, to achieve the ideal correlation of space and light and feeling of the *Girl with a Water Jug* of Vermeer?

One of the Rubenses in the collection—it is indeed only in part by Rubens—is the *Feast of Achelous*, which shows a group of hungry figures round a table piled with food. This seemed to me a metaphor for the visual feast that was offered by New York—by the Frick Collection, with its sublime Bellini and its Titian portraits and its incomparable Ingres, and the National Academy of Design and the Whitney and the Guggenheim, all three of which functioned as exhibition spaces as well as permanent collections, and the Museum of Modern Art, then operating effectively but at a lower tension than when I was first introduced to it by that genius Alfred Barr. A taxi took one to Brooklyn, with its admirable exhibitions and its rewarding permanent collections, or to the Hispanic Society. The visual experiences available were infinite.

I held a second post as professor at the Institute of Fine Arts of New York University, where I taught one class a term while I was at the museum and to which I still return to teach a course each January. From its inception the Institute was concerned with training for higher degrees, not with undergraduate teaching. Before and immediately after the war it had a staff of unparalleled distinction; it included Karl Lehmann, Peter von Blanckenhagen, Erwin Panofsky, Walter Friedländer, Richard Krautheimer, Martin Weinberger, and Richard Offner. Its standards were exigent, and as a repository of knowledge it was unique. All that I knew of the Institute at this time was what I learned from Offner, whose long, silent, Kantian seminars were designed as studies in method not as a means of imparting information. Its director in the postwar period was my friend Craig Smyth, who enjoyed the affection of the students and the staff. I was a trustee of the Institute for some years before I joined its faculty, and had I known as much about its workings then as I do now I could have performed a useful task. The Institute is housed in the Duke House on the corner of Fifth Avenue and Seventy-eighth Street, almost opposite the Metropolitan Museum. The advantage of this position is its proximity to the museum, which affords easy access not only to the galleries but to an excellent library. Its disadvantage is its physical divorce from other departments of New York University, which encourages a not altogether healthy intellectual isolation on the part of both the students and the staff. After working at the Victoria and Albert, where the national art library is (or in my day was) virtually complete, and at the British Museum, where any book, however rare, could be brought to one's desk in fifteen minutes, I found the Institute library disappointing both in coverage and in quality. The procurement of books was slow, and purchases were geared to the ad hoc requirements of the teaching staff. This was the case also with the slide department, which lacked the coverage and consistency that are demanded by undergraduate teaching, and where a high proportion of the slides seemed to have been made, at short notice, from periodicals or books. When I go to teach in New York today I take over with me whatever slides I am likely to require. It was a guiding principle of the Institute that members of the staff should prosecute their own research, and even after the first immigrant professorial generation expired, a great deal of work of prime importance has been undertaken there.

The core of a teaching institution, however, is its students, not its staff. Until I taught there I had no experience of the student body as a whole. The Institute students whom I met in Europe were hyperintelligent, and had been closely supervised by scholars of great distinction. I like to think that they were characteristic of the student body at that time, but it was not true of the student body when I joined the staff. The standard had come down because the level of admissions was too high. The success of seminars is determined as much by the quality of the students as by the quality of the instructor. Only if students are ambitious and anxious to compete with one another do seminars go well. Fortunately I have had a small number of exceptional students who are now working on intrinsically interesting aspects of my own field that I myself shall have no time to cover. Students, even clever students, are curiously bad at choosing appropriate dissertation topics. They settle on some theme that interests them—prostitution in the High Renaissance and its reflection in the visual arts, or an arcane aspect of astrology—which will not, however carefully it is developed, form a useful addition to knowledge or qualify them for later work. The more exigent the standard applied to the dissertation, the more acute the trouble becomes. This is not an exclusively American problem; I have encountered it also in London at the Courtauld Institute of Art. It is no fun at twenty-three or twenty-four to be saddled with an academic topic that will excite no interest when the dissertation is complete. Students have to be guided firmly toward topics which represent a gap in present knowledge and where new results can hypothetically be secured. A successful dissertation is in the last resort a matter of character, and it is vital that the supervisor know the student well enough to judge his stamina as well as his intellectual capacity.

A great many clever students of art history are not natural art historians; they are not, that is, the type of person who will find fulfillment in teaching or in work in a museum or in independent continuing research. But there is a worldwide shortage of art critics, and I believe that provision for their training should be made by including in graduate programs the option of properly planned courses

in aesthetics and in the recent history of art criticism. How much
better to find oneself writing for a daily paper than teaching at a
remote college, where the library is poor and there are next to no
works of art.

What students obtain from facilities like those offered by the Institute of Fine Arts is determined by the shrewdness with which they
pick their courses and the amount of spread that they allow themselves.
It is important that they be skeptical of the whole structure of knowledge in the areas with which they deal, and it is vital that they be
fully literate. It is not enough to say that muddled writing and clear
thinking do not go hand in hand. A knowledge of discriminating
writing, whether it be Proust or Broch, is conducive to discriminating
visual processes. What I myself have gained from teaching in New
York can be summed up in the word "stimulus." It has come from
students, without whom I would have had no contact with the young,
and whom I find challenging and extremely likable, and from the staff.
I am very conscious of what I owe to colleagues who are also long-
standing friends, like Gert Schiff and Edgar Haverkamp-Begemann
and Colin Eisler and Marvin Trachtenberg and Robert Rosenblum
and Kathleen Brand.

The amount of original research that I could undertake while working at the Metropolitan and teaching at the Institute of Fine Arts was
very limited. An important joint project in which both bodies were
concerned was the cataloguing of the collection bequeathed to the
museum by Robert Lehman. It looked, in its installation at that time,
very odd, since the Old Masters were, at Lehman's express wish,
housed in rooms which reproduced the rooms in his house on West
Fifty-third Street. This meant that the best pictures were inadequately
lit, and that undue emphasis was placed on the comparatively weak
nineteenth-century collection. The curator of the collection was a
Hungarian who had been appointed personally by Lehman and who
was regarded on all sides as uncooperative and difficult to deal with.
His attitude was especially uncooperative toward the catalogue ("the
so-called scholarly catalogue," he called it), which was entrusted to a
joint committee, chaired by an Institute of Fine Arts representative,
Haverkamp-Begemann, on which I represented the Metropolitan Museum and Sydney Freedberg acted as consultant. Its other members—
a shrewd man called Alvin Pearson, whose prime concern was that
the catalogue should tell the truth; a clever lawyer who belonged in

the pages of Musil, Paul Guth; and the writer Michael Thomas—represented the Lehman Foundation. Work on its thirteen volumes got going slowly, but contracts for the individual parts of the collection were eventually allotted to a roster of American and European specialists. The first volumes to be completed dealt with Venetian eighteenth-century drawings, which were catalogued by George Knox and Jim Byam Shaw, and the Italian paintings, for which I was responsible. I have always found that two minds on a catalogue are better than one. I applied this principle to the catalogue of sculpture in London, and to the catalogue of sculpture in the Frick Collection, where Anthony Radcliffe worked over the physical constitution of the bronzes. I applied it again to the Lehman catalogue, where my very able research assistant, Larry Kanter, coordinated the technical examination of the paintings. The collection had been heavily studied in the past, and the first catalogue of what was then his father's collection was a gargantuan book prepared by Robert Lehman. The paintings were well known and of high quality, and were, with very few exceptions, what they were claimed to be. Kanter's contribution was substantial, and his name appeared on the title page as those of Lightbown and Radcliffe had done in earlier catalogues.

The other book I wrote in New York was a life of Benvenuto Cellini. My wish to write on Cellini went back thirty years, to 1949, when Bela Horovitz had asked me to write an introduction to Cellini's *Life*. Academically, Cellini is a difficult subject since so few of his works survive, and those which do cannot be understood in any other context than that of their own time. The more carefully I thought over the project, the more evident was it that it must be cast in the form of a biography in the course of which Cellini's work would be described and analyzed. Though I had been in constant touch with people who were working on biographies, I had never written one myself, and it was some time before I felt sufficiently confident in my reading of Cellini's character to give the book the continuity that it required. During a long hot summer in Florence in the Palazzo Capponi, however, the text was written and handed over to the Abbeville Press. In the detail of its production I had the help of a new research assistant, Michael Mallon, who has worked with me in Florence ever since. The book was a success, and in the window of a bookshop on Madison Avenue an articulated model was made up to represent the *Perseus*. The Italian translator disapproved of slang and colloquialisms ("My mother would not understand this," she said), and the text had in part to be revised by my own translator in Florence, Gabriele Natali.

One of the remarkable and to me unexpected things about New York is the sense it gives one of acceptance. It is the only city in the world where you regularly meet people you know walking along the street. "Welcome home," said the porters in my ugly apartment in Park Avenue whenever I returned there from abroad. This is the opposite of the rather standoffish attitude of Londoners, and I found it very welcome. Dinner parties in New York are very different from staid dinner parties in London. They are energizing and consist of people one wants to see. I already had quite a large number of friends there, like Drue Heinz, whom I had known well for many years, and the Wrightsmans, with whom I had often stayed in Florida, and clever, committed Annette Reed, and Brooke Astor, to whose Vuillard-like drawing room in Park Avenue I was bidden whenever I was in New York. Acquaintances soon became close friends. Two of them were Francis Steegmuller, whose work on Flaubert I much admired, and that excellent and subtle novelist Shirley Hazzard. Another was Diana Vreeland, whom I had met many times but did not know well. At a party at John Richardson's she came across the room and gave me a smacking kiss, saying under her breath: "I had to do that to show I know you as well as I say I do." This was the beginning of a genuine friendship. The person of all others who took most trouble to introduce me to like-minded people was also the most sagacious and most discriminating, Nin Ryan, to whom I owe many of my closest New York friends. After I had been a short time in New York I had a letter from Pamela Hartwell in London asking: "Who is your me?" Nin, I replied. When, in Florence, I think about New York, it is her book-lined drawing room, with its view over the East River and its Sisley trembling above the fireplace, that comes first to mind.

In a very different category were owners of works of art with whom friendly links had to be forged. The most important of them were the Linskys, whose apartment in Fifth Avenue was filled with major works of art. I had known them slightly in London, since they came over to bid personally at auctions, thereby saving the commission they would have had to pay if a third party had bid on their behalf. Both Jack and Belle Linsky had an exceptional sense of quality, which was manifest first in a great ceramic collection and in their excellent French furniture, then in their bronzes (where they did, however, make one or two mistakes), and third in their paintings. Their taste was wide-ranging, and they bought without advice. Though their apartment was characteristic of New York—you could smell Jack Linsky's cigar as you left the elevator—the aggregation of works of art that they assembled was European; it could well have been formed before the war in Frankfurt or Berlin. I grew greatly to like Belle Linsky, who was shrewd and unpretentious and not without a certain charm, but she had a chip on her shoulder from the way in which she had been treated by the Metropolitan Museum in Hoving's time, and it was only my position as a newcomer to the New York art world that made it possible to break this down. What I could not break down was her insistence that her works of art be preserved as an integral collection. A number of people fear death less than they fear anonymity.

In London I had sat on a number of nonprofessional boards (boards not directly connected with the posts I held), and before long I found myself in the same position in New York. I was briefly, at the invitation of Lincoln Kirstein, a member of the boards of the New York City Ballet and the School of American Ballet (briefly because, much as I admired their work, I could not give either the time it properly required). At meetings I sometimes sat opposite a placid lady from Utah who was later found guilty of arranging for her father to be murdered by her son. After a year I was invited to become an advisory director of the Metropolitan Opera, and I retained this position throughout my whole time in New York. Many of the warm friendships I formed there, with Dorle Soria, and Alton and Elizabeth Peters, and Sydney and Marit Gruson, grew from a common interest in opera. I served on the production subcommittee and on the art committee (which was concerned with the portraits of opera singers in the front of the house and historic operatic costumes, not with the appearance of the auditorium or with what went on on the stage). There is a tradition that the board of the Metropolitan Opera should not, at its meetings, discuss artistic policy, and this may well be wise. The scale of the whole operation is immensely much larger than at Covent Garden, both in a literal sense (the size of the house itself imposes restrictions on casting and is unsuited to the performance of intimate works) and because the number of performances is greater. Whereas at Covent Garden opera alternates with ballet, the program in New York provides, over a seven-month period, for seven performances a week. The strain of giving six evening performances and one afternoon performance over so long a time is very great, and throughout the ten years I observed them, I was astonished not that certain performances were of poor quality but that the general level of performance was so high. That this was so was due primarily to the musical director, James Levine. At Covent Garden when Colin Davis was asked questions at meetings of the opera subcommittee, his replies were nervous and defensive. Levine, on the other hand, at meetings of the production subcommittee (at which artistic problems could be raised) was lucid and authoritative, and filled me (and I think the other members of the committee as well) with admiration at his intellectual grasp. The running of the opera house was a dictatorship in circumstances in which only dictatorship could work. From time to time in the press the opera house was criticized for failing to recruit other well-known conductors, and Bernard Haitink, when he came to conduct *Fidelio*, was greeted with rapturous enthusiasm, though his performance was sluggish and dull. But with the advent of Carlos Kleiber this agitation has subsided. The Metropolitan Opera orchestra is extremely fine, and in those works undertaken by both Covent Garden and the Metropolitan (like *La Clemenza di Tito* and *Falstaff* and *Parsifal* and *Pelléas* and *Eugene Onegin*) the New York performances were a good deal superior.

At the Metropolitan Opera, as in most opera houses, producers and designers are variable quantities. The chanciest was Ponnelle, who was responsible for some beautiful productions but could at the same time design a *Fliegende Holländer* so false to the whole nature of the work that it elicited the heaviest booing I have ever heard in any opera house, and a *Figaro* in which the singers were confined to the extreme front of the stage with deplorable acoustic and dramatic consequences. There were a number of what can only be looked upon as failed productions, like those of *Erwartung* and *Macbeth* and *Ernani*, and these seemed invariably to be due to the fact that nobody had looked critically at the models and told the designer to think again and produce plans that, in relation to the action of the opera, were more practical. Against these failures, however, must be balanced the *Tannhäuser*, perhaps the best staging of any Wagner opera to be seen today, the *Billy Budd*, Jocelyn Herbert's superb *Lulu*, and David Hockney's ravishing *Rossignol* and *Enfant et les Sortilèges*. The second half of the twentieth century has been a poor period for stage design, and I have often wondered whether it would not be wise to refer back to earlier painted designs (as La Scala did to excellent effect in the 1950s in its use of sets based on Sanquirico). As with the Metropolitan Museum, so with the Metropolitan Opera activity is buoyed up by public criticism and support. The audiences are more mixed than those in London, and knowledge of foreign languages, especially of German and Italian, is more general. This makes for a more lively interplay between the singers and the audience. Subtitles may be required in London, but they are not needed in New York.

The musical resources of New York proved limitless. Avery Fisher Hall is an uncongenial building, visually and acoustically too, but Carnegie Hall has much of the quality of the old Queen's Hall in London. When you sit in it you are unconscious of the other members of the audience, and can listen to the music undisturbed. The most memorable of the many concerts I have been to in it was the last, when Karajan conducted the Bruckner Eighth Symphony with a freedom and intensity I have never heard surpassed. Two blocks away from my apartment was the Ninety-second Street Y, with its regular Schubertiads, to which I often went with Andrew Porter. A great deal of contemporary chamber music was also available, and so were semi-professional performances of rare operas, Peri's *Euridice* at a downtown church, Marschner's *Vampyr* at a church on the West Side, Goetz's *Taming of the Shrew* at the Mannes College of Music, or Dargomyzhsky's *Stone Guest* at Marymount Manhattan College. The quality of the performances was poor to hopeless, but there was something contagious in the enthusiasm that they represented and in the sheer volume of activity.

When moving to New York I held a card of whose value I was unaware, that I was pro-Israeli. The British Museum trustees were a strongly Arabist board; I once suggested the addition of a Jewish member, but the reception was so chilly that I let the matter drop. The climate in New York was very different, and soon after arriving there I received the Torch of Learning Award from the Hebrew University at Jerusalem. At the dinner at which it was presented I spoke about the contribution of refugee scholars in England and in the United States to the study of art history. The major event of the kind was a fund-raising dinner organized by the Bezalel Academy of Jerusalem for the award of the Jerusalem Prize for Arts and Letters. On the first occasion, at which I spoke, the recipient was Meyer Schapiro. Generally such affairs are undiluted pain, but not in this case, since I had boundless admiration for Schapiro and the prize-giving compelled me to reread his published works. On the second occasion I was the recipient and George Weidenfeld was the promoter of the award. It was at the suggestion of George Weidenfeld, moreover, that the Mitchell Prize for Art History was instituted by Jan Mitchell. Initially a single prize was given annually to a volume on art history written in English. Later a second prize was instituted for first publications, and later still a prize was added for art criticism. The selections were made by a committee of three, of which I served as chairman for the first three years. This was a most valuable initiative, through which books of merit gained more notice and a much larger circulation than they would otherwise have had.

In an active museum two constituencies are of particular importance. One consists of dealers and the other of art critics. In my youth art dealing was an ambiguous profession. What counted was not knowledge but the ability to market works of art. By the 1970s, however, effective dealing involved study and research. If you had an Ingres for sale, you did not go to an Ingres specialist and pay for a certificate. You took the first plane to Montauban and spent a week going through Ingres drawings to find out how your picture fitted into the pattern of Ingres's work.

One of the architects of this change was my friend David Carritt in London, who had the gift of instantaneous visual response (his reactions were much more rapid than my own) and whose coruscating wit hid an analytical mind that would have made him a substantial art historian had he not opted for the art market. Contact with him was a delight. When Massenet's *Manon* was first put on in English at Covent Garden after the war, one of the arias opened with the words "Leisure is pleasure," and this, alas, was David's view. As a result, he is remembered now, outside the diminishing circle of his friends, only through one or two lectures and exhibition catalogues and pictures, like the Caravaggio *Concert* in the Metropolitan, for whose discovery he was responsible.

In London, until well after the war, museum officials were trained to despise what was called the trade, and the staff at the National Gallery were discouraged from going to look at dealers' stocks. In the field in which I was then working, apartheid would have been unpractical, since a dealer like Alfred Spero had an instinctive sense for quality in Italian bronzes and Andrew Ciechanowiecki at the Heim

Gallery was the source of a number of fully researched purchases. The concept of research had long been promulgated in New York by European-based dealers like Wildenstein's, but it was some years before it was accepted as a norm. The professionalism of the great auction rooms was a contributing factor. With minor sales, speculation due to undercataloguing tends to raise the price level, but with costly paintings and works of art it is essential that the full facts be known. By the time I reached New York the transformation was complete. Dealers were colleagues, though with a bar sinister. Many of them were sincerely interested in the museum, and I owed much to their criticism and advice.

The power of critics in New York is greater than in any other center in the world. *The New York Times* has a monopoly, and an unfavorable notice there may close an expensive theatrical production after three or four performances. Obviously the hazards that it offers are less great for museums (where its articles normally deal with exhibitions, purchases, or installations) than with the performing arts. Nonetheless press relations are of great consequence. Through the Hoving regime the museum was frequently assailed by Hilton Kramer, whose positive judgments were often wise but whose negative judgments tended to be intemperate. Kramer was succeeded by John Russell, whom I had known well for more than forty years and for whose convictions and discrimination I had unbounded respect. He was incorruptible, in the sense that he was never influenced by what other people thought, and his prose style, formed under the eye of Logan Pearsall Smith, was so flexible and so refined as to communicate shades of disapproval or approval with no need for any megaphone. His sense of occasion was impeccable, and his contribution to the art world in New York has been incalculably great. The wind of critical approval filled my sails throughout my whole time in New York.

My contract with the Metropolitan made traveling in Europe easier than it had been from London, and my ten years there were punctuated not only by my customary summers in Florence but by journey after journey to places that I either did not know or did not know thoroughly. One of the cities I had never been to was Lisbon, where the Gulbenkian Museum had opened some years before. Kenneth Clark, at its inauguration, said publicly how much Gulbenkian would have disapproved of it. The sense it left on my mind was one of disappointment, not at the beautifully arranged Islamic galleries but at the galleries of paintings. Anyone who knows the Kent frame that housed Rubens's full-length portrait of Helena Fourment over a chimneypiece at Houghton must resent seeing it hung low with the bottom of its frame almost on the floor. The Museo de Arte Antigua yielded the only Piero della Francesca I had not seen, the *St. Augustine* from the altarpiece for S. Agostino at Borgo San Sepolcro. In the original (and this may have been a matter of condition) it looked weaker than the panels from the altarpiece in Milan and London and New York, and I wondered if it had not been painted from Piero's cartoon by Signorelli. I had been fairly often, on one pretext or another, to Madrid and Toledo and the Escorial, but my knowledge of Seville and Granada was limited to a single visit, and I drove there from Madrid with Everett Fahy to look not just at the Zurbaráns and Murillos and the Alhambra, but at the Sebastiano del Piombo *Pietà* from Ubeda and the Flemish primitives in the Capilla Real at Granada. On the way down there we stayed at Trujillo with an old friend, Xavier de Salas, a former director of the Prado whom I had known first as the very successful head of the Spanish Institute in London. I remember a captivating day with de Salas at Guadalupe looking at the great cycle of Zurbaráns and at the sacristy painted by Giordano. In Spain, unlike Italy, there is next to nothing to look at between the places you really want to see, so we went by train from Granada to Salamanca, and there picked up another car. Salamanca exerted its old spell (it is one of the most civilized cities in the world), and from it we went on to Valladolid, with its beautifully ordered museum of sculpture, and Palencia, with its great El Greco *St. Sebastian*, and Burgos, where the pleasure of the ornate Gothic sculpture at Miraflores exceeded all anticipation, as did a marvelous day at a site consecrated by Schapiro, San Domingo de Silos. This was a short journey—it must have lasted less than three weeks—but it opened my eyes to a great deal I had not seen before.

Paris was naturally accessible, as it had been from London, for every major exhibition. One slogged round the Grand Palais wondering if the Le Nains were not weaker painters than the French believed, and if Courbet and Renoir were not far better painters than one would, from the ugly exhibitions of their work, have credited. The exhibition I recall most clearly was of Ingres portraits, impeccably displayed by Michel Laclotte in two galleries in the Louvre. My knowledge of the rest of France was patchy, and I redressed this by two long journeys, one to Le Mans and Angers and Tours and Bourges and Autun and Beaune and Besançon and Arc-et-Senans and Bourg-en-Bresse and Lyon; and the other to Toulouse and Montauban and Moissac and Souillac and Conques and Albi and Castres and Béziers and Montpellier and Avignon and Aix and Marseille and Grasse and Grenoble and Chambéry. These were gluttonous journeys, but the sudden changes of level, from the Angers tapestries to the Mantegna at Tours, from Rogier van der Weyden to Fra Bartolommeo, from Ingres to Romanesque sculpture, from Toulouse-Lautrec to Domenichino, from the Aix Annunciation to the Rubenses at Grasse (which were painted for Santa Croce in Gerusalemme in Rome), were enormously invigorating. Another journey started at Antwerp, a city to which I have always felt greatly attached, and continued through Strasbourg and Colmar and Basel and Vaduz to Vienna. Yet another began in Amsterdam, and embraced Bremen, Hanover, Brunswick, Würzburg, Regensburg, Munich, and Innsbruck. I returned to Prague (where the standard of display imposed upon the galleries by Jiří Kotalík is uncommonly high) and spent a fascinating day in the palace at Karlstein, and to Hamburg and West and East Berlin and Munich. My earlier traveling was always done alone, but in my journeys from New York I had with me a friend or a research assistant, to drive, where driving was necessary, as it is in France, and to deal with the practicalities of travel. There were three rules, that every work of art should be looked at, that every available moment should be spent looking, and that if opera were available the evenings should be spent at it. The last stipulation produced a mixed batch of experiences: a decent provincial *Fidelio* in Bremen; an awful *Aida* produced by Götz Friedrich in Berlin, in which, during the prelude, Radames and Aida were shown standing back to back against a sentry box, which in the last scene became their tomb; a coarse *Ariade auf Naxos*, also in Berlin, where the confusion of tone between the two competing entertainments was made needlessly explicit by muddling up the scenery; an inspired *coup de théâtre* in *Tristan*, when the stage was lit with raking light on King Mark's return in the second act; a feminist *Zauberflöte* in Vienna, of which, according to the program, the Queen of the Night was the protagonist; an abominable *Falstaff* in the Smetana Theater in Prague and a beautiful *Rusalka* at the National Theater; a travesty of Handel's *Giulio Cesare* at Zurich; and an excellent *Trittico* in Munich. These and many other performances convinced me that over a great part of the world the vagaries of unintelligent and ambitious directors are slowly changing the character of opera. But the journeys also gave me an up-to-date knowledge of the present state of museums in France and Belgium and Holland and Germany and Austria.

From Florence I have kept up the same practice of traveling—to Dublin (where the ill-maintained National Gallery of Ireland contains many important Italian pictures); and most recently West Berlin (where the standards of display at Dahlem are incomparably high); and East Berlin (where the old Kaiser Friedrich Museum, now the Bode Museum, after four decades of neglect is being slowly brought to life); and Potsdam (which now looks much as it did when I was a child); and Dresden (where despite every physical disadvantage serious curatorial standards have always been properly maintained); and Altenburg (where I had not been for over fifty years, and where the Lindenau primitives are now much better cared for than they were before the war); and Weimar (where the Goethe and Schiller museums and the great collection of Cranachs are ideally well shown). Returning by way of Frankfurt, I went back to Cologne and Aschaffenburg, and from Aschaffenburg to Stuppach, where a little church houses the great *Madonna* of Grünewald, by my calculation the only supreme masterpiece of Western painting I had never seen. One often enjoys paintings in the ratio of the trouble that one takes to see them, and the Grünewald was a revelatory experience. Too revelatory for comfort indeed, for in Florence I live near Santa Felicita, which has in the Capponi Chapel what is perhaps the greatest Italian Mannerist painting, the *Deposition* by Grünewald's contemporary Pontormo. At Stuppach I asked myself, as I had done after each visit to Colmar, whether an aesthetic based primarily on Italian painting did not require to be revised.

13

THE USES OF SCHOLARSHIP

VICTORIAN NOVELS ARE FILLED WITH SCENES SET IN MUSEUMS. IN *Middlemarch* museums are the catalyst whereby the newlywed heroine discovers the aridity of Casaubon: "There is hardly any contact more depressing to a young ardent creature than that of a mind in which years full of knowledge seem to have issued in a blank absence of interest or sympathy." Hilda, in Hawthorne's *Marble Faun*, "her capacity for emotion choked up with a horrible experience," revisits the Roman museums she had so much enjoyed, and for the first time grows acquainted with "that icy demon of weariness who haunts great picture galleries. He annihilates color, warmth, and more especially sentiment at a touch." "Art," she concludes, "cannot comfort the heart in affliction; it grows dim when the shadow is upon us." In Victorian England museums were perilous places where you could lose your faith, as Kingsley's hero Alton Locke comes within an ace of doing in the Dulwich College Picture Gallery. "The rich, sombre light of the rooms, the heavy warmth of the stove-heated air, the brilliant and varied colouring and gilded frames which embroidered the walls, the hushed earnestness of a few artists who were copying, and the few visitors who were lounging from picture to picture, struck me at once with a mysterious awe." One picture attracts his notice above all the rest, and "timidly but eagerly" he goes up to it. It is a painting by Guido Reni of St. Sebastian. "Gazing at the picture since," he reflects, "I have understood how the idolatry of painted saints could arise in the minds even of the most educated, who were not disciplined by that stern regard for fact which is, or ought to be, the strength of Englishmen." For Henry James a museum was filled not with people but presences. Isabel Archer, in *The Portrait of a Lady*, sits down among the "shining antique marbles" in the Capitoline Museum, "regarding them vaguely, resting her eyes on their beautiful blank faces; listening, as it were, to their eternal silence." I wish that museums were still looked on as a litmus paper separating truth from falsehood, as styptics for emotional hemorrhage, as a parable for life or as an assembly of silent friends.

The history of modern museums is, by the standard of the objects they exhibit, a very short one. It is compressed in a period of about a hundred and fifty years, from the middle of the nineteenth century up to today. In the early nineteenth century museums were at a discount. "All that can be done in England," says William Cobbett, the radical MP and author of *Rural Rides*, "by squandering upon galleries and museums is to excite a desire in the vain and frivolous part of the nation to hanker after such things." But in the middle of the century there came into existence a new concept, their educational role. "A museum," we read in a report of 1854, "may be a passive, dormant institution, an encyclopaedia as it were in which the learned student, knowing what to look for, may find authorities; or it may be an active teaching institution, useful and suggestive." The clearest statement of this thesis was proffered by that great pioneer Sir Henry Cole. "The museum is intended to be used," he declares, "to the utmost extent consistent with the preservation of the article; not only to be used physically, but to be talked about and lectured upon. I venture to think that unless museums and galleries are made subservient to the purposes of education, they dwindle into very sleepy and useless institutions." In most museums in Great Britain and the United States this principle still operates. Though some museum staffs gyrate complacently round their collections, like the Rhinemaidens in Wagner's opera swimming round the Rhinegold, it would be generally accepted that their true role is to exploit, for the public benefit, the works of art of which they have temporary charge.

When I was quite young I was introduced to museology by a friend of my mother's, Matthew Prichard, who had been interned at Ruhleben during the First World War. Though he was English, Prichard had joined the staff of the Boston Museum of Fine Arts in 1903, as a specialist in classical antiquities, and there he produced a report, "Current Theories of the Arrangement of Museums of Art," the first intelligent formulation of the problems of the modern museum and the means by which they should be resolved. "The Museum," he wrote, "has to consider a number of different interests, the public and the artist, each seeking inspiration for his life and work; the art student in the spirit of franker imitation; the specialists and the students who apply themselves to some special branch of the collections; the teacher for whom the exhibits are illustrations of his lectures. The balance between all these sometimes conflicting claimants must be held with a steady hand. . . . A museum of art, ultimately and in its widest possible activity, illustrates one attitude toward life. It contains objects which reflect the beauty and magnificence to which life has attained in past times. The fruits of this exalted and transcendent life are gathered within its walls, and it is the standard of this life, with the noble intellectual activity it presupposes, that the Museum offers for acceptance by its visitors. The Museum is for the public, and not for any caste or section of it." In the early 1930s I became familiar with Prichard's views from seminars on aesthetics held by him in the mornings, among shattered glasses, in the Gargoyle nightclub before the *Red Studio* of Matisse. A drypoint of him by Matisse, indeed, looks down at me from my study wall today.

British and American museums grew from the same seed, but they developed very differently. In England educational policy was the directing force. "The founding of museums adapted for the general instruction and pleasure of the multitude," declared Ruskin, "seems in these days to be a further necessity, to meet which the people themselves may be frankly called upon, and to supply which their own power is perfectly adequate, without awaiting the accident or caprice of private philanthropy." Between 1851 and the 1890s there was established a prototype, the South Kensington Museum, and all but a few of the large regional museums. Dependent on public funding, the regional museums rapidly ran down and very seldom did they attract local patronage. No owner of an inherited collection would have looked on them as a fit repository for his works of art. In the United States, on the contrary, private philanthropy was dominant. It was private individuals in Boston in the 1860s who urged "the establishment of a museum of art of the character of that at South Kensington," as an instrument of education, and who in 1876 recorded that "nowhere has the wisdom of giving works of art an educational bearing been more completely shown than in our museums." The same enlightened policy was adopted in New York by the founders of the Metropolitan Museum. Every local American museum I have visited, at Sarasota and Seattle, at Louisville and Fort Worth, at Toledo and Detroit, at Kansas City and Chicago, at Baltimore and Hartford and Indianapolis, carries the same message of enlightened private enterprise directed to the public good. Their contents owe their quality in part to bequeathed private collections and in part (especially at Cleveland, Toledo, and Detroit) to purchases made possible by private generosity. Nowhere has the contribution of private patronage been more apparent than in their architecture. When you have spent much of your life, as I have, wrestling with the egos of dead architects, when you have lived through showdown after showdown with Captain Fowke, and Gottfried Semper, and Sir Aston Webb, when you have watched a building that you once despised becoming, slowly and ineluctably, a work of art, you feel something akin to jealousy of colleagues who have modern buildings in which they can operate, who are not fettered by nostalgia, and for whom display is not rooted in compromise.

But museums are not simply instruments of education; they are repositories of knowledge too, and it is incumbent on each director and each board of trustees to determine how far what is known as scholarship should be encouraged in the museum for which they are responsible. In 1965 I was invited by James Rorimer, then director of the Metropolitan Museum, to discuss this problem in New York at the seventh triennial meeting of an international body known as ICOM (a subsection of UNESCO specializing in museums). I accepted hesitantly, since the audience would be in the main American, and there seemed at that time to be something of a gulf between the scholarly function of museums in Europe and the function they fulfilled in the United States. I reproduce part of the paper here, since it touches on a number of fundamental museum problems and expresses views that I still hold. This is what I said:

> I think I should begin by saying frankly that the title of this paper has been changed. First it was called "The Place of Scholarship in a Museum" and then it was retitled "The Contribution of Museums to Scholarship." The first title was rather a contentious one; it presumed that scholarship had some place in a museum, and members of museum boards might deny that that was so. They might argue that the scope of a museum was educational, and that schol-

arship, if it were admitted, should occupy only a back seat. But the second title, "The Contribution of Museums to Scholarship," reminds us that this attitude is of comparatively recent growth. Before the First World War and for some time after it, it was taken for granted that museums were staffed by scholars, and that one of the functions of museum staffs was to undertake research. The reason why that thesis is now debated is that the character of museums has been transformed. Not of all museums, of course. There are still some which exist as research institutions, and are justified solely or mainly by the scholarly tasks that they perform. Most archaeological museums are in that category. But in fine arts museums a revolution undoubtedly has taken place. Their activities are more diversified and their focus has become more popular, and in these circumstances it seems to me that we must ask ourselves three questions. What are the basic scholarly obligations of the modern museum? How far should museums today encourage scholarship? And if scholarship is to be encouraged, what steps are to be taken to consolidate and to extend the scholarly tradition transmitted to us by the past?

I shall take the first question first, because it can be answered comparatively easily. The basic scholarly obligations of museums are determined by public rights. In the first place, members of the public and a fortiori students have the right to know what they are looking at. In the morass of speculation that surrounds all works of art, their physical condition is frequently the only thing that can legitimately be described as fact. So their physical condition simply must be divulged. I do not mean by that that sculpture in museums should necessarily be stripped of makeup, nor that with paintings the vacant areas should be left void. These are criteria for the archaeologist. I do mean that in all cases where the condition of the object is problematical, or is not what it appears to be, warning of that should be given on the label as well as in the catalogue, and the nature of the damage should be made clear. That is not an academic point. If it is not frankly avowed that certain paintings are gravely damaged, a false impression of the artists who painted them inevitably will result. How reassuring it would be, as we walk round the great picture galleries, to encounter precise statements of what the condition of the paintings is. I suspect that any gallery or museum which sponsored a policy like this would command greater, not less, public confidence.

I am often disconcerted by the vagueness of curators about the constitution of the works under their care. It seems generally to be investigated only when there is some prospect that the work concerned may be restored. But curators have a clear duty in this matter. The condition of the works of art for which they are responsible ought to be investigated, and the findings that result ought to be made freely available. Ignorance of condition is one of the greatest single limiting factors on the development of sound art history, and when paintings pass from private into public ownership, it is inexcusable that speculation should not at last be translated into fact. It is in the museum's interest too that members of its staff should be freely encouraged from the first to look analytically at works of art, because ignorance of condition is accountable for many speculative purchases. There is no room for deception or for self-deception here.

In the second place, the attributions on labels in museums should be such as to inspire confidence. There was a time when the pronouncements of museums had an aura of infallibility. Their contents were a mystery, attribution was an occult pursuit to which a few magicians had the key, and it was not for the ignorant public to question the decisions that were made. Moreover, there was an irrational feeling that works of art acquired an added authenticity through the mere fact of passing into public ownership. One of my predecessors at the Victoria and Albert Museum took the view that he was conscientiously bound to defend all the magniloquent names that had been given to the objects in his charge. Once a Michelangelo, always a Michelangelo for him. Things are rather different now. The public is less ignorant—owing to the spread of popular art-historical teaching it is, over a great part of the world, all but actively sophisticated—and it is an open secret that the attributions of many works of art are much less certain than is suggested by conventional museum labeling. Wrong ascriptions do not become more credible in the ratio of the tenacity with which they are maintained and there is nothing whatever to be gained, and a great deal to be lost, by papering over past mistakes. The names given on labels ought invariably to represent fair-minded dispassionate assessments of the probabilities.

In the third place, it is the duty of museums, whether or not they initiate research themselves, to facilitate research. One means of doing so is to ensure that up-to-date photographs are generally available, and another means by which research can be facilitated is by a liberal policy of access to works of art. In saying that I must admit that I am influenced by the facilities I was myself accorded, as a student, in the Kaiser Friedrich Museum in Berlin. They still seem to me to set a standard by which we today should not fall short.

Till now I have avoided touching on that difficult word "scholarship." But with the question "How far should museums encourage scholarship?" I can do that no more. Nowadays the term is very loosely used. "He is a good scholar," we say of someone of whom there is, indeed, little else that can be said. "This is a scholarly book," we say, meaning that it is stuffed with facts. Unhappily most of the pejorative terms with which the word "scholarship" was once hedged round have dropped into disuse. We no longer refer to "scholarians" meaning "pedants" nor to "scholarism" meaning "pedantry." And the result is that the concept of scholarship embraces a whole range of activities, some of which are useful and constructive while others are eccentric, sterile, and superfluous. I take it we should all agree that in modern museums there is no room for the second category of study, and that steps have to be taken to discourage it. I suppose that that is what colleagues have in mind who tell one that what museums need is not scholars but connoisseurs. Certainly a scholar who is not a connoisseur and has no sense of the relevance of his activities to the museum as a whole can prove a hideous liability. In any case it is only the useful and constructive areas of research that need concern us here. Most fine art museum officials are connoisseurs, and have a connoisseur's acquaintance with some period or class of artifact. But one must distinguish between that and scholarship. Connoisseurship becomes scholarship only when research into specific problems is prosecuted to exceptional depth or when the study is consciously directed toward some larger synthesis. So the question I asked should be rephrased a little differently. "How far should museum directors encourage the connoisseurs on their staffs to develop into scholars in the full sense?"

It goes without saying that research can be indulged in only at the expense of other work, and it would be generally felt in the museums of today that if a clear conflict arose between the competing demands of research and activities which impinge directly on the public interest—display and the like—research ought not to have priority. If the cost of research is an archaic system of display which does not satisfy the public's need or a restricted educational service which inhibits the museum from playing its full part in the life of the community, the price simply is too high. But in large museums there is generally sufficient flexibility to preclude conflicts of that kind, and it is with them that the whole problem takes on actuality. Should the director of one of these museums stimulate research, or should he plead: "My staff is small, and within its limits competent, and I cannot produce the working conditions and facilities through which knowledge can develop into scholarship of a creative kind"?

I believe that considerations of principle and of self-interest lead to the same answer, that he must stimulate (stimulate and not just tolerate) research. For efficient functioning, museums are dependent upon knowledge, and the conviction that fact can be ascertained, that right judgments can be formulated, is the central pillar that supports the edifice. In establishing the disinterested intellectual climate in which facts are likely to be ascertained, and right judgments are likely to be formed, the fostering of scholarship is the only means we have at hand. What a museum gains from the presence of scholars on its staff is not only that vastly overrated commodity, prestige, but the moral qualities of seriousness and pertinacity without which it will generate less than its full force.

It gains tangible advantages as well. Scholarship offers a platform of security. Within the area of the scholar's specialty, the museum can operate with greater confidence. In large museums the interesting, really individual departments are those which have been shaped by the taste and knowledge of some scholar on the staff. But the museum can benefit only if the scholars on its staff receive the support that will enable them to develop their collections as they wish. Unduly rigid trustee control is often an impediment. I cannot help suspecting that museums would develop in a freer, more individual way if boards could be persuaded to accept the hazards of greater flexibility.

Some museums are still responsible for publications of pure scholarship, publications which could be promulgated by a university but are in fact issued by a museum. The *Bulletin of the Museum of Far Eastern Antiquities* in Stockholm and the *Occasional Papers* of the

Freer Gallery in Washington are cases in point. But generally speaking there is a difference between scholarship in a museum and scholarship promoted in a university. The difference can be summed up in the word "practicality." In museums it is hardly ever possible to study problems to that point of no return when useful work becomes a complicated academic exercise. Museum officials, thank heavens, cannot study iconography; time is too pressing and life too short. And since there is a premium on results (not necessarily on positive results, but on clearly defining the conclusions that it is permissible to reach), they cannot have recourse to the smoke screen of footnotes that so often mask a failed attack. The continuous contact with works of art implicit in working conditions in museums ensures that whatever other vices it may have museum scholarship is seldom theoretical.

Those fields of study which involve an aggregated knowledge of technique can be fruitfully pursued only in museums. And if people in museums are negligent in discharging their responsibilities, the deficiency cannot be compensated by research elsewhere. That is one reason why there is a mandatory obligation on museums to exploit the scholarly as well as the recreational and educational potential of their collections.

We have every reason to feel grateful that that obligation was discharged in such a dedicated fashion in the past. To speak only of the field with which I am familiar at first hand, it is astonishing how much our knowledge of Renaissance art alone owes to museum scholarship. If we need information about plaquettes, we turn to Molinier. If we need information about engravings, we turn to Hind. If we need information about majolica, we turn to Rackham. If we need information about medals, we turn to Hill. Rackham's, of course, was specifically a catalogue of the majolica in London, while Molinier and Hind and Hill used the collections of which they were in charge as a bridgehead in an assault on the whole field. In Italian sculpture too the foundations of the study were laid out not in universities but in the Kaiser Friedrich Museum in Berlin, and without the inspiration of Bode and the dedicated work of Schottmüller and Bange no subsequent advance would have been possible. Along with that must be mentioned the Kunsthistorisches Museum in Vienna, whence there emerged not only the catalogues that we still use today but the *Venezianische Bildhauer* and the Riccio monograph of Planiscig. When a catalogue is under way, it is natural that the issues discussed in it should be ventilated in the form of articles. That happened in Berlin—I should not care to guess what proportion of the articles in the earlier volumes of the *Prussian Yearbook* centered round museum objects or were written by members of museum staffs—and it happened also in Vienna, where the curators of the Kunsthistorisches Museum, headed by Baldass and Wilde, made a whole series of carefully cogitated contributions to our knowledge of German and Austrian and Venetian paintings. The yield included books as well; there was Bode in Berlin, writing on artists as remote as Brouwer and Bertoldo, and there was Friedlaender, the peculiar quality of whose *Altniederlandische Malerei* was bound up with the fact that all the earlier volumes appeared while he was working in the Kaiser Friedrich Museum.

Never again will there pour out of museums the spate of publications that appeared between 1880 and the early 1930s. In Europe in the years after the last war the thread of continuity was interrupted by the need to rebuild and reinstall, and in most major museums conditions are now less favorable to scholarship than they were before. Nonetheless it would be wrong to underrate what has been accomplished since 1945. The quantity may have been less, but the quality is in some respects higher than it was. The progress of knowledge is to some extent accountable for that, but another factor is the spread of a sense of scientific objectivity which was not always present in the past. I am bound to mention here the catalogues put out by the National Gallery in London. What they have added to our knowledge is remarkable enough, but still more remarkable when they appeared was the tenacious honest-mindedness by which they were informed. The intention to tell the whole truth and nothing but the truth was never for a moment in doubt. So far as I am aware they were the first recorded case of a picture gallery corporatively coming clean.

Great catalogues force us to recognize that museum publications have bifurcated. Catalogues have become so complex and so expensive to produce that their circulation is in practice limited to scholars and to libraries, and the interests of the public are catered for in other ways. Certainly scholars benefit from that, because they gain room for maneuver which very few of them possessed before. And the public benefits as well, for never has there been a time when responsible popularization was so widespread as it is today. This concept of popular scholarship has quite a long history—in the 1930s it produced a masterpiece in a little book on medieval art by Professor Kitzinger that was issued by the British Museum— and I imagine no one in this audience would still subscribe to the old-fashioned view that knowledge, if it is assimilable, has been vulgarized. An increasingly large number of museum visitors tend to adopt what we may loosely call an art-historical approach to works of art; they see the work of art, that is, in a historical context, and require to be presented with facts. And there is no reason at all why new conclusions should not be promulgated in a way that they can understand. It is healthy that the findings of art history should be submitted to the suffrage of commonsense.

Obviously from the museum's standpoint it is important that cataloguing should be entrusted, where that is possible, to permanent members of the staff. Only in that way can long-term benefits accrue. It is not necessary to wait until you have a scholar. At least as many catalogues have produced scholars as scholars have made catalogues. But nowadays the preparation of a catalogue is quite a serious task. Cataloguing necessarily involves periods of absence to study cognate works elsewhere, as well as subsidies for travel and photographs, and if museum research is to be actively promoted, provision must be made for both. I know that is asking a good deal of both directors and trustees, but I am convinced that an open-handed attitude toward this matter does pay dividends. In the last resort the effectiveness of a museum staff is in the ratio of the extent to which repeated access to works of art abroad can be assured. No director can be expected to promote research by his subordinates if he is not free, at his own discretion, to make liberal grants of leave for approved projects, and if he does not have available a quite substantial travel fund. I say "quite substantial," but of course in relation to the prices paid for works of art the sum involved is minimal. Let it not be forgotten that business criteria are inapplicable here. The fully efficient, really creative museum is the museum that by business standards is overstaffed.

That brings me to my last point. All over the world—in this country, in Italy, I understand also in Holland and Germany, and certainly in England—the students who emerge from art-historical institutes tend to gravitate toward teaching rather than toward museum work. They feel, and in present circumstances they may be correct in doing so, that a larger quota of original research is likely to be produced in university conditions than in a museum post. It goes without saying that that is not an absolute judgment; teaching is far from being an ideal background for research (the number of first books and articles that are never followed by a second is abundant proof of that), and I have always found myself that the feeding of hungry minds is a great deal more sterilizing than life lived with works of art. What the judgment reflects is a belief that conditions of employment in museums are less favorable than in teaching posts; it is not always a question of salary, but rather of imponderables, greater liberty of movement, greater freedom from pressure, a higher premium on the products of the mind. The point has been put to me by students on more occasions than I should care to count that in museums what is expedient is often more important than what is true. I do not want to go into that point in any depth save only to say this. If you scratch the surface of almost any graduate student, you will find something that looks very like idealism underneath. And unless that idealism can be enlisted in the service of museums, unless a museum career can be presented as a vocation and not simply a profession, the quality of recruitment cannot be expected to improve. If the image of fine arts museums as myth-creating, myth-propagating, myth-perpetuating bodies is not dispelled, we shall find museums staffed mainly by installation experts and public relations officers, while the talent by which they should be powered languishes on the campus of some far-off university. The quality of this lost manpower is extremely high, so high that if the situation were put right, if the museum profession could be presented as offering superior opportunities for a fruitful, studious, and constructive life, we could look forward to a time when museum staffs would be more talented, better informed, and more empirically minded than any in the past. But that will occur only if we give visible endorsement to the thesis that the active pursuit of truth is not a luxury, but an essential, without which no museum can maintain its status or its self-respect.

I did not touch on this subject again till 1982, and in the intervening seventeen years much had changed. I had six years of practical experience of life in the United States, and the attitude of the boards and administrative staffs of American museums had been considerably modified. In Washington a center for art-historical research had been established under the same roof as the National Gallery of Art and was already exercising a beneficial influence in the museum field, and in New York the inhibitions that had prevented a close relationship between the Metropolitan Museum and the Institute of Fine Arts were much reduced.

Seen from New York, the position of subsidized museums in England in the 1980s (other than the National Gallery, which acquired an excellent chairman in Jacob Rothschild and a public-spirited patron in John Sainsbury) was a pitiable one. They were, and had long been, underfunded, and at the Victoria and Albert arrears of maintenance threatened the security of the collections. In 1984 the Victoria and Albert's dependence on the Department of Education and Science was terminated, and it was supplied with a body of trustees. There could be no objection in principle to this change, but the trustees were ill selected and ill led. For some years there had been overt antagonism between the director and the staff, and since the chairman of the new board, Lord Carrington, initially supported the director, this resulted in antagonism between the staff of the museum and the board. That radical reform was needed there could be no doubt, but reform could only be effected by a director with professional experience. The staff played what cards they had unwisely, and on every major issue were overruled. My former research assistant in the museum described their morale as that of a people defeated in war. When the post of director became vacant, a number of eligible candidates for the position were interviewed by a committee, and at each interview it was made clear that the trustees were searching not for a professional director but for a manager who would implement the policies of the board. The result was the appointment of a capable librarian named Mrs. Elizabeth Esteve-Coll, who embarked on policies of a brainless vulgarity that would not have been tolerated by any self-respecting museum in the United States.

Hardly was this appointment made when Lord Carrington abandoned the chairmanship of the trustees (in order to move to Christie's) and was succeeded by Lord Armstrong, a successful civil servant whose reputation, thanks to his much publicized testimony in a lawsuit in Australia, was at a low ebb. With his support, a plan for the restructuring of the museum was drawn up by Mrs. Esteve-Coll and was forced rapidly through the board. Its main features were that the organization of museum departments by medium was to be abandoned, a central research department for all media was to be created, and certain key curatorial functions were to be discharged by newly appointed administrative officers. It had a second purpose, to eliminate opposition by members of the staff, and eight senior curators were pressed to accept voluntary retirement. The trouble with dismissing members of a museum staff is that you dispose not just of their personalities but of their knowledge too. This was especially serious in the Department of Textiles, where both the keeper and her deputy were ruthlessly eliminated. The whole matter caused considerable unease, and I felt bound to bring it into sharper focus with a letter to the *Independent*, in which, with my pen dipped in what Lord Carrington, in the House of Lords, primly described as vinegar, I protested at the vulgar popularism of the director's interviews and described the administrative changes as "uneconomical and asinine." A wave of protests against the restructuring proposals, especially from American scholars and museums, made it clear to the trustees that they were dealing with an international, not a domestic institution. I contributed a factual article on the whole matter to the *New York Review of Books*, which was reprinted in the *Guardian* and in Italian, Dutch, and German papers. A debate in the House of Lords, on a motion of Lord Annan, focused on the injustice done to public servants on the staff. Both Lord Armstrong, in replying to the debate, and the deputy chairman, an ex-diplomat called Sir Michael Butler, in a disingenuous article in *The Times*, declared that the changes were designed to encourage scholarship.

The restructuring proceeded, not very effectively since it is difficult for bad employers to recruit good staff, and the Research Department, which was to be the "powerhouse" of the museum, a place where, in the director's vision, younger scholars were to be "seated metaphorically" at the feet of great scholars, was reduced to one official with no research to do and no one to instruct. At some point in this sad story some of the trustees took fright, and a committee that included three members of the staff was appointed to reconsider Mrs. Esteve-Coll's proposals. They recommended, not unnaturally, that the traditional departmental structure be reinstated, and *The Times* of November 9, 1989, reported the result: "Victoria and Albert plans prove unworkable." Mrs. Esteve-Coll was said to be "entirely behind" and "very comfortable" with "the new scheme." It was prejudicial, as the old scheme had been, to scholarship, since it involved the understaffing of curatorial departments and the downgrading of senior curatorial posts, but it preserved a staff structure on which, with wiser direction and more intelligent trustees, the museum might eventually be reconstituted in a useful form.

The central flaw in the thinking behind these muddled policies was the belief that museums in Great Britain can be wrenched into conformity with museums in the United States. Though they spring from the same roots, British and American museums operate on different gauges and serve two different societies. The contents of British national museums are the property of the nation; the contents of civic museums in America are vested in trustees. In the United States there are substantial inducements for board members to contribute generously to the institutions with which they are associated. In Great Britain there is no such machinery. Well-to-do businessmen without professional interests or qualifications who do not make a significant financial contribution to the institution have no place on any museum board. The prime function of museums in England is educational, and the prime role of the trustees is to ensure that they meet this task in an efficient and imaginative way. Unlike the lethargic museum public in Great Britain, the public in the United States is culture-conscious and seducible. Visitors are anxious to avail themselves of the resources that museums have to offer, and are very willing to pay for doing so. There is, therefore, a premium on innovation and vitality, which is supported by the generosity of the trustees. The acceptance of federal subsidies by American civic museums would, in the long term, impair the nature of what are at present independent, creative institutions. Conversely, in Great Britain dependence on individual or corporate subsidies would change the character of bodies which have, under their past terms of reference, made a far from negligible contribution to knowledge and society.

14

KNOWLEDGE AND INTUITION

WHEN SOMEONE ASKS ME WHAT I DO, I REPLY THAT I AM JUST AN art historian. The operative word is "just," and the reason for that is that in the short time I was taught what I still think of as real history, in the orthodox Balliol tradition of the 1930s, it was impressed on me that art history was an inferior discipline. So there I stood, with my feet on Stubbs's Charters and my head allegedly in the clouds, and I have never recovered from a sense of guilt at that predicament. At the time the condescension of one's tutors was not unjustified—there was something rather dilettantish about the combination of archaeology and aestheticism that was fashionable at that time—but I am not convinced that the prejudice is entirely in the past. Even in the United States, where so large an investment has been made in institutional art history, I have been conscious, among historians, of some reserve. It would be argued, if the critics were to come clean, that though a number of learned and clever books about art history were produced, art-historical analysis remained empirical and its results approximate. Nowadays I am sometimes told that conventional art history—the kind of art history that I practice—is in course of being superseded by new and superior types of study. The case is made most often by social historians who claim that the problems presented by art history can be solved by historical research. This is a fallacy. Looking back at the progress of history and art history in the last fifty years, I have no doubt that they are two disciplines, not one. In the past the chain of historical causation behind great works of art may sometimes have been understressed or misinterpreted, but there is, to the best of my belief, no major artifact whose character can be satisfactorily explained through historical study alone. The reason for this is that the work of art results from the interplay of a whole variety of factors; it depends on the requirements of the patron or the commissioning body, it depends on iconographical tradition and on the cultural context in which the commission is placed, it depends on technique, and it depends on the proclivities of the artist. If all of these can be satisfactorily established, there remains the problem of determining the relationship between them if we are to understand exactly why the work of art assumed the form it did. My own interest lies, and has always lain, in what is loosely called artistic personality. This was also the concern of Berenson, but great as is my debt to him, we differed on one essential point. His published writings on art history deal with the relationship between the work of art and the spectator, whereas mine deal (not always effectively) with the relation between the artist and the work of art. How, I ask myself, did the work of art come into existence and why did it assume its actual form?

It is very difficult to approach an artist with a large critical bibliography as though nothing whatever had been written on him. But the art historian is required to do precisely that. The fact that an opinion is widely entertained does not mean that it is correct. To take one instance only, every book about Italian painting tells us that the high altarpiece painted by Duccio for the Duomo in Siena, the *Maestà*, was commissioned in 1308 and completed in 1311. We have irrefutable evidence as to the date of its completion, since early histories of Siena one and all record that it was installed in the Cathedral on June 9, 1311. But the supposed date of the commission depends from a contract referring to the painting which was found early in this century in the Archivio di Stato in Siena. It was at once assumed that this was the initial contract for the altarpiece. But the document is nothing of the kind. It does not specify the form or subject of the painting, and its purpose was to cover a substantial loan made to the artist by the Opera del Duomo. It is concerned solely with the progress of the work, and, if accurately read, clearly refers back to a lost antecedent contract. We have, therefore, no evidence as to the date at which work on the *Maestà* began. This is of more than academic interest, since it changes the time frame for study of the painting. The *Maestà* is an exceptionally complex double-sided altarpiece, and if it were painted in four months less than three years, we would have to suppose either that Duccio planned and executed the whole work with unprecedented speed, or that in the narrative panels on the back he made extensive use of studio assistants. But if work on the *Maestà* extended over five years or six, as is possible and indeed likely, we need have no recourse to either explanation. The altarpiece could well have been painted relatively slowly and have been executed in great part by the artist.

An analogous case is that of the high altar of Sant'Antonio at Padua, for which the bronze statues and reliefs were made by Donatello. There is a record in this case of quite a substantial number of payments but only one master document survives. It provides for the making of four narrative reliefs of scenes from the life of St. Anthony, of a number of other subsidiary reliefs, and of two full-scale bronze statues. The contract for the remaining figures, which consist of a Virgin and Child and four saints, is lost. The problem in this case is how the altar originally looked. It is now generally assumed that there were seven statues on the altar, a Virgin and Child in the center and three saints on either side. But our only account of the altar in its finished state dates from the early sixteenth century; it was written by an intelligent Venetian, Marcantonio Michiel, and what Michiel saw on the altar were five statues, not seven. The altar, as we know because of other payments, was planned as a kind of stage, with a superstructure and supporting columns, and Michiel would therefore have seen the Virgin and Child in the center and a pair of saints at either side. Read in isolation his description would not be conclusive; his visual observation or his memory might have let him down. The only admissible criterion is therefore physical examination of the statues. They were made, as we know from other payments, on the cheap, and the only means of reducing the cost would have been to limit the chasing of the cast figures to the essential minimum. Four of the six saints were indeed treated in this way; chasing of the faces was restricted to the area which would be visible to a spectator standing in front of the altar. With two of the saints, Giustina and Prosdocimus, the right side of the face (from the spectator's point of view) is more highly chased than the left side, and with the other saints, Daniel and Anthony of Padua, the opposite is true. The first pair of saints must therefore have stood to the right and the other to the left. But the heads of the remaining saints, Francis and Louis of Toulouse, are chased evenly and are therefore likely to have stood free so that they were seen frontally. When we apply these observations to the document, it transpires very clearly that the statues on the altar represented the Virgin and Child with the four patron saints of Padua, and that statues of the two Franciscan saints without Paduan associations—that is, Francis and Louis of Toulouse—were commissioned to be shown not on the altar but independently in its vicinity. This is a minority view today, but it seems to me, on the basis of what documents tell us about the works of art and what the works of art tell us about themselves, to be irrefutable.

The greater the work, the larger the problems it presents. To most art historians today, no special problem is presented by the Brancacci Chapel in the Carmine in Florence. There are no documents, but it would be generally agreed that the decoration of the chapel was the joint work of Masaccio and Masolino, that the roles of the two artists could be satisfactorily identified, and that the frescoes were left unfinished in 1427, when Masaccio went to Rome. Till relatively recently only one earlier collaborative work by Masaccio and Masolino was known, a *Madonna and Child with St. Anne* that is now in the Uffizi. Though the parts painted by Masaccio were impressive for their freedom and tactility, it remained surprising that the painters of this impressive but not very confident panel should have been able, a year later in 1425, to embark on the far more coherent frescoes in the lower registers of the Brancacci Chapel. The discovery of a still earlier painting by Masaccio, a triptych of 1422 at Cascia, did nothing to clarify this problem. Its main virtue was the three-dimensionality of the main figures, but it was not otherwise a painting of great distinction. How did the artist of its rather inexpert throne, one asked oneself, learn to project the fictive architectural moldings and pilasters and the solidly built palaces and roofs of the Brancacci frescoes?

There were clues as to the answer, but no mandatory proof. A fresco of the *Dedication of the Carmine* formerly in the cloister of the convent is known to have contained portraits which included likenesses of Donatello and Brunelleschi, and it appeared that Donatello's low relief of the *Ascension with Christ Giving the Keys to St. Peter* in London was originally carved for, but not installed in, the altar of the Brancacci Chapel. This was a hypothesis when it was first advanced—it was based on the fact that the relief showed two scenes which were associated in an Ascension play given annually in the Carmine, but were not represented in the frescoes in the chapel—but it is more than a hypothesis today, since cleaning of the frescoes has revealed a small fresco beneath the window which proves that the original altar was a low freestanding altar in which the ratio of height to width must have been approximately those of the London relief. There is thus some evidence that Donatello was a participant in the whole project. In 1426, moreover, when Masaccio was in Pisa working on an altarpiece for the local Carmelite church (the central panel is a *Madonna* in the National Gallery in London), an eighth of the sum due for the altarpiece was paid to Donatello. The likely reason for this is explained by the London *Madonna*, where the figure of the Virgin resembles works executed by Donatello at this time so closely as to leave little doubt that the model for it must have been made by Donatello. But if the *Madonna* was collaborative in this sense, were the Brancacci frescoes not collaborative too? One conclusive argument seems to show that this must indeed have been the case. The works at Empoli executed by Masaccio's collaborator, Masolino, before work started in the chapel, are couched in a generalized late Gothic style, to which he reverted in Rome and Naples in his later, post-Brancacci paintings. But in the main fresco he executed in the Brancacci Chapel, the *Raising of Tabitha*, the figure style resembles Masaccio's figure style in the *Tribute Money* so closely that a German critic, August Schmarsow, believed Masolino's figures to have been painted by Masaccio. The only reasonable inference is that in the Brancacci Chapel (where uniformity of lighting was of special consequence) a new type of figure painting was introduced to which Masaccio, enthusiastically, and Masolino, reluctantly, alike conformed; it involved the use of plastic models, which in all probability were prepared by Donatello. If this were the case (and I am convinced it was) the decoration of the chapel, with its allusions to antique painting, its solid architecture and its sculptural figures, would be due not simply to two painters but to a group of artists, headed by Brunelleschi, determined to transfer to painting the realistic style that had been introduced in sculpture seven or eight years earlier.

Nowadays the most popular fifteenth-century Italian artist is that enigmatic figure Piero della Francesca. There is something called the Piero della Francesca trail, and tens of thousands of people pursue it every summer, driving rapidly from place to place. John Mortimer, in his novel *Summer's Lease*, describes three tourists leaving their rented house in the Chianti so that they "can do the Resurrection before lunch." They stop briefly at Arezzo to see the frescoes of the *Legend of the Cross*, and the only one who really wants to look—she is called Molly—is puzzled by the story they represent. She sees "round, invariably handsome, always unsmiling figures, looking down with perpetual detachment and even, in the case of the women, a certain contempt." But she does not look at them for long. "Not ten o'clock yet, and we've done Arezzo," one of the party exclaims. "It can't take us long to knock off the pregnant Madonna." And knock it off they do, leaving Molly, in the oratory at Monterchi, scarcely time for a few commonplace reflections on her last pregnancy. Then on to San Sepolcro and the *Resurrection*, where, says one member of the party helpfully, "you can see what all the fuss was about." A hasty lunch, and straight on to Urbino and the *Flagellation*, "the picture Molly had had in her mind all the holiday and had come so far to see." Not unnaturally, Molly sees what she expects to see: "The young lord of Urbino stands, barefoot and serene, between two evil counsellors. What are they plotting, discussing, arguing about? What terrible and irrevocable decision have they come to, no one can tell. What is certain is that they are too involved in their own concerns to notice the act of cruelty which is casually, almost elegantly taking place at the other end of the building."

The first difficulty with Piero della Francesca is one of meaning, and it is as well to tackle it in the *Flagellation*. The identification of the subject is a comparatively recent one; it goes back only to an inventory made when the panel was in the sacristy of the Cathedral at Urbino in 1744. Little could the author of the inventory have guessed that through succeeding centuries the panel he looked at would acquire a longer, cleverer, more learned bibliography than any other Quattrocento painting, and that for every single scholar who wrote on it, for Longhi and Clark and Gombrich and Lavin and Ginzburg, his account of it would have the ring of truth. The painting contains two visually discrete scenes. In the distance on the left is the so-called Flagellation, a static, painless flagellation which contains features that do not appear in any other flagellation scene. The column stands in the center of an inlaid pavement and is brilliantly illuminated by neon-like light, which is restricted to the central section of the coffered ceiling and to the area immediately beneath. Neither the gilded classical figure on top of the column, nor the aureole surrounding the victim's head, nor the brilliant light with which this part of the painting is suffused, is explicable if the scene depicts the Flagellation of Christ. But there is another celebrated flagellation scene to which all three are integral. This is the Dream of St. Jerome, which is described in a famous letter from St. Jerome to Eustochium:

> Suddenly I was caught up in the spirit and dragged before the Judge's judgment seat: and here the light was so dazzling, and the brightness shining from those who stood round so radiant, that I flung myself upon the ground and did not dare to look up. I was asked to state my condition, and I replied that I was a Christian. But He who presided said: "Thou liest, thou art a Ciceronian not a Christian. For where thy treasure is, there will thy heart be also." Straightforward I became dumb, and amid the strokes of the whip—for He had ordered me to be scourged—I was ever more bitterly tortured by the fire of conscience. . . . I began to cry out and to bewail myself saying: "Have mercy upon me, O Lord, have mercy upon me," and even amid the noise of the lash my voice made itself heard. At last the bystanders fell at the knees of Him who presided and prayed Him to pardon my youth and give me the opportunity to repent of my error on the understanding that the extreme of torture should be inflicted upon me if ever I read again the works of gentile authors.

That this is indeed the subject of the left side of Piero's painting can be confirmed from a predella panel of the Dream of St. Jerome by a Sienese artist, Matteo di Giovanni, in Chicago. This must in turn affect our attitude to the three figures in the foreground on the right. Do they represent Judas Iscariot returning the thirty pieces of silver, or Ottaviano Ubaldini della Casa, or Cardinal Bessarion, or Tommaso dell'Agnello, or Filippo Maria Visconti, or Francesco Sforza? Obviously not, there is not a shred of evidence that the intention behind the figures is historical. If the left half of the painting shows the Dream of St. Jerome, and not the Flagellation of Christ, the subject of the discussion on the right cannot be the sufferings of the Church, or the desirability of a crusade, or any other of the magniloquent topics that have been proposed, but can only refer to the Dream of St. Jerome. The subject of St. Jerome's dream was a *locus classicus* for humanists— if it were accepted literally, it struck at the heart of Renaissance thinking—and it is with the resulting compromise that the conversation in the foreground deals. It takes place between a bearded figure on the left and a bald man on the right, and the conclusion that they reach is attested by an angelic figure in the center with bare feet. Not for nothing did the picture once bear on its frame the phrase "*Convenerunt in unum.*" It did so not because of an arcane connection with the Good Friday ritual, as has been suggested, but because the words exactly described its theme: "They came together" or, more colloquially, "Agreement was reached."

There is always a temptation to suppose that great paintings represent more than they appear to do. With some artists and some works of art this is unquestionably true. But not with Piero della Francesca. The *Madonna* at Monterchi illustrates the prayer "Show us the blessed fruit of thy womb, Jesus"; the fresco of the *Resurrection* is a sublime portrayal of the *Resurrection*; and the *Baptism of Christ* in London is a lucid portrayal of the Baptism. Their significance arises from their directness and artistic quality, not from refinements of literary content. In both cases the fit area of investigation is geometry, not iconography. This is well put by Berenson in a late essay, "Piero della Francesca, or the Ineloquent in Art":

> Piero della Francesca seems to have been opposed to the manifestation of feeling, and ready to go to any length to avoid it. He hesitated to represent the reaction which even an inanimate object would have when subjected to force. . . . One is almost compelled to conclude that Piero was not interested in human beings as living animals, sentient and acting. For him they were existences in three dimensions whom perchance he would gladly have exchanged for pillars and arches, capitals, entablatures and facets of walls.

It follows that the method by which Piero's paintings are constructed is a firmer guide to their chronology than is generally supposed. His only securely datable painting is a fresco of 1450 at Rimini, *Sigismondo Malatesta before St. Sigismund*, and the only means we have of determining the date (more strictly, dates) of the vast fresco cycle at Arezzo is to examine them in the light of the Rimini fresco. The choir at Arezzo is very wide, but it is nonetheless widely assumed that the two lateral walls were painted from a common scaffolding. This is improbable, since scaffolding stretching the whole width of the choir would have impeded use of the high altar. It is, moreover, demonstrably wrong. The subject of the lunette at the top of the left wall is the *Exaltation of the Cross*. The center of the composition is void, and the figures, with one exception, are confined to a narrow platform at the front. This is a competent but not an enterprising composition; the vanishing point in the center is about a fifth of the height of the fresco field. With the lunette on the right wall we enter an entirely different world. It shows four scenes which are unified by the spreading branches of a tree in the center of the field. The depth of the foreground is established by the disposition of the figures in monumental poses of astonishing variety and strength; the drapery forms are weighty and authoritative; and the figures bear witness to a close study of classical sculpture, of which there is no trace in the scene opposite. Descending to the second register, we find on the left the scene of discovery of the cross with a schematic view of Jerusalem at the back. The depth of the foreground area is defined by the two crosses, one receding gently and the other sharply into the picture space. To the right is a church façade and beyond it a street, and the action, hemmed in by a kneeling figure at one side and by standing figures at the other, takes place in an area limited by the bier and the extended cross. This fresco once more stands in sharp contrast to the *Meeting of Solomon and the Queen of Sheba* on the right-hand wall, which portrays two separate scenes but is a unitary scheme. The perspective structure has its vanishing point in the focus of action, the Queen kneeling before the wood at the entrance to the palace. In the bottom register the same contrast prevails. On the left is the tightly packed *Victory of Heraclius over Chosroes*, where depth is established in the center and on the left by the reduced size of the rear heads and on the right by the isolated structure of the throne of Chosroes. Opposite on the right wall is the magnificent *Victory of Constantine over Maxentius*, one of the most lucid and most delicately balanced multi-figure compositions in Quattrocento painting. The difference between the two walls is commonly explained by the assumption that the right wall is autograph and that the left wall was carried out with the help of members of the artist's shop. But this cannot be the case. The left wall was clearly designed before the right, and the scaffolding from which it was painted was confined to that wall and did not stretch over the whole width of the choir.

In Piero della Francesca's datable fresco at Rimini, *Sigismondo Malatesta before St. Sigismund*, the design is one of extreme sophistication. At the front and on either side of the inlaid marble floor are strips of light and dark marble of equal width which form the module of the composition. The white marble strips also function as perspective guidelines, with a vanishing point in Sigismondo Malatesta's head. The Rimini fresco, with its advanced Albertian composition, is the only means we have of establishing the relative date of the two walls at Arezzo, and it proves very clearly that the frescoes on the left wall must have been painted before 1450 (they cannot in fact have been begun till 1448, when the previous artist responsible for the choir returned to Florence) and that the frescoes on the right wall were painted, in a second campaign, after 1451. A third campaign was dedicated to the still later frescoes on the altar wall, one of which, the *Dream of Constantine*, is lit in a way that recalls French illuminations from the circle of Jean Fouquet, which Piero would have seen not in Arezzo but at some Central Italian court.

Fresco is normally a rapid medium. The preparatory process, the creative thinking, the making of preliminary drawings and cartoons, might well take time, but the speed of execution was determined by the day or days in which the priming or intonaco could be kept damp enough to absorb paint. After it dried, surface additions could be made *a secco*, but they were recognized to be less durable than the paint layer beneath. Piero della Francesca was a slow painter in every sense. Not only was the execution of his major works protracted over an unprecedentedly long period of time, but in fresco the individual heads were also worked up singly with the utmost care. Modern techniques of infrared and ultraviolet analysis have explained a great deal about his frescoes that was not previously evident. They have revealed the drawings beneath the frescoes in such a way that we can now understand for the first time how a detailed image became the impassive, generalized image that we know. There is no means by which lost retouching can be recovered, but an examination of the *Madonna del Parto* at Monterchi has made it possible to establish the form of the lost *secco* detail, so that we now know that the Virgin wore a headdress that recalls the crowns in Aretine Dugento paintings.

People writing about works of art have a bias toward supposing that great paintings like Piero's must be inspired by great ideas or great events. This is the case with the *Baptism of Christ* in London. In the form in which we know it, it is one of the supreme masterpieces of Italian painting, and it has been argued, simply for that reason, that its meaning differs from that of other Baptisms, that it represents the reconciliation of the Eastern and Western churches, and that it was inspired by the proponent of the Council of Florence, Ambrogio Traversari. But there is no evidence for that, and its uniqueness derives not from the ideas that it embodies, but from the way in which it was produced. Piero may, if a passage in Vasari is to be trusted, have started life as a mathematical prodigy, and his two treatises, on perspective and on the five regular bodies, are milestones in the history of geometry and mathematics. This was, in a sense, an ordinary interest raised to higher power. Cities like Arezzo employed masters of the abacus, who taught arithmetic, geometry, and algebra to the level that was necessary for successful commercial activity. Piero's written work is infinitely more demanding. He knew Euclid thoroughly; and he seems to have believed that the five regular bodies had the cosmological significance ascribed to them in Plato's *Timaeus*. An excellent geometrical analysis by B. A. R. Carter has shown that this was fundamental for the planning of the *Baptism of Christ*. The finality that is evident to the naked eye is due not to the painter's imagination, but to his geometrical consistency. A great many people go to concerts not to listen to the music, but for the thoughts that music promotes, and they do this with Piero too. If they are unsophisticated, like the awful travelers in *Summer's Lease*, they stand in the oratory at Monterchi thinking about childbirth or in the museum at San Sepolcro ruminating before the *Resurrection* about rebirth, the cycle of the seasons, or pagan mysteries. If they are scholars, they roam more widely. They imagine that the Tiber Valley in the background of the *Baptism* is intended as an earthly paradise, that the robed figures in the middle distance, though there are four of them, are the three Magi, that the angels at the side are guests at the Marriage at Cana, and that the catechumen behind Christ is putting on, not taking off, his shirt. They misinterpret every one of the details in the background of the Urbino *Dream of St. Jerome*, and they believe that the curtains in the *Madonna* at Monterchi are lined with ermine, and therefore allude to the Immaculate Conception, not with the commonplace fur which is actually shown. My own heterodox view is that Piero's paintings, great works as they are, mean no more than they appear to mean.

For Giovanni Bellini the geometrical planning of the picture field was no less significant than it was for Piero. Giovanni Bellini's power of description far exceeded Piero's, and the geometry of his paintings is correspondingly less evident. In a relatively late work, the *Baptism of Christ* at Vicenza, the iconography depends from an earlier *Baptism* of Cima in San Giovanni in Bragora in Venice, but the pictorial elements are rationalized as though by a Venetian Piero della Francesca. A strong vertical runs from the top of the panel through the standing Christ, and at a median point between the dove and the head of Christ is the brighly lit baptismal bowl held by St. John. In the sky and on the riverbank are two firmly established horizontals, and above Christ's head are two converging diagonals of hills. The *Coronation of the Virgin* at Pesaro, with its huge square central panel, its square window behind the throne, and its five square predella panels, seems also to have started life as a theorem in geometry, while the *Resurrection* from San Michele in Isola in Berlin is constructed round the firmly stated verticals of the central Christ and the two male figures at equidistant points from the sides of the painting, and the strong horizontals of the lines of rock above and below the tomb and the bands of cloud and sky. Writers on Giovanni Bellini have concentrated on the effect made by the paintings; witness the beautiful passage by Roger Fry on the Naples *Transfiguration*: "To anyone who understands the universal language of pose and gesture, it is evident that these three men—real men who walk the earth with palpable tread—are suddenly perceived by their amazed companions to be of more than human build, are heard to converse with the large serenity of gods. The idea of the invasion of this actual material world by a divine presence has surely never been realised with so intimate an imagination as here." But no thought has been given as to the means by which this sublime image acquired its actual form.

People sometimes complain that there is nothing new to be said about Italian painting. They mean by this there are now monographs on many minor painters and that the work of great artists has been discussed in a large number of books. But the truth is that the raw material of Italian painting is in a constant state of flux. When paintings change through cleaning, our view of the artist who produced them changes as well. The great artists who have been affected most radically by this activity are Michelangelo and Titian. The cleaning of the Sistine Ceiling has proved that old assessments of Michelangelo's palette and intentions were incorrect. In its cleaned form the ceiling has again become what Michelangelo's contemporaries considered it, one of the supreme achievements of mankind. With Titian the revelation started in the National Gallery in London, when the *Bacchus* and *Ariadne* was freed of centuries of dirt and proved to be painted in an altogether different tonality from any that had previously been supposed. It continued in the Scuola del Santo at Padua, where Titian's early frescoes acquired an unsuspected vividness, at Kroměříž, where the *Flaying of Marsyas* took on a quite new character, at Cambridge, where the *Tarquin and Lucretia* proved to be a work of incomparable dynamism, and in Venice with the cleaning of the *Assumption* in the Frari and of the Pesaro altarpiece. Scarcely less important than the surface cleaning of Titian's paintings has been technical examination of what lies beneath. An immense number of his canvases have been investigated from this point of view, and we can now speak with some confidence of the ideas that he rejected and of the method by which the paintings were built up. The way lies open to a survey of this hidden area in Titian's style. Would that these facilities had been available to great art historians of the past.

One of the things about art history that I found puzzling from the first was that clever art historians (there were stupid ones too, of course, but a lot of them were really clever) should reach diametrically opposite conclusions on the basis of a tiny nucleus of evidence. The reason, so far as one could judge, was that the subjective element in art history was disproportionately large. If this were so, it was not only works of art that needed to be looked at in the original but art historians too, since their results were a projection of their personalities. So for some years, I made meeting art historians a secondary avocation.

Though their results may be in part outdated, many of the art historians I have known were indeed great figures, built on a different scale from the narrowly focused art historians of today. Their minds moved freely over a wider span, partly because they were intellectually more confident and partly because less had been written on the artists or works of art with which they dealt. I have a lively sense of indebtedness to the great art historians I have known.

The first in point of time was Kenneth Clark. Though he abandoned ship halfway through his career, his natural talent as an art historian was immense. He wore a mask of practicality or pragmatism, but behind it there was, not exactly an artist, but someone who looked at works of art with an artist's understanding of what they were designed to do and how they had occurred. His private collection was not the collection of an aggregator; it was the collection of someone who loved art. This quality of visual awareness or acuity was among the many gifts he took to the museums with which he was associated. It affected the dormant Ashmolean at Oxford, and at its touch the then inert hulk of the National Gallery sprang to life. At Oxford he bought from Prince Paul of Yugoslavia the *Forest Fire* of Piero di Cosimo, and his first purchase in London was of the magical *Scenes from the Life of St. Francis* by Sassetta, which had been so well described by his mentor Berenson. When he arrived at the National Gallery there was no major work by Ingres, but with the purchase of one of Ingres's most splendid, most uncompromising portraits, *Madame Moitessier*, that gap was filled. This was a masterpiece, and Rembrandt's shimmering *Saskia as Flora* and Rubens's *Watering Place* were masterpieces too. But for K. none of those pictures would be there. As director, he introduced new standards of scientific conservation (they were extended by his successor, under whom they got more than a little out of hand), and he rehung the galleries with an intelligence and visual tact that made them look much more distinguished than they had looked in living memory. His difficulties arose from his relations with his staff. The currency of museum staffs is knowledge, not vision, and at the Gallery the staff could not acclimatize themselves to a director who addressed Leon Battista Alberti and Philip Sassoon on equal terms. K. on his side, quite legitimately as I think, preferred the company of people who were talented, no matter in what profession, to the company of untalented professionals. That was a factor in his decision in 1945 to resign the National Gallery directorship and to become Slade Professor of Fine Art at Oxford. It seemed a regrettable decision at the time—in a sense it seems so still; he was the greatest director of the Gallery in this century—but it freed him to begin the work that constitutes his main claim on posterity.

From the start his publications rested on a unique mixture of inspiration and clearheadedness. His first book, *The Gothic Revival*, dealt with the history of ideas, not with the history of art, but in 1929, the year that it appeared, he began working on the drawings by Leonardo da Vinci in the Royal Library at Windsor Castle. It was a colossal task. There were just over six hundred drawings, among them some of the most beautiful and most closely studied drawings in the world, and the catalogue, when it appeared, revealed a power of logical analysis and a security of judgment which was a breakthrough in Leonardo studies. The general book on Leonardo that he later distilled from this experience has never been surpassed.

From 1945 on, however, the focus of his interests changed. He remained a scholar whom other scholars had to reckon with, but he became increasingly intolerant of the minutiae of scholarship and increasingly impatient with the study of secondary artists. Thenceforth his concern lay with bridge building, not tunneling. His subsequent achievement rested on direct communication. The term "direct communication" suggests a certain speed or superficiality, but the remarkable thing about his published lectures is their self-discipline. The roots of his Rembrandt lectures reached back to an early period when he was working through the Rembrandt etchings at Oxford under the aegis of Charles Bell; *The Nude* was eleven years in gestation; and *Landscape into Art* proceeded from a lifelong immersion in the natural world. For K. the lecture was a distillation of experience, and he became a supreme exponent of the rhetoric of lecturing. The underpinning of each of his books is a stable set of values, human, not just aesthetic values, and again and again the vivid personal accounts of individual paintings offer a near-perfect definition of the mysterious relationship between a work of art and the individual confronting it.

But the story does not stop there. "I believe," he wrote in an early essay, "that those of us who try to make works of art more accessible are not wasting our time. Our hope lies in an expanding elite, an elite drawn from every class and with varying degrees of education, but united in a belief that non-material values can be discovered in visible things." From that order of conviction *Civilisation* was born. A cultural conscience was implanted like a pacemaker deep in K.'s personality. Probably the influence of Ruskin was responsible for that. It went without saying that the television screen was the only vehicle for the task he had in hand, and he had sufficient experience of television to recognize the risks that were involved. Television is rather a coarse medium, but he accepted its hazards, and how right he was, for by virtue of the films he became one of the civilizing forces of the second half of this century. The films were entitled "A Personal View," and it was to one mind, his own, that they owed their breadth and consistency and power of synthesis. They were not addressed only to a historically minded public. They were trained also on a vast heterogeneous public of historical illiterates, to whom the films proved not merely a source of stimulus or pleasure but a fount of inspiration and sustenance. They are K.'s true self-portrait. They show him, in countless different contexts, exactly as he was—sometimes incisive, sometimes extremely funny, sometimes impatient, sometimes intimate, sometimes almost tongue-tied, as he appears to be before the miracle of Vézelay. They record the range of his intellectual interests and the depth of his visual response, and the pulse of his powerful, buoyant, undogmatic mind.

Speaking for myself, I have never felt the urge to abandon the narrow, craggy pathway of art history for the open fields of public communication. That I did not do so was due, above all else, to the influence of Richard Offner. One of the most distinguished members of the generation which created art history as we know it now, Offner is, to the world at large, one of the least known. His major work, *A Critical and Historical Corpus of Florentine Painting*, is a lavish publication that is found only in specialist libraries, and his occasional writings have never been collected in book form. This is unfortunate, first because Offner's work has a unity and an integrity that stemmed directly from his character and second because his method of analysis is applicable to other areas than those with which he dealt. Most art historians meet each other for the first time through the medium of the written word, and that was how, at Oxford in the library of the Ashmolean Museum, I encountered Offner. Many of the students of Italian painting whose work I read (with the exception of Berenson and the partial exception of Adolfo Venturi)—they included Weigelt and Vitzthum and van Marle and Khvoshinsky and Salmi—were working in a single frame of reference; their judgments were subjective and fallible, and the interpretative content of their books was next to nil. But there was one wild card, a book in which paintings were discussed objectively not as relics of material culture but as works of art. It was called *Italian Primitives at Yale University*, and it was by Richard Offner.

It was quite a short book—only forty-three pages long in fact—and though they were not formally separated from each other it consisted of two parts, a nine-page introduction in which the pictures in the Jarves collection were assigned their place in a panoramic survey of Tuscan painting, and a longer section in which the problems presented by specific paintings were discussed. It described the use in the Dugento of "figures without cubic density in space without cubic depth" and of a style that is "a sort of consecration of the surface, to which, by a fine instinct or respect for the flat, the representation remains true." It explained how Bernardo Daddi's *Vision of St. Dominic* "contains the same poetic piety that reappears a century later in Fra Angelico, and a feeling for the alliance of the figure with the flat plane towards similar spatial harmonies," and how the panels of Nardo di Cione "disclose a romantic temperament tinged with a delicate mystery, which he was the first modern artist to seek in the modulations of the face and the insinuations of the eye." And it brought one closer than any other book to Antonio Pollaiuolo, whose *Rape of Deianira* "holds within the tightly knit figures a dynamic tension which was not to find complete release until the later drawings of Leonardo." Alongside it on the library shelf was an earlier book by Offner, *Studies in Florentine Painting*, with immensely accomplished essays on Trecento painters.

When I first met him in Florence, Offner was a dapper figure, in a well-cut snuff-colored suit, with glossy brown shoes and glossy black hair. At our first meeting, in 1936, the seeds of a long and fruitful friendship were sown. I did not, to my regret, become one of his pupils, but I was exposed spasmodically to his tutorial technique, of prompting people to solve problems for themselves. Knowing that I was going to Siena, he told me to study the Trecento panel of the Beato Andrea Gallerani in San Pellegrino, and tell him on my return who painted it. I spent hour after hour looking at the panel, and concluded that it was an early Andrea Vanni. Offner agreed, and encouraged me to publish it. When I go today to Santa Maria Novella to look at the Orcagna altarpiece, I still see it as I saw it then through Offner's eyes.

Till Offner's death I continued to see him frequently both in London and in Florence. We had meals, sometimes agonizing meals together—agonizing because, confronted with some bland risotto at Harry's Bar, he would accuse the waiter of putting pepper in it—and we looked together at works of art. His eye was the most rapid I have ever known, and never was he more impressive than when he was operating off his natural field. Going to Bologna in 1958 for a miscellaneous exhibition of Bolognese Seicento paintings, I found Richard on the platform at the railway station, and we spent the morning looking at the Schedonis and the Mastellettas in the exhibition. By lunchtime I saw them very differently from the way in which I had seen them earlier. This happened again in 1961 at an exhibition of Italian bronze statuettes in London. I went round it with many specialists, but it was Offner alone who realized what the central problems were and how they could be attacked. In his first book he included a chapter on method; it is abstruse and theoretical, and deals with the concepts of shape as the ultimate unit of style, shape as material for the cognitive faculty, and attribution as the recognition of a recurring experience. A clearer definition of method is included in the *Corpus of Florentine Painting*. It rests on a number of simple propositions: first that the history of art is the history of artistic expression, second that the initial stage is deep study of the single object, third that the physical character of the single object, if properly analyzed, will establish its aesthetic individuality, and fourth that conclusions to which this leads have then to be absorbed into a larger synthesis. These principles gave rise to Offner's splendid articles on Masaccio and on the painter known as the Barberini Master, and are the basis of his great essay on the Assisi frescoes, "Giotto, non-Giotto." Forty years have passed since this last article appeared, but it is intellectually impregnable, and in that time no compelling answer to it has been made. It is a barrier which separates Anglo-Saxon art historians (all of whom read it as students) from art historians in Italy.

In Vienna, Offner was a student of Dvořák, and among Dvořák's other students at the time was a Hungarian, Friedrich Antal. Antal was a very different figure; he was an orthodox Marxist, and his concern, throughout a long career, was to establish an equation between society and style. He lived in London in a flat in Marlborough Place, and I used before the war to spend evenings with him discussing problems of art history. Central European in appearance and cast of mind, he had a low, rather mellifluous speaking voice which was in striking contrast to his radical beliefs, and it was difficult to contest his heresies in an undertone. His natural affinities were with Mannerism, and I learned more about Mannerism from him than I did about the Italian fourteenth and early fifteenth centuries, on which he was working at the time. It was indeed reason, not instinct, that had led him to the field. The best of his early articles was an essay on Dutch Mannerism in the *Kritische Berichte* (it has now been translated and is an extremely stimulating piece of work), and his initial intention was to stake out the case for Marxist art history in a volume on the Cinquecento. That this was never written was a serious loss, but he found first that it was impossible to write on the sixteenth century if he had not written on the fifteenth, and then that the fifteenth century could be discussed only after study of the fourteenth. This was the book on which he was working when I knew him. The results were awaited with expectancy, but when the volume finally appeared in 1947 it proved a disappointing work. The difficulty was not that Antal was a Marxist; it was that his whole cast of mind was theoretical, and that he had a kind of pattern-making propensity that caused him to force works of art into a mold. This had been evident a decade earlier, in a strange article called "Studien zur Gotik im Quattrocento," in which he applied the term "Gothic" to a quantity of mid-Quattrocento works of art that had in common only their non-Gothic character. Antal saw what he wished to see. For him Masaccio represented "the peak of upper-bourgeois rationalism in religious art," while Lorenzo Monaco's "extreme late Gothic formal idiom was closely linked with the aristocratizing, polished upper middle class." As a convinced Marxist he captivated Anthony Blunt, and he may at first have regarded me as a possible disciple, but our conversations convinced me that a combination of generalized style history and rudimentary sociology would never produce useful or interesting results.

The crippling effect of Antal's method was the more evident by comparison with the subtler and solider work in the same field of Millard Meiss. I first encountered Meiss's articles at Oxford in 1933. They combined carefully cogitated style analysis with perspicacious but uninsistent iconographical research, and when I met him—in an exhibition at Arezzo—the first impression was that his human personality corresponded exactly with the personality implicit in his written work. The scholar and the man were one, and the qualities they shared were the qualities that made him a great art historian. In art history there is a premium on abstinence. The subject requires great cleverness, but cleverness that never lapses into exhibitionism; it requires imagination, but imagination under rational control; it requires a capacity to formulate that differs from other forms of writing in that it is invalidated if the writer gives way to the seduction of writing for writing's sake. In all those respects Meiss was a paradigm. He could have astonished but refrained from doing so; he could have allowed a powerful imagination to draw him beyond the permissible limits of the evidence; he could have disturbed the careful balance between formulation and the thought that it expressed. But he did none of those things. His style was a mirror of his mind, a means of communicating judgments and conclusions that were balanced and precise and which, though learned, were leavened by historical imagination of a kind few other art historians have possessed. It is sometimes suggested that students of art history can dispense with sensibility, and anyone who is so foolish as to believe that that is so should give close thought to the undertow of pleasure throughout Meiss's work. Nine out of ten articles on iconography are ill-packed suitcases stuffed with superfluous clothes. Only a strong-minded scholar can resist the attractions of the inessential and will confine himself, as Millard invariably did, to analogies that are demonstrably valid and to citations that illuminate. This is not simply a matter of selection, but reflects something more significant, a recognition that our evidence for the way in which Renaissance artists really thought is insufficient to admit of dogmatism, and that only those deductions that faithfully reflect the vagueness of the evidence are in the last resort likely to be correct.

In 1947 three lectures were given at the Warburg Institute by a scholar who was little known in England, Meyer Schapiro. One was about Cézanne, another was about animals tearing each other to pieces on Romanesque portals, and a third dealt with randomness in art. They were marvelous lectures, so smooth, so compulsive, and so perfectly articulated that they inspired incredulity; one wondered if they could possibly be true. After the third, Schapiro, at the instigation of our common friend Fritz Saxl, came to look at the medieval objects in the Victoria and Albert. Only a few of them were displayed, and the bulk of the collection lay in disorder in storage cases in the basement. But as each case was opened, and we removed the ivories, I found to my astonishment that there was not one work Schapiro did not know. One of the things that you get used to in museums is cushioning the fall of specialists, covering up the myriad mistakes they make when they are actually confronted by works of art. But this was quite a different occasion; here was someone whose thought proceeded from the object seen.

I have never known Schapiro well, but I have learned much from his work. His weight of armament is greater than that of any other living art historian. He possesses a computer bank of information and, more important, of visual images, and its essential concomitant, the power of instantaneous recall. The second factor is his scope, by which I mean two things, the range of subjects with which he deals and the variety of analytical techniques that are applied to them. At one end of the spectrum he can write on early mosaics in Israel and the frescoes at Castelseprio and the manuscripts produced at Jarrow in the first half of the eighth century, and at the other he can deal, with great originality, with Mondrian and abstract art. That would be less remarkable if the studies themselves were less percipient and original, but in every case Schapiro leaves us with the sense that he has dug down to the bedrock of the argument. The matter of analytical technique is harder to define. The function of art history is to determine why individual artifacts took the form they did. This task involves a mastery of widely divergent areas of knowledge, which extend from simple history (if any history is simple) to semiotics and psychology. In relation to the ideal requirements of the subject the equipment of most art historians (myself included) is sadly inadequate. They operate in the conventional, clumsy way in which dentists used to drill teeth half a century ago. But with Schapiro one is constantly astonished by the variety of angles from which problems are attacked, and by the lucidity with which his concepts are expressed. His work is at root visual. That is apparent whether the subject is the Moissac tympanum or the *Grande Jatte* of Seurat. But behind the observation a probing mind is constantly at work. In his essays the act of seeing is precisely correlated with the act of thought. He commands at the same time that essential but treacherous weapon, intuition. No art historian can produce new or interesting results without it, but the most rigorous self-criticism is necessary if it is not to cross the frontiers of fantasy, and Schapiro never does. In his books on Cézanne and van Gogh he enters the artists' minds and, with an authority few other art historians or critics have achieved, reconstructs their creative processes.

One of the most distinguished scholars who found a temporary home in England during the war years was Otto Paecht. Quintessentially Viennese, he did not find communication easy, and one had to know him well before one got a clear impression of his originality and depth. His prime area of concern was manuscript illumination, and I remember his giving one devastating lecture at the Courtauld Institute on Panofsky's *Early Netherlandish Painting*. Much of his time in England was spent at Oxford, where he was closely associated with the Bodleian, but he was unhappy there since he was constantly confronted by a competitive professional communicator in the person of Edgar Wind. I found him of absorbing interest in private contacts, and on the last occasion that I saw him, in Vienna, we drove out together to see a Polish exhibition about the Cracow sculptures of Veit Stoss. With his appointment to a chair at Vienna University, he realized himself more fully than had been possible in England, and fortunately left behind him a body of disciples dedicated to his method and his memory.

The position of Johannes Wilde was very different. Also Vienna trained, he was brought to England by Antoine Seilern. I met him for the first time just before the war at the Toksover Hotel in Dulwich. He had a weight of personality that was immediately impressive, a wealth of experience gained in the Kunsthistorisches Museum and a quality of disinterest or otherworldliness that inspired immediate confidence. Unlike Paecht, he was transplantable, and at the Courtauld Institute he was responsible for training a whole generation of able art historians. Though he was long thought of as primarily a historian of Venetian painting, his most important study was of Michelangelo. It gave rise to a number of articles, an excellent set of lectures reprinted in book form, and a highly illuminating catalogue of the Michelangelo drawings in the British Museum. It is difficult to preserve one's balance when working on the greatest artists. In Florence I knew Charles de Tolnay fairly well—we used sometimes to take a taxi from the Casa Buonarroti, where he lived, to lunch together in the Piazzale Michelangelo, looking up at the back and buttocks of a bronze cast of the *David*. But I set no serious store by Tolnay's work on Michelangelo; I could indeed see no close relationship between the views Michelangelo demonstrably held and the views Tolnay ascribed to him. With Wilde, however, there was no trace of faking. What he said rang true.

Some of the most enviable art historians are those so saturated in an artist's work that they respond to every movement of his mind. Once when I was visiting the Fogg I was taken round an exhibition of Rembrandt's graphic work by Jakob Rosenberg. I had always thought his monograph on Rembrandt rather a dull book, but on this occasion, before the prints, I saw him for the first and only time as an interpreter, conscious of the creative inflection behind every change in every state. I wished there were some means of recording the experience.

I owe a recurring debt to the most gifted Italian art historian of the first half of this century, that mysterious figure Roberto Longhi. Whereas the desiccated work of academic Italian scholars like Mario Salmi belongs firmly to the past, Longhi's books and articles remain as fresh, as stimulating, sometimes as shocking as they seemed when they first appeared. I knew him from 1939 until his death, though never very well, and whenever we met I was captivated by his charm, his fluency, and his unpredictability. In his own setting in Via Benedetto Fortini in Florence, he possessed hypnotic powers. About 1950, when I was working on Uccello, I told him I did not understand the basis of his attribution to Uccello of the frescoes in the Cathedral at Prato; it seemed to me inadmissible first on the ground of lack of similarity to Uccello's authenticated works and second because the perspectival structure of the scenes was inconsistent with that of Uccello's frescoes. Longhi opened a drawer full of detail photographs of the frescoes, and at the end of half an hour I was convinced that he was right and I was wrong. But next day I took the precaution of going back to Prato, only to discover that the frescoes looked not as they had done in Longhi's study, but as they looked to me before. When my rather conservative book appeared, Longhi described it as "antidiluviano."

Longhi had relatively little influence outside Italy. One reason for this was the difficulty of his style. Every attempt that I have made to translate or to arrange for the translation of his articles or books has come to grief on the rocks of syntax and terminology. In English they become self-conscious and commonplace. There is now a glossary, for Italian use, of the terms that he employed. The premises behind his work are specifically Italian, and derive from Benedetto Croce. Croce was both historian and critic; much of his literary criticism is of the highest quality, but objection has been rightly raised to what one scholar defines as "the conceptual dissolution of history in criticism and his practical relegation of history to an unimportant secondary role." Croce's concern was to assess the aesthetic quality of the work under discussion and only when this was done to explain its place in history. In Anglo-Saxon literary criticism the normal practice is the opposite. Like Croce, Longhi was a critic of genius. Often his response to paintings is so authentic and so vivid as to be unforgettable. Not long ago, looking in Vicenza at the great *Baptism of Christ* by Giovanni Bellini, I recalled his description of its landscape: *"Nella calculata chiusura d'orizzonte, entro la cerchia dei monti altissimi, i colori acquistano la densità di un respiro che venga dal profondo."* The ability, by the use of words or of word cadences, to persuade readers to look at works of art through the writer's eyes is a rare and covetable gift.

Longhi was also a brilliant philologist, with a flawless memory and an eye of great speed and often of great accuracy. Unlike Berenson, he presented his conclusions as the result of intuition, not of reason, and this had a contagious, often deleterious, influence on his disciples, who accepted the myth that the attributionist was a prestidigitator and that attribution was a conjuring trick. He is the only art historian all of whose published writings (every word even of the most ephemeral of them) have been assembled in a complete edition, and when one reads through them their strengths and weaknesses become self-evident. They are constructed of philology and criticism, and their value is established by the ratio between the two. The early monograph on Piero della Francesca, though now outdated, is an interpretative masterpiece. Elsewhere, even in *Officina Ferrarese*, one of his most imaginative books, the weight of emphasis generally falls on minor painters. In his least sound work, "Giudizio sul Duecento," the preponderant factor is critical, and the study fails in part because the critical criteria applied in it are misconceived and in part because it is, from a philological standpoint, ill observed. In his best work, however, philology preponderates, and the article "Fatti di Masolino e di Masaccio" forms a milestone in the study of Quattrocento style. In Longhi's most substantial writings, on Caravaggio and Caravaggesque painting, criticism and philology move forward hand in hand.

The lack of critical content in current Anglo-Saxon art-historical writing and teaching seems to me a serious defect. One of the few scholars who have attempted to redress it, often with striking success, is my friend Sydney Freedberg, who in his books on High Renaissance painting has described, in terms that are sometimes dismissed as over-personal but that I admire and support, his response to the work of the great Italian artists of the sixteenth century.

On one point all the scholars I have mentioned would, I suspect, agree, that creative processes can be only approximately reconstructed, and that without some concomitant of intuition none of those factors that imperatively require explanation can be explained. I became an art historian through a sense of the mystery of the whole subject, and it is that sense of mystery that has led me to persevere in studies to which no wholly satisfactory outcome is likely ever to be reached. In the words of Henry James: "We work in the dark. We do what we can. We give what we have. Our doubt is our passion, and our passion is our task. The rest is the madness of art."

15

HOME TO FLORENCE

HOUSE HUNTING IS A FRUSTRATING BUSINESS, AND NOWHERE MORE so than in Italy. It is a purgatory you must pass through before a miracle occurs, and the preordained house declares itself. I looked in the summer of 1985 at flats without views or space or air, and in the fall the miracle occurred, when the telephone rang in my bedroom in New York and a voice—it was Flavia Capponi's—said that a suitable apartment had suddenly become available. I flew over at once to look at it. It was in the Palazzo Canigiani (not the palace with a courtyard attributed to Michelozzo, but one immediately to its east, with a courtyard dating from the eighteenth century), and it faced across the Arno in one direction and across the Via de' Bardi in the other. I seized on it immediately. I had a superstitious as well as a practical reason for doing so. My birthday falls on the Feast of St. Lucy, December 13, and I would have a devotion to St. Lucy even were that not so, for she is the patron of the organ by which I live, the eye. Adjacent to the Palazzo Canigiani is the church of Santa Lucia dei Magnoli, to which Benvenuto Cellini carried the offering of a golden eye when, after an accident that almost blinded him, his eyesight was restored.

The appearance of the apartment was unpromising. It was in a filthy, unhygienic state, but it was not on the *piano nobile* and had well-proportioned rooms of human scale. It had other advantages as well: a long L-shaped hall; a circular neo-classical dining room with a coved ceiling; a pretty and reasonably capacious drawing room with a late-nineteenth-century silvered ceiling; and, projecting north-ward, a big room that could be filled with books, with one window looking over the river and the other facing the church of Santa Lucia. Best of all, a steep wooden staircase led up to a terrace the same size as the study beneath. Doing up the apartment was a long, mainly enjoyable operation. Money was a factor, and it seemed to me from the start that there were three areas on which to concentrate. The first comprised the living rooms, whose character would be determined in great part by their curtains. I had curtains for them made in New York, not Florence. The second area was the dining room. It required a circular table, and shooting a bow at a venture I asked a Florentine friend to find me one in porphyry. A long time elapsed, and then there appeared a circular *porfiraccio* table with a sturdy cherry-wood base. In my dining room in New York (and for the matter of that in my dining room in London) guests were subjected to sitting on Renaissance chairs of great discomfort, on which relaxation was impossible. In the new setting these would not do. I found a set of supposedly Genoese Biedermeier chairs in cherry wood, which at least had the merit of looking unlike any chairs I had seen before. The third area was the study, which now houses my library. The bookcases, as one would expect with bookcases designed and built in Florence, are dignified, spacious, and impeccably well made.

One of the pleasures of the move was the craftsmanship exhibited by every artisan who was employed. The painters had the critical acumen of painters in the fifteenth century. Was the yellow one had chosen not a little sharp? they asked. And sure enough it was. Beneath the dirty painted drawing-room floor there proved to be well-preserved terracotta tiling, and in the dining room and study there were patterned wood floors of excellent quality. Of the four bedrooms I adapted one, the smallest, for my own use. Another became an office.

Objects mean more to me than people. It is not that I am frigid or reclusive, but that object-based relationships are more constant than human ones (they never change their nature and do not pall). In New York I looked on despairingly as a gang of powerful packers invaded my apartment, fitting pieces of my life resolutely into a container in the street. How much, I wondered, would one see again and in what state? After an unconscionable lapse of time the boat with the container reached Leghorn and the container itself arrived in Florence. The infinitely helpful staff of the Soprintendenza ai Beni Culturali dealt with the necessary formalities, and since nothing proved to have been damaged, I was free to arrange, in the last house I shall live in, the objects that form an epitome of my whole life.

My bedroom faces east and when I draw the curtains (they are blue brocaded curtains I have known all my life in drawing rooms in London and New York; the only ones like them I have ever seen were at the Durdans and belonged to Lady Sibyl Grant), I look out at the Campanile of Santa Lucia next door and beyond it to an immense magnolia outside the Palazzo Torrigiani. To the right of the window is a tondo of the Virgin and Child by a Lucchese painter, the Stratonice Master. The Child in it looks like a frog, and in another work by him, in the Lederer collection in Geneva, the same frog child appears. I bought the picture in 1936 at Christie's, where it was regarded as a spurious Filippino Lippi. Under it is a little Pax with the Pietà, which has indeed some remote connection with Filippino. It was heavily overpainted when I bought it for ten pounds at the Harris sale, but it was cleaned one afternoon at the Victoria and Albert and has given me uncritical pleasure ever since. The only other painting hangs beside my bed. It is a small, much abraded *Virgin and Child with Saints* by Ugolino da Siena, which I first encountered in the 1930s in a photograph published by Berenson in *Dedalo*. It reappeared not long ago at Sotheby's in New York, as one of the last lots in the sale of the paintings of Florence Jay Gould.

The only sculpture is opposite my bed; it is a good version in pigmented stucco of a group by Antonio Rossellino which was given me by my aunt Susan Birch. Hers was Regency taste and she took no stock in the Renaissance, but I think of her each time I look at it. Beside it are two black painted chairs, which I remember by my mother's dressing table when I was a child. The only object without associations is my bed, a nice Tuscan seventeenth-century four-post bed which was found in the Via de' Fossi in Florence. On the left wall is a tallboy I have known all my life. It is a not very distinguished piece of late-eighteenth- or early-nineteenth-century English furniture that has traveled with me from house to house. On its pediment is a green tin pineapple (I suppose it must be German), which has always stood exactly where it stands today. At the back of the dressing table is a watercolor of my mother by an old Chelsea friend called Hilda Trevelyan. It was painted slowly through endless afternoons, and though the features are not defined, it records, in the way that only affectionate sketches can do, a sense of my mother's presence in a room. Next to it is a photograph of her by Cecil Beaton, taken against a background of disordered furniture when we were moving after the war, and next to that is a languid photograph by Cecil of my brother

James, leaning, one wintry morning, on a sphinx at Chiswick House. It is faithful to what at the time was James's view of himself, as a French romantic washed up in the twentieth century. Beside it is a Beaton photograph of Berenson. It is a confidence-inspiring likeness, and from time to time I ask it: "Have I come up to scratch?"

Otherwise my bedroom walls are filled with drawings by that still underrated sixteenth-century Sienese Barocci-follower, Francesco Vanni. I was given the first by my uncle Wyndham Birch. It is an enchantingly pretty red chalk and bistre drawing for a lost altarpiece surrounded by a frame with the mysteries of the rosary. A copy of it is in Siena in the Palazzo Chigi-Saraceni. Most of the other drawings have specific connotations. One, in soft chalk, shows a beatified Capuchin nun, Pasitea Crogi, one of the *"dévotes et sorcières italiennes"* who followed Maria de' Medici to France, and another is for a picture in the right transept of Monte Oliveto Maggiore, showing Guido Tarlati, Bishop of Arezzo, dedicating the church. By the door is a frame with six engravings by Stefano della Bella. They show pairs of eagles, sometimes feeding hungrily, sometimes with backs turned, and sometimes on the edge of greedy confrontation. I kept this in my offices at the Victoria and Albert and the British Museum as a parable of all the things that can so easily go wrong in a museum staff.

Outside in the passage is another Stefano della Bella, a wash drawing of a puppet show made for the amusement of Ferdinand II de' Medici as Gran Principe, *"suo scolaro."* A whole book of these drawings was brought to me during the war in London, but I was hard up at the time and could only afford one. When the others come up singly for sale, I kick myself for this economy. Two oval mythological paintings belonged to my mother's mother; Roberto Longhi once told me they were by Giacomo del Po and nobody has disagreed with him. Between them is a poor man's Titian, a Polidoro Lanziani *Holy Family with the Young Tobias* from George Spencer-Churchill's collection. I paid no special attention to it at Northwick, but from its easel in the sale room it seemed to be begging to be bought. On the opposite wall is a Cordieri drawing for the statue of Paul V at Rimini and a Beccafumi view of Pisa; the Beccafumi is a theatrical, not a topographical drawing, but shows the Lungarno looking much as it does today. The corridor leads to my book-filled study, where I work at a Spanish walnut refectory table that I saw for the first time in the middle of the 1930s dining with some friends of my mother's called Erskine before a debutante dance. On the only vacant wall is a painting I bought in London as a Francesco Vanni. Sienese specialists tell me it is really an early work of Rutilio Manetti, and they may well be right. Beside it are two uncontested Francesco Vannis, a grisaille oil sketch for an altarpiece at Fabriano and an almost square drawing of the Virgin and Child between SS. Bernardino and Catherine of Siena with a distant panorama of Siena, of which an earlier version is in the Metropolitan Museum. Under them is my piano, a Steinway of Ethel Salter's on which I practiced for the first time in the late 1920s in California Street in Washington. It is a beautiful piano, and since Arthur Salter grudgingly handed it over I have had boundless pleasure from it. On it is the music from which I have always played, Casella's edition of the Beethoven sonatas, which I bought when I was at school, a copy of the Brahms symphonies arranged for four hands which belonged to Arnold Bennett, messy copies of the *Wohltemperierte Klavier* and the English and French suites, Haydn and Mozart sonatas, and Brahms, Schumann, and Scriabin, with a few relics of the moment at which it was fashionable to play from unedited urtexts. My only talent was for sight-reading, and my fingers are too stiff today to sight-read with facility.

Five *pietra serena* steps lead down to the hall, which is lined with Dufour *papiers peints* of the *Legend of Cupid and Psyche* that give pleasure of a temperate, nonassociative kind, and on the vacant walls are two paintings, a Domenichino and an Albani. I admired the Albani the first time I went to Ashburnham, where it formed a pair to a Guercino now in Berlin, and after Lady Catherine's sale I secured it from a dealer who had bought it for its splendid frame. The Domenichino is a sketch model for a ruined altarpiece in the Duomo at Volterra. I once lent it anonymously to an exhibition at Agnew's, where the current Domenichino specialist, Richard Spear, described it in a review as a French copy. On the back of the canvas is a seventeenth-century Italian inscription, and since it is painted in precisely the same way as the Bologna altarpieces of the same date, no one else has doubted it. On top of a cabinet under the Albani is a bronze bust of St. Philip Neri by Algardi. Most of Algardi's busts of St. Philip were made in multiple versions, but this one is unique, and its chasing is of remarkably high quality. It was bequeathed by Henry Harris to his manservant, who became a Catholic and took at his confirmation the name Philip. After Harris died, the manservant took to drink, and about a year later I found the bust in a shop in Kensington Church Street where he had pawned it.

Along a passage to the left are more engravings. Among them is the Agostino Veneziano print of the Roman studio of the sculptor Bandinelli. Unlike most of my contemporaries, I am no friend to Bandinelli, but the silhouettes thrown by candle- and lamplight on the studio walls remind one of the world of fantasy destroyed by the invention of electricity. Opposite is a watercolor sketch by Louisa Lady Waterford, a highly talented artist who has been cold-shouldered by the feminist art historians of today. Made after dinner one evening in 1870 at Forde Abbey, it has the intimacy of a Bonnard. At the other end of the same wall is a little group of Kirsteiniana, two beautiful drypoints by Nadelman which Lincoln Kirstein gave me one day after dinner in New York and a well-known photograph of Lincoln and his sister Mina by George Platt Lynes. They were both a great deal younger at the time the photograph was made than when I knew them, but it commemorates an inexhaustibly enriching friendship. The dining room is circular, and filled with four inbuilt vitrines. On the wall opposite the window is a view of the Lake of Geneva, which used always to hang above my mother's desk. I did not know who painted it until a colleague from Copenhagen came to lunch and identified it as by Simon Malgo, a Dane who worked in the third quarter of the eighteenth century in Rome and in 1776 executed two overdoors for Voltaire at Ferney. The view is taken from the point at which the Musée d'Art et d'Histoire stands today. The vitrines are filled with odds and ends—a German limewood group of three children that used to stand on Paul Wallraf's desk in London, a seventeenth-century Transylvanian backgammon board, an Augsburg traveling canteen, an excellent version of the small Giovanni Bologna bronze self-portrait, some ting and celadon, and an enchanting eighteenth- or early-nineteenth-century Japanese hand-screen of a mounted figure, which used to be in my brother's flat—and between them are excised illuminations. There are stories attached to all of them, but I shall mention only one here. In 1947 I went by appointment to look at some drawings at Alfred Scharf's, a dealer who had written a good book on Filippino Lippi. To get there from the Victoria and Albert you took a No. 28 bus, and sitting on the upper deck I thought, vaguely, of what it would be fun to find. I was working on the Yates-Thompson codex of the *Divine Comedy* at the time, and the thought

passed through my head that the object which would give me greatest
pleasure was one of the seventeen missing illuminations from a Milanese codex of the *Divine Comedy* that was split between the Biblio-
thèque Nationale and Imola. Looking at drawings with Scharf, I forgot
this velleity, but as I was leaving I turned round in the doorway and
asked if he had any illuminations. "Only one," he replied, "it was
brought in this morning," and he handed me the figures of Dante and
Virgil from one of the missing miniatures. The illumination is not
much larger than a large-scale postage stamp (when I lent it to an
exhibition in Milan not long ago it looked indeed ridiculously small),
but I value it not just for what it is but for the message of precognition
it seemed to convey.

The drawing room, like all my drawing rooms, is dominated by a
fine Japanese screen. It was given to my father's father when, as
governor of Hong Kong, he paid a formal visit to Tokyo. My interest
in iconography is limited, and the other day I realized that though I
have lived with the screen for more than half a century I have never
had the scenes on it read or identified. Over it hangs a long panel of
the *Marriage of the Virgin*, which dates from about 1520; it has been
ascribed to Pacchia (wrongly, by Longhi) and its most recent attribution is to Brescianino. If it belonged to someone else, I would have
found out long ago who painted it, but since it is my own I feel no
interest in the problem. It is, nonetheless, a satisfying painting. On
the chimneypiece are Chinese objects—an iron cast statue and a li-
bation pot and some celadon—and over it is a *Mystic Marriage of St.
Catherine* by Carlo Dolci, which was weeded out, in what must have
been a moment of insanity, from the Spencer collection at Althorp.
It is still in a fine English 1740 frame. To its right is a Mola *Baptism
of Christ* from Bridgewater House, and to its left a Marcantonio Fran-
ceschini. In the corner of the room is a Venetian *stile povero* corner
cupboard—the nicest thing about it is that it still has its original glass—
and on another wall is a big Neapolitan cabinet from Maudslie Castle
with glass-fronted drawers. There must originally have been two, as
all the scenes derive from the Old Testament frescoes in the Raphael
Loggia of the Vatican save one, which is from the New Testament.
In one drawer the scenes are replacements—the figures in them look
like the Péllerin Cézannes—and in the middle, concealed behind the
door, is a painting on glass which looks like a Luca Giordano. Over
the radiator are two drawings of fish from the Museo Cartaceo made

in Rome for Cassiano del Pozzo, and between the windows is a
fifteenth-century Sienese *Assumption of the Virgin* by an artist who used
once to be called Pacchiarotto and is now identified as Pietro degli
Orioli, where the white-and-gold-clad Virgin seems really to float up
into the sky.

When I moved to Florence in the autumn of 1986, I had a welcome
sense of being welcomed, first by my nomination as Grande Ufficiale
dell'Ordine del Merito of the Italian Republic, and then by the award
of the Galileo Galilei Prize at the University of Pisa. This very distinguished award was the more gratifying in that its sponsors were a
committee of Italian scholars whose work I respected. The prize, a
bronze by Emilio Greco, stands in my study today.

After so many summers spent in Florence the city should have
seemed familiar, but it did not. There is a vast difference between
visiting places and living in them. When I was working in Florence
in the summer I hardly ever went to shops, save for the chemists and
the bookshops in Via Tornabuoni. But as soon as one bought bathroom
fittings and light fixtures and tables and beds, one entered a new
world. Under almost every palace there were small shop windows,
and if you went inside you discovered room after room with chandeliers hanging from the ceiling and piled-up furniture. The light
fixtures were mainly modern, but in the shops themselves you had
the sense that if you bumped into some Victorian woman novelist
you would feel no surprise. These shops formed a civic infrastructure
of which I had been wholly unaware.

Another thing that I discovered is how life in Italy has been slowed
down by the computer. When you go to the telephone company to
secure a telephone, you find rows of helpful, middle-aged ladies sitting
at computers they do not fully understand. If you have the good luck
to find a subscriber with a superfluous number, they will reallocate
it. But a telephone number is of little use without a telephone. At
first I supposed that, as in London or New York, high-level pressure
would do the trick. But not a bit of it. I got a telephone only when
I mentioned my predicament to a painter friend who in turn had a
friend who was employed by the company. The next day the telephone turned up.

Another difference is more fundamental: that the basis of life in
Italy is not the nation but the historic unit of the city. I am tempted
to write a history of Italian art which does not use the adjective Italian

or the name Italy. One result of life in Florence is that when you visit other cities—large cities like Bologna and Padua or small ones like Faenza and Gubbio and Lucca—you are conscious of how different they are from one another. I used to be aware of what Italian cultural centers had in common. But as an adoptive Florentine, once you are outside Florence, you feel displaced.

In the past I have always been puzzled by the preoccupation of Florentine students with the Florence of the Medici grand dukes, at the expense of the vital, republican Florence that preceded it. But as the statue of Cosimo I in the Piazza della Signoria shows all too clearly—with its scenes of the conquest of Siena and the creation of the grand duchy of Tuscany—this nostalgia has historic roots. The ruler of Florence is the *sindaco*, and the *sindaco*'s office in the Palazzo della Signoria is the Sala di Clemente VII with its splendid historical paintings by Vasari. In Florence there is no escaping history.

The prevailing *campanilismo* is reflected in the local press. You read *La Nazione* at breakfast to find out what strikes are imminent (for life in Italy is punctuated by *scioperi*) and which football teams from the immediate neighborhood have won or lost over the weekend. Only when you open the *Corriere della Sera* (when you admit to reading it, you are asked whether you do not think it much too Milanese) or the *Republica* do you learn about the world, the state of the stock market, or the situation in the Middle East. In the aggregate, in combination with the most expensive and inefficient postal service in the whole of Europe (airmail letters to the United States take longer than letters did by sea before the war), this builds up to a sense of being insulated against reality. But the rewards of life in Florence are very great. In my case part of the pleasure is associative and part professional. The idea of Florence, built up in the nineteenth century, and still alive today, is a synthesis of memories. In the corridor of the Uffizi I think of Shelley's inspired descriptions of the Medici Venus and the other antique sculptures. At the bottom of the Via Maggio I look up at the Brownings' windows in Casa Guidi, and at the bottom of the Via dei Serragli I run into Lamartine. I think of George Eliot, accompanied by a Quattrocento ghost, looking down at the city on a golden morning from San Miniato, and I watch Swinburne running along the Via della Chiesa on his first visit to the poet Landor. Perhaps the most moving statement of the idea of Florence as a refuge is contained in Swinburne's poem about Landor's death:

And thou, his Florence, to thy trust
Receive and keep,
Keep safe his dedicated dust,
His sacred sleep.

From my terrace I look across the river at almost all the buildings with which, at one time or another, I have been concerned. To the right is Santa Croce, with its paper-thin white marble façade tacked onto the west front. Opposite is the roof of the Badia and the tower of the Bargello, and to the left again the cupola of the Cathedral and the hulk of the Palazzo della Signoria. A little further on is the arcade of the Uffizi, and beyond it, if you crane your neck, you see one end of the Ponte Vecchio. Turning right round, you gaze up at San Miniato sitting on its hill.

What lies beyond is unpredictable. On clear days one looks along the river in the direction of Pontassieve and Vallombrosa and across it to Fiesole, with Montebeni in the distance to its left. Always one is conscious of topography and of the curve of protective hills that saved Florence from assault in the early fifteenth century. Never before have I lived beside a river, and the Arno at close quarters, sluggish as it may seem in summer, is powerful and recalcitrant. With a few days of heavy rain it reaches a state of *pre-allarme*, and traumatic memories of the flood of 1966 float to the surface of one's mind. So strong is its identity that one believes (as I have personally not done with other rivers) in the sixteenth-century imagery of propitiatory river gods.

Living in Florence, I am tormented by the things I do not know. Generic explanations that seemed adequate when one was in London or New York, that artist A influenced artist B, or that artist C fell under the spell of artist D, no longer suffice. Florence, you are reminded on every side, was a small, claustrophobic town, in which every artist knew every other artist in the same way that shopkeepers know other shopkeepers today. Artists were living people, not names in documents, walking the streets we walk. Most of them were conservative, as native Florentines still are—there is no audience at the Teatro Comunale for Janáček—and how, you ask yourself, did they respond to innovation when it occurred? It is a useful exercise to stand before Leonardo's unfinished *Adoration of the Magi* in the Uffizi and imagine how it would have looked to you if you had seen it when work was broken off, in storage in the Via de' Benci. When a single gigantic whitewashed figure by Donatello stood on the north flank of the Cathedral, would one have voted that it be retained, or removed, or replaced? There can have been very little privacy. Chapels were sealed off while they were being frescoed, much as the Brancacci Chapel has been till recently, and life-size statues were boarded in under lock and key, but the individual panels of Ghiberti's Gate of Paradise must have been familiar from the time that they were modeled—moles in his overstaffed workshop would have seen to that— though the whole door must have proved a revelation when it was installed. If you were well-to-do and had a superfluity of bed linen or clothes, you bought a chest with, on its front, a scene from classical antiquity treated as a charade in which the figures wore contemporary dress. For gilded and pigmented reliefs for your bedroom you went, if you could afford it, to the fifteenth-century equivalent of Gucci, a shop run by Neri di Bicci in the Via Porta Rossa. The people you are studying led real lives, and this was where their lives were led.

After ten years in New York my eyes were starved, not of works of art, of which one saw if anything too many, but of the natural world. I understand why people in an urban setting are prepared to spend vast sums procuring the vicarious experience of nature that Monet's poplars or haystacks or water lilies can be relied on to supply. But if you have been trained to look, there is something dissatisfying about this kind of response. You want to see the world, not through the tired eyes of some past painter, but through your own.

In London I had two gardens. They were quite small, but they were invaluable, partly for practical reasons—if you deal with works of art it is important to have some means of getting your hands dirty in a clean way—and partly because when you are talking about organic growth in artists' styles it is useful to be in contact with things that really grow. How much I missed gardening when I was in New York I did not realize till I arrived in Florence, where, on my loggia, gardenias and hibiscus and camellias and cassias and plumbago grow quite easily, and where, in terracotta pots, not beds, one can reestablish contact with the mystery beneath the surface of the soil. If you are a person for whom nature means Central Park, it stands to reason that you cannot look. In Florence the results of looking are spectacular.

The light on the buildings across the river changes constantly, and at almost any time of year save the high summer it can give them a Cuyp-like warmth. The foliage of the trees on the near side of the Lungarno varies continually in tone and color, and so does the painted surface of the campanile of the church next door and the outline of the two bells suspended in it. Nothing has been written on the depiction of the sky in Tuscan art. After rain, it lights up like a tangerine, but never from the generality of paintings would one guess that this is so. Save for a brief moment in the 1420s, the skies in Florentine painting are not based on observation, unless, as by Botticelli, the turbulence of nature is put to admonitory or didactic use. When the sun sets, the lights come up on the Lungarno and sparkle in reflection on the river, and if you learn to ignore the lines of commuter motorcars (as the Japanese have learned to ignore the pylons in a landscape) you are transported to the tranquil Florence of the nineteenth century. Next morning you throw open the shutters with expectancy, and in pours the caressing, invigorating sun.

INDEX